Illicit Firearms Markets and Organized Crime

Illicit Firearms Markets and Organized Crime

Global, Regional, and Local Perspectives

Edited by

DAVID BRIGHT

Professor of Criminology, Deakin University, Australia

OXFORD
UNIVERSITY PRESS

OXFORD
UNIVERSITY PRESS

Great Clarendon Street, Oxford, OX2 6DP,
United Kingdom

Oxford University Press is a department of the University of Oxford.
It furthers the University's objective of excellence in research, scholarship,
and education by publishing worldwide. Oxford is a registered trade mark of
Oxford University Press in the UK and in certain other countries

Published in the United States of America by Oxford University Press
198 Madison Avenue, New York, NY 10016, United States of America

British Library Cataloguing in Publication Data
Data available

Library of Congress Control Number: 2024947058

ISBN 9780198902379

DOI: 10.1093/9780198902409.001.0001

Printed and bound by
CPI Group (UK) Ltd, Croydon, CR0 4YY

FSC
www.fsc.org
MIX
Paper | Supporting
responsible forestry
FSC® C013604

The manufacturer's authorised representative in the EU for product safety
is Oxford University Press España S.A. of el Parque Empresarial San
Fernando de Henares, Avenida de Castilla,
2 – 28830 Madrid (www.oup.es/en).

Acknowledgements

The Editor wishes to acknowledge = Dr. Doug Lorman who assisted with editing and proofreading the final drafts of all chapters.

Contents

PART II. INTERSECTIONS BETWEEN ILLICIT FIREARMS MARKETS AND ORGANIZED CRIME

Tables and Figures

Tables

Figures

Contributors

Ashley Allen, Jointly Awarded PhD Candidate in School of Social Sciences, University of Adelaide, Adelaide, Australia. https://orcid.org/0000-0001-6289-9937

Simon Anderson, PhD, MPhil, MSc, MBBCh, FRCP, FESC is Professor of Population Health Sciences and Cardiovascular Medicine, The George Alleyne Chronic Disease Research Centre, Caribbean Institute of Health Research, The University of the West Indies, Barbados, The University of the West Indies, Jamaica. https://orcid.org/0000-0002-8896-073X

Wasiu A. Balogun, PhD is Lecturer, Department of History and International Studies, Lagos State University, Ojo, Lagos, Nigeria. https://orcid.org/0000-0001-8519-2053

Étienne Blais, PhD is Professor, School of Criminology, Université de Montréal, Montreal, Canada. https://orcid.org/0000-0002-1018-1090

Anthony A. Braga, PhD is Jerry Lee Professor of Criminology, Department of Criminology, University of Pennsylvania, Philadelphia, United States

David Bright is Professor of Criminology, Deakin University, Australia. https://orcid.org/0000-0002-4425-9589

Arielle Chainé is Master's student in Criminology, École de criminologie, Université de Montréal, Canada

Piotr Chlebowicz, PhD is Professor in the Department of Criminology and Forensic Science, University of Warmia and Mazury in Olsztyn, Poland. https://orcid.org/0000-0002-9553-7665

David Décary-Hétu is Associate Professor, School of Criminology, Université de Montréal, Canada

Nils Duquet is Director, Flemish Peace Institute, Brussels, Belgium

Anne-Séverine Fabre is Researcher, Data and Analytics Unit, Small Arms Survey, Geneva, Switzerland

Adewunmi J. Falode, PhD is Professor of International Relations and Strategic Studies, Department of History and International Studies, Lagos State University, Ojo, Lagos State, Nigeria. https://orcid.org/0000-0003-0649-1042

Nicolas Florquin, PhD is Head of Data & Analytics, Small Arms Survey, Graduate Institute of International and Development Studies, Geneva, Switzerland. https://orcid.org/0000-0002-4569-8882

Lina Grip is Research Analyst, Research and Evaluation Unit, Swedish Prison and Probation Service, Stockholm, Sweden. https://orcid.org/0000-0001-8976-8718

Mark Halsey is Matthew Flinders Professor, Flinders University, Adelaide, Australia

Callixtus Joseph is Assistant Director, Policy, Strategy and Innovation (Ag.), CARICOM Implementation Agency for Crime and Security, Port of Spain, Trinidad and Tobago

Freddie Kootstra is Datascientist at the Service Regional Information Organization (DRIO), Department of Analysis & Research (A & O), Dutch Police, Unit North-Netherlands, Netherlands

Monique Mann is Senior Lecturer, Institute of Criminology, Victoria University of Wellington, Wellington, New Zealand. https://orcid.org/0000-0001-8372-3797

Annelies Pauwels is Senior Researcher, Flemish Peace Institute, Brussels, Belgium

Carlos A. Pérez Ricart is Assistant Professor in International Relations, Center for Research and Teaching in Economics (CIDE), Mexico City, Mexico. https://orcid.org/0000-0001-9601-552X

Michael E. Picard is Independent Expert, Forum on the Arms Trade, Washington, United States

Joy St. John is former Executive Director, Caribbean Public Health Agency and former Assistant Director-General, World Health Organization, Port of Spain, Trinidad & Tobago

Fenna van der Wijk, MSc is PhD student, Department of Sociology, University of Groningen, Netherlands. https://orcid.org/0000-0002-6604-7501

Introduction

David Bright

Illicit firearms are an enabler of organized criminal groups and of illicit markets. They facilitate battles for market dominance, deter state actors from intervening, and are used to threaten and coerce communities, to extort money from victims, and to facilitate engagement in a range of other organized crimes (del Mercado 2022; UNODC 2020). Firearms are used to gain dominance in conflicts between OCGs, to protect and extend territories, and to facilitate other crimes including kidnapping, extortion, and armed robbery (del Mercado 2022; UNODC 2020). Criminals who are involved in transactions of large sums of money, operate under the threat of heavy penalties if detected, and face well-armed competitors and law enforcement, will use illicit firearms as both defensive and offensive tools (Gagliardi 2012).

Welcome to this edited collection on *Illicit Firearms Markets and Organized Crime*. This book aims to reveal insights into harmful intersections across illicit firearms markets, organized crime, and OCGs. Illicit firearms markets and organized crime are symbiotic beasts. They feed off each other and each is nourished by the co-existence of the other. Illicit firearms markets and organized crime cause significant economic, social, and political harms; the harms caused at their junction are significantly magnified. There is a clear and pressing need for enhanced understandings of how illicit firearms markets are related to other forms of transnational organized crime, including illicit drug trafficking (e.g. del Mercado 2022). This book is the first to explore the interrelationship between illicit firearms markets and organized crime in rich detail at global, regional, and local levels. Among its interlocking themes, the book explores how OCGs are involved in the trafficking of illicit firearms, how the availability of illicit firearms contributes to the social and political power of OCGs, and how the use of illicit firearms can facilitate the operation of a range of other illicit markets, most notably illicit drug markets.

David Bright, *Introduction* In: *Illicit Firearms Markets and Organized Crime*. Edited by: David Bright, Oxford University Press. © Oxford University Press 2025. DOI: 10.1093/9780198902409.003.0001

This edited collection collates cutting-edge, contemporary scholarship on illicit firearms markets and organized crime from scholars across the globe to examine interconnections between illicit firearms markets and organized crime/ OCGs and the significant economic and social harms caused at that nexus. The book weaves together contributions from leading and emerging experts on the intersections between illicit firearms, organized crime, and criminal networks across the disciplines of criminology, law, political science, and economics. This book is an interdisciplinary, global edited collection drawing together cutting-edge research with a specific focus on the interconnections and interrelationships between illicit firearms markets and organized crime/OCGs. This includes, for example: (1) the methods and routes by which firearms enter illicit markets; (2) illicit firearms as facilitators and enablers of other illicit markets and other crime including organized crime; (3) the role of illicit firearms in exacerbating organized crime, and related crime and violence; and (4) policy responses to illicit firearms and the efficacy of such, including unintended consequences. The book employs a regional lens on illicit firearms markets, while concurrently exploring key emerging themes and challenges that lie at the intersection of illicit firearms markets and organized crime, such as the trafficking of firearms by OCGs, and the facilitation of other organized crimes (e.g. illicit drug trafficking) using illicit firearms. The book adopts a broad, global scope on these issues, while also drilling down to examine local harms and impacts. It also addresses emerging challenges and threats, evaluates existing policies, and explores potential alternative policy options to respond to these challenges, threats, and social harms more effectively. In addressing policy issues, the book focuses on contemporary challenges but is also forward-looking, seeking to identify emerging threats and innovative responses to the global 'wicked' problems of illicit firearms markets and organized crime. Each chapter will analyse relevant policies, the efficacy of such policies, and critically examines alternative options that prevent and reduce crime and enhance community safety. In this way, chapters contribute to advances in scholarly and public policy debates within and across countries.

Chapters cover significant breadth with respect to geography, concepts, theory, and substantive content related to illicit firearms markets and organized crime. As an integrated whole, the book provides a coherent narrative on the relationship between the operation of illicit firearms markets and organized crime in five primary ways. First, as previously mentioned, the book integrates existing scholarship on illicit firearms markets and organized crime, including unpacking the relevance of this relationship for other illicit markets, such as drugs. Second, the operation of illicit firearms markets including the trafficking and supply of illicit firearms will be studied as a key activity of organized crime groups. That is, illicit firearms will be studied as one of the primary illicit commodities trafficked by organized crime groups. Third, illicit firearms will be conceived as an important tool used by OCGs to facilitate illicit business. For example, OCGs use firearms for a range of strategic purposes, including to protect illicit business and personnel against competitors or other threats, to coerce and threaten subordinates and competitors, and to ensure compliance from associates and victims. Fourth, illicit firearms are utilized as tools across a range of other organized crimes, such as drug trafficking, people smuggling, and protection rackets. Fifth, the book examines how illicit firearms markets and organized crime activities contribute to conflict and political unrest, particularly in weak states.

Illicit Firearms and Organized Criminal Groups

According to the UNODC, 'firearms are linked to various form of organized crime in several ways: as a tool for gaining and maintaining power, as an instrumentality for the commission of crime, and as a commodity to be trafficked' (UNODC 2012, 101). The use of illicit firearms by members of OCGs manifests across a wide spectrum of instrumental and expressive violence (Masari 2013; Kotze et al. 2022). The acquisition of firearms can become an 'arms race' fought between members of rival OCGs, where illicit profits garnered from illicit market activities are reinvested in firearms to gain precedence over rivals or the state. There are, of course, regional variations in trends of access and use of illicit firearms by OCGs. In Mexico, for example, criminal groups have enjoyed increased availability of high calibre weapons following the 2004 expiry of the ban on federal assault weapons in the United States (Monroy 2019 cited in del Mercado 2022). In Brazil, crackdowns on organized crime by the state have seen increased investment in firearms by OCGs (Dube et al. 2019). High gun-related homicide rates in Latin America, facilitated by the ready availability of firearms, are primarily linked to conflicts between criminal organizations (del Mercado 2022).

Regional Variations in Illicit Firearms Markets and Organized Crime

There is significant regional variation in the structure and dynamics of illicit firearms markets, including the extent of involvement of OCGs. These patterns will be explored across locales, regions, and countries throughout the book, especially in Part I. For now, a couple of prototypical examples will suffice.

In Mexico, most crimes involving firearms are committed by OCGs who access firearms via illicit markets (Vargas and Gonzalez 2022). Shifts in gun production and federal laws in the United States have facilitated much greater access to firearms by Mexican OCGs (see Vargas and Gonzalez 2022). From 2015 to 2020, approximately 69 per cent of all firearms seized in Mexico were manufactured in or legally imported from the United States, similar to proportions observed in Central America and the Caribbean (del Mercado 2022). Consequently, firearms crime overall has increased in Mexico over the last two decades: while less than 20 per cent of homicides were committed with a firearm in 1997, this increased to almost 70 per cent in 2017 (Parsons and Weigend 2018).

In Europe, demand for firearms is from individual firearms owners and collectors, terrorist groups who may have connections with OCGs, and OCGs (Savona and Mancuso 2017). The majority of firearm seizures in Europe involve small-scale shipments, often referred to as 'ant trafficking' or the 'ant trade'. Large-scale shipments are associated with the trafficking of large numbers of firearms, with small groups involved in such trafficking. This finding suggests that a small number of actors are responsible for a large proportion of seizures of illicit firearms (Savona and Mancuso 2017). Organized criminal groups are the main participants in illicit firearms markets in Europe (Spapens 2007). A variety of organized criminal groups across Europe are involved in the trafficking of illicit firearms (e.g. Albanian-speaking OCGs, Outlaw Motorcycle Gangs, the 'Ndrangheta, Balkan OCGs, Russian/Georgian OCGs, Turkish OCGs; Savona and Mancuso 2017). While part of the motivation is financial profit, groups are also motivated to traffic arms to ensure continued reliable access to firearms in order to facilitate the conduct their other illicit activities (Massari 2013).

Defining 'Organized Crime' and 'Organized Criminal Groups'

In this section, I address some of the fraught definitional issues with respect to the contested concept of 'organized crime'. At the outset, it is important to note that the term 'organized crime' originated in political discourse and was not constructed via robust definitional and conceptual development and refinement by social scientists (see Von Lampe 2015). The result is a confused term that is not used consistently by researchers or by law enforcement agencies (see Von Lampe 2023; Finckenaur 2005). Nonetheless, the term is so strongly emplaced in extant scholarship that it is unlikely to be supplanted by some other term, despite its problematic history and contemporary controversies. Some definitions of organized crime emphasize economic gain, others focus on the structure of the groups involved in organized criminal activities, and yet other definitions incorporate aspects of social and political power and influence. The fundamental problem with the term 'organized crime' is related not to the word 'crime' but to the word 'organized' (see Bright and Whelan 2021; Finckenaur 2005). The 'organized' part of the concept means a range of things and is used to refer to a plethora of observations on criminal activities and the groups that commit them. For example, the term is sometimes used to refer to the organization of crime (e.g. how complex drug trafficking activities are structured with multiple phases and roles required), while at other times it is used to refer to the organization of criminals (e.g. criminal network structures). Some definitions of 'organized crime' refer only to the commission of a specific set of criminal activities without mention of the OCGs which undertake such activities. Indeed, some scholars have been critical of definitions that lack reference to OCGs (e.g. Finckenaur 2005; Bright and Whelan 2021). Scholarly debate has also focused on the term 'organized criminal group', with once again a range of definitions proffered. Finckenaur (2005), for example, has argued that OCGs can be represented along a spectrum depending on the extent to which they possess four primary characteristics: (1) criminal sophistication characterized by planning, skills, knowledge, and durability; (2) evidence of organization structure such as division of labour and lines of authority; (3) self-identification with the group; and (4) authority of reputation that allows the group to coerce others without the need for actual violence. One of the most well-known and influential definitions of organized crime, the UNODC definition, is in effect a definition of OCGs: 'a structured group of three or more persons, existing for a period of time and acting in concert with the aim of committing one or more serious crimes or offences' (UNODC 2004, 5). The definitional quagmire has been an impediment to progress in the study of 'organized crime'; scholars need to move beyond arguments about definitions to free the field to move forward (e.g. see Bright and Whelan 2021; Von Lampe 2015).

Klaus Von Lampe (2015) has argued that rather than attempting to achieve a consensus definition of organized crime (or an organized criminal group), scholars should focus on identifying the core attributes of organized crime.

Of course, there is no consensus on these core attributes either. Nonetheless, Von Lampe (2015) developed a framework comprising three core characteristics: (1) criminal activities, (2) the organization of criminals, and (3) extra-legal governance. Note that the use of this framework is contingent on a somewhat artificial separation of the criminal activities that characterize organized crime from a consideration of the social and organizational structures that tend to be observed in OCGs. In reality, the criminal activities can be undertaken more efficiently (and more securely) when particular relational features are observed (see Morselli 2009; Morselli et al. 2007). Von Lampe's (2015) framework offers a useful alternative to debates about definitions and provides a way forward by focusing attention on the key characteristics of organized crime rather than endless and, to date, fruitless searches for a consensus definition. Given its potential utility to our understanding of the interconnections between organized crime and illicit firearms markets, I provide a brief overview of the framework here.

Criminal Activities

Criminal activities can theoretically lie on a continuum from spontaneous, impulsive acts to more complex, integrated crimes that comprise multiple stages of interlocking activities that may take many months to complete. These more complex crimes are difficult or impossible for a sole offender to complete successfully (and efficiently), and therefore often require collaboration among a group or network of offenders (Finckenaur 2005). Three primary classes of criminal activities fall under the umbrella of organized crime, and all have relevance for the study of illicit firearms markets and the use of illicit firearms by OCGs. These three types of criminal activities are: (1) market-based crimes that typically involve the provision of illegal goods and services that are in demand; (2) predatory crimes characterized by the infliction of harm and victim–offender interactions; and (3) regulatory or governance crimes characterized by the establishment and subsequent enforcement of rules of conduct, including the adjudication of disputes.

The Organization of Criminals

A variety of social and organizational structures characterize groups of offenders and can facilitate cooperation and collaboration of actors in undertaking criminal activities. Three primary types of organizational structures emerge from diverse literatures across a range of disciplines including sociology, psychology, economics, and criminology (see Bright and Whelan 2021). First, are market-based relationships between customers and suppliers that usually involve one-off transactions with no obligations for any future transactions. The second type of organization is hierarchies in which members of a group are organized across several hierarchical levels and lower-ranked members are expected to follow established rules and to obey instructions from those who occupy senior positions in the group. Finally, there are network structures in which coordinated action is undertaken among a group of actors who are loosely connected via a range of social ties and in which the structure of the group is 'flat' and without formal hierarchical levels (e.g. familial, co-offending, business ties). It is important to note that these three types are 'ideal' types and that hybrid forms can (and often do) exists (e.g. see Bright et al. 2012).

Extra-Legal Governance

Extra-legal governance relates to the exercise of social and political power by OCGs. The establishment and exercise of extra-legal governance is facilitated by quasi-governmental structures that allow criminals to control the activities of other criminals, regulate behaviour, protect contractual and property rights in illegal contexts, and provide conflict resolution services. Organized criminal groups that engage in extra-legal governance may extract payments in the form of a tax from those within their jurisdiction (e.g. territory or market). Extra-legal governance can involve actual or threatened violence (see e.g. Campana and Varese 2018; Barker 2014; Sergi 2022; Varese 2017) to ensure compliance and to monopolize illicit markets (e.g. Abadinsky 2013).

Before moving on to a discussion of illicit markets, I need to deal with one other definitional issue related to organized crime: the distinction between (street) gangs and OCGs. There is significant scholarship on street gangs and their use of illicit firearms (e.g. Sanders 1994; Contreras 2013; Harcourt 2006). However, our focus in this book is not gangs, but OCGs. While some of the literature on gangs and illicit firearms can be instructive for our aims, and some chapters examine the literature and data on gangs, their use of illicit firearms, and involvement in the trafficking of illicit firearms, street gangs are not our primary focus.

Distinguishing Organized Criminal Groups from Street Gangs

As with organized crime, definitions of gangs are contentious. However, a scholarly consensus has emerged. 'Gangs' are generally defined as being relatively durable, predominantly street-based groups of young people who view themselves as a discernible group. Scholarship on gangs tends to converge on the following key criteria (see Decker et al. 2022): gangs are comprised of a group of actors, use symbols to signify collective identity, are durable across time, have a street or turf orientation, and engage in criminal activities.

Organized criminal groups can be distinguished from gangs in that they are a group of individuals for whom involvement in crime is motivated primarily by personal gain (financial or otherwise). For members of OCGs, crime is arguably their primary occupation (Marshall et al. 2005). This is not the case for gangs. Organized criminal groups and gangs differ in three main ways. First and foremost, OCGs tend to attempt to regulate and control the production and distribution of illicit commodities or services (i.e. they engage in extra-legal governance). Gangs do not attempt to regulate and control illicit markets, although they may participate in such markets. Second, while gangs tend to seek symbolic aims, economic goals are of premier importance to OCGs. Profit-making activities tend to be sporadic and more opportunistic for gangs. Finally, gangs are focused on turf and territory, while OCGs tend to focus far less on territory, aside from attempts to control and regulate geospatially located markets.

In the real world, clear distinctions between OCGs and street gangs can be difficult, and some groups occupy a kind of definitional 'grey zone' showing characteristics of both (e.g. outlaw motorcycle gangs), such that classifying them as either street gang or organized criminal group is fraught with difficulties.

Illicit Markets

At the outset, it is important to acknowledge that firearms differ in important ways from other commodities that are also sold on illicit markets. First, firearms are durable and can be bought and sold both legally and illegally many times over their lifespan. This distinguishes firearms from other illicit commodities such as drugs. Second, firearms have the power to take or protect human life, a significant characteristic, especially in the context of high-risk illicit markets. Third, firearms can be used to coerce, threaten, and even defend communities, groups, and gangs. And fourth, unlike other types of illicit commodities (e.g. drugs) firearms are inextricably linked with social, economic, and political power (e.g. Arsovska and Kostakos 2008).

Firearms can be the primary commodity of an illicit market (i.e. the illicit firearms market) or tools used by members of OCGs to facilitate the operation of other illicit markets (e.g. illicit drug markets; Gagliardi 2012). In this section, I introduce the concept of a 'market' and provide a brief overview of the operation of illicit markets. Markets, whether they be legal or illegal markets, can be defined as 'socially constructed arenas where repeated exchanges occur between buyers and sellers under a set of formal rules and informal understandings that govern relations among competitors, suppliers and customers' (Fligstein and Dioun 2015, 67). In essence, markets are social spaces where goods and services can be bought and sold. Some researchers have argued that 'marketplaces'—the spatially located meeting place—should be the unit of analysis rather than the more esoteric concept of the 'market', and that relationships between actors (buyers and sellers) should be the focus of analysis (e.g. Johnson, Hamid, and Sanabria 1992). It is worth noting here that network approaches can provide rich perspectives on the structure and dynamics of market-based interactions including connections between actors (e.g. buyers and sellers) and flows of commodities (e.g. drugs, weapons, money). A network lens has been applied to the OCGs operating in illicit markets (e.g. Morselli 2009; Bright et al. 2012).

In illicit markets, OCGs are subject to the usual economic and market forces and processes where concepts like supply, demand, monopoly, and price fluctuations are key to the operation of such markets and therefore are primary influences on the activities of the groups. Illicit markets have been conceptualized as being similar in many respects to legal markets, but differ given the illegality associated with the activities (Smith 1980; Haller 1990). Furthermore, and related to their illegality, illicit markets transactions are characterized by a paucity of information about the nature of the exchanges and commodities. For example, the quality of goods and the trustworthiness of those with whom one interacts may be poorly understood or completely unknown. Therefore, actors in illicit markets must create opportunities to reduce such uncertainties and to facilitate trust in contexts where there are opportunities to cheat (and be cheated), and where there is no recourse to legitimate authorities for dispute resolution.

An illicit market is 'an arena for the regular voluntary exchange of goods and services for money where the goods and services themselves, their production, selling and/or consumption violates the law' (Von Lampe 2015

81; see also Arlacchi1998; Beckert and Wehinger 2013). According to Von Lampe (2015), there are two main categories of illicit markets: (1) markets for commodities (goods or services) that are illegal in all circumstances; and (2) markets for commodities that are regulated, involving legal restrictions on who can buy or sell that commodity or where exchange of the commodity involves the payment of a tax or customs duty. There is also a distinction between 'absolute contraband' and 'relative contraband' (Von Lampe 2015), and this is of particular relevance for illicit firearms markets. The terms 'absolute contraband' describes commodities that are prohibited and where there is no extant parallel market (e.g. child pornography). In contrast, the term 'relative contraband' describes commodities where licit and illicit markets can operate in parallel. Buying and selling these commodities is illegal in some contexts and legal in others. One example of relative contraband is firearms. Importantly, and of relevance to the regional analyses that form a large component of this book, the legal restrictions (e.g. on-buying and selling) vary across contexts (e.g. regions, countries, and states) including variations in the type of restrictions that are imposed on the buying and selling of firearms. For example, in some countries, firearms can be sold only by licensed dealers and purchased only by those with a requisite licence for a specific type of firearm. The relative level of restrictions in legal markets tends to influence the differential pricing of commodities, such as firearms, between legal and illegal markets (Naylor 2003). Prices for restricted commodities are usually higher on illicit markets compared with legal markets (although there are exceptions; e.g. see Killicoat 2007). For example, in a heavily regulated firearms context like Australia, firearms purchased on the illicit market are likely to cost significantly more than those purchased legally (see Bright et al. 2022).

Illicit drug markets have been studied in significantly greater depth compared with illicit firearms markets. Therefore, the literature on illicit drug markets may be instructive in understanding the operation of illicit firearms markets (notwithstanding that there are significant differences between the two commodities). In this section, I draw on the work of Peter Reuter and Mark Kleiman and their 'risks and prices' framework (see Reuter and Kleiman 1986). Although the framework was originally conceived for application to illicit drug markets, I use the framework here in the context of any market for illicit goods and services, including illicit firearms markets. The 'risks and prices' framework suggests that interventions of law enforcement agencies against illicit markets operate like a tax on those who operate in such markets, thus inflating the prices of illicit commodities. The inflationary impact is caused by direct costs incurred by market participants (e.g. replacement costs for seized product) and indirect costs such as increased compensation for the risks of operating in such contexts (e.g. risk of arrest and imprisonment). Indeed, enforcement inflates the prices of illicit commodities at all market levels, but because of the multi-level pricing structure of illicit markets, the impact of enforcement is magnified at retail level (for more detail see Reuter and Kleiman 1986). One way of circumventing the risks and uncertainties in illicit markets is to devise ways to facilitate and strengthen trust, often through social embeddedness, nurturing of strong interpersonal ties (Granovetter 1985), and repeat transactions with trusted affiliates (see Von Lampe and Johanson 2004; Gambetta 2009). Social networks can facilitate trust and enhance efficiency of operations while also balancing the need for security (see Morselli 2009; Morselli et al. 2007). Outside of the operation of trust, adversarial forms of illicit governance are often maintained through coercion, fear, and violence (e.g. Jacques et al. 2014), sometimes using tools of fear and coercion such as firearms. Opportunistic predation is often prevented using threats of violence, cultivating a strong reputation and by acts of deterrence (e.g. carrying and displaying a firearm). Of course, when threats are insufficient, and market shares are disputed, acts of conflict and violence can cascade, leading to spirals of retaliatory violence that often involve the use of illicit firearms (e.g. see Papachristos 2009).

It is important to note that there is not a single, global firearms market but rather many different and sometimes intersecting illicit markets for firearms (Duquet and Goris 2018). The structure of illicit drug markets shows significant variability across geographic location, customers, and the characteristics of the criminal group involved in supply (e.g. Eck 1994; Caulkins and Reuter 2006; May and Hough 2004). We can expect similar variation, especially given differences in legal contexts, in illicit firearms markets in different regions and countries. For example, in Denmark firearms are often trafficked in combination with or as payment for illicit drugs, with involvement of Outlaw Motorcycle Gangs and street gangs in some cases. In Peru, OCGs involved in drug trafficking are also involved in the trafficking of firearms (e.g. to those involved in cocoa cultivation).

Trafficking Illicit Firearms

Trafficking in illicit firearms causes significant social, political, and economic harms. For example, the trafficking of illicit firearms escalates civil conflicts and political destabilization, provides tools of coercion for criminals and political extremists, contributes to high crime rates, and can derail humanitarian assistance programmes and post-conflict development strategies (Arsovska and Kostakos 2008; Davis et al. 2001; Dhanapola et al. 1999; see also Florquin 2021). Diverted weapons can enjoy a long life in illicit markets (UNODC 2020). A large proportion of illicit firearms commence life as legally manufactured firearms which are diverted into the illicit market at some stage in their life (UNODC 2020). Methods of diversion to illicit markets include theft, reactivation of deactivated firearms, and technical loopholes in legislation/regulation that facilitate the movement of firearms from licit to illicit markets (e.g. ACIC 2016; Bright et al. 2022; Squires 2022). Internationally, the illicit supply of firearms is dominated by OCGs who utilize their expertise in trafficking other illicit commodities and apply these to firearms. In such endeavours, they utilize established routes and existing contacts, and are frequently assisted in these endeavours by corrupt officials and professionals (Savona and Mancuso 2017). Compared with other illicit commodities, the profitability potential is reportedly not as high for illicit firearms, with some scholars positing that the primary motive for engaging in illicit firearms trafficking is not financial profit, but motivated to ensure access to firearms for personal and criminal use (Savona and Mancuso 2017; see also Sneddon 2022).

Based on global firearms seizures data, illicit firearms tend to be seized outside the country of manufacture, and large proportions of international seizures are detected on shipments that do not travel directly from the country of manufacture to the destination country (UNODC 2020). Not surprisingly, countries which exhibit greater evidence of drug trafficking activities also have a large proportion of firearms seizures that relate to illicit drug trafficking (UNODC 2020). From a global perspective, the crimes most linked with firearms seizures (excluding firearms-related offences) are violent crimes, most notably in Latin America and Africa. In Europe, in contrast, the largest offence category linked with firearms seizures is trafficking illicit drugs (UNODC 2020).

Historically, violent conflicts and wars produce conditions in which firearms can be accumulated. The conclusion of such conflicts tends to see the displacement of firearms into illicit markets and the hands of OCGs and insurgent groups. Although there is no evidence to suggest that there is a current flow of firearms into illicit markets from firearms repositories related to the war in Ukraine, the risk of this type of transmission is relatively high based on recent conflicts (e.g. the Balkan wars in the 1990s and the Soviet-Afghan war in 1988; Buscemi et al. 2018; Galeotti and Arutunyan 2023).

Emerging Threats

There are some emerging threats around illicit firearms markets and trafficking that are worthy of mention. First, privately made firearms, also called 'ghost guns', are those firearms (including firearm parts) that are manufactured by someone other than a licensed manufacturer and do not carry serial numbers, making them difficult to trace (Braga et al. 2022). Converted firearms are objects that resemble firearms and that, as a result of their construction or the material from which they are made, can be converted—without the need for specialized tools, equipment or skills—to expel a projectile or to increase their firepower. Converted firearms are such objects that have been modified or transformed to expel a projectile or increase their firepower (e.g. Jongleux and Florquin 2020). There has been a concerning rise in the availability of such firearms in Europe driven partly by inconsistent legislation across the EU (see Jongleux and Florquin 2020). Issues regarding privately made and converted firearms are addressed in the chapters that form Part I of this volume. 3D-printed firearms are firearms that can be printed using existing 3D-printing technology. There has been a concerning rise in the availability, interception, affordability, and technological sophistication of 3D-printed firearms (e.g. Daly et al. 2021; Schaufelbühl et al. 2024; O'Shaughnessy 2021; see also Chapter 8 of this volume). This has occurred alongside, and partly due to, the increasing accessibility of the digital design files required to manufacture them. Finally, there has been recent concern regarding illicit firearms trafficking on the dark web. However, available evidence suggests that the online market for illicit firearms remains relatively small, while presenting risks of potential expansion (e.g. Paoli et al. 2017). It has been suggested that the scale of the online market for illicit firearms renders it unlikely to be used by OCGs and instead it is a more likely option for individuals and small fringe groups who seek access to guns (Paoli et al. 2017; Florquin and King 2018). Chapter 9 of this volume focuses on dark web trafficking of illicit firearms.

Theoretical Perspectives

In this section, I briefly introduce some relevant criminological theories that can be applied to the study of illicit firearms markets and organized crime. It is important to note that this is not intended to be a comprehensive overview. Instead, this section is aimed to simply foreground some theories that may assist with our understanding of illicit firearms markets and the participation of OCGs in such markets.

For the study of organized crime and illicit markets, the focus on generating financial profit has witnessed the dominance of economic and rational explanations (e.g. Schelling 1971; Cressey 1969; Gambetta 1994). Economic theories (e.g. the risk and prices framework discussed above) are heavily influenced by rational choice theory, which asserts that decisions to commit crime are the product of human decision-making processes in which individuals weigh the potential risks and rewards of engaging in specific criminal activities. In this context, illicit activities are rational alternatives to legitimate activities, and decisions to commit crime are made by rational actors who are motivated by financial profit, and balance the potential profit with the risk of being arrested, convicted, and punished. Of course, individuals do not always act rationally, partly because decisions are made under conditions of uncertainty where risks, rewards, and effort may be poorly perceived, and the probabilities and severity of such risks may be erroneously estimated (see Clarke 1995; Caulkins and MacCoun 2003; Kahneman and Tversky 1979).

Despite the prominence of economic theories, other theories of criminal behaviour have also garnered support (e.g. Merton 1938; Sutherland 1972) and can help to understand the operation of illicit markets. Purely rational explanations of organized crime and illicit firearms markets and trafficking do not fully consider the social and political capital and power that access to firearms can facilitate (Arsovska and Kostakos 2008). Such accounts also do not take full account of relevant socio-cultural considerations. Socio-cultural explanations can provide nuanced accounts of some of the factors and drivers underlying firearms trafficking and use, including why illicit markets and organized crime bloom in particular contexts and at specific times (e.g. see Arsovska 2007; Arsovska and Verduyn 2008). Social and cultural accounts that can explain participation in illicit firearms markets include consideration of social constructs like masculinity (e.g. see Goldsmith et al. 2022). Firearms can also be imbued with significant cultural meanings and symbolism. For example, firearms and firearm ownership may become synonymous with notions of liberty and freedom (e.g. the Balkan region and the United States; see Arsovska and Kostakos 2008). In regions characterized by insecurity, firearms can provide a sense of safety and control (e.g. the Balkans; see Arsovska and Kostakos 2008).

In concluding this section, and segueing to the next section on policy, it is important to note that policy interventions premised on rational choice theory, and which do not take account of relevant social, political, and cultural meanings with which firearms are imbued, risk being ineffective. Simply increasing the risks and reducing the rewards of a criminal activity such as illicit firearms trafficking may not significantly impact the trafficking and use of firearms, because other motivations and drivers are at play (see Arsovska and Kostakos 2008).

Illicit Firearm Policies and Implications for Policy Change

As mentioned previously in this introduction, a major focus of this book is an assessment of the relative effectiveness of existing policies and practice, and the generation of a suite of potential alternative policies and practice. There have been some global attempts to enshrine principles for good policy making aimed at controlling illicit firearms trafficking and associated harms. For example, the UNODC Firearms Protocol offers a framework for countries to control and regulate legal firearms, to prevent the diversion of firearms into illicit markets, and to investigate and prosecute related offences (see del Mercado 2022). Similarly, the UN Arms Trade Treaty, which has been in force since 2014, is designed to regulate licit trade in firearms and to abolish the illicit trade of firearms primarily through globally consistent protocols for the transfer of weapons (Karp 2018). The UN Programme of Action on small arms and light weapons, adopted by UN member states in 2001, has facilitated the adoption of the International Tracing Agreement and a global framework on ammunition (e.g. the development of the International Ammunition Technical Guidelines; see Parker and Wilson 2016).

Despite attempts to enhance global consistency in firearms policy and practice, existing policies aimed at limiting access to illicit firearms and alleviating the social harms associated with the trafficking and use of illicit firearms vary significantly across countries and regions, mostly due to the influence of local contexts, politics, and histories. This book will examine these local and regional variations in firearms policies and will review key similarities and differences. The book will examine the effectiveness of such policies and tender recommendations about alternative policies and practices.

Structure of the Book

The book is divided into two related parts. Part I comprises a series of regional perspectives on illicit firearms markets and organized crime. Part II takes a deep dive into some of the key emerging threats and challenges at the intersections between illicit firearms markets and organized crime.

In the first part of the book, Chapters 1 to 7 provide regional perspectives on illicit firearms markets and intersections with organized crime. Chapter 1, by Anthony Braga, focuses on North America, a region known to be a source of significant numbers of legal and illegal firearms, especially to neighbouring countries. In Chapter 2, Lina Grip contributes a regional analysis of illicit firearms markets in Europe with a focus on Western Europe. Chapter 3, written by Michael Picard, turns the focus to firearms trafficking in Asia and South-east Asia. Chapter 4, contributed by Carlos Perez Ricart, provides an analysis of firearms markets and organized crime in Latin and South America. In Chapter 5 the spotlight turns to Eastern Europe with an emphasis on the conflict in Ukraine, written by Piotr Chlebowicz. In Chapter 6, contributed by Adewunmi Falode and Wasiu Balogun, we explore illicit firearms markets and organized crime in Africa. Chapter 7 concludes Part I of the book with a regional analysis of the Caribbean region, written by Nicolas Florquin, Simon Anderson, Anne-Séverine Fabre, Callixtus Joseph, and Joy St John.

Part II of the book comprises five chapters that focus on key themes at the intersection between illicit firearms markets and organized crime. In Chapter 8, Monique Mann, David Bright, and Ashley Allen document some of the emerging risks and vulnerabilities associated with 3D-printed firearms, with a particular focus on the potential threats emerging from the use of 3D-printed firearms by OCGs. Chapter 9, written by David Decary-Hetu, Arielle Chainé, and Étienne Blais focuses on the emergence of online marketplaces for illicit firearms, including markets on the dark web. In Chapter 10, Fenna van der Wijk, David Bright, and Freddie Koostra employ a network perspective to analyse the structures and dynamics of illicit firearms trafficking. In Chapter 11, David Bright and Mark Halsey examine the use of illicit firearms as 'tools of the trade' by members of OCGs who participate in illicit markets. The final substantive chapter of the book, written by Nils Duquet and Annelies Pauwels, examines illicit firearms markets and the nexus between OCGs and terrorist groups.

The Conclusion draws together themes that emerge across the foregoing chapters, including implications for policy and policing practice related to the operation of illicit firearms markets and intersections with organized crime.

References

Abadinsky, Howard. 2013. *Organised Crime*. 11th edn. Wadsworth ISE.

Arlacchi, Pino. 1998. Introduction to the Panel Discussion, 'Attacking the Profits of Crime: Drugs and Money Laundering', United Nations Office for Drug Control and Crime Prevention, New York, 10 June 1998. *Trends in Organized Crime* 4 (2): pp. 114–116.

Arsovska, Jana. 2007. 'Code of Conduct: Understanding Albanian Organised Crime'. *Jane's Intelligence Review* 19 (8): pp. 46–49

Arsovska, Jana, and Kostakos, Panos A. 2008. 'Illicit Arms Trafficking and the Limits of Rational Choice Theory: The Case of the Balkans'. *Trends in Organized Crime* 11: pp. 352–378.

Arsovska, Jana, and Verduyn, Phillipe. 2008. 'Globalisation, Conduct Norms and "Culture Conflict": Perceptions of Violence and Crime in an Ethnic Albanian Context'. *British Journal of Criminology* 48 (2): pp. 226–246.

Australian Criminal Intelligence Commission. 2016. *Illicit Firearms in Australia*. Canberra: ACIC.

Barker, Thomas. 2014. *Biker Gangs and Transnational Organized Crime*. Routledge: London.

Beckert, Jens, and Wehinger, Frank. 2013. 'In the Shadow: Illegal Markets and Economic Sociology'. *Socio-Economic Review* 11 (1): pp. 5–30.

Braga, Anthony, et al. 2022. 'Privately Manufactured Firearms, Newly Purchased Firearms, and the Rise of Urban Gun Violence'. *Preventive Medicine* 165 (Part A) 107231.

Bright, David, and Whelan, Chad. 2021. *Organised Crime and Law Enforcement: A Network Perspective*. Abingdon: Routledge.

Bright, David A., Hughes, Caitlin E., and Chalmers, Jenny. 2012. 'Illuminating Dark Networks: A Social Network Analysis of an Australian Drug Trafficking Syndicate'. *Crime, Law and Social Change* 57: pp. 151–176.

Bright, David, et al. 2022. '"I Know a Guy and He's Got Guns Galore": Accessing Crime Guns in the Australian Illicit Firearms Market'. *Deviant Behavior* 44 (5): pp. 671–689.

Buscemi, Francesco, et al. 2018. 'Illicit Firearms Proliferation in the EU Periphery: The Case of Ukraine'. In *Triggering Terror: Illicit Gun Markets and Firearms Acquisition of Terrorist Networks in Europe*, edited by Nils Duquet, pp. 461–280. Brussels: Flemish Peace Institute.

Campana, Paolo, and Varese, Frederico. 2018. 'Organized Crime in the United Kingdom: Illegal Governance of Markets and Communities'. *The British Journal of Criminology* 58 (6): pp. 1381–1400.

Caulkins, Jonathan P., and MacCoun, Robert. 2003. 'Limited Rationality and the Limits of Supply Reduction'. *Journal of Drug Issues* 33 (2): pp. 433–464.

Caulkins, Jonathan P., and Reuter, Peter. 2006. 'Illicit Drug Markets and Economic Irregularities'. *Socio-Economic Planning Sciences* 40 (1): pp. 1–14.

Clarke, Ronald V. 1995. 'Situational Crime Prevention'. *Crime Justice* 19: pp. 91–150.

Contreras, Randol. 2013. *The Stickup Kids: Race, Drugs, Violence, and the American Dream*. University of California Press.

Cressey, Donald. 1969. *Theft of the Nation: The Structure and Operations of Organized Crime in America*. New Brunswick, NJ: Transaction Publishers.

Daly, Angela, Mann, Monique, Squires, Peter, and Walters, Reece. 2021. '3D Printing, Policing and Crime'. *Policing and Society* 31 (1): pp. 37–51.

Davis, Ian, Hirst, Chrissie, and Mariani, Bernado. 2001. *Organised Crime, Corruption and Illicit Arms Trafficking in an Enlarged EU: Challenges and Perspectives*. London: Saferworld Arms & Security Programme.

Decker, Scott H., Pyrooz, David C., and Densley, James. 2022. *On Gangs*. Philadelphia: Temple University Press.

del Mercado, Guillermo. V. 2022. *Arms Trafficking and Organised Crime: Global Trade, Local Impacts*. Geneva: Global Initiative Against Transnational Organized Crime.

Dhanapala Jayantha, et al. (eds.) 1999. *Small Arms Control: Old Weapons, New Issues*. Ashgate/UNIDIR.

Dube, Arindrajit, Dube, Oeindrila, and García-Ponce, Omar. 2013. 'Cross-Border Spillover: US Gun Laws and Violence in Mexico'. *American Political Science Review* 107 (3): pp. 397–417.

Duquet, Nils, and Goris, Kevin. 2018. *Firearms Acquisition by Terrorists in Europe. Research Findings and Policy Recommendations of Project SAFTE*. Brussels: Flemish Peace Institute.

Eck, John E. 1994. *Drug Markets and Drug Places: A Case-Control Study of the Spatial Structure of Illicit Drug Dealing*. University of Maryland, College Park.

Finckenauer, James O. 2005. 'Problems of Definition: What is Organized Crime?' *Trends in Organized Crime* 8 (3): pp. 63–83.

Fligstein Neil, and Dioun, Cyrus. 2015. 'Economic sociology'. In *International Encyclopedia of the Social & Behavioral Sciences*, edited by James D. Wright (ed.), pp. 67–72. Amsterdam: Elsevier.

Florquin, Nicolas. 2021. 'Gun Violence: Insights from International Research'. *Global Crime* 22 (4): pp. 288–311.

Florquin, Nicolas, and King, Benjamin. 2018. *From Legal to Lethal: Converted Firearms in Europe*. Geneva: Small Arms Survey.

Gagliardi, Pete. 2012. 'Transnational Organized Crime and Gun Violence. A Case for Firearm Forensic Intelligence Sharing'. *International Review of Law, Computers & Technology* 26 (1): pp. 83–95.

Galeotti, Mark, and Arutunyan, Anna. 2023. *Peace and Proliferation: The Russo-Ukrainian War and the Illegal Arms Trade*. Global Initiative Against Transnational Organised Crime.

Gambetta, Diego. 1994. 'Inscrutable Markets'. *Rationality and Society* 6 (3): pp. 353–368.

Gambetta, Diego. 2009. *Codes of the Underworld: How Criminals Communicate*. Princeton University Press.

Goldsmith, Andrew, Halsey, Mark, and Bright, David. 2022. 'Taking Crime Guns Seriously: A Socio-Material Perspective'. *Criminology & Criminal Justice* 22 (3): pp. 462–479.

Granovetter, Mark. 1985. 'Economic Action and Social Structure: The Problem of Embeddedness'. *American Journal of Sociology*, 91 (3): pp. 481–510.

Haller, Mark H. 1990. 'Illegal Enterprise: A Theoretical and Historical Interpretation'. *Criminology*, 28 (2): pp. 207–236.

Harcourt, Bernard E. 2006. *Language of the Gun: Youth, Crime, and Public Policy*. University of Chicago Press.

Jacques Scott, Wright, Richard, and Allen, Andrea. 2014. 'Drug Dealers, Retaliation, and Deterrence'. *International Journal of Drug Policy* 25: pp. 656–662.

Johnson, Bruce D., Hamid, Ansley, and Sanabria, Harry. 1992. 'Emerging Models of Crack Distribution'. In *Drugs, Crime, and Social Policy: Research, Issues, and Concerns*, edited by Thomas Mieczkowski, pp. 56–78. Boston: Allyn and Bacon.

Jongleux, Benjamin, and Florquin, Nicolas. 2020. 'Monitoring the Response to Converted Firearms in Europe'. Non-Proliferation and Disarmament Papers, no. 70: pp. 1–15.

Kahneman Daniel, and Tversky, Amos. 1979. 'Prospect Theory: An Analysis of Decision Under Risk'. *Econometrica* 47: pp. 263–291.

Karp, Aaron. 2018. 'Estimating Global Civilian-Held Firearms Numbers', *Small Arms Survey*, June 2018, https://www.smallarmssurvey.org/resource/estimating-global-civilian-held-firearms-numbers.

Killicoat, Phillip. 2007. *Weaponomics: The Global Market for Assault Rifles.* (Vol. 4202). World Bank Publications.
Kotzé, Justin, Antonopoulos, Giorgios, and Rahand, Mohammed, M. 2022. 'The Processes, Logics and Economies of Violence in Organised Crime'. *Trends in Organized Crime* 25 (1): pp. 1–7.
Marshall, Ben, Webb, Barry, and Tilley, Nick. 2005. *Rationalisation of Current Research on Guns, Gangs and Other Weapons: Phase 1.* London: Jill Dando Institute of Crime Science, University College London.
Massari, Monica. 2013. 'Guns in the Family. Mafia Violence in Italy.' In *Small Arms Survey 2013: Everyday Dangers.* Geneva: Small Arms Survey. https://www.smallarmssurvey.org/sites/default/files/resources/Small-Arms-Survey-2013-Prelims-Intro-EN.pdf.
May, Tiggey, and Hough, Mike. 2004. 'Drug Markets and Distribution Systems'. *Addiction Research & Theory* 12 (6): pp. 549–563.
Merton, Robert K. 1938. 'Social Structure and Anomie'. *American Sociological Review* 3 (5): pp. 672–682.
Morselli, Carlo. 2009. *Inside Criminal Networks.* New York: Springer.
Morselli, Carlo, Giguère, Cynthia, and Petit, Katia. 2007. 'The Efficiency/Security Trade-Off in Criminal Networks'. *Social Networks* 29 (1): pp. 143–153.
Naylor, Robin Thomas. 2003. 'Towards a General Theory of Profit-Driven Crimes'. *British Journal of Criminology* 43 (1): pp. 81–101.
O'Shaughnessy, Conor. 2021. '3-D Printed Firearms: How We Got Here, The Ever-Changing Threat, and How We Might Prepare for the Future'. *Rutgers Law Record* 49 (2): pp. 136–154.
Paoli, Giacomo Persi, et al. 2017. *Behind the Curtain: The Illicit Trade of Firearms, Explosives and Ammunition on the Dark Web.* RAND Europe.
Papachristos, Andrew V. 2009. 'Murder by Structure: Dominance Relations and the Social Structure of Gang Homicide'. *American Journal of Sociology* 115 (1): pp. 74–128.
Parker, Sarah. and Wilson, Marcus. 2016. *A Guide to the UN Small Arms Process: 2016 Update.* Handbook. Geneva: Small Arms Survey.
Parsons, Chelsea, and Weigend, Eugenio. 2018. 'Beyond our Borders: How Weak U.S. Gun Laws Contribute to Violent Crime Abroad'. *Cap 20.* https://www.americanprogress.org/issues/gunscrime/reports/2018/02/02/445659/beyond-our-borders/.
Reuter, Peter, and Kleiman, Mark A. 1986. 'Risks and Prices: An Economic Analysis of Drug Enforcement'. *Crime and Justice*, 7: pp. 289–340.
Sanders, William. 1994. *Gangbangs and Drive-Bys: Grounded Culture and Juvenile Gang Violence.* New York: Aldine De Gruyter.
Savona, Ernesto U., and Mancuso, Marina. 2017. *Fighting lllicit Firearms Trafficking Routes and Actors at European Level.* Final Report of Project FIRE. Milan: Transcrime.
Schaufelbühl, Stefan, et al. 2024. 'The Emergence of 3D-printed Firearms: An Analysis of Media and Law Enforcement Reports'. *Forensic Science International: Synergy* 8: 100464.
Schelling, Thomas C. 1971. 'What is the Business of Organized Crime?'. The American Scholar, pp. 643–652.
Schelling, Thomas C. 1976. 'What is the Business of Organized Crime?' In *Crime Society: Organised Crime and Corruption in America*, edited by Francis A.J. Ianni and Reuss-Ianni, Elizabeth, pp. 69–82. New York: New American Library.
Sergi, Anna. 2022. *Chasing the Mafia:'Ndrangheta, Memories and Journeys.* Policy Press.
Smith Jr, Dwight C. 1980. 'Paragons, Pariahs, and Pirates: A Spectrum-Based Theory of Enterprise'. *Crime & Delinquency* 26 (3): pp. 358–386.

Sneddon, Simon. 2022. 'Firearms, Terrorism and Organized Crime'. In *Firearms: Global Perspectives on Consequences, Crime and Control*, edited by Helen Poole, and Simon Sneddon, pp. 98–110. New York: Routledge.

Spapens, Tobine. 2007. 'Trafficking in Illicit Firearms for Criminal Purposes within the European Union'. *European Journal of Crime, Criminal Law and Criminal Justice* 15 (3): pp. 359–381.

Squires, Peter. 2021. 'Illegal Firearms, Illicit Markets and Weapon Trafficking'. In *Firearms: Global Perspectives on Consequences, Crime and Control. Routledge*, edited by Helen Poole, and Simon Sneddon, pp. 51–71. New York: Routledge.

Sutherland, Edwin H. 1972. 'The Theory of Differential Association'. In *Readings in Criminology and Penology*, pp. 365–371. Columbia University Press.

UNODC. 2004. *United Nations Convention Against Transnational Organized Crime and the Protocols Thereto*. New York: United Nations.

UNODC. 2012. *Digest of Organized Crime Cases: A Compilation of Cases with Commentaries and Lessons Learned*. Vienna: UNODC.

UNODC. 2020. *Global Study on Firearms Trafficking 2020*. New York: United Nations.

Varese, Frederico. 2017. 'What is Organised Crime?' In *Hart Studies in European Criminal Law*, edited by Carnevale Sefani, Forlati Sserena, and Giolo Orsetta, pp. 27–55. Oxford: Hart Publishing.

Vargas, Eugenio Weigend, and González, Silvia Villarreal. 2020. 'Firearms and Injuries During Home Robberies in Mexico, 2010–2017'. *Trends in Organized Crime* 25 (1): pp. 1–24.

Von Lampe, Klaus, and Johansen, Per Ole. 2004. 'Organized Crime and Trust: On the Conceptualization and Empirical Relevance of Trust in the Context of Criminal Networks'. *Global Crime* 6 (2): pp. 159–184.

Von Lampe, Klaus. 2015. *Organized Crime: Analyzing Illegal Activities, Criminal Structures, and Extra-legal Governance*. Thousand Oaks: Sage.

Von Lampe, Klaus. 2023. 'Organised Crime Definitions'. http://www.organized-crime.de/organizedcrimedefinitions.htm Accessed 23 Jun. 2023.

PART I

REGIONAL PERSPECTIVES ON ILLICIT FIREARMS MARKETS AND ORGANIZED CRIME

1

The Illicit Sources of Guns to Criminal Groups in the United States

Anthony A. Braga

Introduction

Most shootings in US cities are highly concentrated among groups of criminally active individuals who use guns to settle disputes emanating from personal clashes, drug market business, ongoing gang rivalries, and other conflicts (Klein 1995; Howell and Griffiths 2016; Braga et al. 2024). City-level studies have found gang-related motives in more than one-third of homicides in Chicago (Block and Block 1993), half of the homicides in Los Angeles' Boyle Heights area (Tita et al. 2003), and nearly two-thirds of Oakland homicides (Braga et al. 2019). In some cities, such as Baltimore, the violent street scene is characterized by various criminal groups ranging from small informal networks of drug sellers and street robbery crews to more formal gangs to larger drug trafficking organizations (Braga, Kennedy, and Tita 2002). A study of more than twenty cities generally found that, on average, less than 1 per cent of a city's population was involved in gangs, drug crews, and other criminally active groups, but they were connected to over 50 per cent of a city's shootings and homicides (Lurie 2019).

Gang members, drug dealers, robbers, and other serious criminals generally do not obtain their guns by purchase from a licensed dealer, but rather in informal transactions in underground markets supplied by guns diverted from legal commerce (Cook 2018a; Braga et al. 2002). Prominent illegal sources of guns to criminal networks include straw purchasers, unlicensed manufacturers and sellers, corrupt licensed dealers, and theft (Hureau and Braga 2018; Braga et al. 2012). Supply-side interventions seek to further limit illegal transactions and enhance the incentive for gangs and other criminal groups to economize on gun possession and use (Cook 2018a; Braga and Pierce 2005). Unfortunately, despite evidence suggesting gun violence could be reduced by disarming high-risk people, few US cities are invested

Anthony A. Braga, *The Illicit Sources of Guns to Criminal Groups in the United States* In: *Illicit Firearms Markets and Organized Crime*. Edited by: David Bright, Oxford University Press.
 DOI: 10.1093/9780198902409.003.0002

in disrupting the illegal supply of guns (Braga and Cook 2023). Federal, state, and local law enforcement agencies need to sharpen their focus on interdicting traffickers and halting theft. Problem-solving approaches can be applied to understand how criminals acquire guns in specific jurisdictions and implement interventions to shut down underground markets.

This chapter presents a detailed account of the illicit sources of guns to criminal groups and individual offenders in the US It begins by briefly reviewing the legal and regulatory frameworks that govern US firearms commerce and private ownership. Given the strong relationship between community gun prevalence and criminal access to firearms, legal firearms commerce and noteworthy changes in the technology of guns sold in the US are presented. The characteristics and sources of crime guns to prohibited persons and existing research on the illicit pathways through which gangs and other criminally active groups acquire guns are then described. Key sources of crime guns include illegal transfers in underground gun markets, firearms theft, and privately made firearms. The chapter concludes with policy recommendations on gun market disruption strategies to reduce gun violence that are supported by evaluation evidence on effective problem-oriented policing strategies.

Legal and Regulatory Framework

The US government has enacted firearms laws and regulations to reduce the harms of misuse, such as criminal gun violence, while preserving benefits of gun ownership such as for hunting and self-protection. Prominent federal laws are briefly reviewed here (for more details, see Cook 2013; Cook and Goss 2020).

Following alcohol prohibition and the associated surge in gun violence during the 1920s, US Congress passed the National Firearms Act of 1934 (NFA) which required owners of machine guns (fully automatic firearms), sawn-off shotguns, and other weapons to be registered with federal authorities. All transfers of NFA weapons were subjected to a $200 tax, which greatly limited the prevalence of these weapons. In 1986, US Congress banned the manufacture and import of machine guns for civilian use, while preserving the registration requirement of older machine guns already in the hands of citizens.

The Gun Control Act of 1968 (GCA) was enacted following an increase in crime, civil unrest, and political assassinations (Zimring 1975). The GCA strengthened federal licensing of firearms dealers and limited interstate shipments of guns to licensees, to protect states that opted for stronger gun controls from states with lax gun regulations. The GCA also prohibited certain 'dangerous' classes of people from possessing firearms, such as convicted felons, illegal immigrants, people suffering from mental illness, and youths. All firms in the firearms supply chain are required to have a federal firearms licence (FFL) and keep records of firearms shipments. Retail FFLs are required to screen prospective gun-buyers to ensure that they are not prohibited from owning a firearm, ask buyers to fill out forms attesting that they are not prohibited, and keep records of gun transfers. The GCA ensures that a firearm can be traced from an FFL to the first retail purchaser. If, after the first retail purchase, the firearm re-enters regulated commerce, the tracing process may identify additional unlicensed purchasers beyond the first retail purchaser (ATF 2023). These unlicensed secondary purchasers are commonly referred to as the last known purchaser. Finally, the GCA banned the importation of small, low-quality handguns from foreign manufacturers that did not meet a 'sporting purposes' test.

The Bureau of Alcohol, Tobacco, Firearms, and Explosives (ATF) was established as an independent agency in 1972 with responsibility for regulatory enforcement and criminal investigation of firearms trafficking. It is a relatively small agency with some 2,400 special agents charged with investigating federal gun crimes and roughly 800 industry operations investigators responsible for regulating the firearms importers, manufacturers, dealers, and other industry members. In 1986, the Firearm Owners Protection Act limited ATF's ability to inspect FFLs and maintain records that would help identify suspicious purchasing patterns. However, with the surge in gun violence associated with the late 1980s and early 1990s crack cocaine epidemic, in 1994 US Congress passed the Brady Act that enhanced the screening of prospective gun buyers by requiring every firearms purchase from an FFL to be preceded by a criminal background check. It is worth noting here that the Brady Act only applies to purchases made through FFLs. While a few states regulate private firearm sales, federal law does not require criminal background checks to be conducted by unlicensed private owners selling their guns to other citizens. The 1996 Lautenberg Amendment increased the list of prohibitions from possessing a firearm to include people who had been convicted of domestic violence, including misdemeanour offences.

Privately made firearms (PMFs) or 'ghost guns' are homemade, unserialized, untraceable firearms that are produced from nearly finished precursor parts (also see Chapter 7) or 3D-printed using software accessed for free online (Braga et al. 2022; Wintemute 2021; and see Chapter 8). Individuals can purchase pre-packaged kits with finishing and assembly instructions that include all the required parts to build a firearm. Alternatively, they may opt for partially complete kits or 80 per cent kits, which necessitate the purchase of supplemental parts. With no record of their existence and minimal skill needed for their assembly, PMFs represent an attractive entry-point to illicit activity, especially for persons who are prohibited by federal or state laws from possessing a firearm. Following the Covid-19 pandemic surge in gun violence, the Biden Administration enacted Final Rule 2021R-05F in 2022, which required PMFs that enter regulated commerce to be identified through a serial number prior to being transferred by an FFL. Law enforcement agencies are also encouraged to provide serial numbers and other identifying markings on PMFs recovered in crime to ATF for tracing. Further, the 2022 Bipartisan Safer Communities Act included several new federal firearms laws, including enhanced background checks for firearms purchasers under the age of twenty-one, clarifications to FFL requirements, and increased penalties for firearms trafficking, including 'straw purchases' where prohibited persons use proxy buyers who can pass criminal background checks to purchase firearms from FFLs.

Federal laws provide the basic legal framework that shapes firearms commerce in the US and reduces the availability of guns to gangs, drug crews, and organized crime groups. Beyond these federal requirements, some states impose more stringent requirements for firearms transfers. State laws may require buyers to obtain a special permit or licence, and licensed dealers to observe a waiting period before transfer, conduct more extensive record checks, and limit the number of guns that can be sold to any one buyer in a specified period (such as one handgun per month).

Legal Firearms Commerce

Firearms are legal commodities that sometimes end up used in crime, usually in the hands of a person who is prohibited from possessing a gun due to their criminal history, age, or other characteristic. Crime guns often originate from the legal supply chain of manufacture/importation, distribution, and retail sale (Braga, Cook et al. 2002; Cook 2018a). After the first retail sale, guns may change ownership several times. Some transfers may violate gun commerce regulations and can include theft. Knowledge of the legal supply chain is important in understanding the sources of guns to criminals, including members of street gangs and organized crime groups. In principle, any legal possessor could become a supplier of a gun to a proscribed possessor.

Surveys estimate there are more than 350 million guns in private hands in the US, more than enough to provide a gun for every adult citizen. The US stockpile of guns grows annually through the manufacturing and importation of new firearms. In 2020, domestic firearm manufacturers made more than 11 million GCA firearms and more than 240,000 NFA weapons for sale in the US; that same year, more than 6 million GCA firearms were imported for domestic sale (ATF 2022). NFA weapons are not allowed to be imported into the US for sale to private citizens. Between 2000 and 2020, controlling for US population increases, the number of GCA firearms and NFA weapons manufactured for domestic sales increased by 187 per cent, and the number of GCA firearms imported for domestic sales increased by 350 per cent. ATF (2022) noted that these general trends included sharper increases in the percentage of medium and large calibre semi-automatic pistols, assault rifles (including AR-15 and AK-47 variants), short-barrelled rifles, and silencers manufactured in and imported into the US for domestic sales.

Two-thirds of all gun transactions involve purchases from FFLs (Miller et al. 2017). In 2020, there were some 66,000 licensed dealers who sold firearms from a variety of retail outlets including stores that specialize in firearm and ammunition sales, sporting goods stores, department stores, and pawn shops (ATF 2022). These dealers are authorized to sell new and second-hand firearms and, in 2020, were responsible for selling more than 17 million firearms. The remaining one-third of gun transactions include 'private sales' between people that can occur at gun shows and through wanted ads, gifts, and other transfers (Miller et al. 2017).

Private gun ownership is concentrated in the US, with people who own at least one gun averaging about five guns (Miller et al. 2017). Legal US gun owners are more likely to be men relative to women, White relative to Black or Hispanic, and middle class relative to lower income (Cook and Pollack 2017). Increasingly, US residents buy guns for self-protection rather than for hunting or other traditional gun sports (Pew Research Center 2013). Slightly less than one-third of households own a gun, with gun ownership higher in the South and lowest in the North-east (Smith and Son 2015). Gun ownership rates vary greatly across states and localities, ranging from 60 per cent in Mississippi to 13 per cent in Massachusetts (Azrael et al. 2004). In Boston, Massachusetts, less than 4 per cent of households report gun ownership by a current household member (see Braga and Cook 2016). Community gun prevalence influences whether an offender knows someone, or knows someone who knows someone, who would be willing to loan, sell, or share a gun. Community gun prevalence also affects the likelihood that a gun might be yielded from a home burglary or theft from a vehicle as part of the stolen loot (Cook and Ludwig 2003).

The Characteristics and Sources of Crime Guns in the US

Offenders, including members of street gangs, drug crews, and organized crime groups, rarely acquire firearms from FFLs. For instance, a 2016 US government survey of state prison inmates found that fewer than 10 per cent purchased their last firearm at a gun store or pawnshop (see Table 1.1). Gun criminals tend to acquire their firearms from family members, friends, acquaintances, and via connections to the underground economy such as fences, drug dealers, and other 'street' sources (Braga et al. 2002). Firearms purchased through underground market sources have usually changed hands several times (Cook 2018a).

Analyses of ATF firearms trace data provide useful information about patterns of activity in underground markets that supply criminals with guns. Between 2017 and 2021, ATF received trace requests for 1,922,577 crime guns recovered by law enforcement agencies (see ATF 2023). The total yearly number of crime gun trace requests increased by 36 per cent from 337,903 in 2017 to 404,024 in 2021. ATF was able to trace 77 per cent of these trace requests (1,482,861 of 1,922,577) to the last known purchaser. ATF was not able to identify firearms purchasers for several reasons, including incomplete or invalid firearms information provided by the law enforcement agency making the trace request (7 per cent), the firearm was too old to trace (3 per cent), and the serial numbers on the firearm had been obliterated (3 per cent). The presence of obliterated serial numbers is viewed by law enforcement agencies as an indicator of gun trafficking, as this represents an attempt to conceal the source of the recovered crime gun (Kennedy et al.1996; Cook and Braga 2001).

Traced crime guns were predominately semi-automatic pistols with medium and large calibres (ATF 2023). Between 2017 and 2021, pistols accounted for 68 per cent of the 1,922,577 recovered crime guns traced by ATF. Rifles accounted for 12 per cent, revolvers accounted for 11 per cent, and shotguns accounted for 7 per cent of the recovered crime guns. Pistols accounted for an increasing share of crime guns recovered during this period, rising by more than 12 percentage points from roughly 62 per cent in 2017

Table 1.1 Sources of Guns to State Prisoners

Source of Firearm	Count	Percent of all responses	Percent of useful responses
Gun store or pawn shop	86	8%	10%
Flea market or gun show	10	1%	1%
Friend or family	270	24%	30%
Fence, street, or drug dealer	388	36%	44%
Crime scene	132	12%	15%
Unspecified	68	7%	–
Non-response	117	11%	–
Total	1,071	100%	100%

Source: Braga and Cook (2023) computations from US Bureau of Justice Statistics, National Inmate Survey 2016: https://www.bjs.gov/index.cfm?ty=pbdetail&iid=6187

Note: The sample was restricted to prisoners aged eighteen or older who were incarcerated in state correctional facilities within the United States during 2016 who admitted in the survey interview that they had a gun at the time of the offence. The sample was further restricted to inmates who had not been in prison prior to 2014.

to 75 per cent in 2021 (reflecting a 20 per cent increase in the percentage of pistol recovered). Almost half of the traced pistols were 9 mm, with .40 (17 per cent), .380 (12 per cent), and .45 (10 per cent) also accounting for noteworthy percentages of recovered pistols. Many traced pistols were produced by high-quality gun manufacturers. Almost 20 per cent of traced pistols recovered in crime were produced by Glock, followed by Smith & Wesson (14 per cent), Taurus (12 per cent), Sturm Ruger (9 per cent) and HS Produkt (5 per cent). In sum, the top manufacturers accounted for roughly 60 per cent of traced pistols that were recovered in crime between 2017 and 2021.

Crime gun traces provide information of the location of the FFL that transferred the firearm to the final known purchaser and the location of crime gun recoveries (ATF 2023). Between 2017 and 2021, 72 per cent of the traced crime guns were recovered in the same state where they were sourced from and 28 per cent of the traced crime guns were recovered in a different state. Location data generally show that crime guns migrate from states with less restrictive gun controls to states with more restrictive gun controls. States with strong gun controls have higher percentages of traced crime guns last purchased from FFLs in other states (suggesting interstate trafficking), such as New Jersey (82 per cent), New York (80 per cent), and Massachusetts (67 per cent) (ATF 2023). In contrast, states with weaker gun controls have higher percentages of traced crime guns last purchased from FFLs in the same state (suggesting intrastate trafficking), such as Texas (86 per cent), Wisconsin (84 per cent), and Ohio, Virginia, and Indiana (all with 83 per cent) (ATF 2023).

Time-to-crime represents the length of time between the last known purchase of a firearm and its recovery as a crime gun by law enforcement (ATF 2023). A short time-to-crime is regarded as an indicator of firearm trafficking and can provide an important opportunity for law enforcement agencies to investigate recently transferred firearms and disrupt the flow of crime guns from specific licensed dealers and purchasers (Pierce et al. 2004; Braga et al. 2012). ATF (2023) generally uses a three-year time-to-crime cut-off as a firearm trafficking indicator for traced crime guns. Between 2017 and 2021, 46 per cent of traced crime guns were recovered within three years of their last known purchase while 25 per cent of traced crime guns were recovered within one year of their purchase (ATF 2023).

As Figure 1.1 shows, the percentage of short time-to-crime guns increased among all crime guns traced between 2017 and 2021 (ATF 2023). The percentage of traces with a time-to-crime less than one year increased by 12 percentage points from 2019 (20 per cent) to 2021 (32 per cent), representing a

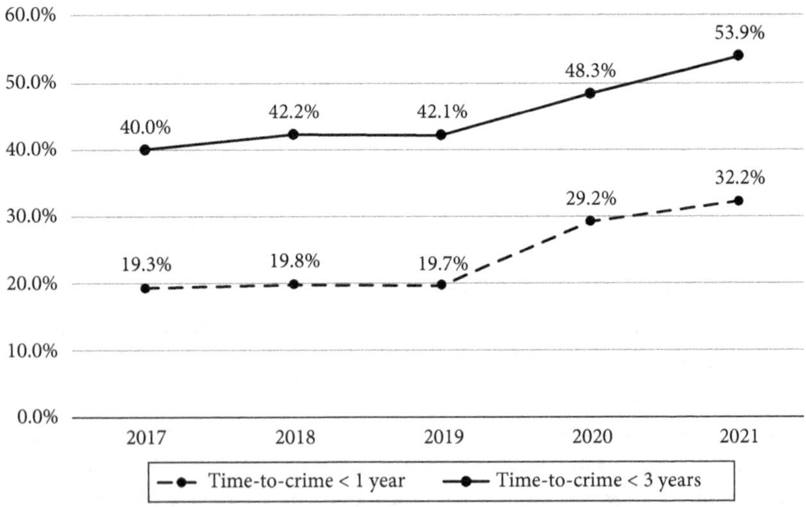

Figure 1.1 ATF firearm traces: recovered crime guns by one-year and three-year time-to-crime groupings
Source: ATF (2023).

64 per cent increase in the share of these very fast time-to-crime guns. The percentage of crime guns with a time-to-crime less than three years also increased by 12 percentage points from 2019 (42 per cent) to 2021 (54 per cent), reflecting a 28 per cent increase in the percentage of these guns. The overall increase in the recovery of fast time-to-crime guns was almost entirely driven by traced guns with time-to-crime less than one year. The average time-to-crime of traced crime guns recovered in specific cities varied considerably across US (ATF 2023). Cities located in states with weak gun controls had recovered crime guns with much shorter time-to-crime. For instance, Richmond, Virginia had the fastest median time-to-crime with 1.5 years. Detroit, Michigan (1.6 years), Columbia, South Carolina (1.7 years), and Phoenix, Arizona (1.8 years) also had very short median time-to-crimes. In contrast, New York City had the longest median time-to-crime with 6.3 years followed by Baltimore, Maryland (5.3 years) and San Jose, California (4.6 years).

Crime guns were disproportionately recovered from younger males. In almost two-thirds of the crime guns recovered and submitted to ATF for tracing between 2017 and 2021, the age of the criminal possessor was determined (ATF 2023). Some 60 per cent of the traced crime gun possessors were thirty-four years old or younger and 24 per cent were eighteen to twenty-four years old. According to the 2020 US Census, residents ages twenty-four and younger represented 45 per cent of the US population and residents ages eighteen to twenty-four represented 9 per cent of the US population. Males possessed a vast majority of the traced crime guns (91 per cent), while females possessed a very small percentage of traced crime guns (9 per cent) during the study period (ATF 2023).

Between 2017 and 2021, very few traced crime guns were recovered in the possession of the last known purchaser. Roughly 58 per cent had a different purchaser than possessor, another 29 per cent were recovered without a known possessor associated with the crime gun, and only 12 per cent had the same purchaser and possessor (ATF 2023). Many of these crime guns that changed hands were quickly recovered in crime, suggesting illegal diversion from lawful commerce. Some 43 per cent of the traced crime guns with a different purchaser than possessor was recovered within three years of purchase, and 22 per cent of traced crime guns with a different purchaser than possessor was recovered within one year of purchase.

Women are underrepresented among the gun-owning population in the US; as such, ATF (2023) views traced crime guns first purchased by women as an indicator of potential firearms trafficking. Between 2017 and 2021, the

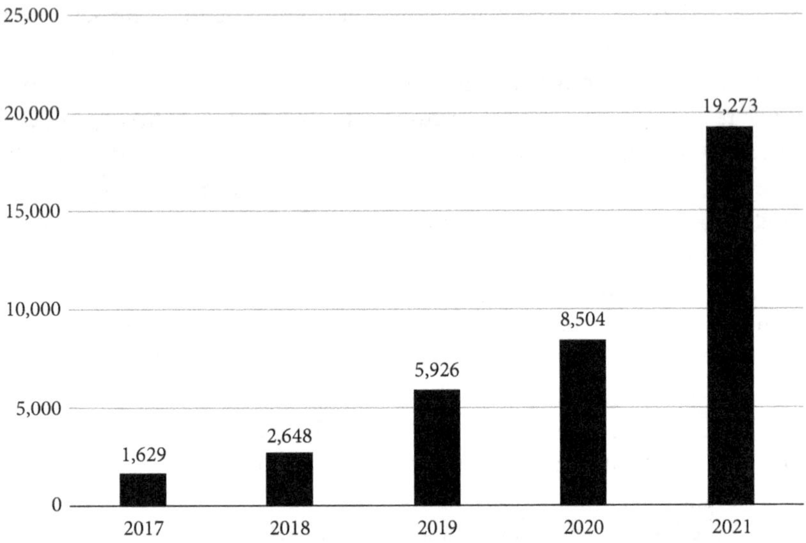

Figure 1.2 Suspected PMFs recovered by law enforcement agencies and traced by ATF
Source: ATF (2023).

median time-to-crime for traced crime guns that were purchased by a female (1.7 years) was notably shorter than traced crime guns purchased by a male (3.1 years).

ATF received 37,980 PMF trace requests between 2017 and 2021. The annual number of PMFs recovered in crime by law enforcement agencies submitted to ATF for tracing increased by nearly 1,100 per cent, from only 1,629 in 2017 to 19,273 in 2021 (Figure 1.2). The dramatic rise in PMF trace submissions reflects both increased criminal use of these firearms and enhanced awareness among law enforcement agencies resulting from ATF education, outreach, and training efforts (ATF 2023). Pistols were the most common type of PMF traced (59 per cent), followed by rifles (14 per cent) and fully automatic machine guns (12 per cent). PMF pistols were primarily 9 mm and .40 calibre firearms. PMF rifles were often fashioned as AR-15 and AK-47 style assault rifles with .223, 5.56 mm, and 7.62 mm being the most popular calibres. Some 56 per cent of PMF trace requests did not identify a manufacturer. For those that did specify a manufacturer, Polymer80, Inc. accounted for more than 88 per cent of the recovered crime guns submitted for tracing (ATF 2023).

There are very few academic studies of PMF use in crime in the US: as of the writing of this chapter, these were limited to two studies conducted in California. In Oakland, Braga et al. (2022) analysed 585 PMFs recovered in crime between 2017 and 2021. During this period, the percentage of PMFs among all recovered crime guns increased from 1 per cent in 2017 to almost 25 per cent in 2021. The most frequently recovered PMF was the 9 mm semi-automatic pistol. A multivariate analysis found that, relative to crime guns made by traditional firearms manufacturers, PMFs were significantly more likely to be recovered in violent crime. Braga et al. (2022) suggested that Oakland gun criminals seemed to prefer PMFs that cannot be traced, when committing violent acts such as fatal and non-fatal shootings. In Hayward, a separate study also observed a dramatic increase in the proportion of PMFs among recovered crime guns, rising from less than 1 per cent in 2015 to nearly 19 per cent in 2021 (Jackson et al. 2023).

Analyses of ATF firearm trafficking investigation data provide information on the types of gun trafficking channels that supply criminals in the US ATF (2024) recently released a report on 9,709 firearms trafficking investigations initiated and closed between 2017 and 2021. The most frequent types of trafficking channels identified in ATF investigations were unlicensed firearms dealing by private persons (40.7 per cent) and straw purchasing from FFLs (39.5 per cent) (Table 1.2). ATF investigations revealed a variety of illegal diversions from lawful firearms commerce, including trafficking in firearms through online marketplaces (3.6 per cent) such as Craigslist, OfferUp, eBay, Armslist, and Gunbroker; at gun shows, flea markets, or auctions (3.0 per cent); social media platforms (2.7 per cent) such as Facebook and Instagram; and through peer-to-peer applications (1.0 per cent) such as WhatsApp, TikTok, and Tinder. ATF investigations also revealed the trafficking of firearms through illegal exports (7.8 per cent) and illegal imports into (0.9 per cent) the United States.

ATF case agents established the total number of firearms trafficked in about 80 per cent of the trafficking investigations (see ATF 2024). In these investigations, ATF estimated that almost 230,000 firearms were trafficked (7,770 of 9,709). On average, these investigations involved almost thirty trafficked firearms each. However, most ATF trafficking investigations involved small numbers of firearms. Approximately 57 per cent of cases involved five or fewer trafficked firearms, and these investigations accounted for roughly 4 per cent of the total number of trafficked firearms between 2017 and 2021. While only fifty-five investigations involved the trafficking of more than 250 firearms (0.7 per cent of 7,770), these higher volume cases accounted for

Table 1.2 Total Number and Percentage of Cases by Firearm Trafficking Channel Types Identified in ATF Investigations, 2017–21

Trafficking Channel	**No. of Cases**	**% Total Cases**
Trafficking in firearms by an unlicensed dealer (private person)	3,404	40.7%
Trafficking in firearms by a straw purchaser or straw purchasing ring	3,305	39.5%
Trafficking in firearms stolen from an FFL	1,452	17.3%
Trafficking in firearms stolen from private persons	664	7.9%
Trafficking in firearms illegally exported from the United States	649	7.8%
Trafficking in firearms through online marketplaces	298	3.6%
Trafficking in firearms through unlicensed making (PMFs, etc.)	253	3.0%
Trafficking in firearms at gun shows, flea markets, or auctions	250	3.0%
Trafficking in firearms through social media platforms	227	2.7%
Trafficking in firearms by an FFL(s)	136	1.6%
Trafficking in firearms through peer-to-peer applications	83	1.0%
Trafficking in firearms illegally imported into the United States	75	0.9%
Trafficking in firearms stolen from a common carrier	50	0.6%
Trafficking in firearms through the dark web (e.g. via TOR or VPN concealer)	5	0.1%
Trafficking in firearms through printed classified or trade magazines	5	0.1%
Trafficking in firearms stolen from law enforcement or the military	4	0.0%

Source: ATF (2024)

Note: Categories are not mutually exclusive.

almost 59 per cent of the total number of trafficked firearms during the study period. This included an outlier case involving 103,111 firearms trafficked.

ATF trafficking investigations show that firearms may be stolen and subsequently trafficked from a variety of sources, including FFLs (17.3 per cent), private persons (7.9 per cent), common carriers (0.6 per cent), and law enforcement or the military (<0.1 per cent). ATF investigates firearms thefts from FFLs and common carriers but does not have direct jurisdiction to investigate theft of firearms from private persons. State and local police departments have primary jurisdiction to investigate theft of firearms from private persons. Firearms thefts from private citizens greatly outnumber firearms stolen from FFLs. From 2017 to 2021, 1,074,022 firearms were reported stolen (ATF 2023). About 3 per cent (34,339) were stolen in FFL thefts, 1 per cent (13,145) were stolen in interstate shipments, and almost 96 per cent (1,026,538) were stolen in thefts from private citizens. Very few offenders report that they personally stole their most recently acquired firearm (Cook et al. 2015). However, stolen firearms may be sold subsequently by individuals and groups specializing in firearms trafficking or by those fencing stolen goods (Cook 2018b).

Guns, Gangs, and Criminal Groups

Adult and juvenile illegal gun possessors, when asked directly, usually report wanting guns for self-protection (eg see Fagan and Wilkinson 1998; Lizotte et al. 1994; Sheley and Wright 1995; Wright and Rossi 1994). The meaning of 'self-protection' is somewhat murky but generally suggests a calculated choice to gain a strategic advantage in potential criminal encounters with victims, other aggressors, and sometimes the police (Hureau and Braga 2018). Gangs and other criminal groups serve as important contexts in shaping demand for guns. Gangs and criminal groups are important mechanisms in explaining the stability of gun violence in disadvantaged neighbourhoods (Papachristos et al. 2013) and generate a bulk of gun homicides in most cities (Klein 1995; Braga et al. 2024). Research also reveals that gangs and criminal groups facilitate gun ownership and illegal gun carrying among their members and associates (Bjerregaard and Lizotte 1995; Thornberry et al. 2003).

A study of the illegal supply of guns to Boston gang members found that their guns tended to be medium calibre (9 mm, .380) semi-automatic pistols made by reputable manufacturers such as Glock, Smith & Wesson, and Sturm Ruger (Hureau and Braga 2018). Traced guns seized from gang members were more likely to be older firearms (median time-to-crime was fourteen years) relative to guns seized from non-gang members (ten years median time-to-crime). Traced guns recovered from gang members were also more likely to have been purchased by someone else and more likely to have been purchased at FFLs in states with weak gun controls such as nearby New Hampshire and Maine, as well as Interstate 95 southern states including North Carolina, South Carolina, Georgia, and Florida. Interviews with Boston gang members and drug dealers revealed that they tended to acquire older handguns diverted by illicit gun runners who exploit unregulated secondary market transactions in states with weak gun controls (Hureau and Braga 2018). Further analyses found that Boston crime guns with trafficking indicators were more likely to be recovered from gang members, drug sellers, and other high-risk offenders who faced the greatest risk of both committing shootings and suffering gunshot wounds (Ciomek et al. 2020).

Boston gang members and drug dealers also reported paying inflated prices for handguns diverted by gun traffickers exploiting unregulated private transactions, and that they paid significant price premiums for high-calibre semi-automatic pistols (Hureau and Braga 2018). Relative to legal market prices for similar handguns, gang members and drug paid a near 200 per cent mark-up over fair market value. New guns did not command a price premium relative to their fair market value when compared to second-hand guns. The increased age of traced guns recovered from Boston gang members suggested that these firearms had changed hands several times before being acquired by their most recent owner. Interviews with gun traffickers suggested that they directly and indirectly supplied these high-risk networks with second-hand guns purchased from licensed and unlicensed sellers in states with weaker gun control laws (Hureau and Braga 2018). Traffickers preferred purchasing second-hand firearms because these 'used' guns were more difficult to trace and less likely to identify the person responsible for the illegal diversion.

A study of high-risk young adults in the Bronx and Brooklyn boroughs of New York City found that most subjects also reported that many crime guns in their neighbourhoods originated from I-95 Southern states with lax gun laws (Braga et al. 2021). The study participants regularly referred to 'the south' or 'down south' when speaking about the flow of illegal guns into their neighbourhoods (Braga et al. 2021, 11). The respondents identified three primary pathways for illegal guns reaching Bronx and Brooklyn neighbourhoods: high-volume gun brokers, middlemen, and individuals who make episodic low-level acquisitions from straw purchasers in other states. However, subjects suggested that most illegal firearm acquisitions occurred through low-level individual transactions on the street; many observed that illicit gun sales were not centralized to a handful of individuals, but rather, were spread out among many market participants. For example, one gang member explained: 'it's not like one person. It's widespread. It's various people that have [them (guns)] and various people that know people who have [them]' (Braga et al. 2021, 12). No subjects identified theft as a meaningful source of crime guns.

Many participants in the New York City study (57 per cent) reported that getting firearms was somewhat difficult (Braga et al. 2021). However, the ease of acquiring firearms was mediated by whether the respondent reported gang membership. The interviewees suggested that gang members have established supply lines and, as such, have easier access to guns when compared with their non-gang counterparts. For example, a gang member explained, 'basically, people in gang . . . they got guns ready . . . They know more people . . . got more connects (potential dealers).' Furthermore, an individual gang member's access to guns was not restricted to merely their own personal networks; rather, gang members shared 'connects.' As another gang member illustrated, '[someone in] a gang knows more people. I might know a couple, you might know a couple, he might know a couple. That might add up' (Braga et al. 2021, 11).

An analysis of ATF trace data for crime guns recovered by the Chicago Police Department between 2009 and 2013 found that the guns recovered from gang members were relatively old (median age was ten years from first retail sale), suggesting that they had gone through a series of secondary transactions before being acquired by the gang owner (Cook, Harris et al. 2015). What is more, some 60 per cent of traced guns associated with Chicago gang members were first purchased from licensed dealers in other states, especially in nearby Indiana—a state known for its permissive gun laws. Cook, Harris et al. (2015) concluded that if law enforcement is to be effective at reducing access to guns by gang members, it should focus on the intermediaries in the underground market—straw purchasers, brokers, and traffickers.

An earlier qualitative study in Chicago analysed prospective gun searches by an array of various underground market actors, such as thieves, sex workers, drug dealers, and gang members (Cook et al. 2007). The authors found evidence of considerable frictions in the market for guns due primarily to the fact that the underground gun market was both illegal and 'thin', indicating that the number of buyers, sellers and total transactions was small, and relevant information on reliable sources of guns was scarce (Cook et al. 2007). Importantly, a main characteristic of the research was the high number of failed searches—many actors, even within the criminal underworld of a disadvantaged Chicago neighbourhood, could not successfully purchase a gun. These findings, in conjunction with the relative ease with which some others acquired guns (i.e. gang members), suggest gun markets should not be expected to operate under the law of one price, but that price—and access—will be impacted by 'who you know'.

Policy Recommendations on Disrupting the Illegal Supply of Guns to Criminals

Very few gun offenders acquire their most recent firearm directly from a licensed gun dealer. This provides prima facie evidence that legislation and regulatory schemes can be effective in keeping guns out of the wrong hands. Studies show that interstate gun flows change in response to new legislation and regulation. For instance, Cook and Braga (2001) noted a large change in sources of crime guns to Chicago following the adoption of the Brady Act in 1994; the percentage coming from the deep South states, where gun stores for the first time were required to run background checks, dropped abruptly by 15 points, replaced by in-state sales. Braga (2017) showed the likelihood that a Boston handgun would be traced to a Virginia FFL nearly doubled after Virginia repealed its law limiting consumers to one handgun per month.

It is important to consider whether these changes in gun flows affected violence. The screening of retail gun purchasers required by the passage of the Brady Act did not result in significant reductions in the homicide rate in affected states (Ludwig and Cook 2000). Unregulated private transfers in secondary firearm markets undermined the provisions of the Brady Act; closing the 'private sale loophole' seems necessary to reduce criminal access to firearms. As suggested by the studies of gang members in Boston, New York, and Chicago, secondary firearm transfers represent an important supply line of guns to very risky people who generate a bulk of fatal and non-fatal shootings in cities. Unfortunately, US Congress has not passed legislation requiring regulation of private firearms transfers (i.e., universal background checks). As such, law enforcement efforts to disrupt underground markets serving gang members and other dangerous people need to be pursued.

A central goal for policing underground markets is to reduce the proportion of a typical criminal career in which the offender has access to guns. Criminal careers are usually short, with one estimate suggesting five years as the average career for people who begin committing crimes during their youth (Blumstein et al. 1982). Gun offenders often own several firearms over the course of their career, with gaps of time when they do not own a gun

(Cook 2018a). Interviews suggest that offenders sell guns when they need cash, loan guns to friends, and lose guns to theft and police confiscation. As suggested by trace data analyses reviewed above, guns tend to be quickly used in crime and removed from the street through police recoveries. Given the high turnover in gun ownership, law enforcement agencies seeking to shut down supply lines of guns to criminals should focus on transactions in underground markets rather than merely possession. Gun market disruption strategies seek to increase the price of guns sold to prohibited persons and increase the 'effective price' of acquiring guns—the time and hassle required to make a connection to buy guns (Braga and Pierce 2005; Moore 1973). In underground markets, effective law enforcement could increase the search time needed to locate a willing gun seller and enhance perceptions of legal and personal risk in participating in gun transactions.

There is promising evidence that local police departments can be effective in disrupting underground markets if they engage in strategic partnerships with ATF and other federal and state law enforcement agencies and take a problem-oriented policing approach when designing interventions (Braga 2008; Braga and Cook 2023). This approach places a premium on the comprehensive collection and analysis of crime gun intelligence to understanding the workings of underground gun markets. Gun market analyses are seriously undermined when local jurisdictions do not comprehensively process all recovered crime guns and related evidence. Without these comprehensive data, it is not possible to develop an accurate assessment of the sources of illegal guns and their use in violent crime. Law enforcement agencies at the local, state, and federal levels need to conduct a thorough review of their internal directives related to the processing of the crime guns and related evidence. Policy procedures should include processing for ballistic evidence as well as DNA, latent fingerprints, and trace evidence from firearms; processing projectiles and casings through the ATF National Integrated Ballistics Information Network (NIBIN); conducting firearms traces; and reporting to the National Crime Information Center (NCIC) (see Gagliardi 2019). The passage of federal legislation requiring universal criminal background checks on all firearms transfers would also generate critical information that could be used to monitor suspicious purchase and sale patterns in the secondary firearm market.

Boston's Operation Ceasefire intervention serves as an important example of a problem-oriented approach to disrupt underground gun markets (Braga and Pierce 2005). Based on an analysis of the local illegal gun market operating during the 1990s, the resulting strategy was appropriately focused on the illegal diversion of new handguns from retail outlets in Massachusetts, Southern states along Interstate 95, and elsewhere. The key elements of the Ceasefire gun market disruption strategy (summarized from Kennedy et al. 2001) were:

- Expanded focus of local, state, and federal authorities to include *intrastate* firearms trafficking in Massachusetts in addition to interstate trafficking.
- Focused enforcement attention on traffickers of the makes and calibres of handguns most used by gang members.
- Focused enforcement attention on traffickers of handguns that had short time-to-crime intervals and, thus, were most likely to have been trafficked. The ATF Boston Field Division implemented an in-house tracking system that flagged handguns whose traces revealed a short time-to-crime interval.
- Focused enforcement attention on traffickers of handguns used by the city's most violent gangs.
- Attempted to restore obliterated serial numbers of confiscated handguns and subsequently investigate trafficking based on these restorations.
- Supported these enforcement priorities through strategic analyses of data generated by the Boston Police Department and ATF's comprehensive tracing of crime guns and by developing leads from the systematic debriefing of gang-affiliated arrestees and those involved in violent crime.
- Deliberate communication of successful investigation and prosecution of gun traffickers to deter others from diverting firearms from retail sources to criminals and youth in Boston.

A quasi-experimental evaluation found that Operation Ceasefire's focus on close-to-retail diversions of handguns was associated with significant decreases in the percentage of handguns recovered by the Boston Police that were new (Braga and Pierce 2005). While data on street prices of new handguns paid by criminals were not available, the evaluation findings suggest that the supply-side enforcement strategy increased the 'effective price' of new handguns by making it riskier to acquire these firearms for illegal possession and criminal use. The Boston supply-side approach was implemented in conjunction with a powerful deterrence-based demand-side strategy to reduce youth violence (Braga et al. 2001). Therefore, the gun-trafficking investigations and prosecutions followed the implementation of a very successful deterrence strategy, and their effects on gun violence could not be independently established. Nevertheless, the results provide some much-needed research evidence that supply-side strategies can be used to good effect in shutting down direct pipelines of illegal guns to criminals.

In the early 2000s, the Los Angeles Police Department (LAPD), ATF, and the RAND Corporation initiated a research and development programme to understand the nature of illegal gun markets operating in Los Angeles (Ridgeway et al. 2008). The primary goal of this project was to determine whether a data-driven, problem-solving approach could yield new interventions aimed at disrupting the workings of local illegal gun markets serving criminals, gang members, and juveniles in the LAPD's 77th Street Policing District area (South Los Angeles). Problem analyses revealed that many crime guns recovered in the target area were first purchased at local licensed dealers. That is, rather than the conventional wisdom that crime guns were being trafficked across state borders from places with less stringent regulations such as Arizona and Nevada, most crime guns were purchased in Los Angeles County.

Based on their investigative experience, LAPD detectives and ATF case agents suggested that the local nature of the market was driven by prohibited possessors who were having local friends or family members conduct straw purchases for them (Ridgeway et al. 2008). Since the persons making the straw purchases did not have a criminal history forbidding them from making legal purchases, investigators believed this population could potentially be deterred from initiating this illegal activity. In partnership with the California Department of Justice, the LAPD and RAND researchers organized a 'letter campaign' intervention that attempted to dissuade legal firearm purchasers from selling or transferring their firearms to others without filing the necessary paperwork with the state. New gun buyers received a notification letter during their ten-day waiting period, before they picked up their newly purchased firearm, that informed them of their responsibilities as a gun-owner and that firearms can be traced back to them if used in a crime. The key idea of this new gun market disruption strategy was to deter small-scale straw purchasers from picking up their firearms and from making other illegal purchases in the future.

A rigorous evaluation found that the rate at which guns were reported stolen for those who received the letter was more than twice the rate for those who did not receive the letter (Ridgeway et al. 2011). Of those receiving the letter, nearly 2 per cent reported their gun stolen during the study period, compared to only 1 per cent for those who did not receive the letter. The percentage of guns reported stolen in these neighbourhoods is high, indicating a high rate of true gun theft, a regular practice of using stolen-gun reports to separate the gun buyer from future misuse of the gun, or some blend of both. This research suggested that simple, targeted gun law awareness campaigns can modify new gun-buyers' behaviours.

There are other examples of law enforcement efforts to shut down the illegal diversion of guns from retail commerce (Braga and Gagliardi 2013). Unfortunately, very few have been evaluated. Those that have been evaluated have shown notable changes to local gun market dynamics. For instance, in Detroit and Chicago, the number of guns recovered within a year of first retail sale from someone other than the original purchaser was sharply reduced after undercover police stings and law suits targeted scofflaw retail dealers (Webster, Zeoli et al. 2006). In Milwaukee, the number of guns recovered within a year of first retail sale from someone other than the original purchaser decreased dramatically after voluntary changes in the sales practices of a gun dealer who had received negative publicity for leading the US in selling the most guns recovered by police in crime (Webster, Vernick et al. 2006).

Very little is known about the post-theft supply chain in the US. While gang members and other violent criminals usually don't acquire their guns by committing burglaries and breaking into vehicles, stolen guns enter underground markets through fences and other middlemen (Cook 2018b). Problem-oriented policing approaches have been shown to be effective in controlling a wide range of theft problems including residential and retail establishment burglary, thefts from cars, and shoplifting (Clarke 1997; Scott and Clarke 2020). This approach has also been used to analyse and diminish markets for stolen goods (Sutton 2010). The practical lessons learned from these experiences could be applied in specific jurisdictions to address guns stolen emanating from residential burglaries, 'smash and grab' theft operations that target licensed dealers, and street fences who transfer stolen guns to criminals.

It is possible that the important pathways of illegal guns for specific gangs and criminally active groups of offenders at any given moment may not be important in a year's time. As mentioned earlier, there is mounting evidence that PMFs represent an emergent source of guns for dangerous people, potentially including members of gangs and organized crime groups. Individuals with criminal records and others who would not pass background checks to obtain guns can assemble them at home—often with the help of online videos and instructions—after legally buying kits and individual parts. The potential for substitution is precisely the reason that developing problem-oriented methodologies to analyse local gun markets is key to improving the capacity of local jurisdictions to respond to illegal gun supply lines. If proven methodologies exist to identify pathways of gun trafficking, law enforcement agencies can reassess the situation, diagnose the alternative supply channel, and implement a response to reduce the flow of guns to the street (Braga and Cook 2023).

Conclusion

The available evidence suggests that stemming the flow of illegal guns to gangs and other violent groups may indeed reduce gun violence. A measurable impact on firearms trafficking and related violence requires an adequate commitment of resources, however. For further gains, the firearms supply chain must be better secured through adequate regulation and enforcement. Success against underground gun markets will only be achieved by separating firearms trafficking strategy from gun politics. However, until the United States implements more rational gun control policies, local police departments should take a problem-oriented approach to understand how criminals access guns in their jurisdictions, and should collaborate with federal and state law enforcement partners to implement interventions to shut down specific gun trafficking pathways.

References

Azrael, Deborah, Cook, Philip J., and Miller, Matthew. 2004. 'State and Local Prevalence of Firearms Ownership'. *Journal of Quantitative Criminology* 20 (1): pp. 43–62. DOI:10.1023/B:JOQC.0000016699.11995.c7 Accessed 23 Jul. 2024.

Bjerregaard, Beth, and Lizotte, Alan J. 1995. 'Gun Ownership and Gang Membership'. *Journal of Criminal Law and Criminology* 86 (1): pp. 37–58. https://doi.org/10.2307/1143999 https://www.jstor.org/stable/1143999 Accessed 23 Jul. 2024.

Block, Carolyn Rebecca, and Block, Richard. 1993. *Street Gang Crime in Chicago*. Washington, DC: US National Institute of Justice.

Blumstein, Alfred, Cohen, Jacqueline, and Hsieh, Paul. 1982. *The Duration of Adult Criminal Careers*. Washington, DC: US National Institute of Justice.

Braga, Anthony A. 2008. Problem-Oriented Policing and Crime Prevention. 2nd edn. Boulder, CO: Lynne Rienner Publishers.

Braga, Anthony A. 2017. 'Long-Term Trends in the Sources of Boston Crime Guns'. *RSF: The Russell Sage Foundation Journal of the Social Sciences* 3 (5): pp. 76–95. DOI: https://doi.org/10.7758/RSF.2017.3.5.04 Accessed 23 Jul. 2024.

Braga, Anthony A., et al. 2001. 'Problem-Oriented Policing, Deterrence, and Youth Violence: An Evaluation of Boston's Operation Ceasefire'. *Journal of Research in Crime and Delinquency*, 38 (3): pp. 195–225.

Braga, Anthony A., and Cook, Philip J. 2016. 'The Criminal Records of Gun Offenders'. *The Georgetown Journal of Law and Public Policy* 14 (1): pp. 1–16. https://link.gale.

com/apps/doc/A482055774/AONE?u=anon~3ef96042&sid=googleScholar&xid=9ba0d4d2 Accessed 22 Jul. 2024.

Braga, Anthony A., and Cook, Philip J. 2023. *Policing Gun Violence: Strategic Reforms for Controlling Our Most Pressing Crime Problem.* New York: Oxford University Press.

Braga, Anthony A., Cook, Philip J., et al. 2002. 'The illegal supply of firearms'. In *Crime and Justice: A Review of Research*, vol. 29, edited by Michael Tonry, pp. 319–352. Chicago, IL: University of Chicago Press.

Braga, Anthony A., Kennedy, David M., and Tita, George. 2002. 'New Approaches to the Strategic Prevention of Gang and Group-Involved Violence'. In *Gangs in America*, edited by C. Ronald Huff, pp. 271–286. Thousand Oaks, CA: Sage Publications.

Braga, Anthony A., et al. 2012. 'Interpreting the Empirical Evidence on Illegal Gun Market Dynamics'. *Journal of Urban Health* 89 (5): pp.779–793.

Braga, Anthony A., et al. 2019. 'Street Gangs, Gun Violence, and Focused Deterrence: Comparing Place-Based and Group-Based Evaluation Methods to Estimate Direct and Spillover Deterrent Effects'. *Journal of Research in Crime and Delinquency* 56 (4): pp. 524–562.

Braga, Anthony A., et al. 2021. 'Underground Gun Markets and the Flow of Illegal Guns into the Bronx and Brooklyn: A Mixed Methods Analysis'. *Journal of Urban Health* 98 (5): pp. 596–608. https://doi.org/10.1007/s11524-020-00477-z Accessed 23 Jul. 2024.

Braga, Anthony A., et al. 2022. 'Privately Manufactured Firearms, Newly Purchased Firearms, and the Rise of Urban Gun Violence'. *Preventive Medicine* 165: p. 107231, https://doi.org/10.1016/j.ypmed.2022.107231 Accessed 21 Jul. 2024.

Braga, Anthony A., and Gagliardi, Peter L. 2013. "Enforcing Federal Laws Against Firearms Traffickers: Raising Operational Effectiveness by Lowering Enforcement Obstacles." In *Reducing Gun Violence in America: Informing Policy with Evidence and Analysis*, edited by Daniel W. Webster and Jon S. Vernick, pp. 143–156. Baltimore, MD: Johns Hopkins University Press.

Braga, Anthony A., MacDonald, John, and Tita, George. 2024. 'Defund the Police? Considerations for Reducing Gang Violence'. In *Oxford Handbook of Gangs and Society*, edited by David Pyrooz, James Densley, and John Leverso, pp. 849–869. New York: Oxford University Press.

Braga, Anthony A., and Pierce, Glenn L. 2005. 'Disrupting Illegal Firearms Markets in Boston: The Effects of Operation Ceasefire on the Supply of New Handguns to Criminals'. *Criminology & Public Policy* 4 (4): pp. 717–748.

Ciomek, Alexandra, Braga, Anthony A., and Papachristos, Andrew V. 2020. 'The Influence of Firearms Trafficking on Gunshot Injuries in a High-Risk Social Network'. *Social Science & Medicine* 259: p. 113114, https://doi.org/10.1016/j.socscimed.2020.113114 Accessed 21 Jul. 2024.

Clarke, Ronald V. 1997. *Situational Crime Prevention.* 2nd edn. New York: Harrow and Heston.

Cook, Philip J. 2013. 'The Great American Gun War: Notes from Four Decades in the Trenches'. In *Crime and Justice* vol. 42, edited by Michael Tonry, pp. 19–73. Chicago, IL: University of Chicago Press.

Cook, Philip J. 2018a. 'Gun Markets'. *Annual Review of Criminology* 1 (1): pp. 359–377.

Cook, Philip J. 2018b. 'Gun Theft and Crime'. *Journal of Urban Health* 95 (3): pp. 305–312.

Cook, Philip J., and Braga, Anthony A. 2001. 'Comprehensive Firearms Tracing: Strategic and Investigative Uses of New Data on Firearms Markets'. *Arizona Law Review* 43: pp. 277–309.

Cook, Philip J., and Goss, Kristin. 2020. *The Gun Debate: What Everyone Need to Know.* New York: Oxford University Press.

Cook, Philip J., and Ludwig, Jens. 2003. 'The Effects of Gun Prevalence on Burglary: Deterrence Versus Inducement'. In *Evaluating Gun Policy*, edited by Jens Ludwig and Philip J. Cook, pp. 74–118. Washington, DC: Brookings Institution Press.

Cook, Philip J, and Pollack, Harold. 2017. 'Reducing Access to Guns by Violent Offenders'. *RSF: Russell Sage Foundation Journal of the Social Sciences* 3 (5): pp. 2–36.

Cook, Philip J., et al. 2007. 'Underground Gun Markets'. *The Economic Journal* 117: pp. 558–588.

Cook, Philip J., et al. 2015. 'Some Sources of Crime Guns in Chicago: Dirty Dealers, Straw Purchasers, and Traffickers'. *Journal of Criminal Law and Criminology* 104 (4): pp. 717–759.

Cook, Philip J., Parker, Susan T., and Pollack, Harold A. 2015. 'Sources of Guns to Dangerous People: What We Learn by Asking Them'. *Preventive Medicine* 79: pp. 28–36.

Fagan, Jeffrey, and Wilkinson, Deanna L. 1998. 'Guns, Youth Violence, and Social Identity in Inner Cities'. In *Crime and Justice*, vol. 24, edited by Mark Moore and Michael Tonry, pp. 105–188. Chicago, IL: University of Chicago Press.

Gagliardi, Pete. 2019. *The 13 Critical Tasks: An Inside-Out Approach to Solving More Gun Crime*. Quebec, CA: Ultra Electronics Forensic Technology.

Howell, James, and Griffiths, Elizabeth. 2016. *Gangs in America's Communities*. Thousand Oaks, CA: Sage.

Hureau, David M., and Braga, Anthony A. 2018. 'The Trade in Tools: The Market for Illicit Guns in High-Risk Networks'. *Criminology* 56 (3): pp. 510–545.

Jackson, Summer, Rippy, Michelle, and Chaplin, Toney. 2023. 'Troubleshooting Violence: An Evaluation of Ghost Guns, Firearm-related Violence, and Law Enforcement Policy in a Bay Area City'. *Policing* 17: https://academic.oup.com/policing/article-abstract/doi/10.1093/police/paac114/7160216 Accessed 23 Jul 2024.

Kennedy, David M., Braga, Anthony A., and Piehl, Anne M. 2001. 'Developing and Implementing Operation Ceasefire'. In *Reducing Gun Violence: The Boston Gun Project's Operation Ceasefire*. Washington, DC: US National Institute of Justice.

Kennedy, David M., Piehl, Anne M., and Braga, Anthony A. 1996. 'Youth Violence in Boston: Gun Markets, Serious Youth Offenders, and a Use-reduction Strategy'. *Law & Contemporary Problems* 59 (1): pp. 147–196.

Klein, Malcom. 1995. *The American Street Gang: Its Nature, Prevalence, and Control*. New York: Oxford University Press.

Lizotte, Alan J., et al. 1994. 'Patterns of Adolescent Firearm Ownership and Use'. *Justice Quarterly* 11 (1): pp. 51–74.

Ludwig, Jens, and Cook, Philp J. 2000. 'Homicide and Suicide Rates Associated with Implementation of the Brady Handgun Violence Prevention Act'. *JAMA* 284 (5): pp. 585–91.

Lurie, Stephen. 2019. 'There's No Such Thing as a Dangerous Neighborhood'. *CityLab* 26 February 2019. https://www.citylab.com/perspective/2019/02/broken-windows-theory-policing-urban-violence-crime-data/583030/ Accessed 23 Jul 2024.

Miller, Matthew, Hepburn, Lisa, and Azrael, Deborah. 2017. 'Firearm Acquisition Without Background Checks: Results of a National Survey'. *Annals of Internal Medicine* 166: pp. 233–39.

Moore, Mark H. 1973. 'Achieving Discrimination in the Effective Price of Heroin'. *American Economic Review* 63 (1): pp. 193–206.

Papachristos, Andrew V., Hureau, David M., and Braga. Anthony A. 2013. 'The Corner and the Crew: The Influence of Geography and Social Networks on Gang Violence'. *American Sociological Review* 78 (3): pp. 1–31.

Pew Research Center. 2013. *Why Own a Gun? Protection Is Now Top Reason*. Washington, DC: Pew Research Center.

Pierce, Glenn L., et al. Koper. 2004. 'The Characteristics and Dynamics of Illegal Firearms Markets: Implications for a Supply-side Enforcement Strategy'. *Justice Quarterly* 21 (2): pp. 391–422.

Ridgeway, Greg, et al. 2008. *Strategies for Disrupting Illegal Gun Markets: A Case Study of Los Angeles*. Santa Monica, CA: RAND Corporation.

Ridgeway, Greg, et al. 2011. 'Intervening in Gun Markets: An Experiment to Assess the Impact of Targeted Gun Law Messaging'. *Journal of Experimental Criminology* 7 (1): pp. 103–109.

Scott, Michael, and Clarke, Ronald V. 2020. *Problem-Oriented Policing: Successful Case Studies*. New York and London: Taylor and Francis.

Sheley, Joseph F., and Wright, James D. 1995. *In the Line of Fire: Youth, Guns, and Violence in Urban America*. New York, NY: Aldine de Gruyter.

Smith, Tom W., and Son, Jaesok. 2015. *General Social Survey Final Report: Trends in Gun Ownership in the United States, 1972–2014*. Chicago: NORC. https://www.norc.org/content/dam/norc-org/pdfs/GSS_Trends per cent20in per cent20Gun per cent20Ownership_US_1972-2014.pdf Accessed 21 Jul. 2024.

Sutton, Michael. 2010. *Stolen Goods Markets*. Problem-Oriented Guides for Police Problem-Specific Guides Series No. 57. Washington, DC: US Department of Justice.

Thornberry, Terence P, et al. 2003. *Gangs and Delinquency in Developmental Perspective*. New York: Cambridge University Press.

Tita, George, et al. 2003. *Reducing Gun Violence: Results from an Intervention in East Los Angeles*. Santa Monica, CA: RAND Corporation.

US Bureau of Alcohol, Tobacco, Firearms, and Explosives (ATF). 2022. *National Firearms in Commerce and Trafficking Assessment, Volume I: Firearms in Commerce*. Washington, DC: US Department of Justice.

US Bureau of Alcohol, Tobacco, Firearms, and Explosives (ATF). 2023. *National Firearms in Commerce and Trafficking Assessment, Volume II: Crime Gun Intelligence & Analysis*. Washington, DC: US Department of Justice.

US Bureau of Alcohol, Tobacco, Firearms, and Explosives (ATF). 2024. *National Firearms in Commerce and Trafficking Assessment, Volume III: Firearm Trafficking Investigations*. Washington, DC: US Department of Justice.

Webster, Daniel W., Zeoli, April, Bulzacchelli, Maria, and Vernick, Jon. 2006. 'Effects of Police Stings of Gun Dealers on the Supply of New Guns to Criminals'. *Injury Prevention* 12: pp. 225–230.

Webster, Daniel W., Vernick, Jon, and Bulzacchelli, Maria. 2006. 'Effects of a Gun Dealer's Change in Sales Practices on the Supply of Guns to Criminals'. *Journal of Urban Health* 83: pp. 778–787.

Wintemute, Garen J. 2021. 'Ghost Guns: Spookier than You Think They Are'. *Injury Epidemiology* 8 (13): https://doi.org/10.1186/s40621-021-00306-0. Accessed 23 Jul. 2024.

Wright, James D., and Rossi, Peter H. 1994. *Armed and Considered Dangerous*. 2nd edn. New York: Aldine de Gruyter.

Zimring, Franklin. 1975. 'Firearms and Federal Law: The Gun Control Act of 1968'. *Journal of Legal Studies* 4: pp. 133–198.

2
Organized Crime and Illicit Firearms in Europe

Lina Grip

Introduction

Criminal groups are widely recognized as the primary force behind the illicit firearms market in Europe. Firearms may hold both symbolic and practical significance for organized criminal groups (OCGs). In Europe, firearms are used to protect and advance the interests of OCGs, particularly in the drug trade (Europol 2021a). Firearms and illicit drugs cause approximately equal number of fatalities in Europe each year, with both resulting in over 6,000 deaths annually (European Monitoring Centre for Drugs and Drug Addiction 2023; Flemish Peace Institute 2019). While in most European countries firearms exist more in the background compared to illegal drugs, they still have indirect consequences and repercussions similar to drugs. By enabling and exacerbating criminal activities and acts of violence, firearms play a significant role for OCGs (Europol 2021a).

The expansion of the European Union (EU) and the removal of internal borders have created new opportunities for OCGs at the regional level. Starting in the 1990s, intensified intra-regional trade facilitated the emergence of a regional market for illicit firearms (Council of Europe 2014). The trade in illicit firearms and related services, such as weapon conversion, now operates on a fully European arena. While firearms are believed to be smuggled and dispersed using the same routes and networks as other illegal products, more recent knowledge suggests that firearms markets operate in a manner different to illicit drug markets.

Europe has historically been a significant producer of firearms. While firearms trafficking and their violent use may not generate substantial financial revenue or widespread impact, they play a crucial role for the operations of many OCGs (Savona and Riccardi 2015). The correlation between

Lina Grip, *Organized Crime and Illicit Firearms in Europe* In: *Illicit Firearms Markets and Organized Crime*. Edited by: David Bright, Oxford University Press. © Oxford University Press 2025.
DOI: 10.1093/9780198902409.003.0003

firearms trafficking and criminal activity is strong (Global Initiative Against Transnational Organized Crime 2023). OCGs' access to firearms is a significant factor in enabling serious acts of violence. Furthermore, the nature of violent incidents seems to be evolving, with an increasing number of criminals employing violence more aggressively (Europol 2021a).

Like other regions, Europe is not a homogeneous place. There are vast differences in the effects of OCGs and firearm violence between countries, as well as within countries. Based on open-source data, this chapter provides an overview of the current state of knowledge regarding the nexus of organized crime and illicit firearms in Europe. Following this introduction, the chapter describes the main characteristics of OCGs in Europe, before taking a closer look at the structures of the illicit firearms markets in Europe. Subsequent sections lay out the main sources of weapons and look at the violent use of firearms by OCGs. The final sections look at European policy responses and provide conclusions.

Organized Crime in Europe

Europe is less affected by organized crime compared to other regions. Not only are organized crime levels lower, but resilience is also greater, resulting in a smaller overall societal impact than in countries with similar crime levels but weaker institutional responses (Global Initiative Against Transnational Organized Crime 2023). Nevertheless, organized crime has a significant negative impact on internal security, public trust, and economic development. An estimated 60 per cent of OCGs in the EU use violence (Europol 2021a). To intimidate and coerce their victims, OCGs typically use firearms. In the 1990s, OCGs were primarily divided along national lines. European OCGs have since become more international and multi-ethnic as people, services, and money flow more freely. Europol estimates that over two-thirds of the OCGs in Europe are active in more than three countries. OCGs are also embedded in the formal economy: over 80 per cent of the European OCGs utilize legal businesses in their operations (Europol 2022a). Interception of the encryption tool EncroChat in 2020 improved our understanding of how OCGs are structured, particularly in relation to illicit drugs and other serious crimes. For instance, significant information was disclosed regarding the perpetration of violence aimed at rivals, witnesses, or former members (Europol 2021a; Europol 2023a).

There is no tangible current evidence in public sources of specific European OCGs who use firearms trafficking as a substantial source of income and who systematically trade significant quantities of firearms and ammunition for military, political, or economic purposes. Nonetheless, various types of OCGs are involved either in the trafficking of illicit weapons and firearms modifications or as end-users, as part of their criminal repertoire (European Commission 2020; Europol 2021a). Mafia-style groups in Albania, Bulgaria, Russia, Italy, and Turkey have been known to deal extensively in illicit firearms and ammunition. However, firearms smuggling does not constitute their primary business (Savona and Riccardi 2015). For at least some of them, arms trafficking has been replaced by drug trafficking and infiltration into the legitimate economy (Fijanaut and Paoli 2004). Italian mafia groups have in the past trafficked firearms at scale for profit, and sold them in Europe, the Middle East, and North Africa (UNODC 2020). Armed conflicts between Italian mafia organizations in the 1990s also meant that they were sourcing firearms to protect themselves and the markets they controlled (Savona and Riccardi 2015). Italian mafia groups were early adopters of firearms trafficking from the Western Balkans (Albania, Bosnia and Herzegovina, Kosovo, North Macedonia, Montenegro), and they are still active in firearms trafficking in the region today (Savona and Riccardi 2015; Vázquez del Mercado 2022). They use the firearms in their own criminal operations or trade them with other criminal groups in exchange for other illicit goods. The 'Ndrangheta and other mafia groups are still considered well armed, possessing a wide range of firearms and even having their own stockpiles in rural areas. Yet, lethal firearms violence linked to Italian OCGs has declined sharply (Strazzari and Zampagni 2018; Duquet and Vanden Auweele 2021).

Outlaw motorcycle gangs are mostly associated with northern Europe, including Denmark, Germany, and Sweden (Global Initiative Against Transnational Organized Crime 2023). A rivalry exists between the two major clubs, Hells Angels and the Bandidos, which in the mid-1990s led to armed conflict where firearms had a prominent role in the killings on both sides (Fijanaut and Paoli 2004). Outlaw motorcycle gangs are on the rise in Europe (Europol 2022a). Motorcycle gangs have been known to traffic firearms throughout the EU, including between South-west Europe and the Nordic countries, as well as drawing on other OCGs to access illicit firearms (European Commission 2020; Savona and Riccardi 2015; UNODC 2020). In Germany, the Culum brothers and Bandidos have been involved in trading firearms from the Balkans and supplying them in Austria and Switzerland (Vázquez del Mercado 2022).

Firearms are an important marker of status for criminal (youth) gangs. Gangs use firearms violence as a means to strengthen and protect their own position of power in the criminal environment and in defence to protect themselves from victimization (Brå 2016). The supply of illicit firearms fuels urban gang conflicts (Europol 2021a). Gang-related firearms violence is on the rise in parts of Europe, most prominently in Sweden (Global Initiative Against Transnational Organized Crime 2023).

In Germany, clan-based groups are becoming more prominent in organized crime. Clan-based criminal groups are large family-based networks of, for example, Arab or Turkish origin. They are active in a variety of crimes such as armed robberies, money laundering, and drug trafficking. Clan groups in Berlin and Brandenburg have lately been associated with illegal weapon deals (Gerken 2022).

Data Limitations

There is very little accessible primary European data on the role of firearms in organized crime. A major obstacle to analysis is that situational and contextual factors of weapons seizures and violent crimes are not compiled at the national level in most countries. The data in this report comes from EU institutions, the South-eastern and Eastern Europe Clearinghouse for the Control of Small Arms and Light Weapons (SEESAC), previous research, reports published by national law enforcement, and interview studies with both offenders and law enforcement.

Despite many years of regional cooperation there is no consolidated European data. At the national level, three factors confuse understandings and analysis. First, there is a conflation of the contexts of organized crime and the broader term 'criminal milieu'. Several country studies report lethal violence by firearms in criminal milieus. Criminal milieu typically excludes domestic violence, and sometimes also other sub-categories of crimes like robberies but is still wider than the term 'organized crime'. Secondly, there is a tendency to combine all forms of lethal and non-lethal violence linked to organized crime. Annual national reports on organized crime, for example, include data on shootings and other violence resulting in death or injury, without segregation. Thirdly, firearm seizures are typically not categorized by type of actor or situational context. The lack of contextual and situational information is a significant obstacle for research and the development of evidence-based practices.

The Illicit Firearms Market—Structure, Methods, and Access

Regional Aspects

The European firearms market supplying weapons to OCGs is contained both geographically and in terms of the scope of weapons and actors involved. Relatively few actors are trading modest amounts of firearms to a limited number of end-users, resulting in comparatively little revenue. Firearms trafficking is considered a supplementary source of income (UNODC 2020).

While European OCGs have no need to smuggle firearms from other regions, they often depend on intra-regional cross-border supply of firearms (Duquet and Vanden Auweele 2021). For example, 95 per cent of firearms seized by Swedish police in 2021 were assumed to have been smuggled into the country, based on the country of origin and firearm types for which there is no legal market in Sweden (Swedish Police 2023). In 2010 in the Netherlands, 50 per cent of seized pistols, 25 per cent of revolvers, and 13 per cent of automatic firearms originated in Belgium, Germany, or Italy alone. Other firearms used in violence in the Netherlands were produced in mainly Balkan and former Soviet states (Liem and Krüsselmann 2022). Within the European market, producers, stockpilers, smugglers, and end-users operate within a regional market. Widespread production and a strong gun culture in Europe mean that there are also enough people with the skills needed to modify firearms. OCGs in both end-user and source countries are involved, as well as in transit countries (Fijanaut and Paoli 2004; Bruinsma and Spapen 2018).

While lucrative, firearms trafficking is relatively small-scale in terms of financial turnover. As there is not the same magnitude of profitability compared to the illicit drug trade, violent conflicts during firearms smuggling are not as prevalent as in the illicit drug market. There is little reason for competitors to 'snitch' on each other. Firearms traffickers largely operate 'under the radar' (Brå 2019). The illegal trade in firearms is typically instrumental rather than profit-oriented (Duquet and Vanden Auweele 2021). However, there are some indictors of a proliferation in actors involved in firearms trafficking and relatedly, the number of firearms being trafficked. There have, for example, been several joint law enforcement operations, resulting in very large seizures and the disruption of for-profit illicit firearms trade (see below).

Access via Networks

OCGs' access to firearms occurs in a web of social networks, and criminals source firearms within 'their' networks (see Chapter 10 on illicit firearms trafficking networks). Trafficking operations usually involve a few well-connected individuals embedded in OCGs that coordinate the purchase and transfer of firearms (Ćopić and Dokmanović 2022). Small groups or individuals work together but often have specialized roles such as to source, transport, modify, stock, or sell the firearms to end-users. The trafficking of firearms is not run by large OCGs controlling each aspect of the distribution chain. There is a level of specialization, with certain aspects requiring particular skills (Duquet and Goris 2018). Sometimes, relatively small operations make large weapon supplies to major OCGs. In Austria, a small group confessed to supplying 800 handguns and sixty automatic rifles to Italian mafia organizations between 2016 and 2018 (UNODC 2020). While large OCGs are the end-users, a leader of such an organization would not buy firearms directly from the source but place an order via a broker, to maintain distance from the firearms. The smuggling depends on a level of trust—the risks traffickers face include getting caught, the firearms being used against them, or arming 'the wrong side', resulting in retaliation (Europol 2023b). A transaction requires that the seller and the buyer already know each other, or that there is an intermediary who can vouch for them (see Chapter 11 for a deeper consideration of these issues). The knowledge that a weapon used in a shooting can be traced back to the seller if the buyer cooperates with the police necessitates some form of insurance (Brå 2019). In several European countries, law enforcement agencies have observed that firearms traffickers often use contacts within their extended families in the source countries (UNODC 2020).

In some countries, there is also domestic supply of firearms to OCGs. Such supply schemes are characterized by a concentrated group having access to a larger arsenal of firearms, which they source and distribute through established networks and personal contacts (Bruinsma and Spapen 2018). Some large OCGs are assumed to have their own arms suppliers, and Europol has identified firearms pools (Duquet and Van Alstein 2016). Elsewhere, there are no signs of criminal actors maintaining large stockpiles to control or dominate supply, rather the smuggled firearms are quickly transferred to end-users to reduce the risk of detection (Brå 2016).

Status and Access to Guns

Firearms are status markers for members of OCGs. This is presumably linked to the fact that firearms are not available to everyone. OCGs' access to firearms fluctuates in different countries and locations. Sellers, brokers, and fixers of firearms enjoy a high status in OCGs. They are relatively sheltered thanks to their access to firearms and intimate knowledge of homicides and other criminal shootings (Brå 2019).

Status within a criminal group and of the group itself predict access to weapons and what types of firearms are available. Criminal connections are a necessary but insufficient condition to buy an illicit firearm in most European states (Duquet and Goris 2018). Given that access to firearms largely depends on contacts, personal networks, and the earning of trust and loyalty, firearms ownership can be seen to reflect on one's personal characteristics and level of experience (Brå 2016). The types of firearm that are owned may also reflect their intended use. More established OCGs that use firearms in their operations prefer weapons with a 'good' reputation, such as Glock pistols (Duquet and Goris 2018). Weapons that are found less commonly, for example MP-5, Glock, Luger, or Smith and Wesson, are associated with higher status in criminal circles. The increase in demand for weapons from Western Europe and the USA (see Chapter 1 for a discussion of illicit firearms trafficking in the USA) is probably a reflection of the advancing age of Eastern European weapons that have dominated the criminal market for decades: 'You no longer settle for old rusty Kalashnikovs that don't work because they've been buried in the ground for fifteen years. If you really intended to use the weapon, and not just threaten with it, then it must not click' (Brå 2016, 64, translated from original language).

Trafficking Methods

The Ant Trade

Over the past couple of decades, the illicit firearm market in Europe has largely been characterized by what is known as the 'ant trade', where up to fifteen firearms at a time are trafficked, but most often between one and five weapons are carried by a single individual or small group at a time (UNODC 2020). According to Europol, the smuggling of very large weapons caches to the EU is rare (Europol 2022b). Nonetheless, since firearms cross-border trafficking occurs regularly and has done for a very long time, a substantial number of firearms have been trafficked (Spapens 2007).

Border seizures and offender interviews have shown that smuggling of firearms is largely undertaken using motor vehicles or hidden in legitimate cargo in trucks (Spapens 2007; Liem and Krüsselmann 2022). The 'ant trade' can be an instrumental way of setting up a larger smuggling scheme while dividing the risk of detection into smaller shares. However, in cases of small firearms seizures, the link to OCGs is typically not reported and may not even be a focus of the police investigation. In contrast, when large or very large seizures of firearms occur, connections to OCGs are often exposed. The Italian 'Ndrangheta mafia group has, for example, been associated with large-scale firearms trafficking (Strazzari and Zampagni 2018).

While most trafficking is done overland via motor vehicles, or shipped by boat, there is also trafficking of firearms by courier and post. This is especially common in the trading of firearms components and alarm weapons. Alarm weapons are blank-firing firearms used, for example, in sporting events as starting pistols. To avoid the same legislative controls as firearms, alarm weapons must not be capable of being modified using ordinary tools to expel a projectile (European Commission 2019). While the Dark web was used for purchases previously (and see Chapter 9 of this volume), there has been a shift to open Messenger services and encrypted chats (BKA 2022).

Forum Shopping

In Europe, the harmonization of national legislation has often fallen behind market liberalization (Council of Europe 2014). Making use of non-regularization in Europe is one of the key ways OCGs access firearms (Dressler et al. 2021). 'Forum shopping' refers to the flexibility of OCGs to identify and make use of loopholes and source firearms in different locations depending on temporary ease of access. Utilizing divergent legal frameworks in Europe, OCGs have frequently sourced convertible blank-firing weapons and poorly deactivated firearms in countries where they are legally sold without a requirement for either a licence or registration. Such loopholes have at different times been found in Italy, the Baltic states, and Turkey with regard to alarm and gas pistols, and Czechia and Slovakia with regard to deactivated firearms and Flobert guns. The firearms are bought legally in one country, often using false identity documents. They are transported to another location where individuals or a larger facility convert, modify, or reactivate either to restore the weapon to its original capacity or modify it into a higher calibre weapon. This stage is always illegal unless the facility has a firearms manufacturing licence. The firearms are then transported to various destinations and sold to end-users, who almost always have criminal intent (de Labbey et al. 2022; Duquet and Vanden Auweele 2021; Liem and Krüsselmann 2022; Jongleux and Florquin 2020).

While national implementation of EU harmonized standards (even in countries outside the EU, like Turkey) incrementally close loopholes, the firearms are already on the market and will stay in criminal circulation for years to come (Europol 2021a). The modus operandi of forum shopping shows that OCGs are flexible and opportunist in trading and accessing firearms. OCGs are known to leverage similar loopholes in other areas, such as port procedures and vulnerabilities in logistics chains (Europol 2023e).

Firearm Reuse

An alternative to sourcing firearms for OCGs is to buy a used firearm already in the criminal milieu. The age of many weapons used in crime suggests that a substantial share of illicit firearms have been in criminal circulation for a long time (Brå 2016). The recycling of firearms occurs frequently in Europe and is thought to reflect a lack of access to new firearms. However, firearms reuse could also reflect a lack of money to purchase new firearms. Even in contexts where firearms are accessible to criminals, they are not freely accessible. Interview studies have found that criminals only ever get rid of a firearm after a serious crime such as murder, simply because of the cost of buying a new one (Brå 2016). A police intelligence-based report compiled firearm reuse in OCG shootings in Stockholm 2015–19 (Table 2.1), including thirty-two murders. In total, one-fifth of the firearms had been reused. Many of the shootings included more than one firearm, and in almost half of the shootings (42 per cent) one of the firearms had been reused. Typically, the firearms that had been reused had been used in two different shootings during the period. However, closer to a third had been used in between three and five shootings (Sturup 2020).

Table 2.1 Identified firearms linked to shootings in Stockholm 2015–19

Weapon use	2015–19
Total number of shootings	563
Total number of used firearms	444
Unknown weapons	247
Reused but not seized weapons	52
Seized weapons used in one (1) shooting	107
Seized and reused weapons (used in > 1 shooting)	39
Total number (share) of reused weapons	91 (20%)
Total number (share) of shootings with reuse of at least 1 weapon	187 (42%)

Source: Swedish Police. 2020. *Illegal vapenanvändning i polisregion Stockholm Strategisk rapport (Polismyndigheten: polisregion Stockholm).*

Origin and Types of OCG Firearms

This section describes the types of firearms OCGs in Europe use and the most common origins of the weapons.

Former Military and Police Stockpiles

The fall of the Soviet Union and several other communist regimes in Europe, along with the Balkan wars in the 1990s, can be described as a perfect storm for OCGs and firearms diversion. Countries like Czechoslovakia and Yugoslavia had significant small arms and light weapons (SALW) industries when they were divided (Vázquez del Mercado 2022). The fall of communism and the subsequent division of Czechoslovakia in 1993 contributed to a diversion of firearms to OCGs in Europe. While many of the Czech weapons were traded to conflict zones in other continents, substantial numbers also found their way to organized criminals in Europe, usually involved in drug trafficking and prostitution. The Czech weapons most in demand by OCGs were the 9 mm Česká Zbrojovka CZ 75 and CZ 85 pistols, Škorpion and other sub-machine guns, and AK-47 rifles. Czechoslovakia also had clandestine production including assembly factories where serial numbers were removed, and workshops for de- and reactivation of weapons (Sagramoso 2001). These activities still occur in Czechia and Slovakia today (Duquet and

Vanden Auweele 2021; Dressler et al. 2021; de Labbey et al. 2022; Liem and Krüsselmann 2022). Czech weapons remain some of the most frequently used in shootings related to OCGs in Sweden (Brå 2016).

High levels of firearm diversion also occurred in Albania following the toppling of the government there in 1997. In a few months, an estimated 652,000 weapons and 1.5 billion rounds of ammunition were looted from weapons depots. Amnesty periods over the following years are believed to have recovered only about one-third of these weapons (Saferworld 2005). Some of the looted weapons were smuggled early on into Western Europe through collaborations between Albanian OCGs and the Italian 'Ndrangheta at high profit. Some remained in Italy, where they fuelled the bloody mafia wars of the 1990s (Savona and Riccardi 2015).

Firearms from former military stockpiles in Yugoslavia have leaked into European criminal markets incrementally since the 1990s, and smuggled weapons have now remained in criminal circulation across Europe for up to thirty years (Vázquez del Mercado 2022; BKA 2022; Sagramoso 2001; Spapens 2007). While many of the firearms were diverted from military stockpiles, small workshops and factories also operated during the war producing Serbian Zaztava pistols, Yugoslav AK-47s, Croatian Agram sub-machine guns, and Croatian HS pistols, and later diverted to Western Europe. Croatian workshops were also involved in restoring deactivated CZ pistols and Russian Makarov pistols, which were sold in the Austrian and German criminal markets (Sagramoso 2001). Roughly 3,000 Croatian HS and Serbian Zaztava pistols were smuggled to the Netherlands annually at that time (Sagramoso 2001). The smuggling was linked to Croatian OCGs (Spapens 2007).

Most military-grade firearms held by European OCGs today originate from the Western Balkans. Military-grade weapons make up a small part of seized weapons in Europe (Savona and Mancuso 2017), more so in the Western Balkans than elsewhere (SEESAC 2023a). While the criminal use of fully automatic weapons, such as sub-machine guns and automatic rifles, remains rare (UK NCA 2022), the use of military-grade firearms is more intimately connected to OCGs compared to other weapon types (Duquet and Goris 2018). According to ballistics analysis, 'prohibited weapons' (including military-grade firearms) accounted for 29 per cent of all firearms used in the context of OCGs in Belgium between 2006 and 2020 (de Labbey et al. 2022). Europol has observed an increase in the availability of heavy weapons in criminal milieus (Europol 2021a). Economic crisis and a reduced need to retain firearms in the Balkan region might have increased cross-border trafficking (Duquet and Vanden Auweele 2021). However, it is not certain that the surge in armed violence linked to some OCGs is a result of increased trafficking from the Balkans, given that so many of the weapons are already in circulation. In the past few years, law enforcement authorities in Sweden have seized more firearms linked to OCGs than Serbian authorities have seized firearms regardless of contexts. Between 2012 and 2016 a total of 7,048 firearms were seized in Serbia, the majority of them pistols and revolvers (52 per cent) and rifles (21 per cent). Only a small part was seized at border-crossings (Swedish Police and Customs 2023; Ćopić and Dokmanović 2022). A majority of the firearms in Sweden linked to OCGs are old firearms from the Western Balkans and Czechoslovakia. While Balkan weapons are still often used in shootings in Sweden, seizures of such firearms peaked in 2017 and have declined since (Swedish Police and Customs 2023).

Reactivated Weapons

Firearms that were originally designed to fire live ammunition can be modified to prevent them from expelling projectiles. This can be done through firearms deactivation or by converting them into blank-firing weapons, Flobert guns, or acoustic expansion weapons. In the past, deactivated weapons were not regulated by EU firearms legislation and could be traded freely in most member states. Furthermore, in certain European countries, the deactivation process for firearms was not thorough, making it easy to reactive the weapons (Duquet and Vanden Auweele 2021).

Reactivated firearms constitute a significant proportion of the firearms used by OCGs in Europe, and seizures have included reactivated handguns, semi-automatic rifles, and assault rifles (Florquin and King 2018; Europol 2021a; Swedish Police and Customs 2023; de Labbey et al. 2022). Poorly deactivated weapons have been reactivated and used in crime in Europe since at least the 1990s. In the UK during that time, most shootings involving automatic weapons were carried out using reactivated firearms, specifically 9 mm Uzi sub-machine guns and MAC 10 sub-machine guns. OCGs were identified as the primary users and traders of these firearms (Sagramoso 2001). In the late 1990s, junk dealers in Austria legally purchased large quantities of deactivated service weapons, reactivated them, and sold them to OCGs. Croatian OCGs acquired significant numbers of deactivated Makarov pistols previously used by the East German police, and converted them into functioning firearms. By 2000, over 20,000 Makarov pistols, which had been legally bought in the Czech Republic, had been smuggled into the Netherlands.

The main end-users were OCGs (Sagramoso 2001). In 2021, Swedish law enforcement seized Walther, Makarov, FEG, and Tokarev pistols multiple times in connection with various crimes by criminal networks (Swedish Police and Customs 2023). Reactivated pistols have also been used by OCGs in Belgium (de Labbey et al. 2022). Over the last decade, Europol has observed a significant increase in the supply of poorly deactivated and reactivated firearms to criminals in Europe (Europol 2021a).

Converted Firearms

OCGs in Europe to a growing extent rely on modified weapons for their relative ease of access and low price (Duquet and Goris 2018). Convertible alarm and gas pistols, which have circulated widely since the 1990s, now make up a large share of seized firearms used in shootings. In 2017, 91 per cent of firearms seizures in Lithuania involved assembled or converted firearms (Duquet and Vanden Auweele 2021; BKA 2022; Europol 2021a). Shooting incidents have also increased. Almost 20 per cent of the firearms used in shootings in Belgium between 2006 and 2020 involved modified firearms (de Labbey et al. 2022). In the Netherlands, gas or alarm pistols accounted for at least thirty shootings in 2015–19, several resulting in injury or death. In the past decade, convertible blank-firing firearms from Turkey, the Ekol and Atak Arms/Zoraki, have become widely popular among criminals, including OCGs (Duquet and Vanden Auweele 2021). In 2021, Atak Arms was the most seized firearm in Sweden related to crimes, the vast majority in connection to OCGs (Swedish Police and Customs 2023). In the past, converted alarm pistols were associated with young and low-ranking criminals, and much of the crime was assumed not to be directly connected to OCGs. However, as the quality of converted gas pistols has improved, while prices have remained low and products accessible, they are partly replacing semiautomatic pistols—the weapon of choice for OCGs. Convertible firearms also challenge some of the existing dynamics of the illegal firearms market, which was traditionally not profit-oriented and concentrated within closed personal networks. Since 2020, there have been several very large seizures of converted firearms related to OCGs. The initial risk for trafficking gas pistols is lower, while profit margins are higher. Gas pistols can be bought for €150 or less and sold for €500 and above (Duquet and Vanden Auweele 2021; Europol 2021a). As it becomes easier to source, transport, and convert the product, there is also more interest for OCGs in owning 'the full chain', from source to end-use.

3D-Printed Firearms

In the past decade, 3D-printing technology has advanced while the technology costs have been reduced (for more discussion see Chapter 8 of this volume). The 3D-printing technology used to manufacture a firearm or essential components (so-called hybrid weapons) can now create more robust firearms compared to the early simpler plastic single-shot pistols. Police seizures of 3D-printed components and firearms are increasing, and workshops have been dismantled across Europe, including in the UK, Finland, the Netherlands, Germany, and Spain (Duquet and Vanden Auweele 2021). Recent seizures have included examples of fully and semi-automatic submachine guns of the type FGC-9.10. Swedish police seized ten 3D-printed firearms during January and February 2023, as many seized 3D firearms as throughout 2022 (Swedish Police and Customs 2023). Law enforcements believe it is highly likely that criminals, including OCGs, have a growing interest in hybrid 3D-printed firearms (UK NCA 2022; BKA 2022).

Firearms Violence in Organized Crime

Illicit firearms are a regional problem in Europe, but the impact of firearms in national contexts varies significantly. Many countries, including Spain and Poland, are used for the transit or modifications of firearms. In 2020, Spain reportedly seized more firearms (7,782) than any other European country outside of Russia (UNODC 2022). The transit countries are necessary to supply new firearms to end-users, for example, in the Nordic region, the Netherlands, and Belgium, but do not themselves suffer much of the consequences in terms of violence. The firearm homicide rates in Poland, Germany, and Spain are the lowest on the continent (Krüsselmann et al. 2023).

Narcotics Trade

The best-documented overlap between illicit firearms violence and organized crime is in the illicit drug trade, and the subsequent rivalry between suppliers. Most criminal firearms violence in Europe occurs within the drug milieu (UNODC 2020). In 2020, 56 per cent of firearms incidents (sixty-eight) reported in the context of organized crime in the SEESAC countries were connected to narcotics (SEESAC 2023b). In the UK, 99 per cent of firearms seizures are reportedly linked to drug wars, and most firearms discharges correspond with crime groups and street gangs involved in drug supply (UNODC 2020). In Spain, most homicides and firearms injuries are linked to drug trafficking and disputes (Vázquez del Mercado 2022; Duquet and Vanden Auweele 2021). Law enforcement authorities in Denmark, Belgium, the Netherlands, and Sweden are also reporting a rise in firearms possession and violence in narcotic crimes and that the police more often seize firearms as part of drug investigations (De Schutter and Duquet 2023). In Sweden, gun violence is strongly concentrated to locations with open drug markets, particularly drug markets located in disadvantaged areas (Gerell et al. 2021; Magnusson 2023). The European drugs trade is primarily driven by cocaine from Latin America, followed by cannabis and synthetic drugs. Record cocaine seizures have been reported across European ports in the last two years (EMCDDA 2023). The leading discourse explains the local upsurge of firearms violence in the Netherlands and Belgium as caused by the increase in drug trafficking in and around ports and the emerging rivalry between OCGs for dominance and profits (Europol 2023e), along with an intensification of firearm access by OCGs active in the drug trade exacerbating the effects of criminal conflict (De Schutter and Duquet 2023). The past few years have seen an increase in demand for, and use of, firearms within the European drug trade (Vázquez del Mercado 2022). People involved in the drug trade are more often armed compared to other criminals (Duquet and Vanden Auweele 2021). When firearms are used in the context of drug crime, they are more likely to lead to injury or death, compared to when they are used in armed robberies. Drug-related firearms violence is more likely to include automatic rifles and other types of military-grade firearms (De Schutter and Duquet 2023).

Armed Robbery

Many armed robberies in Europe do not involve either firearms or OCGs. Instead, armed robberies are more often carried out with a knife or an other form of weapon. To estimate the scale of armed robberies involving a firearm and committed by an OCG is impossible, given that no European countries publish such data. However, armed robberies by mobile OCGs operating in multiple countries are on the rise in Europe, especially active Western and Northern Europe (Europol 2023d). Jewellery stores and other businesses selling highly valuable and compact goods are key targets for OCGs which engage in armed robberies. Law enforcement operations targeting mobile OCGs have seized firearms (Europol 2023d). Firearms are used to intimidate owners, staff, or witnesses in organized robberies. Yet robberies resulting in firearms injuries are relatively uncommon (de Labbey et al. 2022). While handguns are most often used in armed robberies involving a firearm, high-profile robberies sometimes involve automatic rifles (Duquet and Vanden Auweele 2021).

Homicides Linked to Organized Crime

Lethal firearms violence has decreased in almost every country in the EU since the 1990s, even though the EU has nearly doubled its membership during that time. The annual average homicide rate per 100,000 of the population in Europe dropped from 7.7 in 2000 to 2.8 in 2018. The European rate of firearms homicide (0.3 per 100,000 population) is well below the global average (3.1 per 100,000 population) (UNODC 2019). Significant improvements have been seen in countries with high homicide rates, such as the Baltic states, Bulgaria, and Kosovo (UNODC 2023a; Duquet and Vanden Auweele 2021).

European states do not typically compile data on the typology of crimes. For example, only thirteen European countries submit data to United Nations Office on Drugs and Crime (UNODC) on homicides linked to OCGs or gangs, and most of them reported zero murders linked to organized crimes or gangs in 2022. Only Italy and France reported any significant number: thirty murders in Italy in 2022 and fifty-six in 2021. However, the number of homicides committed with a firearm is not specified (UNODC 2023b). In general, firearms are reportedly used in 12 per cent of all homicides in Europe (compared to the global average of 40 per cent). Only 6 per cent of the homicides by firearms were conducted in the context of OCGs (including gangs). In 2019, only 5.5 per cent of homicides in Italy were ascribed to the mafia, compared to one-third in the early 1990s (Duquet and Vanden Auweele 2021).

Many EU member states report firearm violence as rare in the context of OCGs. Slovenia has 'up to five' murders and manslaughters linked to OCGs in a year. However, that includes all forms of lethal violence, including firearms (Communication between the author and Slovenian Criminal Police Directorate 13 March 2023). The low level of firearms homicides linked to OCGs is believed to be influenced by the tighter control of firearms and violence in more top-down, hierarchical OCGs, compared to the looser network structures found in Sweden and the Netherlands (Duquet and Vanden Auweele 2021).

Sweden has experienced an unparalleled rise in fatal gang violence, arguably driven by socio-economic marginalization, the drug trade, and illegal firearms (Global Initiative Against Transnational Organized Crime 2023). Since 2017, about fifty people per year have been killed by firearms (Swedish Police 2024). An estimated 88 per cent of the fatal shootings during the same period have been linked to criminal networks (Swedish police include gangs in their definition of criminal networks) (Author interview with Swedish Police 2023). During the last decade, there has been a sharp increase in fatal shootings connected with OCGs (BRÅ 2020). In 1990–95, only 20 per cent of fatal shootings were linked to criminal environments (BRÅ 2020). For homicides in Stockholm's criminal environments, in the years 2013–17, the murders were committed with firearms in 95 per cent of the cases (Brå 2020). Many shootings have been retaliation shootings, a result of conflicts between rival gangs (Sturup el al. 2017). In Sweden, homicides by firearms are almost always connected to OCGs in socioeconomically weak areas. For most of Sweden, firearms homicides are actually lower than the European average (0.2 per 100,000 men), but in vulnerable areas the frequency is up to ten times higher (Brå 2020).

In Denmark, almost all shootings in public spaces are believed to be linked to OCGs (Grip 2018). Over the years, the share of firearm homicides in the criminal milieu, such as disputes, have increased (Krüsselmann et al. 2023). Police report a substantial decline in gang conflict related shootings in public spaces. However, the number of deaths related to organized crime, of all types, have not shown the same development. The drop in firearms shootings and the lack of decline in deaths presumably result from law enforcement targeting firearms and publicly displayed violence, rather than reducing gang conflict (Figure 2.1).

In the Netherlands, firearms are the primary modus operandi for homicides that occur in the context of OCGs. Reportedly, 90 per cent of all homicides linked to OCGs were carried out with a firearm (UNODC 2020). Between 2013 and 2015, ninety-eight targeted shootings linked to OCGs took place, including a number of retaliation shootings. There is an assumed arms race among OCGs, linked to the production or distribution of illicit drugs. Close to 60 per cent of the firearms homicides between 2015 and 2019 took place in the criminal milieu. The locations of the shootings suggests a clear link to drug markets, trafficking, and criminal disputes (Liem and Krüsselmann 2022).

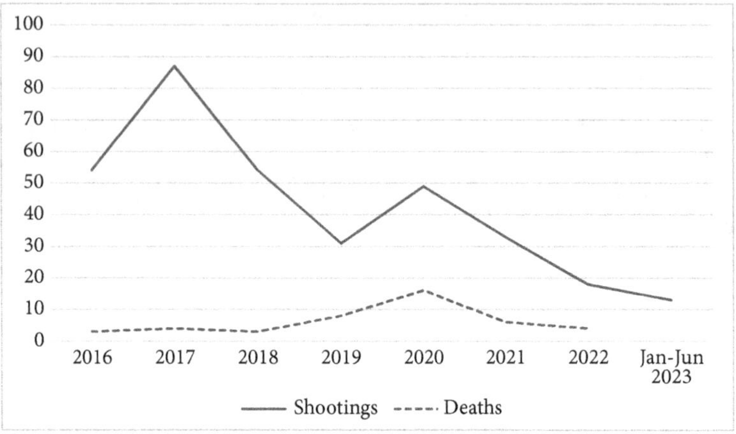

Figure 2.1 OCGs related shootings in public spaces 2016–22
Sources: Politi Nationalt Efterforskningscenter *Rocker- og bandesituationen i Danmark (2016–2023),* https://politi.dk/aktuelt/statistik/bander-og-rockere

Based on ballistic data, more than half of all lethal (62.3%, n = 91) and non-lethal (59.2%, n = 221) shootings in the Netherlands between 2015 and 2019 involved pistols. A Glock pistol was used in about 20 per cent of analysed shootings against individuals, followed by a Zastava pistol (15%). The second most prevalent category was automatic firearms, including rifles such as the AK-47 or (sub-)machine guns such as the Uzi or the Škorpion. Given what is known about criminal access to firearms like Glock pistols, Uzis, or the Škorpion in Europe, a significant share of lethal and non-lethal shootings can be assumed to have taken place in the context of organized crime (Liem and Krüsselmann 2022).

Policy Responses

European regional responses to prevent OCGs having access to firearms, and to reduce associated violence, are relatively advanced. In 2002, the United National Development Programme and the Stability Pact for Southeast Europe launched SEESAC to combat SALW trafficking in the Western Balkans. SEESAC has been successful in supporting national institutions, reducing firearms stockpiles (342,000 firearms have been destroyed since the onset), and monitoring SALW violence in the region. Funding comes from European states, the USA, and the EU. Since 2002, the EU has been providing financial assistance to the Western Balkans for small arms control projects worth almost EUR 30 million (European Commission 2020). During the early period, a major concern was the involvement of European OCGs in the trafficking of SALW with ongoing conflicts outside of Europe, which violated UN embargoes (Council of Europe 2004). Starting with the European Security Strategy in 2003, which determined that organized crime (including illicit firearms) was a threat to European internal security, there was a sharp shift toward preventing the flow of illicit firearms within Europe, with the aim of curbing organized crime.

While patchy and with loopholes, the EU initially started to harmonize firearms legislation among EU member states in 1991. The EU Firearms Directive (Directive 1991/477/EC) has been amended twice (in 2008 and 2017). It has raised the minimum standard of legislation in a number of EU countries, including by prohibiting private ownership of military-grade weapons, certifying registration, and licensing procedures, ensuring that deactivation standards are sufficiently robust, and that any convertible weapon is considered a firearm under the law. Later amendments have, for example, incited changes to national legislation in Czechia, Lithuania, and Slovakia to address the availability of convertible alarm pistols and Flobert firearms (de Labbey et al. 2022). Partly motivated by a series of terrorist attacks in Europe and the presence of more powerful OCGs, the European Commission has stepped up its policy responses to fight illicit trafficking in firearms and organized crime since 2013 (Duquet and Vanden Auweele 2021; also see Chapter 12 for discussion of terrorist groups and access to illicit firearms). In the last few years, the European Commission has adopted strategies and action plans to curb OCGs and firearms trafficking (European Commission 2020; European Commission 2021). In practice, this has inter alia involved amending the legal framework, funding over a dozen studies, and increasing cooperation with South-east Europe (European Commission 2024).

Law enforcement agencies in EU and SEESAC member states have developed strategies for cooperation, the current scheme being called European Multidisciplinary Platform Against Criminal Threats (EMPACT). EMPACT is the EU's instrument for multiagency operational cooperation to fight organized crime at an EU level. One of the work areas is to target criminal networks and individual criminals involved in the illicit trafficking, distribution, and use of firearms. One of the coordinated activities is so-called 'Joint Action Days', cross-border law enforcement operations targeting serious international and organized crime. Results have varied a lot over the years (Europol 2023c). Between 2018 and 2021, EMPACT operations resulted in the seizure of 16,607 firearms and weapons (Council of the EU 2022). To target firearms trafficking remains one of the priority areas for 2022–25, but

Table 2.2 EMPACT results on firearms trafficking

Year	Arrests	Seized firearms	Seized ammunition	Investigations initiated
2019	1,069	6,072	31,369	NA
2020	154	2,480	10,528	NA
2021	404	4,020	17,468	501
2022	57	757	NA	395

Source: Europol EMPACT results fact sheets 2019-2022 (published 2020–23).

results have plummeted in this policy cycle (see Table 2.2). Presumably, the Joint Action Days are not specifically targeting illicit firearms, at least not to the same extent as before.

Conclusions and Policy Recommendations

Cross-border trafficking is a common way for OCGs to source firearms. Firearms trafficking to OCGs in Europe is regional and organized. Smaller smuggling schemes take advantage of the open borders, the differences in national firearm laws, personal networks generated from intra-European migration, and large, accessible stockpiles of firearms. The trafficking of firearms in Europe is characterized by international specialized criminal networks, utilization of loopholes, and modern communications technology. The markets also rely on tight social networks, trust, and loyalty. Although remarkably stable over time, there have been several recent developments in the illicit firearms markets in Europe. These developments are presumably linked to a reduced reliance on armed violence by large OCGs, partial dismantling of large hierarchical OCGs, and the emergence of a multitude of criminal networks, in combination with new technologies. Today, OCGs arguably need to rely less on corruption to source firearms and can use looser criminal contacts or their own means to source modified firearms and 3D-printed firearms. Homicides by firearms in the context of OCGs are unevenly distributed in Europe. Sweden, Italy, the Netherlands, and parts of the Balkans see the highest rates of firearms homicides related to OCGs. When homicides do occur in the context of OCGs, firearms are typically the modus operandi.

Policy Recommendations

Based on the foregoing, several key policy recommendations emerge:

- European policy documents describe illicit firearms as a major security threat that is intimately connected with organized crime. Yet, few countries have any statistics to back this up and many European countries do not report any homicide by firearms in the context of OCGs. To enhance knowledge, EU institutions and member states need to better and more accurately describe the problem of the contemporary relations between OCGs, illicit firearms, and gun violence in Europe. One area in need of improvement is to capture the nuances of the problem, reflecting on the large differences that exist within and between countries. This includes avoiding sweeping and alarmist statements for Europe or the EU in favour of richer descriptions of local challenges. Interventions could be targeted to local contexts and 'hot spots'.
- Over the past few decades, countries and institution have made significant progress in reducing armed violence, including that by OCGs. Such cases provide opportunities for learning from best practice and positive developments. To identify relevant cases, national and regional actors need to keep better track of progress and emerging trends.
- Given the recent decline in seized firearms and arrests under EMPACT, there is a need to re-focus on illicit firearms in joint operations under EMPACT. A better knowledge base allows for the targeting of interventions to local contexts and 'hot spots'.
- Almost all European states need to improve data and start sharing statistics to inform the public, facilitating exchange across state borders with regards to firearms crime by OCGs. Such data is necessary to enable researchers to take on some of the above tasks to improve knowledge and allow for the development of evidence-based practice.

References

Brottsförbyggande rådet (Brå). 2016. *Kriminella Nätverk och Grupperingar Polisers Bild av Maktstrukturer och Marknader*. Rapport 2016:12. Stockholm: Brå.

Brottsförbyggande rådet (Brå). 2019. *Skjutningar i Kriminella Miljöer: En Intervjustudie*. Stockholm: Brå.

Brottsförbyggande rådet (Brå). 2020. *Dödligt Våld i den Kriminella Miljön*. Stockholm: Brå.

Bruinsma, Monique, and Spapen, Toine. 2018. 'Terrorist Access to Firearms in the Netherlands'. In *Triggering Terror: Illicit Gun Markets and Firearms Acquisition of*

Terrorist Networks in Europe, edited by Nils Duquet, pp. 285–326. Brussels: Flemish Peace Institute.

Ćopić, Sanja, and Dokmanović, Mirjana. 2022. *A Snapshot of Illicit Firearm-Trafficking and Gun Violence in Serbia.* Project Target report. Flemish Peace Institute: Brussels.

Council of Europe. 2004. *Organised Crime Situation Report 2004: Focus on Cyber-Crime.* Strasbourg: CoE. https://www.coe.int/t/dg1/legalcooperation/economiccrime/organisedcrime/Organised%20Crime%20Situation%20Report%202004.pdf Accessed 27 Jul. 2024.

Council of Europe. 2014. *White Paper on Transnational Organised Crime.* Strasbourg: CoE. https://edoc.coe.int/en/organised-crime/6837-white-paper-on-transnational-organised-crime.html Accessed 27 Jul. 2024.

Council of the European Union. 2020. *EMPACT—EU Policy Cycle to Tackle Organised and Serious International Crime.* Publications Office: Brussels. https://www.consilium.europa.eu/en/documents-publications/publications/empact/ Accessed 27 Jul. 2024.

Council of the European Union. 2022. *Results of the EU's Fight Against Crime (2018–2021).* https://www.consilium.europa.eu/en/infographics/fight-against-organised-crime-2018-2021-results/ Accessed 27 Jul. 2024.

de Labbey, Quitterie, Vanden Auweele, Dennis, and Duquet, Nils. 2022. *Firearm Trafficking and Gun Violence in Belgium.* Brussels: Flemish Peace Institute.

Dressler, Matteo, Duquet, Nils, and Eckelmann, Julia. 2021. *Forgotten Weapons? Non-Regularised Firearms in the European Union.* Brussels: Flemish Peace Insitute.

Duquet, N, and Goris, Kevin. 2018. 'The Illicit Gun Market in Belgium: A Lethal Cocktail of Criminal Supply and Terrorist Demand'. In *Triggering Terror. Illicit Gun Markets and Firearms Acquisition of Terrorist Networks in Europe*, edited by Nils Duquet. Brussels: Flemish Peace Institute.

Duquet, Nils, and Van Alstein, Maarten. 2016. *Guns for Sale: The Belgian Illicit Gun Market in a European Perspective.* Brussels: Flemish Peace Institute.

Duquet, N, and Vanden Auweele, Dennis. 2021. *Targeting Gun Violence and Trafficking in Europe.* Brussels: Flemish Peace Institute.

European Commission. 2019. 'Commission Implementing Directive (EU) 2019/69 of 16 January 2019 Laying Down Technical Specifications for Alarm and Signal Weapons under Council Directive 91/477/EEC on Control of the Acquisition and Possession of Weapons'. *Official Journal of the European Union* L15: pp. 22–26. https://eur-lex.europa.eu/legal-content/EN/TXT/?uri=CELEX%3A32019L0069 Accessed 27 Jul. 2024.

European Commission. 2020. Communication from the Commission to the European Parliament, the Council, the European Economic and Social Committee and the Committee of the Regions 2020-2025 EU Action Plan on Firearms Trafficking. COM/2020/608 final. https://eur-lex.europa.eu/legal-content/EN/TXT/?uri=CELEX%3A52020DC0608 Accessed 27 Jul. 2024.

European Commission. 2021. Communication from the Commission to the European Parliament, the Council, the European Economic and Social Committee and the Committee of the Regions on the EU Strategy to Tackle Organised Crime 2021–2025. COM(2021) 170. https://eur-lex.europa.eu/legal-content/EN/TXT/?uri=CELEX%3A52021DC0170 Accessed 27 Jul. 2024.

European Commission. 2024. Trafficking in Firearms. DG Migration and Home Affairs, https://home-affairs.ec.europa.eu/policies/internal-security/organised-crime-and-human-trafficking/trafficking-firearms_en Accessed 25 Apr. 2024.

European Monitoring Centre for Drugs and Drug Addiction (EMCDDA). 2023. *Drug-Induced Deaths—The Current Situation in Europe.* European Drug Report 2023. European Union Drug Agency: Lisbon. https://www.euda.europa.eu/publications/

european-drug-report/2023/drug-induced-deaths_en#:~:text=The%20mortality%20rate%20due%20to,population%20aged%2015%20to%2064. Accessed 27 Jul. 2024.

Europol. 2021a. *European Union Serious and Organised Crime Threat Assessment. A Corrupting Influence: The Infiltration and Undermining of Europe's Economy and Society by Organised Crime.* https://www.europol.europa.eu/publication-events/main-reports/european-union-serious-and-organised-crime-threat-assessment-socta-2021 Accessed 27 Jul. 2024.

Europol. 2021b. '18 Arrested as Police Across Europe Seize 350 Firearms' 6 Oct. 2021. https://www.europol.europa.eu/media-press/newsroom/news/18-arrested-police-across-europe-seize-350-firearms. Accessed 23 Jul. 2024.

Europol. 2022a. *Outlaw Motorcycle Gangs.* https://www.europol.europa.eu/crime-areas/outlaw-motorcycle-gangs Accessed 23 Jul. 24.

Europol. 2022b. *EMPACT 2021 Results Factsheets.* https://www.consilium.europa.eu/media/58310/2022_291_empact-factsheets-2021_web_final.pdf Accessed 27 Jul. 2024.

Europol. 2023a. 'Dismantling Encrypted Criminal EncroChat Communications Leads to over 6 500 Arrests and Close to EUR 900 million Seized' (27 June 2023), https://www.europol.europa.eu/media-press/newsroom/news/dismantling-encrypted-criminal-encrochat-communications-leads-to-over-6-500-arrests-and-close-to-eur-900-million-seized Accessed 27 Jul. 2024.

Europol. 2023b. *Crime Areas: Illicit Firearms Trafficking.* https://www.europol.europa.eu/crime-areas/illicit-firearms-trafficking (europa.eu) Accessed 23 Jul. 2024.

Europol. 2023c. *EMPACT 2022 Results Factsheets* (4 Oct. 2023). https://www.europol.europa.eu/publications-events/publications/empact-2022-results-factsheets Accessed 27 Jul. 2024.

Europol. 2023d. *Mobile Organised Crime Groups.* https://www.europol.europa.eu/crime-areas/mobile-organised-crime-groupsAccessed 10 Jan. 2024.

Europol. 2023e. *Criminal networks in EU ports Risks and challenges for law enforcement.* Joint report of Europol and the Security Steering Committee of the ports of Antwerp, Hamburg/Bremerhaven and Rotterdam.

Federal Criminal Police Office of Germany (BKA). 2022. *Waffenkriminalität Bundeslagebild 2022.*

Fijanaut, Cyrille, and Paoli, Letizia. (eds.) 2004. *Organised Crime in Europe: Concepts, Patterns and Control Policies in the European Union and Beyond.* Dordrecht: Springer.

Flemish Peace Institute. 2019. *Firearms and Deaths by Firearms in the EU: Fact Sheet.* Brussels. https://vlaamsvredesinstituut.eu/wp-content/uploads/2019/04/factsheet_firearms_and_deaths_in_eu.pdf Accessed 27 Jul. 2024.

Florquin, Nicolas, and King, Benjamin. 2018. *From Legal to Lethal Converted Firearms in Europe.* Geneva: Small Arms Survey.

Gerell, M., Sturup, J., Magnusson, M. M., Nilvall, K., Khoshnood, A., and Rostami, A. 2021. 'Open Drug Markets, Vulnerable Neighbourhoods and Gun Violence in Two Swedish Cities. *Journal of Policing, Intelligence and Counter Terrorism* 16 (3): pp. 223–244. https://doi.org/10.1080/18335330.2021.1889019

Gerken, Jessica. 2022. 'Clan Criminality: Germany's Ignored Transnational Organized Crime Risk?', *Global Initiative* 16 Sep. 2022. https://globalinitiative.net/analysis/germany-crime-ocindex/#:~:text=German%20clan%20criminality%20is%20not,were%20active%20in%20other%20countriesAccessed 23 Jul. 2024.

Global Initiative Against Transnational Organized Crime. 2019. *Hotspots of Organized Crime in the Western Balkans: Local Vulnerabilities in a Regional Context.* https://globalinitiative.net/wp-content/uploads/2019/05/Hotspots-Report-English-13Jun1110-Web.pdf Accessed 27 Jul. 2024.

Global Initiative Against Transnational Organized Crime. 2023. 'Criminal Markets, Actors and Resilience: Understanding the Dynamics' in *Global Organized Crime Index 2023: A Fractured World*. https://globalinitiative.net/wp-content/uploads/2023/09/Global-organized-crime-index-2023-web-compressed-compressed.pdf Accessed 27 Jul. 2024.

Global Initiative Against Transnational Organized Crime. 2023. *Global Organized Crime Index 2023: A Fractured World*. https://globalinitiative.net/wp-content/uploads/2023/09/Global-organized-crime-index-2023-web-compressed-compressed.pdf Accessed 27 Jul. 2024.

Grip, Lina. 2018. 'Illegal Weapons, Gangs and Violent Extremism in Denmark'. In *Triggering Terror: Illicit Gun Markets and Firearms Acquisition of Terrorist Networks in Europe*, edited by Nils Duquet, pp. 123–168. Flemish Peace Institute: Brussels.

Jongleux, Benjamin, and Florquin, Nicolas. 2020. *Monitoring the Response to Converted Firearms in Europe*, Non-Proliferation and Disarmament Papers, no. 70. https://www.nonproliferation.eu/wp-content/uploads/2020/10/EUNPDC_no-70.pdf Accessed 27 Jul. 2024.

Krüsselmann, K., et al. 2023. 'Firearm Homicides in Europe: A Comparison with Non-Firearm Homicides in Five European Countries'. *Global Crime* 24 (2): pp. 145–167. https://doi.org/10.1080/17440572.2023.2211513

Liem, Marieke, and Krüsselmann, Katharina. 2022. *The Way of the Gun: Firearm Trafficking and its Impact on Violence in the Netherlands*. Leiden University: Project Target report.

Magnusson, Mia-Maria. 2023. 'Predicting Gun Violence in Stockholm, Sweden, Using Sociodemographics, Crime and Drug Market Locations'. *European Journal on Criminal Policy and Research* https://doi.org/10.1007/s10610-023-09560-y Accessed 23 Jul. 2024.

Saferworld. 2005. Turning the page: Small arms and light weapons in Albania (seesac.org). Accessed 1 Nov. 2024.

Sagramoso, Domitilla. 2001. *The Proliferation of Illegal Small Arms and Light Weapons in and Around the European Union: Instability, Organised Crime and Terrorist Groups*. London: Saferworld.

Savona, Ernesto, and Mancuso, Marina. 2017. *Fighting Illicit Firearms Trafficking Routes and Actors at European Level. Final Report of Project FIRE*. Milan: Transcrime. https://fireproject.eu/wp-content/uploads/2017/03/FIREFinalReport.pdf Accessed 27 Jul. 2024.

Savona, Ernesto, and Riccardi, Michele (eds.). 2015. *From Illegal Markets to Legitimate Businesses: The Portfolio of Organised Crime in Europe. Final Report of Project OCP—Organised Crime Portfolio*. Trento: Transcrime–Università degli Studi di Trento. https://www.transcrime.it/wp-content/uploads/2015/04/executive.pdf Accessed 27 Jul. 2024.

The South Eastern and Eastern Europe Clearinghouse for the Control of Small Arms and Light Weapons (SEESAC). 2004. *South Eastern Europe SALW monitor*.

The South Eastern and Eastern Europe Clearinghouse for the Control of Small Arms and Light Weapons (SEESAC). 2023a. *In Focus Armed Violence Monitor on Weapon Seizures in South East Europe in 2022* (seesac.org). Accessed 1 Nov. 2024.

The South Eastern and Eastern Europe Clearinghouse for the Control of Small Arms and Light Weapons (SEESAC). 2023b. *In Focus Armed Violence Monitor on Firearm incidents in the Criminal Context in South East Europe in 2022* (seesac.org). Accessed 1 Nov. 2024.

Spapens, Toine. 2007. 'Trafficking in Illicit Firearms for Criminal Purposes within the European Union'. *European Journal of Crime, Criminal Law and Criminal Justice* 15 (3): pp. 359–381.

Strazzari, Francesco, and Zampagni, Francesca. 2018. 'Between Organised Crime and Terrorism: Illicit Firearms Actors and Market Dynamics in Italy'. In *Triggering Terror: Illicit Gun Markets and Firearms Acquisition of Terrorist Networks in Europe*, edited by Nils Duquet. Brussels: Flemish Peace Institute.

Sturup, Joakim, Rostami, Amir, Gerell, Manne, and Sandholm, Anders. 2017. 'Near-Repeat Shootings in Contemporary Sweden 2011 to 2015'. *Security Journal* 31 (1): pp. 73–92.

Sturup, Joakim. 2020. *Illegal Vapenanvändning i Polisregion Stockholm Strategisk Rapport (Polismyndigheten: Polisregion Stockholm).*

Swedish Police. 2023. *Regeringsuppdrag Slutredovisning, Kartläggning av Förekomsten av Illegal Vapenhandel, Vapensmuggling och Annan Införsel med Illegala Syften till Sverige.*

Swedish Police. 2024. *Confirmed Shootings per Region and Month 2017–2023*, https://polisen.se/om-polisen/polisens-arbete/sprangningar-och-skjutningar/ Accessed 23 Jul. 2024.

Swedish Police and Customs. 2023. *Nationell Lägesbild Gällande Skjutvapen i Kriminella Miljöer.*

UK National Crime Agency. (NCA). 2018. *National Strategic Assessment of Serious and Organised Crime 2018.* https://www.nationalcrimeagency.gov.uk/who-we-are/publications/173-national-strategic-assessment-of-serious-and-organised-crime-2018/file Accessed 27 Jul. 2024.

UK National Crime Agency (NCA). 2021. *National Strategic Assessment of Serious and Organised Crime 2021.* https://www.nationalcrimeagency.gov.uk/who-we-are/publications/533-national-strategic-assessment-of-serious-and-organised-crime-2021/file Accessed 27 Jul. 2024.

UK National Crime Agency (NCA). 2022. *National Crime Agency Annual Report and Accounts 2020–21.* https://www.nationalcrimeagency.gov.uk/who-we-are/publications/606-national-crime-agency-annual-report-2021-2022/file Accessed 27 Jul .2024.

UK National Crime Agency (NCA). 2023. *National Strategic Assessment 2023.* https://www.nationalcrimeagency.gov.uk/images/NSA_2023_Website_-_PDF_Version_1.pdf Accessed 27 Jul. 2024.

United Nations Office of Drugs and Crime (UNODC). 2019. *Global Study on Homicide: Understanding homicide.* Vienna: United Nations. Microsoft Word - Booklet 3 _ED_2_reviewAM_workinglayout_aug1 (unodc.org) Accessed 1 Nov. 2024.

United Nations Office of Drugs and Crime (UNODC). 2020. *Illicit Trafficking in Firearms, their Parts, Components and Ammunition to, from and across the European Union. Regional Analysis Report.* Vienna: United Nations. https://www.unodc.org/documents/firearms-protocol/2020/UNODC-EU-Report-A8_FINAL.pdf Accessed 26 Jul 2024.

United Nations Office of Drugs and Crime (UNODC). 2022. *Firearms Trafficking Arms Seizures.* https://dataunodc.un.org/dp-firearms-arms-seized Accessed 5 Jan. 2024.

United Nations Office of Drugs and Crime (UNODC). 2023a. *Global Study on Homicide 2023.* Vienna: United Nations.

United Nations Office of Drugs and Crime (UNODC). 2023b. Data Victims of Intentional Homicides. dp-intentional-homicide-victims | dataUNODC Accessed 4 Nov. 2024.

Vázquez del Mercado, Guillermo. 2022. *Arms Trafficking and Organized Crime: Global Trade, Local Impact. Policy Brief.* Global Initiative Against Transnational Organized Crime.

3

Illicit Firearms, Organized Crime, and Illegal Economies in South-east Asia

Michael E. Picard

Introduction

Recent scholarship and journalism have examined the complex interplay between firearms and organized crime in South-east Asia, where government structures, private interests, and illicit business often fuse together in violent ways (Lin 2023; Lintner 2002). There are complex relationships between illicit economies, organized crime, corruption, and state-building throughout the region (Baker and Milne 2015). In general, South-east Asia has been the setting for a wide range of criminal economies, such as drug trafficking, human smuggling and trafficking, various environmental crimes (such as wildlife trafficking, illegal logging, illicit mineral resource extraction, and illegal fishing), illegal casinos, prostitution, scam centres, extortion rackets, counterfeit goods, piracy, kidnapping, hired murders, and so on.

However, there has been little research conducted in recent years that examines the role of illicit firearms in the region's diverse criminal economies, as well as arms trafficking as a criminal economy in its own right. As such, the basic elements of illicit firearms, organized crime, and illicit economies in South-east Asia are not well documented or analysed. This chapter aims to provide a brief scoping of how illicit firearms intersect with organized crime and illicit economies in contemporary South-east Asia. The chapter seeks to answer basic questions—the who, what, when, where, and how—of firearms trafficking in the region with respect to criminal economies. It also provides a basis for examining a set of more concentrated questions about the interplay of these elements. Namely, what are the methods and routes whereby firearms enter the illicit market in South-east Asia? How do illicit firearms facilitate and enable other illicit economies in South-east Asia? How do illicit firearms exacerbate organized crime, criminality, and

Michael E. Picard, *Illicit Firearms, Organized Crime, and Illegal Economies in South-east Asia* In: *Illicit Firearms Markets and Organized Crime*. Edited by: David Bright, Oxford University Press.
 DOI: 10.1093/9780198902409.003.0004

violence? And how have states responded to illicit firearms, and what impact have these measures had?

This chapter is structured into six sections. First, the introduction describes the methodology of this overview. Second, the contextual background synthesizes recent literature on illicit firearms, organized crime, and illegal economies in order to identify the key regional dynamics that shape these overlapping subjects. The third section introduces the case data and provides 'snapshots' of illicit firearms and criminality in each country. The fourth section addresses the five basic elements (the who, what, when, where, and how) based on these snapshots, while the fifth section answers the research questions stated above. The chapter concludes with a set of policy recommendations for state actors combatting illicit firearms and organized crime in South-east Asia.

To answer the questions raised in the introduction, this chapter compares three bodies of information: a small dataset of almost 200 documented firearms seizure and trafficking incidents occurring between 2016 and 2024 as reported by media and government sources throughout the region; policy reports examining specific South-east Asian criminal economies produced by prominent international and non-governmental organizations; and recent scholarship and long-form journalism on organized crime and illicit economies in the region. The dataset provides a snapshot of arms trafficking trends in South-east Asia that can be compared against the established literature.

The dataset is composed of 174 cases of firearms seizure and trafficking incidents occurring between 2016 and 2024 (most after 2021) as reported by prominent national media outlets and government agencies. This dataset also includes twenty-five reports about government responses to arms trafficking and other criminal economies. Each case documents either the seizure of an illicit firearm by law enforcement agencies, or the use of a firearm in an illicit activity. Each case is analysed to identify the actors involved, where the incident occurred, the types of firearms involved, the trafficking methods employed, the presence of other illicit economic activities, other crimes involved, types of violence employed, as well as the government response that led to or resulted from the incident. Each case was also analysed to determine if an organized criminal element was involved, and if the case was part of a broader trend of conflict, organized violence, or civil unrest.

These cases are analysed against a large body of academic literature and long-form journalism on organized crime and illicit economies in South-east Asia. The analysis drew on almost twenty recent policy reports examining specific illicit economies from prominent international and non-government organizations focused on combatting organized crime.

Contextual Background

Several factors enable and sustain organized crime, arms trafficking, and other illicit economies in South-east Asia. An intricate web of porous land and sea borders shape South-east Asia's illicit economies, providing traffickers with an abundance of potential supply sources and trafficking routes, regardless of the commodity (Munro 2012; Luong 2020). To this day, governments possess limited control over such areas, sustaining a vacuum that is often exploited by armed groups, criminal organizations, and trafficking networks (Dahari et al. 2019; Chouvy 2013).

The region's physical geography is further punctuated by its human geography. Many of the region's remote borderlands are inhabited by cross-border ethnic minorities who are often economically and politically marginalized if not outright discriminated against by their respective governments (Van Uhm and Grigore 2021; Luong 2020). Such communities often possess unique knowledge of the local terrain, robust cross-border social networks, and an aversion to the authorities. Just as remote mountains or rivers may determine certain production areas and trafficking routes, these communities provide traffickers with social pathways for sourcing illicit products and moving them across borders (Luong 2020). Similarly, overseas ethnic communities (including refugee populations) in foreign economic centres provide human networks, infrastructure, and market access for traffickers.

Geographic factors are exacerbated by limited state capacities. The ability of South-east Asian governments to capture revenues and finance security institutions varies greatly (Larsson 2013). Several states struggle to provide adequate resources (ranging from physical assets like patrol vessels to liveable salaries) to security agencies, and the selective allocation of limited resources sustains geographic enclaves where state presence is weak or compromised (Larsson 2013; Munro 2012). It also reinforces patronage and corruption within state institutions as officials compete for limited resources and personnel seek to supplement meagre incomes. Such weaknesses provide pathways for traffickers and can lead to collusion or even tacit alliances between state personnel and criminal networks (Baker and Milne 2015).

The region is also shaped by past, ongoing, and emerging conflicts, which elevate both the supply and demand for illicit firearms. Several countries possess large legacy stockpiles from past conflicts ranging from colonial-era struggles and World War II, post-colonial conflicts (such as the Vietnam War), to modern subnational/secessionist insurgencies (also see Chapters 2, 5, and 6). At the same time, increasing geopolitical competition between traditional arms suppliers like China, Russia, and the United States, and the emergence of new arms-exporting states like South Korea, Israel, and Turkey is increasing the sources and opportunities for governments to acquire arms and ammunition (Picard et al. 2019). This can lead to surplus stockpiles which are easier to divert. All of these factors ensure that there are consistent pockets of high demand for illicit firearms, as well as diverse and fairly reliable supply sources (Picard 2021).

Beyond firearms, the region's past and present conflicts fuel other illicit economies. Armed groups throughout the region are financed to varying degrees by direct and indirect participation in criminal activities. These forms of financing lead to criminal convergence between illicit economies, armed groups, and criminal networks.

Convergence is further shaped by South-east Asia's rapid and extensive digitization as well as regional economic integration. The rise of social media and e-commerce has transformed the consumption habits of the region's millions of inhabitants. Social media have effectively digitized illicit markets: participants can advertise, buy, sell, pay, coordinate activities, and exchange knowledge concerning illicit and restricted goods through e-commerce sites as well as messaging apps like Line, WhatsApp, Facebook, Telegram, and so on (Picard 2023). App-driven delivery services as well as traditional courier companies allow participants to ship illicit products with minimal exposure. Sites like Twitter and YouTube allow market participants to exchange knowledge on how to carry out illicit operations, such as converting an airsoft or blank-firing gun to fire live ammunition, or packaging contraband so it can be shipped without detection (Picard 2023).

The cumulative effect of digitization is that more participants can access illicit markets, boosting supply and demand opportunities as well as the frequency and volume of transactions (Picard 2023). Market participants face fewer risks when participating in illicit markets (except for victims of online scamming, which relies heavily on social media and e-commerce platforms), especially as national law enforcement agencies struggle to adapt investigative methods and evidence protocols to digital marketplaces (Phaicharoen and Boonreak 2023). In any case, the diversity of platforms available to traffickers and participants as well as the ease of creating and deleting profiles ensures that illicit online markets are resilient, adaptive, and innovative against sporadic law enforcement interventions (see Chapter 9).

Efforts by the Association of Southeast Asian Nations (ASEAN) to create an integrated free trade bloc have increased the flow of goods between states (Luong 2020). Despite the prosperity that this undoubtedly has generated, it has also facilitated trade in illicit goods, which are just as likely to be trafficked in bulk through established trade corridors than via cross-border ant trade of small shipments following remote routes (Luong 2020). Special economic zones—typically cross-border trade hubs that are governed under special tax and legal regimes—also help facilitate the large-scale flow of illicit goods and services between countries by laundering profits generated from illicit sources, benefiting from relaxed oversight and scrutiny by the authorities (OHCHR 2023).

The special economic zones intersect with another key feature that shapes South-east Asia's illicit arms flows and other forms of trafficking: uneven laws and markets for illicit and restricted goods. In the case of firearms, the governments of the region take vastly different approaches to regulating civilian firearms ownership (Picard 2021). The disparate approaches to policing civilian firearms ownership create uneven markets across borders, with arbitrage opportunities that traffickers can exploit. Traffickers can reportedly purchase Glock pistols in Thailand for around $450 and sell them in Malaysia for three times the price (The Star 2024a). Laotians have reportedly purchased firearms over social media from Thailand, where they are more widely available (see Laotian Times 2022).

Other legislative issues reinforce this dynamic. Some national gun laws are relatively outdated and contain exploitable loopholes. States in the region have also done little to update their gun laws to account for the digitization of arms trafficking and emerging technologies like 3D printing (see Chapter 8; Picard 2023). International arms control treaties like the Arms Trade Treaty (ATT) and the UN Programme of Action (UNPoA) aim to reduce trafficking opportunities by harmonizing the key elements of national gun laws and closing off exploitable legal loopholes within and between states. However, such efforts clash with ASEAN's non-intervention principle concerning the internal affairs of its constituent members, which limits opportunities for regional cooperation in combatting arms trafficking and other forms of organized crime (Mok Shen Yang 2020).

Description of Cases and Country Snapshots

Over 170 cases of recent firearms seizure and trafficking incidents from across South-east Asia illustrate these dynamics at play. This section provides an overview of the cases when aggregated at the national level in order to provide a snapshot for each country.

Brunei

This study identified nine cases of reported arms seizure incidents in Brunei, entailing just fifteen weapons and some ammunition, occurring between 2019 and 2022 (no cases were identified since 2023). All of the seized weapons were craft-produced, some of which entailed rudimentary designs built from simple household or workshop materials, and used toy marbles as ammunition (these are nevertheless considered firearms under local laws). This reflects the country's small population and extremely strict gun laws, which effectively outlaw all civilian gun ownership (Picard 2021). Where information about the seizure was provided, police seized some of the weapons from apparent drug users, and to a lesser extent from suspected illegal hunters and an alleged thief. This analysis did not identify any cases with a clear organized crime intersection.

Cambodia

About twenty cases from Cambodia were considered for this analysis. The cases occurred mostly between 2021 and 2024 (with the inclusion of one unique case from 2016) and involved almost 300 weapons. Several of the cases are noteworthy for their size and composition; over half of the reported seizures entailed dozens of weapons each, and the overall count includes around 120 assault rifles (mostly Russian and Chinese AK-pattern rifles), fifty Soviet grenades, three US M79 grenade launchers, one heavy machine gun, one Soviet sub-machine gun, thirty-six industrially produced handguns, and thirty-one craft-production firearms. Most of the cases involved clear elements of organized crime, mostly in the form of Thai, Vietnamese, Chinese, and Taiwanese gangs and drug trafficking groups. Five cases involved arms trafficking operations (mostly in the form of localized supplier networks, though some involved cross-border movements, particularly towards Thailand) while ten cases intersected with drug trafficking. Many of the weapons were seized in connection with reported thefts, murders, kidnappings, and drug use.

Cambodia is considered one of the main sources of trafficked weapons in the region owing to its large Cold War-era weapons stockpiles (which is reflected in the seizure cases), conflict history, and lingering governance issues (Lintner 2002). The Small Arms Survey estimates there are over 700,000 weapons in (illicit) civilian possession (Karp 2018). However, not all the weapons are relics of the Khmer Rouge or the Vietnam War; a considerable number are from more recent sources—such as converted blank-firing pistols—that have widely proliferated throughout the region, especially in Thailand (Harmer and Peck 2023).

Indonesia

Some twenty-seven cases occurring between 2023 and 2024 were identified for Indonesia. The cases entailed at least 203 seized weapons and thousands of rounds of ammunition. The provenance of these weapons is diverse, ranging from colonial-era Dutch rifles to modern civilian AR-15s widely exported by American, Turkish, and European manufacturers. Three military assault rifles were seized. Authorities also seized a wide array of craft-production weapons, including rudimentary gas weapons, converted airsoft and blank-firing guns, and semi-skilled artisanal firearms. Almost half of the cases involved diverse organized crime networks that included street gangs, separatist armed groups, terrorist networks, drug traffickers, foreign criminals, and state employees. Many of these weapons were seized when authorities dismantled digitally enabled arms trafficking networks. Some were used in drug trafficking and alcohol smuggling operations; many were linked to West Papua's separatist conflict. One case involved a poaching network suspected of killing a quarter of the world's remaining Javan rhino population since 2021 (Karmini 2024).

Indonesia's proximity to past and present conflicts, its large urban population, security sector corruption, and geographic position as a crossroads between Asia and Oceania shape its diverse pool of illicit firearms. Papuan separatists have reportedly used diverted local development funds to purchase weapons from corrupt police and military personnel (Lamb and Teresia 2023). They have also apparently sought to source weapons from the Philippines (IPAC 2024). On the other side of the country, one case demonstrated how drug traffickers used maritime routes to import assault rifles and sixteen tons of methamphetamines from Thailand's conflict-affected deep south before being caught (Wijaya 2023). The authorities have also dismantled multiple networks of online gun sellers active in densely populated West Java (Soeriaatmadja 2023).

Laos

This study identified seventeen cases from Laos occurring between 2019 and 2024 and encompassing only about twenty weapons (though some cases did not specify the amount seized). Most of the specified seized weapons were pistols, with occasional shotguns. Many of the weapons were seized as their illicit owners travelled across borders, namely to or from Thailand and Vietnam. Almost all of the cases included elements of organized crime, namely drug traffickers (several from Thailand). Several incidents involved armed robberies of jewellery stores, which are a frequent target of extortion.

The identified incidents illustrate three key trends. Almost all the cases involved individuals using a single firearm for personal protection or coercion; there was only one case involving a sizable seizure of weapons intended for sale (see Laotian Times 2022). This indicates a lack of established arms trafficking networks and methods in the country. It also seemed that many of the weapons originated from Thailand—the aforementioned seizure involved an online seller who sold over thirty weapons purchased in 'a neighboring country' to clients in Vientiane, just across the Mekong from Thailand (Laotian Times 2022). Two other cases involved weapons explicitly sourced from Thailand. Finally, eight incidents involved firearms seized alongside drug shipments, with most seemingly moving in an eastward direction. Western Laos includes the infamous Golden Triangle region (shared with Myanmar and Thailand), which has long been a global drug production hub for opium/heroin and amphetamines (Van Uhm and Nijman 2022; Lintner 2002). Five seizures involved Laotian traffickers transporting shipments into Vietnam.

Malaysia

This study identified twenty-four cases occurring between 2020 and 2024 (most took place in 2023 and 2024) in Malaysia. These incidents included about sixty weapons, mostly handguns, shotguns, and craft-production rifles seized in small numbers. Ten cases involved organized criminal groups, often drug traffickers (though occasionally poachers and robbery gangs). A recent case involving an alleged French-Israeli mobster who was arrested with four locally sourced pistols drew extensive media attention (see Reuters 2024). Nine cases intersected with other criminal economies—namely drug trafficking, but also various forms of contraband smuggling, such as undeclared cigarettes, rice, and alcohol. About half of the seizures coincided with drug, poaching, terrorism, and violence-related crimes. One case involved a terrorist network sympathetic to the Islamic State that had planned an attack on a Hindu temple (Malay Mail 2023; see Mizan Aslam 2020).

The Small Arms Survey estimates there were over 140,000 registered (legal) firearms alongside almost 75,000 weapons in illicit circulation in 2017 (Karp 2018). The seizures indicated some regional variation: nine seizures took place in Malaysia's remote Borneo provinces and were more likely to involve craft-production weapons. Seizures in more populated areas near Kuala Lumpur, Malacca, and Johor (across the border from Singapore) typically involved industrially produced pistols. Eight cases were clustered in the states bordering Thailand, coinciding with frequent reports of arms and drug trafficking from Thailand through its restive southern provinces (Dahari et al. 2019). Police in Kelantan State (which includes the eastern end of the Thai-Malay border) reported seizing eighteen pistols in 2023, often in connection with drug busts (Mahsinah Abdullah 2023). One press report indicated that Glock pistols can be bought in Thailand and resold in Malaysia for three times the original price, and that such weapons are often smuggled through discreet routes in the wetlands surrounding Sungai Golok (The Star 2024a).

Myanmar

Monitoring illicit firearm trends in Myanmar using conventional media sources is challenging due to the country's raging civil war and oppressive media conditions set out by the country's military-controlled government (RSF n.d.). The country's gun laws date back to the colonial era and technically allow licensed ownership of certain handguns by private citizens, though only well-connected individuals are reportedly able to acquire licences from the military-controlled government (Kway Lin Htoon 2018; Eleven Myanmar 2023). Needless to say, these laws hold little sway in areas beyond the junta's control, and certain military units may even flaunt these laws in order to arm local allies in exchange for nominal territorial control (Idris 2019).

Myanmar's fractured anti-government and ethnic armed groups allow varying degrees of information about firearms in their areas of control to be reported. The armament of such actors varies from group to group, though all essentially involve a mix of weapons captured on the battlefield from junta forces, smuggled from abroad, purchased from other armed groups, or produced through robust craft industry. Armed groups located in the country's border areas, such as the Arakan Army or Karen National Liberation Army, often exhibit military-grade weapons likely sourced from neighbouring countries like India and Thailand (see War Noir 2023; VOA News 2021). The United Wa State Army, which controls areas bordering China, Thailand, and Laos, has exhibited unique Chinese weapons like FN-6 MANPADS (the group is believed to have close connections with China's government; Davis 2019). Some groups are able to produce relatively high-quality military weapons on a near-industrial scale, such as the UWSA in the Shan State (Weng 2008). Groups without access to borderland smuggling routes, such as anti-government People's Defence Force cells in the country's heartland, have employed experimental and adaptive craft weapons workshops to produce anti-tank weapons, rifles, and improvised explosives (Frontier Myanmar 2022). Myanmar is one of the few countries in the region where 3D-printed weapons have been continuously documented in the hands of armed groups (Ortiz 2023).

Philippines

The research identified about fifty cases occurring in one month in 2024 in the Philippines alone. This staggeringly high occurrence is largely due to the Philippines' rich (anglophone) media environment as well as the commendable practice by military units and law enforcement agencies of publicizing firearms seizures, providing a detailed view into the varied composition of the country's illicit weapons. Half of the cases were directly related to the Philippines' ongoing armed conflicts. These cases typically involved military-grade assault rifles, light machine guns, rifles (including powerful craft production sniper rifles), grenades, improvised landmines, RPGs, and sub-machine guns ranging from WWII-era guns to more modern weapons. Three cases involved violent feuds between clans in the Bangsamoro region, while four cases involved current or retired military or police personnel who had trafficked or were in possession of illicit weapons. Such cases also often involved military weapons. Ten cases involved clear elements of organized crime—typically networks involved in drug trafficking but occasionally illicit gambling entities and one human trafficking operation (CIDG 2024). These cases were more likely to include small quantities of handguns.

The sheer volume of cases demonstrates that the Philippines faces extensive challenges in combatting illicit weapons. The sources of such weapons are numerous, and include the civilian market, diverted state weapons, and skilled craft production. In any given year, gun owners fail to renew tens of thousands of firearm licences, rendering these weapons illicit (Dalizon 2024; Cabrera 2024). Furthermore, local elected officials have influence over local police units and can enrol their supporters and associates as security auxiliaries (Lingao 2010; HRW 2010). This allows 'private armies' affiliated with political families to acquire weapons (including older state weapons) which can be used to intimidate voters, assassinate rivals, and enforce control over illicit economies (Lingao 2010; HRW 2010). The Philippines is also home to a robust craft-weapons industry (Gutierrez 2019). Craft producers are able to manufacture sub-machine guns, anti-materiel sniper rifles, landmines, and possibly RPG-2-style launchers, all of which have been documented extensively with armed groups in the Bangsamoro region (see Western Mindanao Command, AFP 2024).

Singapore

Only five cases were identified in Singapore between 2019 and 2024. Singapore has very strict gun laws that allow licensed civilian firearms only in a limited number of gun clubs within the city-state (Picard 2021). With its small size, efficient bureaucracy, and well-resourced security apparatus, Singapore strictly enforces these laws. Where information was available, the seizures included one pistol smuggled in from Malaysia, two revolvers stolen from security companies by employees, and an attempt to smuggle in almost two dozen undeclared replica firearms. Two of these incidents included elements of organized crime, namely a gang dispute as well as a robbery to repay debts to unlicensed money lenders. Another incident involved the use of a firearm during a piracy incident on a vessel in the Singapore Strait (shared with Malaysia and Indonesia; Today Online 2020). A security analyst noted that increased tensions in the South China Sea may divert Indonesian naval assets away from the Strait, reducing patrols and creating more opportunities for maritime thefts (Today Online 2020).

Thailand

This study identified almost forty cases for Thailand occurring between 2022 and 2024 entailing thousands of seized weapons and hundreds of thousands of rounds of ammunition. The cases include a heavy machine gun, one underbarrel grenade launcher, dozens of military assault rifles, hundreds of commercially available rifles, shotguns, and handguns, as well as a wide variety of craft production and modified weapons. This last category includes modified pellet guns, airsoft weapons, and blank-firing pistols converted to fire live ammunition. Almost thirty of the cases involved some organized crime element, including drug traffickers, online scam centres, illegal casinos, student gangs, hired hitmen, foreign criminals, and occasionally state officials. More than a dozen incidents involved arms trafficking networks, most of which used online platforms to conduct business. Ten incidents involved drug trafficking, while a small number of incidents involved illegal gambling, money laundering, as well as rice, contraband, and counterfeit currency smuggling. These weapons fuelled homicides (including hired murders), gang violence, armed robbery, and violence against the authorities. Several incidents included weapons smuggled out to neighbouring countries (namely Myanmar, Laos, Malaysia, and Indonesia) as well as drugs being smuggled in (namely from Myanmar and Laos).

This data demonstrates how Thailand lies at the centre of regional trafficking dynamics. The country is both a source as well as a transit point for illicit weapons (Picard 2021). Thailand has the highest gun ownership rate in South-east Asia with approximately six million licensed weapons and an estimated four million illicit weapons in circulation (Karp 2018). Licensing is particularly permissive for state officials and security personnel, who are able to acquire personal firearms at a special discount, ostensibly so they can use the weapons while on duty (Riley et al. 2023). Some officials and personnel have abused this 'gun welfare' system to resell subsidized firearms for profit (Riley et al. 2023). Craft-production weapons are also widely available, as are converted firearms. There have been several high-profile mass-shootings involving such weapons in recent years, and this has generated public concern as well as official promises about strengthening gun laws and cracking down on illicit firearms (Peter 2023).

Vietnam

Some twenty-two cases occurring between 2019 and 2024 were identified for Vietnam. The cases involvled hundreds of weapons, particularly pistols and revolvers. Many of the weapons were either craft-production or non-lethal firearms converted to fire live ammunition. Fifteen of the cases involved an organized criminal element, typically drug traffickers or low-level gangs engaged in armed robberies of businesses. At least six cases involved the online sale of firearms and conversion services. Nine of the cases intersected with drug trafficking. Several cases involved the use of firearms in armed robbery, while one large case involved a local insurrection against the authorities in a rural province in 2022 that led to a large weapons seizure that included grenades (Slow 2024). Several of the cases appeared to involve weapons smuggled into Vietnam from Laos or Cambodia.

The large proportion of converted non-lethal weapons and craft-production firearms in the case data suggests that Vietnamese authorities are committed to restricting access to industrially produced weapons. The cases nevertheless show a significant demand for trafficked firearms, particularly in urban centres like Ho Chi Minh City and highly populated areas like the Mekong Delta provinces. Several cases involved law enforcement agencies dismantling distribution networks that operated online, suggesting a significant degree of market digitization. Several cases also involved small amounts of firearms used by Laotian drug traffickers as they moved their illicit goods from Laos to Vietnamese cities using established transport corridors.

Basic Elements of Illicit Firearms and Organized Crime

These cases and snapshots illuminate the key actors, weapon types, temporal and geographic dimensions, and methods of illicit firearm use and trafficking in South-east Asia. The cases show a diverse and diffuse set of actors engaged in arms trafficking and other illicit economies. Some of these actors are clearly criminal in nature, while others play a more general enabling or supporting role in broader trafficking economies. Many of the cases involved relatively small seizures from low-level actors, such as localized gangs engaged in petty criminality (such as drug dealing, armed robberies, and extortion), drug users, and rural familial/clan networks involved in transporting contraband or protecting illicit/semi-licit income sources. While these elements may entail only a handful of individuals operating with relative autonomy, they are nevertheless part of a broader network of criminal actors who help operationalize illicit economies like drug trafficking.

Incidents involving larger firearm seizures, drug busts, or raids of illicit businesses help illuminate more 'organized' criminal elements involved in illicit firearms use and trafficking. Chief among them are online firearms sellers, which can range from an individual singlehandedly modifying and selling weapons to a general online clientele, to more structured operations that involve coordinated sourcing and distribution systems. Such groups may also participate in other illicit activities (namely drug sales), though many appear to be devoted only to trafficking firearms. The cases also revealed dozens of incidents involving criminal groups composed of foreign nationals. Most of these cases involved small networks of migrants from neighbouring countries, though some involved suspected criminals from countries like Canada, China, France, Israel, Japan, Mexico, New Zealand, South Korea, Taiwan, Turkey, and the UK. These groups appear to be focused on other illicit economies like drug and human trafficking, money laundering, illicit gambling, and scam centres rather than arms trafficking.

Corrupt government officials and personnel are an important group in this constellation of actors. They appeared in over a dozen cases, several of which involved major trafficking operations. In Thailand, several cases involved state officials and personnel allegedly exploiting the 'gun welfare' programme to sell weapons on the black market, including to Myanmar (e.g. see Thai PBS World 2022). Such networks are occasionally referred to as 'mafias' in the Thai press and can also be involved in the embezzlement of state contracts and other illicit businesses (see Fronde 2023). In Cambodia, the authorities arrested seven military officers, including a brigadier-general and two division deputy commanders, in connection with a seizure of over fifty assault rifles and three grenade launchers in 2021 (Khmer Times 2021). In Indonesia, Papuan separatists claim they are able to buy weapons from police and military personnel (Briantika 2020).

Armed groups are another key actor as they drive a near-constant demand for arms and ammunition, as frequent arms movements to Indonesia's Papua and Myanmar's conflict zones illustrate. Efforts by isolated terrorist cells in Indonesia to acquire arms also illustrates how such groups drive demand (see Chapter 12). Armed groups can also occasionally act as suppliers, as demonstrated by recent arms seizures in the Philippines' Bangsamoro region in which former Moro rebels attempted to sell light machine guns and assault rifles to undercover law enforcement (see Bandera News 2024). In the Philippines, private militias affiliated with prominent politicians and clans are key vectors of arms trafficking, as they are seemingly armed by elected officials and engaged in enforcing and protecting illicit economic interests associated with their patrons (Lingao 2010).

The cases also demonstrate the role of various marginal and transnational communities, including expatriates and immigrants, cross-border ethnic groups, refugee populations, and maritime-subsistence communities. Several of the cases involved criminal groups embedded in Vietnamese or Chinese expatriate communities engaged in drug or human trafficking (see CIDG 2024). Burmese and Thai-origin weapons have recently been documented in India's Manipur region where the cross-border Kuki are affected by ethnic violence on both sides of the India-Myanmar border (Singh 2023). In Thailand, refugees from Myanmar have allegedly helped source arms and ammunition to send back to armed groups fighting the regime (Thai Rath 2023). Several cases also involved small maritime vessels transporting weapons and other contraband (such as drugs, fuel, and cigarettes) across borders in Cambodia, Indonesia, Malaysia, the Philippines, and Thailand.

The cases also illustrate the wide variety of weapons in illicit circulation and how they intersect with illicit economies and organized crime. At least fifteen incidents involved exclusively military weapons (including light and heavy machine guns, grenade launchers, grenades, and some assault rifles) leaked from state stocks. Such weapons were often seized as they were being shipped to conflict-affected areas of the region, though a few cases involved military assault rifles presumably being used to protect drug supplies. About half of the cases involved commercially available firearms, namely industrially produced rifles (including semi-automatic assault rifles), shotguns, pistols, and revolvers. Such weapons were commonly seized in large quantities from online traffickers and officials abusing Thailand's 'gun welfare' system (see Thai PBS World 2022). Smaller quantities were seized from mid- and low-level criminals, especially those engaged in drug trafficking and sales as well as armed robbery. Such weapons were also occasionally seized from other criminal enterprises, such as scam centres and illegal casinos.

The data also revealed the widespread use of non-lethal firearms—particularly air guns and blank-firing pistols—converted to fire live ammunition, which were seized in at least twenty cases. Such weapons were commonly seized from online traffickers, some of whom appeared to specialize in modifying and selling converted weapons, while some individuals were able to use online resources to convert firearms using parts they ordered themselves. Furthermore, craft production and homemade firearms were seized in at least thirty-three cases, ranging from crudely improvised handguns to consistent, high-quality semi-industrial rifles. Such weapons were more commonly seized from drug users and individuals without an explicit criminal connection, though the consistency and quality of some craft-production weapons (such as 'Thai Pradit', or Thai-made handguns) indicate a large, organized production and distribution capacity for such weapons.

The frequency of (reported) firearms seizures provides some indication of the extent of illicit firearms proliferation. In the Philippines, local news sources, police agencies, and army units report dozens of individual firearms seizure incidents every month—by far the highest level of disclosure of any South-east Asian country. Reports of illicit firearms seizures are also frequent in Thailand (with over a dozen reported incidents every month) and to a lesser extent Indonesia and Vietnam. Reports are less frequent in Malaysia, Cambodia, and Laos, while reports from Singapore and Brunei are extremely rare.

The cases also reveal a general geography of illicit firearms use and trafficking. Seizure and trafficking incidents are particularly common in urban centres, notably cities and highly populated areas with high levels of tourism like Pattaya, Thailand; Bali, Indonesia; or Nha Trang, Vietnam. Such areas coincide with other illicit economies—namely drug trafficking but also prostitution, illegal gambling, and scam centres—as reflected in several of the seizure incidents. Seizure incidents that targeted established firearm trafficking networks in Thailand, Indonesia, and Vietnam demonstrate that urban centres were often both the source and destination of trafficked firearms (e.g. see Vy 2023).

Several cases involved weapons seized as they were physically crossing borders from one country into another. Many of these utilized established border crossing and transportation routes linking urban centres in different countries, such as the First Thai-Lao Friendship Bridge linking Nong Khai, Thailand with Vientiane, Laos; the Ban Klong Luek border crossing connecting Aranyaprathet, Thailand and Poipet, Cambodia; or the Lao Bao border crossing that connects Savannakhet, Laos with Hue, Vietnam. Some cases also made use of remote crossing points, such as the wetlands surrounding Sungai Golok between Thailand and Malaysia; or the remote hills separating Chang Mai Province, Thailand and Shan State, Myanmar. Maritime routes were also common, particularly in archipelagic Indonesia and around Sihanoukville, Cambodia, which effectively sits between the Bay of Bangkok in Thailand and Vietnam's populous Mekong Delta. Finally, several seizures also involved conflict-affected or adjacent areas, such as the Philippine's Bangsamoro region or Thailand's restive southern provinces.

The cases also provide insight into how weapons are trafficked into the illicit domain. In essentially every South-east Asian country (especially Thailand, Vietnam, Indonesia, and the Philippines), the black market for firearms is extensively digitized. Over two dozen cases explicitly involved some form of online interaction, whether to sell or purchase weapons or related services, share information related to trafficking (such as how to convert a non-lethal firearm to fire live ammunition), or to send an illicit shipment or payment. This overlaps heavily with another key trend—the use of courier or parcel services to send illicit shipments relatively anonymously, which was identified in at least six cases. There were nevertheless many cases in which participants acquired an illicit weapon without online mediation, whether through a personal acquaintance, inheritance, theft, coordinated drop-offs, and so on. Traffickers also made use of fake documents (such as consignment lists, licence plates, identity documents, etc.) as well as various concealment methods (such as hiding weapons in sacks of rice).

Discussion

These cases shed light on the methods and routes of illicit firearm proliferation in South-east Asia. The most significant source of trafficked firearms appears to be the civilian market as the makes, models, and types of firearms appearing in these reports correspond closely with those permitted for licensed civilian use. The second most significant source is craft production weapons and modified/converted non-lethal firearms, which are less strictly controlled in some countries and can be converted with relative ease. State weapons diverted by corrupt or collusive government officials and personnel appear to be another significant source of illicit firearms, albeit less widespread than commercially available and craft production/modified weapons (except possibly in the Philippines and Myanmar). Corrupt officials have also acted as straw buyers and traffickers of commercially available firearms, as demonstrated through numerous abuses of Thailand's 'gun welfare' program (Riley et al. 2023).

Trafficking networks appear to be relatively small and highly decentralized as market participants are able to take advantage of diverse arms sources and trafficking routes, ensuring resilience against government interventions. Part of this is due to the increasing importance of online platforms in facilitating arms trafficking, which law enforcement agencies have struggled to police effectively (Phaicharoen and Boonreak 2023; Ngankham 2014). Over two dozen cases (many of which entailed large weapons seizures) involved illegal online sales using social media platforms and e-commerce sites; traffickers also made use of online courier services to ship weapons locally. Larger movements are facilitated using both established transit corridors where high volumes of goods and people cross national borders as well as small 'ant-trade' routes that exploit complicated terrain and rural, marginalized communities with knowledge of the border and connections on the other side. Maritime corridors are also an essential component of trafficking routes, especially in countries with numerous communities that rely on the sea for economic subsistence. Such communities may rely more heavily on illicit activities (including smuggling) for subsistence when faced with aggressive competition over marine resources from industrial fishing fleets (Chapsos et al. 2019).

This review illuminates the critical role that illicit firearms play in facilitating and enabling other illicit economies in South-east Asia. Over fifty cases involved firearms used to facilitate drug trafficking, where traffickers used them as a means of protection and coercion. The region's armed conflicts—especially in Myanmar—create conditions for large-scale drug production and trafficking, which armed groups tax to finance operations and arms acquisitions (Lintner 2002; Chouvy 2013). A small number of cases also involved the use of firearms as a means of protection and enforcement in other illicit businesses, such as illegal casinos, illegal nightlife venues, and scam centres. Armed groups will also tax these businesses for financing, as seen in Myanmar's Shan State (Tower and Clapp 2024). Firearms were also used to smuggle various contraband across borders, including alcohol, tobacco products, rice, and fake currency. Several cases also involved firearms used for poaching and illegal hunting. Finally, firearms were seized very rarely in connection with human trafficking and people smuggling operations, possibly because traffickers can rely on other forms of coercion (such as the threat of deportation or abandonment) to ensure their victims comply (Nguyen et al. 2020; Rizki Akbari 2015). Nevertheless, firearms used in conflict-related and criminal violence can elevate demand for people smuggling services by civilians seeking safety and security, and this can expose them to human trafficking risks (such as debt bondage, sex slavery, passport confiscation, and so on; Wahab and Khairi 2020).

This review shows how illicit firearms exacerbate organized crime, criminality, and violence in South-east Asia. The cases reveal that armed groups, private militias, and terrorist networks have access to diverse sources of illicit firearms, fuelling conflict and insecurity. Such groups may violently contest state authority, intimidate political opposition and rivals, or target civilians in acts of mass violence. Over a dozen cases involved violence against the authorities. Less visible but nevertheless present are instances in which such groups use firearms to extort commercial enterprises and civilians, enforce illicit businesses, or protect smuggling routes that are essential to their financing. Extortion is said to be a key source of financing for Papuan separatists in Indonesia as well as Communist insurgents in the Philippines (IPAC 2022; Lopez 2024). Armed groups may also form alliances with traffickers and criminal organizations as a means of securing financing from illicit economies as well as sourcing arms and ammunition, as is widely reported to be the case among the ethnic armed groups in Myanmar (Lintner 2002; Chouvy 2013 Meehan 2015). Furthermore, corruption by state officials provides criminal networks with special access to firearms and a degree of impunity from law enforcement. In some cases, state forces may even aid, abet, and benefit from criminal economies, as is said to be the case in Cambodia with respect to illegal logging (Milne 2015; GITOC 2022). With such impunity, organized crime groups are able to engage in inherently violent criminal activities like armed robbery, hired killings, political violence, piracy, and kidnappings, which were reflected in over thirty cases. Illicit firearms also contribute to gender violence, such as intimate partner killings, forced prostitution, rapes, and domestic violence, as seen in at least four cases.

States have attempted to combat illicit firearms with a variety of methods that were evident in the analysed cases as well as from additional research. As the cases demonstrate, the proliferation of illicit firearms is as much a transnational challenge as it is domestic, and law enforcement agencies are constrained by their national borders (arguably more so in South-east Asia than in other regions due to the ASEAN principle of non-intervention; Mok Shen Yang 2020). Nevertheless, states have made efforts to increase regional cooperation and to harmonize countertrafficking efforts through accession to international treaties like the ATT and UNPoA. ASEAN also provides a high-level mechanism for discussing and coordinating countertrafficking efforts through the Senior Officials Meeting on Transnational Crime (SOMTC), which includes a working group on arms trafficking among other illicit economies (Mok Shen Yang 2020). Perhaps spurred on by these high-level efforts, bilateral cooperation between law enforcement agencies and multilateral operations have yielded some high-profile take-downs of transnational trafficking networks (see The Star 2024b).

Within national boundaries, law enforcement agencies show varying degrees of capability and approaches to combatting illicit firearms. Arms trafficking networks appear to be resilient to sporadic and limited interventions by the authorities due to their highly networked and decentralized nature. Several countries, such as Thailand, Vietnam, Malaysia, and Indonesia, utilize special investigative units to target arms trafficking networks in coordinated takedowns. Philippine authorities frequently use entrapment operations and complaint hotlines to seize firearms and other illicit goods. However, it is unclear how effective such units are against increasingly digitized illicit markets in which participants can shift between profiles and platforms to evade detection. Some countries employ extremely punitive measures against illicit firearm owners and traffickers. Most countries (except for the Philippines and Cambodia) reserve capital punishment for severe firearm-related crimes. Brunei, Malaysia, and Singapore employ corporal punishment for more moderate offences, in the form of caning. Few countries use more cooperative measures to reduce illicit firearm possession. Philippine security forces collect some dozens of military-grade weapons each week through an open-ended firearm amnesty/buyback system for weapons possessed by Communist and Islamist rebels as well as conflict-affected communities throughout the country, particularly in the Bangsamoro region. Thai and Vietnamese authorities have employed sporadic, limited firearms amnesties following high-profile gun incidents.

Policy Recommendations

There are several shortcomings to government efforts at combatting illicit firearms, given the increased integration and digitization of regional economies. As noted earlier, notions of non-intervention limit states' abilities to collaborate and disrupt arms trafficking networks beyond their borders, which is essential given their transnational nature. National law enforcement agencies must also adapt to better police and prosecute digitized black markets, as many illicit firearm transactions take place through e-commerce sites, social media platforms, courier services, and digital payment apps. As online platforms have made illicit firearms more accessible to users, it also appears that citizens who are unaware of gun laws can acquire firearms without fully understanding legal gun ownership requirements. Heavy punishments for illicit gun ownership may reduce opportunities for controlling illicit firearms as reluctant gun owners lack a means for safely and legitimately disposing their weapons. In any case, entrenched corruption provides arms traffickers and criminal actors with a pathway for evading law enforcement or even sourcing weapons from state-controlled stocks.

To counteract these trends, South-east Asian governments can pursue initiatives at the regional/international, national, and local level. In line with international instruments like the UNPoA, states should harmonize their national firearm laws and regulations in order to ensure that loopholes are closed, particularly as it concerns emerging technologies (like 3D printing), novel trafficking methods (such as the use of digital platforms), or legal grey areas (such as the status of craft-production weapons; see Pornchookiet et al. 2021). States should also expand multilateral and bilateral cooperation efforts, such as joint border operations, coordinated investigations to dismantle transnational networks, or border access rights during pursuit operations (particularly in the maritime domain). States could also use multilateral fora to share experiences, capacities, and intelligence to tackle new trafficking techniques and actors.

At the national level, governments should ensure firearm laws and regulations are updated to account for emerging technologies and trafficking techniques, such as the conversion of non-lethal weapons to fire live ammunition. They should also assess whether punitive measures impede opportunities for civilians to surrender illicit firearms, such as through gun amnesty and buyback programmes. Governments should also engage companies that provide online services used by traffickers to ensure digital spaces are more secure from criminal activity. Governments could also benefit their own policy-making and legislative processes by improving reporting related to illicit firearms. This could include requiring law enforcement agencies to publicly disclose firearms seizures, publishing annual firearms seizure and destruction figures, as well as reporting prosecution statistics concerning firearms-related crimes. National governments should also take an aggressive approach to minimizing the effects of corruption on stockpile security and arms control. This can take the form of setting up independent oversight units either within or alongside law enforcement agencies with the power to investigate and prosecute corruption-related crimes, strengthening whistleblower and complaint mechanisms, or digitizing record systems to ensure corrupt officials cannot fraudulently alter or issue key records and documents.

On the local level, the authorities should make active efforts to educate citizens about the risks and dangers of illicit firearms. Such efforts should particularly target younger citizens who may be exposed to trafficking opportunities online, as well as rural communities who may not be aware of gun ownership requirements. Governments could also employ localized gun amnesty or buyback campaigns, particularly through engaging local officials and community-based leaders (such as religious figures or tribal/clan heads), as the Philippines has effectively done in Mindanao. Conducting such campaigns over an extended period of time could also provide useful indications to officials about the extent of illicit firearm proliferation as well as the sources of illicit weapons that could inform additional policy changes. Local police forces should also utilize anonymous complaint hotlines to collect actionable information on firearms-related criminal activity.

References

Baker, Jacqui, and Milne, Sarah. 2015. 'Dirty Money States: Illicit Economies and the State in Southeast Asia'. *Critical Asian Studies* 47 (2), pp. 151–176.

Bandera News. 2024. '1 Dead, 3 Arrested in Firearms Buy Bust Operation in Talayan Mag Sur' [Facebook Post] (26 April 2024), https://www.facebook.com/radyobanderacotabato/posts/pfbid02LPZEHsFw4rw9DhmmCMEq3Gkp38QMbT32Wb4KRu6LUBHF37WoLgdZjHy1jHsDRFA8l

Briantika, Adi. 2020. 'Ketika Aparat Menyuburkan Konflik di Papua dengan Berdagang Senjata'. *Tirto* (14 Nov. 2020), https://tirto.id/ketika-aparat-menyuburkan-konflik-di-papua-dengan-berdagang-senjata-f6WE Accessed 23 Jul. 2024.

Buan, Lian, Bolledo, Jairo, and Gavilan, Jodesz. 2024. 'The Duterte Dynasty: Powered by Guns'. *Rappler* (11 Mar. 2024), https://www.rappler.com/newsbreak/investigative/duterte-dynasty-powered-by-guns/ Accessed 23 Jul. 2024.

Cabrera, Romina. 2024. 'DILG: Surrender, Renew Expired Licenses of Firearms'. *The Philippine Star* (10 Feb 2024), https://www.philstar.com/headlines/2024/02/10/2332278/dilg-surrender-renew-expired-licenses-firearms Accessed 23 Jul. 2024.

Chapsos, Ioannis, Koning, Juliette, and Noortmann, Math. 2019. 'Involving Local Fishing Communities in Policy Making: Addressing Illegal Fishing in Indonesia'. *Marine Policy* 109. October.

Chouvy, Pierre-Arnaud. 2013. *An Atlas of Trafficking in Southeast Asia: The Illegal Trade in Arms, Drugs, People, Counterfeit Goods and Natural Resources*. London: IB Taurus.

CIDG (Criminal Investigation and Detection Group). 2024. 'CIDG Rescues Victims and Apprehends 7 Chinese Nationals Involved in Illegal Activities 2024'. [Facebook post] (3 May. 2024), https://www.facebook.com/cidg.pio/posts/pfbid02MsQ86HEhKXZ7MJ13QgzAhRrdudnqxPLGYzugNyazfgohEr9VJh6L1JbcjzSZqysal

Dahari, Rafidah, Idris, Nor Azizan, and Othman, Zarina. 2019. 'Influencing External Factors for Small Arms Light Weapon Smuggling at Malaysia-Thailand Border'. *Asian Social Science* 15(3): pp. 14–26.

Dalizon, Alfred P. 2024. '85K expired law enforcers' gun papers renewed in '23'. *Journal News* (5 Feb. 2024), https://journalnews.com.ph/85k-expired-law-enforcers-gun-papers-renewed-in-23 Accessed 23 Jul. 2024.

Davis, Anthony. 2019. 'China's Mobile Missiles on the Loose in Myanmar'. *Asia Times* (28 Nov. 2019), https://asiatimes.com/2019/11/chinas-mobile-missiles-on-the-loose-in-myanmar/ Accessed 23 Jul. 2024.

Eleven Myanmar. 2023. 'Ministry of Home Affairs Issues an Order on Amending Possession of Arms'. *Eleven Myanmar* (11 Feb. 2023), https://elevenmyanmar.com/news/ministry-of-home-affairs-issues-an-order-on-amending-possession-of-arms Accessed 23 Jul. 2024.

Fronde, Neill. 2023. 'Police Target Kamnan Nok Mafia Networks Linked to Extortion'. *Thaiger* (10 Sep. 2023), https://thethaiger.com/hot-news/crime/thai-police-target-kamnan-nok-mafia-networks-linked-to-extortion-from-overloaded-trucks Accessed 23 Jul. 2024.

Frontier Myanmar. 2022. '"Ready to kill": Inside the weapons factories of the resistance'. *Frontier Myanmar* (26 Oct. 2022), https://www.frontiermyanmar.net/en/ready-to-kill-inside-the-weapons-factories-of-the-resistance/ Accessed 23 Jul. 2024.

GITOC (Global Initiative on Transnational Organized Crime). 2022. *Branches of Illegality: Cambodia's Illegal Logging Structures*. Geneva: GITOC. September.

Gutierrez, Jason. 2019. 'A Family Craft With a Deadly Toll: Illegal Gun Making'. *The New York Times* (7 Apr. 2019), https://www.nytimes.com/2019/04/07/world/asia/philippines-illegal-guns.html Accessed 23 Jul. 2024.

Harmer, Jerry, and Peck, Grant. 2023. 'Deadly Thai Mall Shooting Exposes Murky Trade in Blank Handguns that are Turned into Lethal Weapons'. *Associated Press* (5 Oct. 2023), https://apnews.com/article/blank-handguns-gun-control-lethal-weapons-038d4dc5b9a16790471d06e6aa1436b9 Accessed 23 Jul. 2024.

HRW (Human Rights Watch). 2010. *'They Own the People': The Ampatuans, State-Backed Militias, and Killings in the Southern Philippines*. New York: Human Rights Watch. https://www.hrw.org/report/2010/11/16/they-own-people/ampatuans-state-backed-militias-and-killings-southern-philippines Accessed 27 Jul. 2024.

Idris, Iffat. 2019. *Drivers and Enablers of Serious Organised Crime in Southeast Asia*. K4D Helpdesk Report 655. Brighton: Institute of Development Studies (30 August 2019), https://assets.publishing.service.gov.uk/media/5d9b5b4c40f0b607ec50cc1a/655_Drivers_and_Enablers_of_Serious_Organised_Crime_in_Southeast_Asia.pdf Accessed 27 Jul. 2024.

IPAC (Institute for Policy Analysis and Conflict). 2022. Escalating Armed Conflict and a New Security Approach in Papua. Jakarta: IPAC. https://understandingconflict.org/en/publications/escalating-armed-conflict-and-a-new-security-approach-in-papua Accessed 27 Jul. 2024.

IPAC. 2024. *Managing Conflict in Papua: Suggestions for a New President*. Jakarta: IPAC. https://understandingconflict.sgp1.digitaloceanspaces.com/dashboard/IPAC-Report-91-Managing-Conflict-in-Papua-Suggestions-for-a-New-President_06-02-2024.pdf.pdf Accessed 27 Jul. 2024.

Karmini, Niniek. 2024. 'Indonesian Police Arrest 6 Suspected Poachers over the Killing of 26 Endangered Javan Rhinos'. *Associated Press* (12 Jun 2024), https://apnews.com/article/indonesia-javan-rhino-poachers-fdebd5747c5c74061a13edb071deef7f Accessed 23 Jul. 2024.

Karp, Aaron. 2018. *Global Firearms Holdings Dynamic Map*. Geneva: Small Arms Survey. https://www.smallarmssurvey.org/database/global-firearms-holdings Accessed 23 Jul. 2024.

Khmer Times. 2021. 'Two More Military Officers Involved with Weapons Trafficking Arrested'. *Khmer Times* (22 Nov. 2021), https://www.khmertimeskh.com/50974957/two-more-military-officers-involved-with-weapons-trafficking-arrested/ Accessed 23 Jul. 2024.

Kway Lin Htoon. 2018. 'Firearms and the Law in Myanmar'. *Frontier Myanmar* (2 Aug. 2018), https://www.frontiermyanmar.net/en/firearms-and-the-law-in-myanmar/ Accessed 23 Jul. 2024.

Lamb, Kate and Teresia, Ananda. 2023. 'How Indonesian Village Aid Funds Weapons for Papua's Rebellion'. *Reuters* (7 Jun. 2023), https://www.reuters.com/world/asia-pacific/how-indonesian-village-aid-funds-weapons-papuas-rebellion-2023-06-08/Accessed 23 Jul. 2024.

Laotian Times. 2022. 'Police Arrest Arms Dealer in Vientiane After Exchange of Gunfire'. *Laotian Times* (15 Jul. 2022), https://laotiantimes.com/2022/07/15/police-arrest-arms-dealer-in-vientiane-after-exchange-of-gunfire/ Accessed 23 Jul. 2024.

Larsson, Tomas. 2013. 'The Strong and the Weak: Ups and Downs of State Capacity in Southeast Asia'. *Asian Politics and Policy* 5(3): pp. 337–358.

Lin, Leo. 2023. 'Understanding Asian Organized Crime'. In *Asian Organized Crime and the Anglosphere: Advanced Sciences and Technologies for Security Applications*, edited by L. Lin, Springer.

Lingao, Ed. 2010. *Ampatuans Used Public Office to Amass Mostly Illegal Guns*. Quezon City: Philippine Center for Investigative Journalism. https://pcij.org/2010/02/03/ampatuans-used-public-office-brto-amass-mostly-illegal-guns/ Accessed 23 Jul. 2024.

Lintner, Bertil. 2002. *Blood Brothers: The Criminal Underworld of Asia*. New York: Palgrave Macmillan.

Lopez, Alexander. 2024. 'Army Foils NPA Extortion Try on Agusan Norte Small-Scale Miners'. Philippine News Agency (13 Mar. 2024), https://www.pna.gov.ph/articles/1220688 Accessed 23 Jul. 2024.

Luong, Hai Thanh. 2020. 'Drug Trafficking in the Mainland Southeast Asian Region: The Example of Vietnam's Shared Borderland with Laos'. *International Annals of Criminology* 58, pp. 130–151.

Mahsinah Abdullah, Sharifah. 2023. 'Kelantan Police Concerned about Firearms Smuggling along Border'. *New Straits Times* (27 Jun. 2023), https://www.nst.com.my/news/crime-courts/2023/06/924746/kelantan-police-concerned-about-firearms-smuggling-along-border Accessed 23 Jul. 2024.

Malay Mail. 2023. 'Ex-Leader of Daesh Cell 'Wolf Pack' Charged with Eight Counts of Terrorism-Related Offences Ordered to Enter Defence'. *Malay Mail* (12 Dec. 2023), https://www.malaymail.com/news/malaysia/2023/12/12/ex-leader-of-daesh-cell-wolf-pack-charged-with-eight-counts-of-terrorism-related-offences-ordered-to-enter-defence/107137 Accessed 23 Jul. 2024.

Meehan, Patrick. 2015. 'Fortifying or Fragmenting the State? The Political Economy of the Opium/Heroin Trade in Shan State, Myanmar, 1988–2013'. *Critical Asian Studies* 47(2): pp. 253–282.

Milne, Sarah. 2015. 'Cambodia's Unofficial Regime of Extraction: Illicit Logging in the Shadow of Transnational Governance and Investment'. *Critical Asian Studies* 47(2): pp. 200–228.

Mizan Aslam, Mohd. 2020. 'Malaysian Terrorist Organizations and Potential Involvement in Criminal Acitivities'. *Journal of Al-Tamaddun* 15(2): pp. 15–27.

Mok Shen Yang. 2020. 'ASEAN and Transnational Crime: Gains and Challenges in Tackling Drug Trafficking'. *Wimaya Interdisciplinary Journal of International Affairs* 1(1): pp. 31–38.

Munro, Peter. 2012. 'Harbouring the Illicit: Borderlands and Human Trafficking in South East Asia'. *Crime, Law and Social Change* 58: pp.159–177.

Ngankham, Wassayos. 2014. 'Police Net 26 in Pen Gun Probe'. *Bangkok Post* (10 Nov. 2014), https://www.bangkokpost.com/thailand/general/442371/police-net-26-in-pen-gun-probe Accessed 23 Jul. 2024.

Nguyen, Dung Van, Nguyen, Cuong Huu, Lec, Toan Quang, and Dod, Thanh Danh. 2020. 'Human Trafficking in Vietnam: The Issues and Responses of the Vietnamese Government'. *International Journal of Innovation, Creativity and Change* 13(7): pp. 135–152.

OHCHR (United Nations Office of the High Commissioner on Human Rights). 2023. *Online Scam Operations and Trafficking Into Forced Criminality in Southeast Asia: Recommendations for a Human Rights Response*. Bangkok: OHCHR.

Ortiz, Miguel. 2023. '3D-Printed Guns are Being Used in the Myanmar Civil War'. *We Are The Mighty* (25 July 2023), https://www.wearethemighty.com/tactical/3d-printed-guns-are-being-used-in-the-myanmar-civil-war/ Accessed 23 Jul. 2024.

Peter, Zsombor. 2023. 'One Year After Nursery Massacre, Thailand Waiting for Gun Reform'. *Voice of America* (9 Oct. 2023), https://www.voanews.com/a/one-year-after-nursery-massacre-thailand-waiting-for-gun-reform/7302547.html Accessed 23 Jul. 2024.

Phaicharoen, Nontarat, and Boonreak, Kunnawut. 2023. 'Thai PM Pledges to Tighten Gun Regulations after Mass Shooting at Mall'. *Benar News* (4 October 2024), https://www.benarnews.org/english/news/thai/shooting-update-10042023124929.html Accessed 23 Jul. 2024.

PIA Bukidnon. 2024. 'The 403rd Infantry Peacemaker Brigade, led by BGen Michele B. Anayron Jr. and 4ID Commander MGen Jose Maria Cuerpo II, arranged a "Friends Rescued" forum today at the 403rd Infantry Brigade camp in Malaybalay City for the 44 CPP-NPA rebel leaders and combatants who surrendered' [Facebook post] (7 May. 2024), https://www.facebook.com/permalink.php?story_fbid=pfbid02QSh9sD5R7rc4dDg5E32UR7fVQEMAdA72kSVKMeNx5BwNR5GojRyBFcHmvw4kbYaCl&id=61556770299596 Accessed 23 Jul. 2024.

Picard, Michael. 2021. 'Small Arms Proliferation Challenges and Solutions in South and South-east Asia'. In *Gun Trafficking and Violence*, edited by D. P. Esparza, et al. Oxford: Palgrave Macmillan.

Picard, Michael. 2023. 'Thailand's Mall Shooting Shows That Authorities Must Address Online Black Markets'. *The Diplomat* (7 Oct. 2024), https://thediplomat.com/2023/10/thailands-mall-shooting-shows-that-authorities-must-address-online-black-markets/ Accessed 23 Jul. 2024.

Picard, Michael, Holtom, Paul, and Mangan, Fiona. 2019. *Trade Update 2019: Transfers, Transparency, and South-east Asia Spotlight*. Geneva: Small Arms Survey.

Pornchookiet, Ekkamon, Kanyajit, Sunee, Sinloyma, Patchara, Suwannanon, Apasiri, and Junprasert, Thasuk. 2021. 'Homemade Gun Control and Management: Source of Problem and Solution'. *Turkish Online Journal of Qualitative Inquiry* 12(6): pp. 9357–9364.

RA (Republic Act) No. 10591. 2012. Comprehensive Law on Firearms and Ammunition, https://lawphil.net/statutes/repacts/ra2013/ra_10591_2013.html Accessed 23 Jul. 2024.

Reuters. 2024. 'Israeli Man Pleads Not Guilty to Firearms Offences in Malaysia'. *Reuters* (12 April 2024), https://www.reuters.com/world/asia-pacific/israeli-man-pleads-not-guilty-firearms-offences-malaysia-2024-04-12/.

Riley, Michael, Kocieniewski, David, and Fan, Eric. 2023. 'How the US Drives Gun Exports and Fuels Violence Around the World'. *Bloomberg* (24 July 2023), https://www.bloomberg.com/graphics/2023-us-made-gun-exports-shootings-violence-sig-sauer/ Accessed 23 Jul. 2024.

Rizki Akbari, Anugerah. 2015. 'Explaining Crimmigration in Indonesia: A Discourse of the Fight Against People Smuggling, Irregular Migration Control, and Symbolic Criminalization'. *Indonesia Law Review* 5(3): pp. 276–290.

RSF (Reporters Sans Frontieres). n.d. 'Myanmar'. Press Freedom Index. Paris: Reporters Sans Frontieres. https://rsf.org/en/country/myanmar Accessed 23 Jul. 2024.

Sampurno Soewondo, Slamet, and Kadarudin. 2022. 'Prevention and Eradication of Transnational Organized Crime in Southeast Asia'. *Scholars International Journal of Law, Crime and Justice* 5(2): pp. 37–44.

Schloenhardt, Andreas. 2001. 'Trafficking in Migrants: Illegal Migration and Organized Crime in Australia and the Asia Pacific Region'. *International Journal of the Sociology of Law* 29: pp. 331–378.

Singh, Jitendra Bahadur. 2023. 'Arms Used for Violence in Manipur Smuggled Via Myanmar, Procured by Insurgent Groups: Sources'. *India Today* (27 Jun. 2023), https://www.indiatoday.in/india/story/weapons-used-in-manipur-violence-supplied-via-myanmar-route-intelligence-sources-2398477-2023-06-27 Accessed 23 Jul. 2024.

Slow, Oliver. 2024. 'Vietnam Rebel Attacks: 98 Go On Trial Accused of Killing Nine People'. *BBC News* (17 Jan. 2024), https://www.bbc.com/news/world-asia-67995372 Accessed 22 Jul. 2024.

Soeriaatmadja, Wahyudi. 2023. 'Indonesian Police Uncover Illegal Sales of Firearms on Popular E-Commerce Platforms'. *The Straits Times* (19 Aug. 2023), https://www.straitstimes.com/asia/se-asia/indonesian-police-uncover-illegal-sales-of-firearms-on-popular-e-commerce-platforms Accessed 23 Jul. 2024.

Thai PBS World. 2022. 'Thailand's CSD Police Apprehend Arms Trafficking Gang, Arresting 17 Suspects'. *Thai PBS World* (14 Jun 2024), https://www.thaipbsworld.com/thailands-csd-police-apprehend-arms-trafficking-gang-arresting-17-suspects/ Accessed 23 Jul. 2024.

Thai PBS World. 2023. 'Kamnan Nok Scandal Lifts Lid on Thai Bureaucracy's Corruption Crisis'. *Thai PBS World* (14 Sept. 2024), https://www.thaipbsworld.com/kamnan-nok-scandal-lifts-lid-on-thai-bureaucracys-corruption-crisis/ Accessed 23 Jul. 2024.

Thai Rath. 2023. 'รวบสาวมอญพร้อมปลอกกระสุน M-16 และแมกกาซีน หลังมีพัสดุส่งมาจากชลบุรี'. *Thai Rath* (17 Sep. 2023), https://www.thairath.co.th/news/local/central/2725824?gallery_id=1 Accessed 23 Jul. 2024.

The Star. 2024a. 'Glocks Being Smuggled through Sg Golok'. *The Star* (4 May. 2024), https://www.thestar.com.my/news/nation/2024/05/04/glocks-being-smuggled-through-sg-golok Accessed 23 Jul. 2024.

The Star. 2024b. 'M'sian Kingpin Held in Laos'. *The Star* (3 Jan. 2024), https://www.thestar.com.my/news/nation/2024/01/03/msian-kingpin-held-in-laos Accessed 23 Jul. 2024.

Today Online. 2020. 'Sea Robbery Incidents in Singapore Strait Hit 4-Year High'. *Today Online* (16 Jan. 2024), https://www.todayonline.com/singapore/sea-robbery-incidents-singapore-strait-hit-4-year-high Accessed 23 Jul. 2024.

Tower, Jason, and Clapp, Priscilla. 2024. *China Forces Myanmar Scam Syndicates to Move to Thai Border*. Washington DC: US Institute for Peace. https://www.usip.org/publications/2024/04/china-forces-myanmar-scam-syndicates-move-thai-border Accessed 23 Jul. 2024.

UN Women. 2020. *The Gendered Dynamics of Trafficking in Persons Across Cambodia, Myanmar, and Thailand*. Bangkok: UN Women.

Van Uhm, Daan, and Grigore, Ana. 2021. 'Indigenous People, Organized Crime and Natural Resources: Borders, Incentives and Relations'. *Critical Criminology* 29: pp. 487–503.

Van Uhm, Daan, and Nijman, Rick. 2022. 'The Convergence of Environmental Crime with other Serious Crimes: Subtypes within the Environmental Crime Continuum'. *European Journal of Criminology* 19(4): pp. 542–561.

VOA News. 2021. 'Myanmar Border Gun Seizures Stoke Fears of Illicit Post-Coup Arms Trade'. *Voice of America* (12 June 2021), https://www.voanews.com/a/east-asia-pacific_myanmar-border-gun-seizures-stoke-fears-illicit-post-coup-arms-trade/6206939.html Accessed 26 Jul. 2024.

Vy, Lan. 2023. 'Mekong Delta Woman Helms Weapon Ring that Sells 600 Guns'. *VN Express* (11 Aug. 2024), https://e.vnexpress.net/news/news/mekong-delta-woman-helms-weapon-ring-that-sells-600-guns-4640709.html Accessed 23 Jul. 2024.

Wahab, Andika Ab, and Khairi, Aizat. 2020. 'Smuggling of Rohingyas from Myanmar to Malaysia: A Threat to Human Security'. *Akademika* 90(3): pp. 27–37.

War Noir. 2023. 'Rather Interesting Photos Posted by People's Defense Forces (#PDF) after an Ambush against Tatmadaw'. [X post] (22 Dec. 2023), https://x.com/war_noir/status/1738135682265051272 Accessed 23 Jul. 2024.

Weng, Lawi. 2008. 'AK-47s—Made in Wa State'. *The Irrawaddy* (16 Dec. 2008), https://www2.irrawaddy.com/article.php?art_id=14804 Accessed 23 Jul. 2024.

Western Mindanao Command. 2024. 'Locals Surrender 36 Loose Firearms in Maguindanao del Sur' [Facebook post] (4 May. 2024), https://www.facebook.com/westmincomafp2021/posts/pfbid0MiZ67rN1iJUKXdCzNsLsVDYeccW7qEV6vrJFAUnAdK5daLAeUgW7u6JkkrcmwLinl Accessed 23 Jul. 2024.

Wijaya, Stefani. 2023. 'Satgas P3GN Polri Temukan Penyelundupan 2 Pucuk Senpi oleh Jaringan Narkoba'. *Berita Satu* (18 Oct. 2023), https://www.beritasatu.com/nasional/1072632/satgas-p3gn-polri-temukan-penyelundupan-2-pucuk-senpi-oleh-jaringan-narkoba Accessed 23 Jul. 2024.

4

The Nexus of Firearms and Organized Crime in Latin America

Carlos A. Pérez Ricart

Introduction

Viewers were stunned. Were they watching a performance? Was it a joke? Was it a surprise from the afternoon news? What were those individuals doing on screen? They had never seen anything like it before. A dozen hooded figures appeared on the television screen. They wore caps and ski masks that covered their faces. They brandished pistols, grenades, rifles, and other explosives. The news presenters, who until recently had read the news with their warm voices, now approached the cameras to urge the police to intervene immediately. Were they actors? No one could tell.

It is 9 January 2024. The clock has just struck 14.15 in Ecuador. What the viewers see is not a show—or at least not the one they expected to see. It is the live, full-colour entrance of a criminal group into the TC (*Televisora Central*) channel studio in Guayaquil, the main television station in the country's second-largest city. In front of their televisions, before the transmission was cut off and for about fifteen minutes, millions of Ecuadorians witnessed the takeover of a television channel and the kidnapping of its employees. The armed criminals aimed to send a message to the entire country. They succeeded.

The day before, on 8 January, José Adolfo Macias, also known as Fito, leader of one of the most feared gangs, 'Los Choneros', had escaped from a prison in Guayaquil. Across the rest of the country, bombings, shootings, and murders began to intensify. Over a hundred kidnappings were reported in six prisons across the country. Hospitals and police stations were looted, with dozens of cars set ablaze. The government announced a curfew and

Carlos A. Pérez Ricart, *The Nexus of Firearms and Organized Crime in Latin America* In: *Illicit Firearms Markets and Organized Crime*. Edited by: David Bright, Oxford University Press.
 DOI: 10.1093/9780198902409.003.0005

urged the population not to leave their homes. Following the takeover of the television channel, President Daniel Noboa declared a state of emergency due to an 'internal armed conflict'. Noboa took the opportunity to designate twenty-two criminal gangs as terrorist groups; 'We are at war', he stated.

Until a few years ago, Ecuador was a relatively peaceful country. Its homicide rate was below the regional average. To many, the country was a model of coexistence. Its seventeen million people lived in relative peace, far from the organized crime problems that plague some of its neighbours. In 2018, Ecuador recorded 995 homicides, a rate of 5.8 homicides per hundred thousand inhabitants. In 2023, there were more than 7,500 homicides, a 650 per cent increase from five years earlier. In half a decade, Ecuador had become one of the most dangerous countries in Latin America.

Ecuador is an extreme case, but not an exceptional one. Colombia, Venezuela, Mexico, Brazil, and other countries in Central America and the Caribbean have serious problems with organized crime. Over the past two decades, entire regions of these and other countries have fallen completely under the control of criminal structures. Why has this happened? What explains the violence in the region and the disproportionate penetration of criminal networks that were once small and incapable of directly challenging state authority? What is the role of firearms in the reconfiguration of organized crime in Latin America? This chapter seeks to answer these questions.

The chapter's central hypothesis is that the extraordinary expansion of organized crime in the region cannot be explained without considering the increasing circulation of firearms, most of which originate in the United States. Firearms have been a key factor in explaining the diversification of criminal activities by organizations previously dedicated solely to drug trafficking. As the case of Ecuador shows, criminal groups have been able to maximize their firepower and intervene in other criminal markets, such as human trafficking and extortion. In short, firearms have been the vector that has enabled criminal diversification and, consequently, the territorial expansion of organized crime in Latin America.

In addition to analysing the relationship between firearms and organized crime, the chapter has a second objective: to review public policies aimed at addressing the problem of firearms circulation. Thus, the chapter reviews public policies implemented in Latin America, and makes some policy recommendations for the future. Finally, the chapter emphasizes that any national effort will be insufficient unless the central source of the problem for Latin America is addressed: the availability of firearms from the United States, the largest and most unrestricted firearms market in the world.

Violence in Latin America

Latin America has the highest homicide rate in the world. In the region, 75 per cent of homicides in 2021 were committed with a firearm, also the highest proportion in the world (UNODC 2023a, 131). There is a wealth of data to illustrate the extent of the violence. Here are just three: (1) In 2022, eight of the ten countries with the highest homicide rates were in Latin America (UNODC 2023b); (2) In 2023, forty of the fifty cities with the highest homicide rates in the world were in a country in Latin America and the Caribbean. Of the top ten, nine were located in Latin America and eight were Mexican (Seguridad Justicia y Paz 2023); (3) Although only 8 per cent of the world's population lives in the region, about one-third of homicides occur there. One characteristic of the homicide phenomenon in Latin America is its extreme variability. Whether due to the dynamics of criminal activity or changes in the functioning of the police or judicial system, countries can experience drastic changes in their absolute numbers. Brazil, for example, went from 63,000 homicides per year in 2017 to just under 40,000 in 2023. The reasons for the decline are still difficult to understand. An extreme case is El Salvador, where the 'iron fist' policies of President Nayib Bukele have managed to reduce the homicide rate from over 100 per hundred thousand inhabitants in 2015 to less than five in 2023. But the human rights cost has been enormous.

Before proceeding, it is important to note the existence of regional differences in Latin America. The problem of homicide is not uniform in all areas, nor does it stem from the same causes. Broadly speaking, the region can be divided into three main blocs. The first is made up of countries with an average homicide rate of more than twenty per 100,000 inhabitants over the last three years. Brazil, Mexico, Venezuela, and Colombia are the most important. These four countries alone account for approximately a quarter of the world's intentional homicides.

Of the four countries, the most dramatic case is Venezuela, a country that has experienced exorbitant peaks in the last decade. In this first bloc, we must also include Ecuador and other Caribbean and Central American countries with even higher homicide rates. This is the case of Jamaica, the Bahamas, and the Turks and Caicos Islands, which in 2022 had a homicide rate of more than seventy per 100,000 inhabitants (see Chapter 7 for more details overview of illicit firearms in the Caribbean). As we will see below, the high homicide rates in these countries are linked to the problem of drug trafficking in the region. The Caribbean is one of the regions most affected by the struggle between criminal organizations. Traditionally peaceful places such as the Turks and Caicos Islands, Saint Vincent and the Grenadines, and Trinidad and Tobago have seen their homicide rates rise dramatically in recent years. In 2022, they had homicide rates above thirty per 100,000 population. Jamaica deserves special mention, with a homicide rate of fifty-three per 100,000 people in 2022.

The second bloc includes countries with average homicide rates above ten but below twenty per 100,000 inhabitants. This category includes some Central American countries (Guatemala, Costa Rica, Panama) and Uruguay. These countries have managed to maintain a low level of homicidal violence, but they may be affected in the medium term by the expansion of certain criminal activities. As we will show later, preventing this means denying criminal organizations access to a steady source of firearms.

Finally, there are several countries, such as Bolivia, Peru, Argentina, and Chile, that do not have a significant problem of high homicide rates and may have rates similar to those in Europe. Paradoxically, some of these states do have serious problems with crime and public safety, but this has not had a significant impact on homicide rates.

From this initial segmentation, it is clear that Latin America has more regional variations than the collective imagination often recognizes. It is a region as vast as it is diverse, with enormous differences between urban and rural areas. Nevertheless, the issue of organized crime is becoming increasingly prevalent in the region. While not all countries experience it in the same way, there is no country in Latin America where organized crime is not a growing problem (Bergman 2018; 2023). The next section focuses on this issue.

Organized Crime in Latin America

Latin America produces virtually all the world's coca leaf. In 2021, an all-time high of 2,304 tons of coca leaf was cultivated (UNODC 2023c). The Andean region, which includes Ecuador, Peru, Bolivia, and parts of Colombia, has been a coca leaf production zone since the 1970s, but it has never produced as much as it does now. For a long time, demand was concentrated almost exclusively in the US market, but for a little more than a decade, Brazil has been the second most important cocaine market in the world.

Mexico, on the other hand, serves as a bridge for cocaine trafficking from South America to the United States, and since the 1970s has been a major centre for the cultivation of marijuana and opium poppies favoured by the US market (Smith 2021). To make matters worse, in the last decade, Mexico and some countries in Central America have become production zones for methamphetamine and other synthetic drugs such as fentanyl (Pérez Ricart and Ibarrola García 2023). The fact that Mexico shares a border of more than 3,000 kilometres with the United States suggests that the problem will continue to grow in the coming decades. Mexico's geographic location is inescapable, especially when one considers that the country is the main recipient of US firearms (a topic we will discuss in a later section).

Under these circumstances, it is clear that much of the criminal activity in the region is related to drug trafficking. Much of the violence, including homicides, in Latin America is the result of competition among different criminal organizations for control of the illegal drug market. While it is true that not all drug markets lead to violent dynamics (Daudelin and Ratton 2018; Daudelin 2017), there is sufficient evidence to argue that drug prohibition and lack of regulation are factors that incentivize the resolution of conflicts by violent means. Latin America is a region that has experienced this phenomenon particularly acutely (Pérez Ricart 2021).

Nevertheless, drug trafficking is not the only illegal market in the region, and in some areas, it is not even the most important. In Central America, for example, organized crime groups have opted for other types of business. In particular, extortion stands out as a 'socio-economic feature in the daily life of citizens, businesses and the institutional fabric of the state' (InSight Crime 2019, 1). Extortion is a covert crime based primarily on the threat of future violence. Low reporting rates make it impossible to measure rigorously. Victimization surveys indicate that eight out of ten extortions in Central America go unreported (InSight Crime 2019). In Mexico, the unreported crime rate reached up to 97 per cent in 2021 (INEGI 2022).

In the countries of Central America's northern triangle (El Salvador, Guatemala, and Honduras), extortion has become both the main source of income for gangs (the famous '*maras*') and the most serious threat to the state. In some cases, extortion networks are supported by complex financial structures and transnational money laundering tactics. At its peak in 2014, it was estimated that the private sector in El Salvador paid the equivalent of 3 per cent of national GDP in extortion (InSight Crime 2019, 3).

Unlike drug trafficking, which can operate clandestinely in some parts of the region without disrupting community life too much, extortion cuts across all social and economic strata. It affects entrepreneurs and the most vulnerable alike. Grocers, egg-sellers, and vendors of avocados, meat, and fried chicken must pay extortion groups to avoid harassment. In some areas of Mexico, the problem is more complex, affecting Internet services and the use of public transportation. In Guatemala and Honduras, it is hard to find a more dangerous job than driving taxis or buses—they are constant victims of extortion.

Inevitably, the crime of extortion encourages the emergence of 'parasites' or 'copycats', who benefit from the reputation of the 'real' criminals. These types of networks are more common in Mexico, Panama, or Costa Rica, where street gangs (MS13 and Barrio 18) have less territorial presence than in neighbouring countries. The copycats often operate by telephone. In Mexico, 90 per cent of extortion cases take place over the phone, and according to a victimization survey, in 9 per cent of cases the victim complies with the criminal's demands (INEGI 2022).

At its highest level, territorial expansion of organized criminal groups is a form of criminal governance (Arias 2017). This means that criminal groups exercise control over territory. Their power is manifested in people's daily lives, and political authority is shared with other figures, from religious leaders to elected officials. Again, as we will see later, firearms have been a factor in the expansion of this crime.

Lastly, it is worth mentioning that the growth in the flow of migrants from around the globe to the United States since 2018 has had the unintended effect of increasing the coffers of criminal groups, via kidnapping and people smuggling. There are many modalities, although what predominates is the express kidnapping of migrants and their release (in the best-case scenario) in exchange for several hundred dollars paid by relatives in poor areas. In the dynamics of this market, firearms have played a prominent role (Weigend Vargas et al. 2024).

In conclusion, the challenge that Latin America faces regarding organized crime is significant. In several regions, organized crime and the state are not separate and clearly identifiable entities. They feed off each other: members of the armed forces, police, or bureaucrats play a central role in extortion dynamics, as well as in drug trafficking circuits and human trafficking (Garay-Salamanca 2020). Particularly in Central America and in some regions of Mexico, the distinction between organized crime and the state is not as clear as it might be. Rather than being a phenomenon that emerges when the state is absent, organized crime should be understood as a phenomenon that emerges precisely because the state is present. This configuration has been enhanced by the presence of firearms in the region, a topic that will be explored in greater detail in the following pages.

Firearms: The Key for Organized Crime Expansion

It is evident that weapons in Latin America have been used not only to kill, but also to facilitate the expansion of criminal networks in the region. Firearms have enabled small-scale organized crime groups to challenge state authority to an extent that was previously unimaginable. Firearms have been the factor that enabled the growth of small networks into large armies capable of dominating cities. Without firearms, territorial expansion would not have been possible.

Over the past two decades, the proliferation of firearms has contributed to the diversification of the criminal market in Mexico and Central American countries. For decades, there were numerous groups engaged in drug trafficking without involvement in other crimes. The absence of firearms (and other weapons) constrained their capacity for action, and the types of illegal markets to which they had access were restricted. The ease of access to firearms allowed them to acquire a broad enough dispensary that made it simple to enter other businesses. The rationale was straightforward: given the availability of firearms, it was logical to exploit them for other purposes.

In accordance with this rationale, groups initiated the pursuit of new business ventures, including the trafficking of humans, extortion, protection rackets, the robbery of businesses, and the assassination of individuals. A comprehensive range of criminal activities was perpetrated. They acted in accordance with their capitalist principles, seeking to identify and exploit opportunities. They besieged entire cities and further challenged the already overburdened local police forces, which were unable to effectively respond to the influx of weaponry from the North.

The uninterrupted flow of weapons from the United States to Mexico and the proliferation of criminal organizations have compelled countries across the continent to adopt stringent policies to address the challenge. The direct consequence has been the militarization of public security at various levels (Pion-Berlin 2016). Over the past decade, virtually all countries in Latin America have militarized their public security, creating a vicious cycle of continuous reinforcement between the firepower of criminal groups and state forces (Padilla Oñate and Pérez Ricart 2023). This occurs in a context where the intertwining between organized crime and the state is total (or nearly total) in some regions, resulting in horrifying consequences.

Illegal Arms Trafficking from the United States to Latin America

Despite the region's strict firearms control policies, illegal firearms have circulated extensively in Latin America for decades (Sanjurjo 2020). Soviet-origin weapons were instrumental in fuelling civil wars in Central America in the 1980s, particularly in El Salvador, Guatemala, and Nicaragua. In Peru and Colombia, Soviet and German weapons were pivotal in prolonging their respective civil conflicts well into the twenty-first century. The region also produces arms. Brazil, for instance, has a flourishing firearms industry, with domestically produced firearms being circulated within the country, although these are often illicitly obtained. The tri-border region between Brazil, Paraguay, and Argentina has historically been a natural area for the illicit circulation of firearms.

That said, it is evident that the region's most significant challenge is situated along the border between Mexico and the United States. The border is an extreme case of opposing jurisdictions. While even large-calibre firearms can be purchased in Arizona, Texas, or New Mexico at the age of eighteen with only a driver's licence, in Mexico (and other countries in the region), it is practically impossible to obtain medium-calibre firearms legally (Pérez Ricart et al. 2021; Pérez Esparza and Weigend 2015). This makes it extremely attractive for organized crime groups in Mexico and the rest of Latin America to acquire firearms legally in the United States and then traffic them illegally into Mexico.

The United States is the world's leading producer, importer, and exporter of weapons. The market is also the largest in the world. As will be demonstrated below, the behaviour of this market has significant implications for Latin America and is largely responsible for the high levels of homicide in the region, as well as for the diversification of organized crime activities.

From 1994 until 2004, a federal law in the United States (the Federal Assault Weapons Ban, or AWB) prohibited the production of assault weapons. Following the expiration of the aforementioned legislation in 2004, the arms industry in that country experienced a new period of growth. For instance, in 2006, 4.99 million firearms were manufactured and imported to the United States. By 2012, this figure had increased to 12.13 million, representing 146 per cent growth. According to official data from the Bureau of Alcohol, Tobacco, Firearms, and Explosives (ATF), in 2021, the United States produced 6.75 million pistols, 3.93 million rifles, 1.16 million revolvers, 675,000 shotguns, and 1.28 million miscellaneous firearms. In total, 13.8 million weapons were produced (Bureau of Alcohol, Tobacco, Firearms, and Explosives 2023).

It is a thriving industry. Between 2000 and 2020, the United States saw a 187 per cent increase in firearms production. Concurrently, the number of producers grew from just over 2,000 to nearly 17,000 by 2020 (Bureau of Alcohol, Tobacco, Firearms, and Explosives 2022b, 168). In the year 2000, a total of 3.9 million firearms were manufactured. This equates to 1,397 firearms per 100,000 inhabitants. Twenty years later, in 2020, the number of firearms produced per 100,000 inhabitants was 3,410 (Bureau of Alcohol, Tobacco, Firearms, and Explosives 2022b, 14).

It is of significant consequence to note that while the population of the United States had increased by 18 per cent, the number of firearms produced increased by 187 per cent. The issue is not simply one of increased firearms production in general, but rather the specific type of firearm being produced. It is therefore essential to comprehend the significance of rifle production in comparison to other firearms. In the year 2000, 1,559,000 rifles were manufactured. In 2016, 4.247 million rifles were manufactured, representing a 173 per cent increase in just sixteen years.

A significant proportion of these weapons were destined for the US market, while a considerable number were illicitly trafficked south of the Rio Grande. By 2022, the United States had 77,813 individuals or companies licensed to sell firearms (FLL). By way of comparison, this figure is greater than the total number of McDonald's, Burger King, Subway, and Wendy's outlets in the United States (Everytown Research and Policy 2023). FLLs range from expansive department stores to modest gun shops with consistent operating hours, typically from 09.00 to 17.00. In the majority of cases (55 per cent), however, the individual in possession of an FLL licence is actually a private citizen residing in a residential house (Everytown Research and Policy 2023). A large portion of FFLs are located on the border between Mexico and the United States. As research has shown, these stores legally sell firearms, although they know that the destination of these firearms is Mexico (Weigend Vargas et al. 2023).

It is impossible to know with certainty how many firearms arrive in Latin America illegally, but we have some data to make estimates. The most serious study on the subject (although somewhat dated) has suggested that around

253,000 firearms are trafficked illegally each year (McDougal et al. 2013). Or, to put it another way, about twenty-eight per hour. According to official Mexican government estimates, in the last decade, more than two million guns have been illegally exported from the United States to Mexico. The majority of these exports originated from Texas, Arizona, and California.

A primary source of information regarding these figures is the ATF's statistics based on firearms trace examinations found at crime scenes in Mexico, the Caribbean, and Central America. For over a decade, data from the ATF has indicated that approximately 70 per cent of firearms discovered at crime scenes in Mexico were either manufactured in the United States or imported into the country prior to being trafficked to Mexico. It is possible that the figure is in fact higher, as there is a significant percentage of firearms (approximately 15 per cent) whose origin could not be determined. The same methodology has been applied to Central American countries. The same firearms tracing method indicates that approximately 55 per cent of the firearms originate from the United States. The distinctions between Central American countries are not insignificant, however. In Guatemala, for instance, the percentage is only slightly above 38 per cent. The explanation for this discrepancy can be found in the prolonged period of civil wars that the region endured in the 1980s, coupled with the prevalence of Soviet-made weapons (Bureau of Alcohol, Tobacco, Firearms, and Explosives 2022).

As demonstrated in Chapter 7, the situation is even more pronounced in Caribbean countries, where the prevalence of firearms manufactured or imported initially to the United States and subsequently trafficked illegally to the islands is exceptionally high. In the case of the Bahamas, the prevalence is 99.2 per cent, in the Dominican Republic 86.2 per cent, in Haiti 84.8 per cent, in Jamaica 69.4 per cent, and in Trinidad and Tobago 51.7 per cent. It is evident that the proximity of an island to the United States is correlated with a higher prevalence of illicit firearms originating from that country.

Criminal groups of all sizes are involved in the trafficking of firearms from the United States to Mexico. In some cases, it is the Mexican cartels themselves that manage to maintain their own steady source of firearms (Kinosian 2023) In other cases, those responsible for illegal trafficking are citizens (often women) who sell to intermediaries and act as suppliers of weapons to various cartels. A recent publication (Bureau of Alcohol, Tobacco, Firearms, and Explosives 2023) revealed that individuals or entities involved in the illicit transfer of firearms into illicit markets were predominantly white (53 per cent), male (84 per cent), and US citizens (95 per cent). It is erroneous to suggest that the primary perpetrators are foreign nationals.

In recent years, a novel modus operandi has emerged: the shipment of gun parts by courier to Mexico for assembly. In 2023, the Western District Attorney's Office in Texas accused an individual named Chandler Britain Bradford of trafficking parts and components of AR-15 rifles from the United States to Mexico between 2018 and 2022 .(United States District Court 2023). The accusation states that Bradford would ship or directly transport the seventy parts and components that make up an AR-15 to Monterrey, Nuevo León, Mexico. His partners in Mexico were responsible for the assembly work. He also provided the raw materials independently. The prosecution asserts that, over the course of four years, Bradford received approximately $3.5 million in remuneration for his role in these operations. Bradford's partners in Mexico would have been able to assemble at least 4,800 semi-automatic rifles in Monterrey over four years.

The consequences of this influx of firearms cannot be overstated. Although it is accurate to state that prior to the relaxation of gun policies in the United States in 2004 and 2005, there was a significant crime problem in Latin America, the problem exploded starting in 2007 (Escalante Gonzalbo 2011; Merino, Zarkin, and Fierro 2013; Zepeda Gil and Pérez Ricart 2022). Due to its proximity to the US market, Mexico offers the most striking example of the impact of weapons on armed violence. In 2007, Mexico recorded 8,868 homicides. By 2009, this figure had increased by 58 per cent to reach 14,006 homicides annually. In 2009, the figure rose to 19,803, and in 2010, to 25,757. This means that over a four-year period, Mexico saw the absolute number of homicides increase by 190 per cent. The majority of these fatalities were the consequence of conflict between organized crime groups and confrontations between some of these groups and state security forces.

This represents a growth that exceeds all forecasts and trends. The growth is attributable to several factors, and it is important to note that it is not limited to the increase in the circulation of firearms. Nevertheless, several studies have already demonstrated a causal relationship between the growth in gun production in the United States and the increase in violence in Northern Mexico (Dube, Dube, and García-Ponce 2013). Furthermore, the impact extended beyond Mexico, reaching Central America and the Caribbean also. A regression analysis of a recently published study revealed that the manufacture or importation of one million firearms in the United States was associated with an annual increase of 1.42 firearm homicides per 100,000 inhabitants in Central America and the Caribbean (Weigend Vargas et al. 2023).

Public Policy Experiences and Recommendations

Latin America is currently grappling with a significant challenge in the form of arms trafficking and organized crime. Over the past decade, numerous countries in the region have endeavoured to address this issue in various ways, with varying degrees of success. The following section will present an overview of the main regional approaches to firearms policy, after which recommendations for future public policy will be presented.

Regional Experiences

The conventional response by governments to restrict the circulation of firearms has been the implementation of voluntary disarmament campaigns in exchange for monetary compensation or other goods. These initiatives have been implemented since the 1990s in virtually all countries in Latin America. Unfortunately, these programmes have all reached a similar conclusion: even the most successful voluntary disarmament campaigns are, at best, short-term solutions. At worst, they represent a form of self-deception.

This does not imply that there have been no successful examples. For example, the 'Campanha do Desarmamento' in Brazil resulted in the destruction of over a million firearms between 2003 and 2009 (Associated Press 2011). This stands as the largest example of voluntary destruction of civilian firearms in the world (Karp 2009, 31).

In Argentina, a campaign designed in the wake of a mass shooting at a school in 2007 led to the voluntary surrender of 175,000 firearms and 1.5 million rounds of ammunition over a period of ten years (Angerosa 2016). This initiative was awarded the Future Policy Award in 2013. Despite these undeniable success stories, it is important to note that in most of these campaigns, including the examples of Argentina and Brazil, the majority of surrendered weapons were old or were, at the time of surrender, obsolete. As anticipated, criminals typically do not participate in these programmes or surrender their firearms.

Furthermore, the issue of the scale and scope of these campaigns must be considered. To illustrate, consider the case of Mexico. The Mexican disarmament campaign, known as the 'Campaña de canje de armas de fuego', was responsible for the destruction of approximately 90,000 firearms between 2013 and 2017. This equates to an average of approximately 18,000 firearms per year. If we accept the conservative estimate of seventeen million firearms currently in circulation in Mexico, it will take the government of that country 944 years to confiscate all firearms, assuming that no additional firearms are produced or imported during that period.

In collaboration with international organizations, particularly the United Nations Regional Centre for Peace, Disarmament and Development in Latin America and the Caribbean (UNLIREC), several countries have initiated programmes to enhance the ballistic analysis capabilities of police forces and implement new conventional arms control programmes. The intervention of UNLIREC in promoting good governance in the private security sector by implementing internationally accepted standards, norms, and best practices is noteworthy. In a context of little collaboration between countries, UNLIREC has also served as a focal point for strengthening coordination between police forces from two or more countries (e.g. UNLIREC 2018).

Over the past decade, several countries in the region have made significant investments in cutting-edge technology with the aim of enhancing border security. Brazil has set an example with the implementation of the Integrated Border Monitoring System (SISFRON), a programme initiated by the Brazilian Armed Forces in 2012, with full operation expected to continue until 2035. A sophisticated system of radar, sensors, and communication systems enables the Brazilian Army to receive real-time information about physical movements occurring along the land border between Brazil and its ten neighbouring countries. SISFRON has been instrumental in reducing arms and drug smuggling along the Amazonian border (Zaparolli 2019). However, such programmes are only accessible to countries like Brazil and are not within the reach of other countries in the region.

It is evident that no other nation has invested as heavily in cutting-edge technology to secure its borders as Mexico and the United States. Along the border, a multitude of sensors, cameras, drones, and other forms of aerial surveillance are in place, with routes carefully mapped out by civilian and military authorities. Moreover, the United States government continues to invest in the improvement of border infrastructure. In 2022, the budget requested by President Biden exceeded $1 trillion for these purposes (Asher-Schapiro 2022) Unfortunately, all this investment is aimed at preventing the passage of migrants and drugs from the south to the north, not to stop the illegal flow of weapons from the United States to Mexico.

Recommendations for Public Policy

It is incumbent upon each country in the region to devise and implement state policies aimed at curbing the illicit flow of arms and the violence perpetrated with them. In this section we make recommendations for future policies in the region directed at controlling illicit firearms and their use by organized criminal groups.

First and foremost, it is imperative that countries establish reliable databases and protocols for the registration of homicides and injuries. In certain countries, such as Mexico and Guatemala, weapon registries are outdated and under the control of the military. Without a realistic estimate of the number of weapons in circulation in each country, it is impossible to generate coherent public policies to address the problem.

Secondly, except for a few countries such as Chile, most states lack the presence of a national coordinating agency for firearms. A potential solution would be to establish civilian authorities with a specific focus on firearms issues, akin to the Bureau of Alcohol, Tobacco, Firearms, and Explosives in the United States. The authority should be responsible for formulating and coordinating firearms control policy at the national level, with a particular focus on disrupting the firearms market in its criminal policy. In addition, this agency should regulate private security companies and share information with analogous agencies. The key to success in this endeavour lies in the establishment of regional coordination through agencies that possess the requisite budgetary and investigative capabilities. Only through such measures can programmes for tracking and sting operations designed to detect transnational firearms trafficking networks be implemented.

The third step is arguably the most pertinent. It is imperative that governments in Latin America take the initiative to implement policies with a prevention focus. One illustrative example is the hospital-based injury and violence prevention programmes in the United States, which focus on vulnerable groups, including individuals who have been shot but have not died from their wounds (Cooper, Eslinger, and Stolley 2006). Without policies targeted at demographic groups with significant potential for joining organized criminal groups, the rest of the efforts are insufficient. In Mexico City, the implementation of these programmes in recent years has been particularly successful, as evidenced by the Alto Al Fuego initiative.

The fourth step focuses on the United States. That country represents the primary source of firearms in the region. Latin American countries could establish robust diplomatic coalitions with the objective of coordinating and advocating policies that would result in more stringent firearms control within their borders. In a similar vein, governments in the region could emulate Mexico's actions in 2022 by initiating legal proceedings against firearms distributors and sellers (e.g. those in the United States) for their culpable conduct in the design, production, and sale of their products (Raymond 2024).

Finally, policies should be forward-looking. For many decades, public policy in Latin America has been two steps behind trends in organized crime and the flow of illicit firearms. A comprehensive policy against armed violence should seek to establish policies that can address emerging challenges and threats. For example, policies are needed to address the emergence of 3D-printed firearms (see Chapter 8), firearms that can be assembled from purchased parts or kits, and novel methods of firearms trafficking across borders.

References

Angerosa, Martín. 2016. 'Demilitarizing Gun Control in Argentina'. *Small Arms Monitor* 8 (5): pp. 3–4.

Arias, Enrique Desmond. 2017. *Criminal Enterprises and Governance in Latin America.* Cambridge: Cambridge University Press.

Asher-Schapiro, Avi. 2022. 'Surveillance Tech Makes U.S.-Mexico Border Even Deadlier'. *Context* (23 Nov. 2022), https://www.context.news/surveillance/surveillance-tech-makes-us-mexico-border-even-deadlier Accessed 26. Jul. 2024.

Associated Press. 2011. 'Brazil: Gun Buyback Campaign Begins'. *The New York Times* (6 May 2011), https://www.nytimes.com/2011/05/07/world/americas/07briefs-ART-Brazil.html Accessed 26 Jul. 2024.

Bergman, Marcelo. 2018. *More Money, More Crime: Prosperity and Rising Crime in Latin America.* Oxford: Oxford University Press.

Bergman, Marcelo. 2023. *El Negocio Del Crimen: El Crecimiento Del Delito, Los Mercados Ilegales y La Violencia En América Latina.* Buenos Aires: Fondo de Cultura Económica.

Bureau of Alcohol, Tobacco, Firearms and Explosives. 2022a. 'Firearms Trace Data: Central America 2020'. https://www.atf.gov/resource-center/firearms-trace-data-central-america-2020 Accessed 26 Jul. 2024..

Bureau of Alcohol, Tobacco, Firearms and Explosives. 2022b. 'National Firearms Commerce and Trafficking Assessment: Firearms in Commerce'. https://www.atf.gov/firearms/docs/report/national-firearms-commerce-and-trafficking-assessment-firearms-commerce-volume/download. Accessed 26 Jul. 2024.

Bureau of Alcohol, Tobacco, Firearms and Explosives. 2023. 'Annual Firearms Manufacturing and Export Report Year 2021' https://www.atf.gov/resource-center/2021-annual-firearms-manufacturers-and-export-report-afmer Accessed 26 Jul. 2024.

Cooper, Carnell, Eslinger, Dawn M., and Stolley, Paul D. 2006. 'Hospital-Based Violence Intervention Programs Work. *J Trauma*, doi:10.1097/01.ta.0000236576.81860.8c Accessed 26 Jul. 2024.

Daudelin, Jean. 2017. 'Not Killer Methods: A Few Things We Get Wrong When Studying Violence in Latin America'. In *Violence in Latin America and the Caribbean: Subnational Structures, Institutions, and Clientelistic Networks*, edited by Tina Hilgers and Laura MacDonald, pp. 39–58. Cambridge: Cambridge University Press.

Daudelin, Jean, and Ratton, José Luiz. 2018. *Illegal Markets, Violence and Inequality: Evidence from a Brazilian Metropolis.* Basingstoke: Palgrave.

Dube, Arindrajit, Dube, Oeindrila, and García-Ponce, Omar. 2013. 'Cross-Border Spillover: U.S. Gun Laws and Violence in Mexico'. *American Political Science Review* 107 (3): pp. 397–417.

Escalante Gonzalbo, Fernando. 2011. 'Homicidios 2008–2009 La Muerte Tiene Permiso'. *Nexos*, January 2011. https://www.nexos.com.mx/?p=14089 Accessed 27 Jul. 2024.

Everytown Research and Policy. 2023. 'Inside the Gun Shop: Firearms Dealers and Their Impact'. https://everytownresearch.org/report/firearms-dealers-and-their-impact/ Accessed 30 Jul. 2024.

Garay-Salamanca, Luis Jorge. 2020. *Aparatos Estatales y Luchas de Poderes: de la Captura a la Cooptación y a la Reconfiguración.* Bogotá: Fundación Heinrich Böll.

INEGI. 2022. 'Encuesta Nacional de Victimización y Percepción Sobre Seguridad Pública 2022'. INEGI.

The Global Initiative against the Transnational Organized Crime & InSight Crime. 2019. 'Una Cultura Criminal: Extorsión En Centroamérica.' https://globalinitiative.net/wp-content/uploads/2019/10/GITOC_extortion_PR-2.pdf Accessed 5 Nov. 2024.

Karp, Aaron. 2009. 'Surplus Arms in South America: A Survey'. Small Arms Survey. https://www.smallarmssurvey.org/sites/default/files/resources/SAS-WP7-Surplus-Arms-in-South-America.pdf Accessed 26 Jul. 2024.

Kinosian, Sarah. 2023. 'How a Factory City in Wisconsin Fed Military-Grade Weapons to a Mexican Cartel'. Reuters (9 Dec. 2023). https://www.reuters.com/investigates/special-report/mexico-usa-guns/ Accessed 26 Jul. 2024.

McDougal, Topher, Shirk, David A., Muggah, Robert, and Patterson John H. 2013. 'The Way of the Gun: Estimating Firearms Traffic Across the U.S.-Mexico Border'. Igarapé Institute and University of San Diego. https://igarape.org.br/wp-content/uploads/2013/03/Paper_The_Way_of_the_Gun_web2.pdf Accessed 26 Jul. 2024.

Merino, José, Zarkin, Jessica, and Fierro, Eduardo. 2013. 'Marcado para morir'. *Nexos* (1 Jul. 2013). https://www.nexos.com.mx/?p=15375 Accessed 26 Jul. 2024.

Padilla Oñate, Sergio, and Pérez Ricart, Carlos A. 2023. 'The Militarization of Public Security in Mexico: A Subnational Analysis from a State (Local) Police Perspective'. *Alternatives: Global, Local, Political*, pp. 1–18 https://doi-org.ezproxy-b.deakin.edu.au/10.1177/03043754231177349 Accessed 26 Jul. 2024.

Pérez Esparza, David, and Weigend, Eugenio. 2015. 'The Ilegal Flow of Firearms from the United States to Mexico: A State-Level Trafficking Propensity Analysis'. *Journal of Trafficking, Organized Crime and Security* 1 (2): pp. 115–125.

Pérez Ricart, Carlos A. 2021. 'Mexico and Central America: Flexibility and Frameworks'. In *Transforming the War on Drugs*, edited by Annette Idler and Juan Carlos Garzón, pp. 161–188. Oxford University Press.

Pérez Ricart, Carlos A., and García, Arantxa Ibarrola. 2023. 'La Transición Hacia El Fentanilo Cambios y Continuidades Del Mercado de Drogas En México (2015-2022)'. *Revista de Ciencias Sociales* 36 (53): pp. 15–36.

Pérez Ricart, Carlos A., Castillo, Jerónimo, Curry, Alex, and Serrano, Mónica. 2021. 'Guns in Latin America: Key Challenges from the Most Violent Region on Earth'. In *Gun Trafficking and Violence: From the Global Network to the Local Security Challenge*, edited by David Pérez Esparza, Eugenio Weigend Vargas, and Carlos A. Pérez Ricart, pp. 93–122. Basingstoke: Palgrave Macmillan.

Pion-Berlin, David. 2016. *Military Missions in Democratic Latin America.* Basingstoke: Palgrave Macmillan.

Raymond, Nate. 2024. 'US Appeals Court Revives Mexico's $10 bn Lawsuit against Gun Makers'. Reuters (23 Jan. 2024). https://www.reuters.com/world/us/us-appeals-court-revives-mexicos-10-billion-lawsuit-against-gun-makers-2024-01-22/ Accessed 26 Jul. 2024.

Sanjurjo, Diego. 2020. *Gun Control Policies in Latin America.* Basingstoke: Palgrave Macmillan.

Seguridad Justicia y Paz. 2023. *Ranking (2023) de Las Ciudades Más Violentas Del Mundo.* https://geoenlace.net/seguridadjusticiaypaz/archivo/27f959_0f34f8c7ef.pdf Accessed 26 Jul. 2024.

Smith, Benjamin T. 2021. *The Dope: The Real History of the Mexican Drug Trade.* London: Ebury Press.

United States District Court, Western District Texas, San Antonio Division. 2023. 2nd Superseding Indictment, Chandler Britain Bradford.

UNLIREC. 2018. *United Nations Regional Centre for Peace, Disarmament and Development in Latin America and the Caribbean: Report of the Secretary-General.* https://unlirec.org/wp-content/uploads/2019/05/N1821739.pdfAccessed 29 Jul. 2024.

UNODC. 2023a. *Global Study on Homicide 2023.* https://www.unodc.org/unodc/en/data-and-analysis/global-study-on-homicide.html Accessed 26 Jul. 2024.

UNODC. 2023b. *UNODC Global Study on Homicide 2023: Homicide and Organized Crime in Latin America and the Caribbean.* https://www.unodc.org/documents/data-and-analysis/gsh/2023/GSH_2023_LAC_web.pdf. Accessed 26 Jul. 2024.

UNODC. 2023c. *World Drug Report.* United Nations. https://www.unodc.org/unodc/en/data-and-analysis/world-drug-report-2023.html Accessed 27 Jul. 2024.

Weigend Vargas, Eugenio, et al. 2023. 'Firearm Manufacturing and Imports in the U.S. and Their Association to Firearm Homicides in Central America and the Caribbean, 1991–2019'. *Injury Prevention.* https://injuryprevention.bmj.com/content/early/2024/02/01/ip-2023-045055 Accessed 27 Jul. 2024.

Weigend Vargas, Eugenio, et al. 2024. 'Firearms and Extortions in Mexico, 2012 to 2021'. *Journal of Interpersonal Violence*, 1–16. https://doi.org/10.1177/08862605241246005 Accessed 26 Jul. 2024..

Zaparolli, Domingos. 2019. 'Vigilancia En La Frontera'. *Revista Pesquisa* (Aug. 2019). https://revistapesquisa.fapesp.br/es/vigilancia-en-la-frontera/ Accessed 26 Jul. 2024.

Zepeda Gil, Raúl, and Pérez Ricart, Carlos A. 2022. 'Effects of Long-Term Development and Schooling Expansion on the Decline in Homicide Rates: Mexico from 1950 to 2005'. *Journal of Crime and Justice*, 1–23 https://www.tandfonline.com/doi/full/10.1080/0735648X.2022.2050277#d1e205 Accessed 26 Jul. 2024.

5

Illicit Firearms Markets and Organized Crime in Eastern Europe

Piotr Chlebowicz

From a criminological point of view, organized crime in Eastern Europe has features that differentiate it from organized crime in Western European countries. Consequently, there appears to be potentially interesting divergences of methodologies used in criminological research and the use of conceptual frameworks employed by Western scientists to describe the origins and development of crime in Eastern Europe after the fall of communism. Given the international spread of organized crime, geographical and cultural contexts also play a key role. It is worth mentioning that between 1945 and 1990, authoritarian regimes controlled the societies of Eastern European countries. This had a significant influence on the development of different forms of crime in Eastern Europe. At the same time, criminology as a field of science was marginalized in these countries for ideological reasons, even though Polish scientists had some input into the evolution of European criminology (e.g. Leon Radzinowicz and the development of criminology at Cambridge University; Widacki 2019; Hood 2001). In sum, the differences in observations about organized crime in Eastern Europe, compared with observations elsewhere, mainly result from:

- the varied origins of organized crime in Eastern and Western Europe;
- the absence of certain organized crime types, such as urban gangs, motorbike gangs, and other groups modelled after the Italian mafia;
- little relevance of terrorist organizations (see Chapter 12 for discussion of illicit firearms and acquisition by terrorist groups).

Political changes which took place after 1990, especially economic and political reforms leading to liberalization, democracy, and economic freedoms, generated a powerful stimulus for changes in Eastern European societies.

Piotr Chlebowicz, *Illicit Firearms Markets and Organized Crime in Eastern Europe* In: *Illicit Firearms Markets and Organized Crime*. Edited by: David Bright, Oxford University Press.
 DOI: 10.1093/9780198902409.003.0006

However, this period also saw the emergence of new, previously unknown forms of crime. This applies especially to the emergence of criminal groups and criminal organizations, which started to develop rapidly in the 1990s. During this period, the appearance of the free market was accompanied by the emergence of illegal markets for alcohol, cigarettes, and stolen cars, as well as trafficking of humans, drugs, and firearms. Cases of drug-related crime, human trafficking, and firearms trafficking represented new and emerging criminal activities. Eastern European law enforcement agencies were not equipped to tackle these crimes effectively due to lack of experience, equipment, and suitable legal measures, besides insufficient funding and institutional corruption.

During this period, one can identify some interesting principles connected with the first stage of organized crime development in Eastern Europe. This phase can be characterized as one when criminals were joining together into organized groups which were often strengthened by the addition of professional criminals from other countries. There were also attempts to emulate the organizational patterns of criminal groups operating in the West and, consequently, contacts were made with organized criminal groups in Germany, Spain, Belgium, and Turkey, as well as with those operating in the Western Balkans.

Over this period, organized criminal groups expanded and attempted to gain control over new black markets. In border areas, organized criminal groups competed to control smuggling channels. Depending on the country, the control was aimed at monopolizing illicit markets for stolen cars, alcohol, tobacco, illicit drugs, prostitution, and human trafficking (Kuzior 2009. As opposing criminal groups tried to acquire dominant positions and monopoly power in local illegal markets, the use of violence increased. The use of physical power, knives, and baseball bats was only successful with victims of robberies and extortion; it ceased to be effective in conflict with opposing criminal groups. This precipitated the demand for firearms by organized criminal groups. It should be emphasized that strict firearms rationing was a characteristic feature of Eastern European countries of the communist era and, practically speaking, it meant a ban on the possession of firearms. Those rules remained in force after the political changes of the 1990s. This meant that few firearms were owned by citizens. The low level of firearms ownership in Eastern European societies caused criminal groups to seek alternative sources of illegal firearms.

The black market for firearms in Eastern Europe in the 1990s was characterized by fierce rivalry between organized criminal groups. As mentioned previously, criminal groups created both the demand for arms and the supply, through the operation of smuggling routes and methods. During this period, the illicit firearms trade was not the primary activity for organized criminal groups because it did not provide high income, in comparison with the illicit drug trade, human trafficking, and other illicit markets. Some available data suggest that some organized criminal groups had firearms at their disposal, though it appears that they did not create illegal arsenals (Chlebowicz, Buczyński 2023). Single illicit transactions typically involved small numbers of firearms, mainly handguns, sometimes machine guns.

It is worth emphasizing that according to criminological research the illegal firearms trade is not the main source of income for organized criminal groups across Europe (Duquet 2022). Only a few organized criminal groups deal only with illicit firearms trading, treating firearms primarily as commodities, and not as equipment or 'tools of the trade' (see Chapter 11). Nonetheless, for many organized criminal groups, firearms also serve as tools for committing crimes, compelling obedience both outside (e.g. extorting payments from businessmen) and inside the group (maintaining the hierarchy and discipline in the group), personal protection, and creating status within the group.

A separate phenomenon, which also generated the demand for illegal firearms, was an increase in the occurrence of violent crime against property. There was an increase in violent crimes such as armed robberies (e.g. bank robberies, currency exchange robberies, and lorry robberies), which saw an increase in demand for illicit firearms (Nowicka 2004). Starting in the 1990s, violence, including firearms violence, was included in criminal statistics in Eastern Europe.

The development of Eastern European countries, the introduction of Western standards in legal systems, improvements in police tactics, along with the development of international police cooperation led to the establishment of more effective strategies in combatting organized crime. Violent groups were quite quickly disrupted through police actions. Therefore, violent groups started to adapt by modifying their methods of operating, eliminating, or limiting the use of violence. The use of firearms was especially limited because any incidents of homicide and other violent acts with firearms tended to mobilize law enforcement agencies to conduct intense investigations, especially when public opinion demanded action from the police and governments. Consequently, committing violent crimes, especially those with firearms, became increasingly risky for organized criminal groups.

Organized criminal groups in Eastern Europe after 2000 began investing illegal money in business ventures, becoming active in areas characteristic of white-collar crime (e.g. tax fraud, financial fraud, money laundering, and trafficking). The integration of the Eastern European countries into the European Union (EU) opened new possibilities for money laundering, financial fraud, and other crimes targeting EU financial institutions. In this emerging context, firearms violence was gradually losing its *raison d'etre*.

Data Limitations

Organized crime in Eastern Europe is an area that is difficult to research, primarily due to data limitations. For example, in some countries, police crime data is not available to academic researchers. Moreover, statistics prepared by the police, prosecutors, or courts do not include data which would allow for a rich analysis of the context behind individual incidents with the use of firearms and for establishing the origin of a specific firearm used during a crime. For example, based on the data available, it is impossible to assess if a firearm used during a crime is a legally held firearm or one sourced from illicit markets. What is more, there is a lack of systematic criminological research, as the illicit firearms trade is rarely in the scope of criminological interests and priorities of Eastern European countries.

Difficulties connected with access to data also result from the fact that the illicit firearms trade, especially firearms trafficking, is combated by law enforcement agencies, as well as counterintelligence and intelligence services. Illicit firearms transfers are considered not only a threat to law and order but also a potential threat to state security. Consequently, the regulations governing counterintelligence and intelligence services forbid the disclosure of information concerning the detected and neutralized transactions on the black market of firearms. This represents a further barrier to access to data by academic researchers.

Finally, there is still also a language barrier that prevents systematic research on illicit firearms markets. The scientific literature containing results of research on organized crime in Russia, Belarus, Ukraine, Poland, Slovakia, Czechia, and the Baltic states, mentioning local black markets for firearms and detected instances of firearms trafficking, is usually published only in national languages, which makes comparative studies difficult (Sarnecki, Kotowska, Chlebowicz 2018).

The Emergence of Illicit Firearms Markets in East Europe

The expansion of organized criminal groups and organized crime activities in Poland, the Baltic states, Czechia, and Slovakia accelerated after 1990 when the region liberated itself from the influence of communism. The transformation of political systems brought about profound social and economic changes. The emergence of new forms of crime, including organized crime, was a by-product of the rapid transformation in the political and economic systems (Laskowska 2011). The beginnings of organized crime in Poland were associated with a rapid growth in violent crime, especially armed robberies, and extortion. Organized criminal groups generated demand for firearms and ensured their supply. At the same time, the increasing rivalry between organized criminal groups was an impetus for the emergence of a new type of criminal activity: revenge crime (also known as 'reckoning crime'; Kulicki 2000). It manifested itself, for example, in acts of attempted murder with firearms and explosives aimed at members of rival organized criminal groups (Chlebowicz 2015). From this perspective, the development of local illicit firearms markets resulted from the expansion of organized crime and organized criminal groups.

The situation was different in the former Soviet republics, which became independent states after the fall of the USSR. The end of the Cold War and the collapse of the Soviet Union created new opportunities for criminal entrepreneurs with governmental and military connections to involve themselves in large-scale shipments of illegal firearms (UNODC 2019). Ubiquitous corruption, as well as the economic and political crisis, brought about the decomposition of the internal security systems in Russia, Ukraine, and Belarus. Belarus, in the years 1992–95, was said to be ruled by two forces—the government and criminals (Laskowska 2021).

Organized criminal groups monopolized black markets in Ukraine and invested their criminal profits in legal business activities, whereby they gained influence over political authorities (UNICRI 2022). Similar processes intensified in Russia, where the expansion of organized criminal groups resulted in effective infiltration of state and business structures, facilitated by overwhelming corruption. The presence of so-called '*vor v zakone*' or 'thieves-in-law', members of a recidivist subculture, was a feature common to Ukrainian and Russian organized criminal groups. Organized criminal groups in Russia and former Soviet republics are often described as comprising three main components: the 'thieves-in-law' (i.e. professional criminals), members of the authorities and special services, and so-called 'oligarchs' (i.e. beneficiaries of the political and economic transformations; Mądrzejowski 2008).

A gradual decrease in violent crime intensity was observed in Poland and in the Baltic states after 2000. This decrease was linked to two main factors. First, the transformation within organized criminal groups, which evolved towards the commission of economic and financial crime. The second factor was the development of more effective police forces, which learned how to combat aggressive crime, owing to such measures as the implementation of Western standards in the legislative, organizational, and technical areas. One of the consequences of improving the effectiveness of law enforcement policy and practice was a gradual decrease in the demand for illicit firearms. The relatively high risks associated with firearms trafficking acted as a disincentive for organized criminal group participation in these markets (Europol n.d.).

It is worth noting that unlike Western Europe, local terrorist groups did not find favourable conditions for their development in Poland, Czechia, Slovakia, or the Baltic states. Furthermore, the firearms that such groups purchased were not used to attain their political goals, only criminal ones. Therefore, it seems that this reduced the extent of the illicit firearms market. However, the acquisition of weapons by members of terrorist groups has been noted.

New Sources of Firearms

Diversion from Military Stocks

The fall of communism was followed by the Soviet withdrawal from East Germany, Czechoslovakia, and the Baltic states in the early 1990s. This process had a unique criminological dimension, as both Soviet soldiers and officers are known to have sold large numbers of firearms and ammunition during the withdrawal. This created opportunities for organized criminal groups to acquire firearms from military personnel, whose discipline deteriorated during the withdrawal from Poland, facilitating these illicit transactions. In the early 1990s, firearms acquired from Soviet soldiers found their way to organized criminal groups in Poland. The role of Ukraine as an 'epicentre of post-Soviet arms trafficking' is highlighted in Overton's analysis of firearms trafficking (Overton 2015). We return to Ukraine later in the chapter.

'Dirty Archaeology'

Illicit firearms sources in Eastern Europe seem to have specific features that are rather absent from firearms black markets in Western Europe and the USA. This observation concerns firearms sources dating back to World Wars I and II. Excavations in the areas of battles fought during World Wars I and II—so-called 'dirty archaeology' or 'black digging', the illicit excavation of weaponry or explosives—are an important source of firearms and their parts in Poland, Belarus, and Ukraine. Such firearms, when found by citizens, are often handed over to family members or sold. Although it has been almost eight decades since World War II ended, firearms from that period are still in circulation in illicit markets (Chlebowicz 2015). There has also been an emergence of 'dirty archaeology' in Estonia (James and Hillier 2022).

The scale of the problem is illustrated by the case of an organized criminal group in Podkarpacie, Poland, which accumulated several hundred firearms made in France, Germany, USA, Finland, Belgium, Switzerland, and Czechia (including sub-machine guns, Mausers, PPSCH-41 guns), along with several thousand items of ammunition and grenades. Some items were so unique that forensic specialists suggested that they be donated to a museum (Chlebowicz 2015). Such firearms are sought by collectors and may be sold after restoration (Kasprzak and Brywczyński 2013). The excavation of firearms from battlefield sites is a seasonal activity, usually conducted from April to October. The following months of autumn and winter are the time for restoration and sale of firearms (Kasprzak and Brywczyński 2013). Organized criminal groups are known to be involved in searching for World War II firearms, their restoration, and sale on the black market. Buyers are typically both collectors and criminals, including those connected with organized crime. Trzciński points out that factors that facilitate the growth in this activity include the availability of specialist geodetection equipment and specialist guides for searchers. Similar activities are also conducted in Ukraine by people nicknamed 'black diggers' (Trzciński 2010).

Diversion and Conversion

Transnational crime researchers stress that diversion of firearms can take various forms, including the conversion of firearms. This is a diverse category, which includes the reactivation of deactivated firearms, the modification of semi-automatic firearms into fully automatic ones, the conversion of replicas, and the conversion of blank-firing firearms (Savona and Mancuso 2017).

A problem still exists with converting gas weapons and blank weapons to fire live ammunition. It is especially the latter category that provides considerable opportunities for modification. Blank firearms are cheap, easy to modify, and are legal in most countries. According to police experts, converting them is 'child's play—a moderately skilful turner can bore a stopper in the barrel and replace it with what is needed there' (Starink and Beemsterboer 2010). This trend is also found in Eastern Europe. For example, Operation Mars identified 100 Flobert weapons traced to purchases made by a registered Slovakian arms dealer (Empact,2022). This issue also emerged in Ukraine. Ukrainian police observed a considerable increase in the number of modified Zoraki 914 blank pistols being the objects of illicit trade. Large numbers of these firearms were imported from Turkey at the relatively low price of 100 euros each (Martyniuk 2017). It is not difficult to convert these objects to firearms. Conversion of gas pistols from Turkey to live firearms has also been observed in Poland.

Overall, the sources of illicit firearms in Eastern Europe include the following (Spapens 2007):

- firearms sales by legal owners to unauthorized individuals;
- lack of security in state-managed warehouses used to store firearms;
- firearms being stolen from military or police warehouses or shooting ranges;
- acquisition of firearms and their parts from areas of fighting during World War II;
- restoration of deactivated arms;
- conversion of other items into firearms.

Impact of the Military Conflict in Ukraine on Illicit Arms Markets

Experts have noted that Ukraine was saturated with firearms, including illicit ones, even before the conflict in Ukraine broke out in 2014 (Overton 2015). Among the many reasons for this was the presence of military bases inherited from the USSR (including many weapons arsenals), the strong influence of organized criminal groups, widespread corruption, a geographic position which favoured the development of trafficking routes, and poor border controls in the east of the country. Some of the firearms trafficked by Viktor Bout (one of the most infamous international arms dealers) originated from Ukrainian warehouses. The political crisis and the outbreak of war in 2014 changed the situation in illicit firearms markets in Ukraine, both by increasing the availability of firearms and by expanding the range of available firearms types, including advanced military weapons, such as MANPADS (man-portable air-defence systems) and guided armour-piercing ammunition.

Initially, following the outbreak of war, firearms from Ukrainian military and police warehouses were used to supply groups of volunteers fighting to defend the territorial integrity and sovereignty of Ukraine. As all of this happened during a time of war, little care was taken to control and track the issued arms, some of which were diverted to the illicit market. Many reservists retained their weapons when they returned from the front. Ukrainian organized criminal groups thereby gained access to a wide range of firearm types. Firearms warehouses were plundered in the east of Ukraine, and some of the stolen firearms found their way to the separatist groups backed by the Russian Federation. Before 2022, there were cases of joint firearms smuggling enterprises run by soldiers and functionaries, both from the Ukrainian side and separatists from the so-called 'Donetsk People's Republic' and the 'Luhansk People's Republic'. Firearms trafficking was also conducted by Ukrainians who were not linked to organized crime (Buscemi et al. 2018). They conducted this illicit retail trade for economic reasons, and it was used by some Ukrainians as an additional source of income. This means that the level of saturation of Ukrainian society with firearms is very high.

Following the Russian Federation's invasion of Ukraine in February 2022 Ukrainian citizens armed themselves to defend against the aggressors, who have frequently committed war crimes against civilians. Since 2022, the number of firearms in Ukraine has also been increased by supplies from Poland, the USA, and the UK for the Ukrainian army. There is insufficient data to evaluate how firearms from these supplies are protected against loss and transfer to illicit markets. However, there is historical precedent that some firearms supplied by third-party countries tend to be diverted to the black market. Jawor points out that 'One of the consequences of each war is the appearance of superfluous arms, which become the object of illicit trade conducted by crime groups. This is a phenomenon inherently associated with military conflicts. Examples of such situations include the war in the Balkans, in which nearly 6 million firearms appeared on the market after the military operations ended in the states of the former Yugoslavia' (Jawor 2022). Therefore, unfortunately, it seems probable that the Yugoslav scenario will be repeated in Ukraine. The former territory of Yugoslavia is still the main source of illicit arms for organized criminal groups and terrorists. According to Duquet, 'Ukraine, as well as Syria and Libya, could fall into a similar predicament, where weapons in the region may end up being trafficked elsewhere' (Duquet 2022).

In terms of firearms availability, it appears that the Ukraine is now flooded with small firearms. It also seems that there are no legal, financial, or human resources to control such firearms proliferation in this part of the world, especially in the context of the current war. The Interpol chief, Jürgen Stock, has predicted that illicit firearms will flood the black markets after the end of the war in Ukraine (Stock,2022). Given this increase in availability, one can assume that smuggling will be the most important channel for firearms proliferation in future. The Polish border guard, responsible for Poland's border security, is cognizant of the threats caused by the war in Ukraine. Analysts at the Ministry of Internal Affairs diagnosed in 2015 that:

> The prolonged armed conflict in Ukraine and the constant intensified terrorist threat related to, inter alia, attacks in France, Germany, as well as in other countries, have resulted in an increased demand for goods, technologies and services of strategic importance for state security, i.e. arms, ammunition, explosives, uniforms . . . protective equipment (helmets) . . . and heavy equipment . . . which can be used for military purposes.
>
> [The report also stated that:] Criminal groups increasingly often try to organize channels for smuggling arms and ammunition from the territory of Ukraine into Poland and then to distribute them into the territory of the European Union. Due to the absence of internal borders within the European Union, members of organized crime groups, who are reasonably suspected of being able to smuggle firearms, their parts or ammunition, can take advantage of the freedom of movement within the EU to the detriment of the freedom and security of the European community. (Ministry of Internal Affairs 2016)

When the current war ends, Ukraine's battlefields could and will become a new 'arsenal of anarchy', potentially arming a rage of groups from insurgents in Africa to gangsters on the streets of Europe (Global Initiative Against Transnational Organized Crime 2023). Therefore, the illicit firearms trade in the Ukrainian context is no longer an issue associated only with public order to be resolved with local police measures. Currently, it is a central issue for the security of Poland and the other EU countries.

Intersections Between Legal and Illegal Markets

Regardless of the geographic context, any attempt at describing and characterizing illicit firearms markets must consider the links between the legal and illicit firearms markets. The vast majority of firearms bought and sold on the illicit market were originally bought and sold on the legal market. This was captured by Marsh (2002), when he described the relationship between the white and black markets as two sides of the same coin.

The moment of transition of firearms from the white to the black market is often defined in the literature as 'diversion'. The criminal legal system in a country can be said to be an important criterion separating the sphere of legal from illicit arms ownership and trade. The term 'black market' is closely connected to the legal system—both domestic and international. This factor is decisive in establishing whether a specific case of firearms sale or ownership is of a criminal nature (i.e. illicit). Although the legal orders in Eastern European countries which joined the EU are largely shaped by community law principles, the regulations are not identical. This also has an impact on legislation which focuses on regulating the trade in firearms. The differences in the legal systems and legislation of different Eastern European countries hinder not only the coordination of illicit arms trade controls but also the determination of whether a specific transaction is defined as a crime. For example, in Poland, legal regulations concerning the firearms trade and firearms ownership are strict, and there are criminal penalties for violation of the trade rules (Chlebowicz et al. 2022). The situation is completely different in Ukraine. Martyniuk argues that the Ukrainian legal framework concerning firearms is imprecise and full of gaps, which means that it is often impossible to establish the legal status of a firearm. Firearms—especially smoothbore weapons and hunting rifles—are often given as presents or inherited without the requirement for formal recognition or documentation of the change in ownership (Martyniuk 2017).

The impact of legal factors on firearms proliferation in the region is particularly apparent in the border zone between Poland, Czechia, and Slovakia. Permissive approaches to firearms purchase and possession mean that there is potential for legal firearms to make their way onto the illicit market. Some Czech and Slovak business entities hold permits for trade in firearms and they operate websites in Polish and physical shops in the border zone (see Chapter 9 for a discussion of access to illicit firearms via the dark web). The firearms are transited to Poland (e.g. by post) where they undergo modifications. This creates the foundations for the illicit market for modified firearms.

The liberal regulations in Czechia and Slovakia create opportunities for local organized criminal groups, which buy large numbers of firearms originally deprived of the utility features (i.e. deactivated) and restore them to their original state (a process called 'reactivation'). The activities of these groups aim to supply firearms to foreign illicit arms markets. In 2012, the Polish Internal Security Agency, in cooperation with the Czech Bureau for Combatting Organized Crime at the Police Criminal Service, dismantled one such group and disrupted the trafficking route from Czechia to Poland (TVN24 2012).

It is noteworthy that the effectiveness of combatting the illicit firearms trade depends not only on the legal system but also on the infrastructure that makes applying legal regulations possible. For firearms trade control, forensic databases and registers are of key importance, as that is where details of individual firearms are kept for identification purposes. Notably, Ukraine does not have a central firearm registering system (Martyniuk 2017).

Policy Recommendations

The effective combatting of illicit firearms trafficking depends primarily on the effectiveness of international police cooperation. There is also a need for enhanced cooperation between police forces and intelligence services, which are often reluctant to share information regarding illicit firearms trade, especially with other countries. These cooperative partnerships should also involve customs services and border guards. Such cooperation certainly poses major challenges related to coordination and legal issues (e.g. consistency of legal provisions across countries). However, it seems that only unified and systemic actions can offer the potential to control the flow of illicit firearms not only from Ukraine but also from the Russian Federation, which may start to use illicit arms as a tool to destabilize countries in the EU. This is a well-founded fear, since the Russian Federation treats organized crime as one of its tools of foreign policy (Chlebowicz 2021). Therefore, the cooperation of police forces, border, and customs services as well as counterintelligence and foreign intelligence services of Eastern European countries should be politically supported by all the countries concerned. In the case of Eastern European countries, all of these activities should be focused on monitoring the current situation regarding illicit transactions in firearms and ammunition which may begin to spread from Ukraine to the EU countries.

In addition to the above, the following key policy recommendations flow from the foregoing discussion:

- Interventions that improve the sharing of information on illegal firearms transactions detected by law enforcement agencies, border guards, customs services, and intelligence agencies of the Eastern European countries, especially those constituting NATO's eastern flank (Poland, Lithuania, Latvia, Estonia, Hungary, Romania, Bulgaria, and Finland).
- Improving and updating databases concerning firearms dealers, organized criminal groups, their modus operandi, cases of detected arms trafficking, types and models of illicit firearms that have been seized or detected, as well as their sources.
- Increased resources and financing for forensic labs to determine the origin of each illegal, smuggled firearm, including any known connection with a specific crime.
- Increase the employment and training of strategic crime analysts within law enforcement agencies, border guard and customs services, with a specific focus on intelligence collection and analysis regarding illicit firearms markets.

Conclusions

At the time that this conclusion is being written (April 2024), it is not possible to predict when or how the war in Ukraine will end. Undoubtedly, an armed conflict in a country bordering the EU generates uncontrolled flows of not only small firearms but other advanced weapons systems that are of interest to non-state actors such as terrorist organizations and organized criminal groups. The black market for firearms in Ukraine could be a destabilizing factor for public order and security in the region in the future. This necessitates developing a strategy for combatting the flows of illicit firearms originating from Ukraine. Poland is currently sealing its eastern border, which is effectively the eastern border of the EU. A wall has been erected along the Polish-Belarusian border, whereby the Polish border guard can more effectively thwart attempts at trafficking firearms. Similar installations are to be built along Poland's border with the Russian Federation (Kaliningrad Oblast). However, a question arises as to how to secure the borders with Ukraine, given the alliance between the two countries. Given that the war in Ukraine and its consequences extend beyond Eastern Europe, interventions to combat firearms trafficking in the region should include the participation of the diplomatic, law enforcement, customs, and secret services of Ukraine, EU countries, the UK, the USA, and Interpol.

References

Buscemi, Francesco, et al. 2018. 'Illicit Firearms Proliferation in the EU Periphery: The Case of Ukraine'. In *Triggering Terror: Illicit Gun Markets and Firearms Acquisition of Terrorist Networks in Europe*, edited by Nils Duquet, pp. 461–475. Brussels: Flemish Peace Institute.

Chlebowicz, Piotr. 2015. *Nielegalny Handel Bronią. Studium Kryminologiczne* ['Illicit Arms Trade. A Criminological Study']. Lex a Wolters Kluwer business: Warszawa.

Chlebowicz, Piotr. 2021. 'Organized Crime as a Political Influence Tool of the Russian Federation'. *Internal Security* 13 (2): pp. 175–186. https://doi.org/10.5604/01.3001.0015.6557 Accessed 21 Jul. 2024.

Chlebowicz, Piotr, and Buczyński, Szymon. 2023. 'Tracing the Shadows: Inside the European Illegal Arms Market—The Case of Poland'. *Archiwum Kryminologii* [Archives of Criminology] 45 (1): p. 84.Chlebowicz, Piotr, Buczyński, S., Safjański, T., and Moszczyński, J. 2022. 'The Success Story? An In-Depth Analysis of Illicit Firearm-Trafficking and Gun Violence in Poland'. In *Pulling the Trigger: Gun Violence in Europe*, edited by Nils Duquet. Brussels: Flemish Peace Institute.Duquet, Nils (ed.). 2022. *Pulling the Trigger: Gun Violence in Europe. Country Reports.* Project Target. https://vlaamsvredesinstituut.eu/wp-content/uploads/2022/10/TARGET-7CountryReports-FPI-def.pdf Accessed 26 Jul. 2024.

Europol, n.d. *Illicit Firearms Trafficking*. https://www.europol.europa.eu/crime-areas/illicit-firearms-trafficking Accessed 19 Apr. 2024.

Empact 2022 Results. Factsheet. https://www.europol.europa.eu/publications-events/publications/empact-2022-results-factsheets Accessed 26 Jul. 2024.Global Initiative against Transnational Organized Crime. 2023. *Global Organized Crime Index 2023: A Fractured World* https://globalinitiative.net/wp-content/uploads/2023/09/Global-organized-crime-index-2023-web-compressed-compressed.pdf Accessed 26 Jul. 2024.

Hood, Roger. 2001. 'L Radzinowicz 1906–1999'. *Proceedings of British Academy* 111: pp. 637–655.

James, Paul, and Hillier, Declan. 2022. *Firearm-Related Violence and Trafficking in Estonia.* Project Target Report. Brussels: Flemish Peace Institute.

Jawor, A. 2022. *Broń dla Ukrainy. Kontrola a wojenna rzeczywistość* [Weapons for Ukraine. Control and the war reality] https://infosecurity24.pl/za-granica/bron-dla-ukrainy-kontrola-a-wojenna-rzeczywistosc Accessed 11 Dec. 2022r.).

Kasprzak, Jerzy, and Brywczyński, Wiesław. 2013. *Nielegalne Posiadanie Broni i Amunicji. Studium Prawno-Kryminalistyczne* ['Illicit Arms and Ammunition Ownership. A Legal and Forensic Study']. Poland: Temida.

Kulicki, Mariusz. 2000. 'Przestępczość Porachunkowa—Przedmiot Badań i Definicja' ['Reckoning Crime—The Subject of Research and Definition']. In *Przestępczość Porachunkowa Jako Przejaw Przestępczości Zorganizowanej* ['Reckoning Crime as a Manifestation of Organized Crime'], edited by Marek Zajder, Mariusz Kulicki, and Wiesław Pływaczewski. p. 236. Szczytno: Wyższa Szkoła Policji w Szczytnie.

Kuzior, Patryk. 2009. 'Przestępczość w Krajach Bałtyckich: Litwie, Łotwie i Estonii Ze Szczególnym Uwzględnieniem Przestępczości Zorganizowanej' ['Crime in the Baltic States: Lithuania, Latvia and Estonia, Especially Taking into Account Organized Crime']. *Prokurator* ['Prosecutor'] 1 (29): pp. 97 and 112.

Laskowska, Katarzyna. 2011. 'Etiologia Przestępczości Zorganizowanej w Polsce' ['Etiology of Organized Crime in Poland]'. In *Przestępczość Zorganizowana* ['Organized Crime'], edited by E.W. Pływaczewski, pp. 166–167. Warszawa: Wydawnictwo C. H. Beck Sp. z o. o.

Laskowska, Katarzyna. 2021. *Przestępczość na Białorusi. Przeszłość i teraźniejszość* ['Crime in Belarus. Past and Present'].

Mądrzejowski, Wiesław. 2008. *Przestępczość Zorganizowana. System Zwalczania* ['Organized Crime. A System for Controlling it']. Warszawa: Wydawnictwa Akademickie i Profesjonalne.

Marsh, Nicholas. 2002. 'Two Sides of the Same Coin? The Legal and Illegal Trade in Small Arms'. *The Brown Journal of World Affairs* IX (1): pp. 217–228.

Martyniuk, Anton. 2017. 'Measuring Illicit Arms Flows. Ukraine'. Briefing Paper. Geneva, Switzerland: Small Arms Survey.

Ministry of Internal Affairs. 2016. *Security in Poland Report*. Warszawa: Ministry of Internal Affairs.

Nowicka, Izabela. 2004. *Rozbój Drogowy Jako Przejaw Zorganizowanej Przestępczości* ['Road Robbery as a Manifestation of Organized Criminal Activity']. Kraków: Zakamycze.

Overton, Iain. 2015. *Gun, Baby, Gun: A Bloody Journey into the World of the Gun*. Edinburgh: Canongate Books.

Sarnecki, Jerzy, Kotowska Monika, Chlebowicz Piotr 2018. 'Warto być kryminologiem: z Profesorem Jerzym Sarneckim rozmawiają Monika Kotowska in Piotr Chlebowicz'. *Biuletyn Kryminologiczny* 25: pp. 7–14.

Savona, Ernesto, and Marina, Mancuso (eds.). 2017. *Fighting Illicit Firearms Trafficking Routes and Actors at European Level*. Final Report of Project Fire. Milano: Transcrime—Università Cattolica del Sacro Cuore.

Spapens, Toine. 2007. 'Trafficking in Illicit Firearms for Criminal Purposes within the European Union'. *European Journal of Crime, Criminal Law and Criminal Justice* 15 (3): pp. 359–381.

Starink, Laura, and Beemsterboer, Toon. 2010. 'Kwitnie Pistoletowy Biznes' ['The Pistol Business Is Booming']. *Voxeurop Polski*. https://voxeurop.eu/pl/kwitnie-pistoletowy-biznes/ Accessed 10 Dec. 2022.

Stock, J. 2022. https://www.theguardian.com/world/2022/jun/02/ukraine-weapons-end-up-criminal-hands-says-interpol-chief-jurgen-stock Accessed 11 Dec. 2022.

Trzciński, Maciej. 2010. *Zjawisko Przestępczości Przeciwko Zabytkom—Kontekst Kryminalistyczno-Kryminologiczny* ['Offences Against Heritage—The Criminological and Forensic Context']. In *Co Nowego w Kryminalistyce—Przegląd Zagadnień z Zakresu Zwalczania Przestępczości* ['What's New in Forensic Science—A Review of Crime Combatting Issues'], edited by Ewa Gruza, Mieczysław Goc, Taduesz. Tomaszewski, pp. 357–367. Stowarzyszenie Absolwentów Wydziału Prawa i Administracji UW.

TVN24. 2012. 'Kupowali niedziałającą broń, przerabiali, sprzedawali. Rozbita grupa handlarzy' ['They bought non-functional weapons, modified them, and sold them. A group of traders has been broken up']. https://tvn24.pl/polska/kupowali-niedzialajaca-bron-przerabiali-sprzedawali-rozbita-grupa-handlarzy-ra289053-ls3512605. Accessed 10 Dec. 2022.

United Nations Interregional Crime and Justice Research Institute (UNICRI). 2022. *The Conflict in Ukraine and its Impact on Organized Crime and Security. A Snapshot of Key Trends*. https://unicri.it/News/Conflict%20-Ukraine-impact-on-organized-crime-and-security Accessed 26 Jul. 2024.

United Nations Office on Drugs and Crime (UNODC). 2010. *The Globalization of Crime. A Transnational Organized Crime Threat Assessment.* https://www.unodc.org/documents/data-and-analysis/tocta/TOCTA_Report_2010_low_res.pdf Accessed 26 Jul. 2024.

United Nations Office on Drugs and Crime (UNODC). 2019. *The Illicit Market in Firearms.* https://www.unodc.org/documents/e4j/Module_04_-_The_Illicit_Market_in_Firearms_FINAL.pdf Accessed 26 Jul. 2024.

Widacki, Jan. 2019. 'The Polish Years of Leon Radzinowicz: A Contribution to Biography'. *Archiwum Kryminologii* ['Archives of Criminology'] XII (2): p. 377.

6

Illicit Firearms Markets and Organized Crime in Africa

Adewunmi J. Falode and Wasiu A. Balogun

Introduction

This chapter analyses illicit firearms markets, organized criminal groups, and crime in Africa. It shows the important nexus between the proliferation of small arms and light weapons (SALWs) and organized criminality on the continent. The chapter shows that illicit markets for firearms thrive extensively in the different regions of the continent. The easy accessibility to illicit firearms, the result of a combination of a range of internal and external factors, creates favourable grounds for the establishment of organized criminal groups which have proven to be resistant to disruption by sovereign and legitimate actors. The chapter argues that the proliferation of illicit firearms and the organized criminality that it encourages has serious short- and long-term effects on the political stability, economic development, and sovereign integrity of states in Africa. The chapter shows that illicit firearms have spawned and ensure the sustenance of organized crime activities including firearms trafficking, drug trafficking, piracy, natural resource trafficking, and human trafficking. In addition, the proliferation of illicit firearms is a major factor in the outbreak of incessant conflicts in Africa. The chapter concludes by arguing that states in Africa must adopt proactive and holistic measures that can simultaneously tackle the issues of illicit firearms markets and organized crime.

Illicit Markets and Organized Crime in Africa

Illicit firearms markets and organized crime, both of which are opaque and complex in nature, constitute a major threat to security and stability in Africa. Given the elasticity of Africa's conflict landscape, combined with organized

Adewunmi J. Falode and Wasiu A. Balogun, *Illicit Firearms Markets and Organized Crime in Africa*
In: *Illicit Firearms Markets and Organized Crime*. Edited by: David Bright, Oxford University Press.
 DOI: 10.1093/9780198902409.003.0007

crime activities which are facilitated by porous borders and fragile territories, it is unsurprising that a multi-million-dollar illicit firearms market has proliferated in the continent. Such a robust illicit economy in firearms accentuates the already deeply entrenched fault lines and security challenges ravaging the continent and compromises the path to a sustainable future. With over 100 million SALWs in circulation, Africa is an epicentre of global illicit firearms trafficking with an active and extensive market (UNODC 2020; Agbegbedia 2022, 12). East Africa has the most active firearms market in the continent (Adeniyi 2017). South Africa, Mozambique, and Zimbabwe all have sizeable illicit firearms markets in Southern Africa (Global Initiative Against Transnational Organized Crime 2022). West Africa's arms trafficking market is concentrated around Mali, Niger, Burkina Faso, and Nigeria, where gangs, criminal networks, and armed ideological extremist groups extract arms from government stockpiles for criminal and violent activities (Falode 2021). The Democratic Republic of Congo (DRC) and the Central African Republic (CAR) form the hub of illicit firearms markets in Central Africa, with the two countries ranked among the ten largest arms trafficking markets in the world (ENACT Report 2021).

Irrespective of their location on the continent, illicit firearms markets in Africa share unique characteristics. Illicit firearms markets develop within formal politico-economic structures, feed into legitimate arms market, operate primarily within informal and clandestine economic settings, and encompass a wide range of weapons from diverse sources (Falode 2020). These markets enjoy a degree of uniformity in their organization, with the active participation of various organized criminal groups on the continent cutting across regions. Some of these organized criminal groups that traffic in illicit weapons include the Akasha brothers of Kenya, the Abergil crime family of Morocco, and the Mai-Mai Yakutumba criminal group of the DRC (Falode and Faseke 2024). Their operations are characterised by cross-border mobility, networks of contacts, and adaptability that protects illicit market participants from arrest and interdiction. But significant variations exist in levels of arms trade across the continent, especially in terms of volume and the flows of illicit firearms, which suggests that illicit arms markets in Africa are both complex and segmented.

The infiltration of the illicit firearms market by organized crime facilitates the sustenance and resilience of this illicit market in Africa. Organized criminal networks with links to other illicit activities such as drug trafficking, oil theft and piracy, wildlife poaching, and cattle rustling, facilitate the illicit firearms trade by acting as intermediaries between suppliers and buyers, providing technical knowledge and financing for illicit operations, undermining the law enforcement capacity of states, and navigating complex logistical challenges, thereby ensuring smoother and more covert illicit transactions (ENACT Report 2021; Africa Centre for Strategic Studies 2020). The profit margin in the illicit firearms trade can be substantial, making it financially attractive for organized criminal groups. For example, on the Criminal Market Scores Index for Arms Trafficking, Nigeria, Libya, and South Africa scored 8.5, 9.0, and 8.0 out of a possible 10, respectively (ENACT 2023)

Africa's geography of conflict, violence, and war provides a ready attraction for organized criminal groups who indulge in arming conflicts and accentuating violence. These organized criminal groups see such wars as providing ready markets for their deadly wares and avenues for easy profits (Kinsella, 2014). It is therefore unsurprising that Africa is witnessing some of the deadliest and longest-running conflicts and wars in the world. From Libya and Sudan in the north to Ethiopia and Eritrea in the east, to the Sahelian states of Burkina Faso, Niger, Mali, to Chad, Cameroon, the DRC, and the CAR in Central Africa, and to Nigeria in West Africa, the proliferation of illicit arms facilitated by the activities of organized criminal groups has created conditions that fan the flames of war and violence. In the sections following this introduction, this chapter dwells extensively on the origin, nature, and dynamics of the illicit firearms market in Africa, and delves into its relationship with organized criminal groups. The study also examines the drivers of the illicit market, key actors in the market, and considers the national and regional security implications, including recommendations on how to combat both illicit arms proliferation and organized criminal groups in Africa.

Illicit Firearms Trafficking and Organized Crime in Africa

Africa is a major hub of illicit firearms trafficking. Of an estimated forty million firearms in the possession of civilians across the continent in 2017, about 5.8 million were officially registered and sixteen million were unregistered (Small Arms Survey 2017). SALWs such as pistols, rifles, rocket launchers, and machine guns make up most of the firearms and other weapons in the illicit markets (Falode 2021). The availability of such weapons, due to factors such as porous borders and corruption of state-embedded agents like police officers and army personnel, has both encouraged and sustained the high incidence of conflicts on the continent and the proliferation of entrenched criminal groups. The volatility and fragility of the region, its ungoverned spaces, extensive and embedded activities of organized criminal groups, and absence of effective governmental controls are crucial drivers of the illicit firearms market. The explosive nature of some parts of the continent, due partly to the 'war against terror' in the Sahel and part of West Africa and insurgency in Central Africa feeds into the operation of an extensive and flourishing black market for firearms, with the troubled Sahel region particularly notorious as a buyer's market for guns (TOCTA 2022). The illicit firearms market in Africa has two layers: first, the illicit arms black market and secondly the illicit grey market. A different range of actors operate in each of these two layers (Wood and Danssaert 2020). While the arms trafficking black market is dominated by organized criminal groups, the illicit grey market involves the participation of governments, and their clients and agents, exploiting loopholes or intentionally circumventing national and international regulations and conventions on the arms trade.

There is an intertwined and complex relationship between organized criminal groups and illicit firearms in Africa. Trafficked firearms serve two important purposes: as a means to an end and as an end in itself. As a means to an end, the illicit firearms market is a source of considerable wealth for organized criminal groups on the continent. Substantial profits are made by these groups from trafficking firearms. As an end, the existence of these markets and the easy accessibility of weapons makes it possible for such criminal groups to defend their illicit commodities and territories and ensure their survival (also see Chapter 11 of this volume for discussion of the utility of firearms for organized criminal groups). The activities of these organized criminal groups and the proliferation of illicit markets (including illicit firearms markets) are responsible for significant political, economic, social, and military instability on the continent.

Illicit Firearms Markets in Africa: A Regional Perspective

A regional analysis of Africa's illicit firearms markets shows significant variations in distribution and volume of firearms trafficking. For instance, in the southern African region, there are an estimated 3.8 million unregistered illegal firearms shared among South Africa, Mozambique, and Zimbabwe, with the three countries holding over one-fifth of the sub-region's unregistered firearms (Irish-Qhobosheane 2021). Not only do they have a substantial number of illegal firearms, but their shared history also serves to ensure an interlinked illicit weapons trade that continues to fuel violence and instability in the region. South Africa has the largest pool of illegal firearms in the region, with an estimated 2.35 million such weapons, followed by Mozambique, with an estimated 1.33 million unregistered firearms, and Zimbabwe, with an estimated 264,315 weapons (Irish-Qhobosheane 2021). East Africa has a robust and complex illicit arms market because of the long-running insurgencies of both al-Shabaab (Somalia and Kenya) and the Lord's Resistance Army (Uganda) making it the epicentre of illicit arms trafficking in Africa (ENACT report 2021). The continued volatility of the region and fragility of its states, consequences of long-term political instability, conflicts, and criminal activities, have created a flourishing corridor for illicit firearms trafficking in East Africa. A corridor is a border region that connects two or three African states and makes possible the transfer or proliferation of illicit weapons due to its porousness. For example, the Seme Corridor between Nigeria and Benin Republic is known for the trafficking of various illicit commodities.

In West Africa, Mali, Niger, Burkina Faso, and Nigeria each provide the necessary conditions for the emergence of a thriving regional illicit firearms market. Ideological extremist groups, such as Boko Haram in Nigeria and al-Qaeda in the Sahel, facilitate conflict and violence through ease of access to firearms, including access to stockpiles of weapons that proliferated following the collapse of Gaddafi's regime in Libya (Varisco, Wezeman, and Kuimova 2022). Decades of conflict have created a rich context for the illicit smuggling of firearms, making the region the tenth-largest arms trafficking hub in the world (Pinson 2022).

The number of deaths in South Africa connected with illegal firearms was 21,022 between 2018 and 2019 and 21,325 between 2019 and 2020. On average, fifty-eight people were murdered every day during these periods (Africa Check 2020). A recent development in Mozambique, the emergence in 2017 of what is believed to be an ISIS-linked insurgency in the northern Cabo Delgado province, has further compounded the problem of illicit firearms in Mozambique, resulting in a renewed proliferation of firearms in the area (Irish-Qhobosheane 2021).

Though illicit arms trafficking had been a constant in Africa for decades, the collapse of Gaddafi's stronghold in Libya and the ongoing conflicts in Syria have given rise to illicit arms trafficking and other criminal activities. Moreover, the infiltration of organized crime including trans-border networks, and the escalation of geopolitical rivalries in the Middle East, have not only created new opportunities for the illicit firearms trade in Africa, they have ensured firearms proliferation in the continent, especially in the Sahel.

Drivers of the Illicit Firearms Markets in Africa

Several factors are responsible for the growth and spread of the illicit firearms markets in Africa. We consider the following factors below: (1) ongoing conflicts in Africa, (2) transborder arms trafficking, (3) diversion of firearms, (4) ungoverned spaces, (5) poor regulation of local arms, and (6) corruption.

Ongoing Conflicts in Africa

The African continent has a history of colonial wars, wars of independence, and secessionist and separatist conflicts which have created the image of a continent in perpetual crisis. As decolonization struggles and geopolitical wars intensified across the continent in the 1970s, 1980s, and 1990s, the demand for firearms grew, especially in Southern Africa (Schmidt 2013). In the twentieth century, there were five notable wars in Africa: the Somali civil war (1991), Nigerian civil war (1967), Rwandan genocide (1994), the Lord's Resistance Army Insurgence (1987), and Ethiopian-Eritrean war (1998) (Stockholm International 2020). These wars created a significant arms build-up and an environment that traumatized civilians physically and psychologically. In the twenty-first century, the rapid growth and spread of non-state actors such as criminal groups and terrorist groups like Boko Haram in West Africa and al-Shabaab in Somalia, and different organized criminal groups in the sub-regions, have ensured a steady stream of illicit firearms (and other weapons) on the continent (see Chapter 12 for a discussion of illicit firearms and terrorism). Most of these groups rely extensively on SALW procured from these illicit markets to prosecute their campaigns.

Transborder Trade in Arms

Cross-border firearms trafficking is a critical component of the illicit firearms trade in Africa (Small Arms Survey Annual Report 2022). Across Africa there are notable arms trafficking corridors which provide the pathways for trafficking of illicit commodities including firearms (Adeniyi 2017). The Sahel region is a tangled web especially because of the presence of large ungoverned spaces, weak and fragile states, and a multitude of illicit activities such as drug trafficking, human trafficking, and mineral trafficking which feed on the availability of firearms. Also, vast swathes of Libya's countryside provide a steady supply of firearms across the Sahel (Mangan and

Nowak 2019). Most of these firearms were procured by the former Libyan leader Muammar Gaddafi between 1970 and 2009; after his death in 2011 the stockpiles were looted (Shihundu 2022, 64). In West Africa, the Nigeria-Benin Republic land border and West Africa-Sahel corridor represent notoriously active illicit firearms belts, while the Somalia-Wajir-Kenya corridor and Kenya-Ethiopia corridor, in Northern Kenya, and South Sudan-Lake Turkana-Kenya corridor have continued to serve the East African regional illicit firearms markets.

While porous land borders remain the preferred route for illicit arms trafficking, maritime lanes are also commonly used (Ugwuibe, Idoko, Nwogbo, and Ezinna 2023). Turkish arms and mercenaries find their way into Libya across the Mediterranean Sea, and both the Gulf of Guinea in West Africa and the waters off the Somali coast in the Indian Ocean are particularly notorious for shipments of illicit firearms and maritime piracy (Bahadur 2021). Illegal arms trafficking and other maritime security threats have also been extensive in the Red Sea and the waters surrounding the Horn of Africa.

Diversion of Firearms

The diversion of small arms is a major driver of the illicit firearms trade in Africa. Diversion usually occurs when firearms (and other weapons) that have been legitimately procured by the state end up in both black and grey markets due to official corruption by state embedded personnel like the police and the armed forces. The problem of firearms diversion is accentuated by poor firearms management and lack of thorough planning, disregard for safe storage, and, in some cases, poor handling (TOCTA 2022). Poor national inventory practices by recognized security agents of the state inevitably create problems with the identification of surplus firearms. In Africa, diversion of arms tends to include the entirety of the security architecture of states because of the multitude of government agencies that bear arms. In Africa, police, army, and other government agencies and institutions, such as customs, immigration, correctional services, and national intelligence agencies have members who are licensed to bear firearms. In South Africa, more than 47,028 licensed civilian firearms were reported lost or stolen between 2013/14 and 2018/19 (Mercado 2022), with police officials often accused of complicity in the disappearance of police-issued firearms. Cases also abound of theft of recovered firearms stored in police armouries, representing a glaring instance of looting of arms. In the northern part of Mozambique, cases of poor storage and security and protection of firearms have aggravated arms theft, especially by insurgents who have repeatedly targeted the Forcas Armadas de Defesa de Mocambique or Mozambique Defence Armed Forces (FADM)'s military formations because their vulnerability (Haysom 2018). Cases of arms theft and diversion are reinforced by the socio-political and economic structures of states which create the market and consequential conflict environment that emboldens different shades of criminality and undermines further the capacity of states to combat arms proliferation.

Ungoverned Spaces

Ungoverned spaces are territorial areas within states where there is an absence of state capacity and authority (Ejiofor 2022). Large ungoverned spaces attract organized criminal groups who sometimes cross state borders with firearms through ungoverned spaces such as forests. The Sahel region, especially the Niger-Nigeria-Chad corridor, has vast expanses of ungoverned space which has proved attractive to criminal and terrorist groups such as Boko Haram and other dangerous non-state actors (Ejiofor 2022; and see Chapter 12). Ungoverned spaces and unregulated forests that link Zamfara, Niger, Kaduna, Kebbi, Katsina, and Sokoto states are controlled by a range of armed groups, an example of illicit governance. This includes Sambisa, Alagarno, Kamuku, Kudaru, Kuyambana, Burwaye, Ajja, Dajin Rugu forest, Fagore forest, Dutse forest, and Rijana forest (Adewuyi and Daful 2021). The illicit firearms markets in these various regions are both a means to an end and an end in themselves. As a means to an end, trafficked firearms are used to generate funds to ensure the sustenance of these criminal groups. As an end, such illicit weapons are used to illicitly govern the conquered territories and protect the groups from other malign actors. These ungoverned spaces have further facilitated the proliferation of firearms used by the armed groups and provide opportunities for illicit appropriation and extraction of natural resources, particularly gold in Zamfara, Nigeria.

Thriving Black and Grey Markets

Grey and black markets are important sources of illicit firearms (and other weapons) in Africa. Grey markets refer to firearms being sold or purchased in the illicit economy by legitimate state actors (Zweifel 2012). They allow legitimate state actors to trade in trafficked firearms under the guise of anonymity. States under arms embargo, and which cannot buy weapons legally from the international market, can source firearms from other state actors through such markets (Karp 1994). Black markets, on the other hand, involve the trade in illicit weapons, trafficked by non-state actors such as Boko Haram and al Shabaab (Kinsella 2014). Such markets exist in border regions in Mali, Niger, and Nigeria, and the port cities of Dakar, Conakry, Abidjan, and Lagos (Jesse 2023). There is a thriving black market for illegally acquired weapons in Africa. Weapons in such black markets in the Sahel usually sell for between $700 and $2,500. For example, in 2019, assault rifles from Libya flooded black markets in Libya and could be procured for prices that ranged between $700 and $1300 (TOCTA 2022)

Poor Regulation of Local Arms Production

A major driving force behind firearms proliferation in Africa is poor regulation of local firearms produced clandestinely by craftsmen or artisans. In several African states, local arms production is poorly regulated, and in some cases, there are no control mechanisms. In most West African countries, locally made weapons are widespread, and are used to commit a range of crimes (Christoper 2011). In the eastern part of Nigeria, locally made weapons produced by craftsmen or artisans, such as Beretta-like pistols and fabricated double-barrelled guns, constitute the bulk of illegal arms that sustain the activities of the Eastern Security Network (ESN), a pro-Biafra separatist movement (Nowak and Gsell 2018). It is estimated that 60 per cent of illegal arms in south-east Nigeria are produced locally, with some communities renowned for illegal arms fabrication (Nowak and Gsell 2018) while local blacksmiths have developed skills and capacity to manufacture assorted and sophisticated rifles such as AK-47s, revolvers, improvised explosive devices, among others (Baiyewu 2021). In Mali, local gunsmiths have the capacity to produce over 5,000 weapons a year, while over 200,000 weapons are produced annually in Ghana. Though lucrative, the industry is artisanal and clandestine, animated by blacksmiths whose knowledge and expertise are recycled across generations (Institute for Security Studies (ISS) 2017).

Corruption

Corruption, especially among government officials, is a major driver of the illicit firearms market in Africa. Corrupt government officials, including law enforcement officers, customs officials, and military personnel, drive the illicit trade in firearms, and there are frequent arrests and prosecutions for such activities (Malami, Abdullah, and Yusoff 2021). While this collusion is evident in all regions in Africa, it has been documented for East and Southern Africa (UNODC 2023). For instance, in January 2018 a 20-foot container loaded with military camouflage uniforms and suspected weapons disappeared at the Tin Can Terminal in Apapa (Vanguard Newspaper, 17 January 2018), though the customs agent who had cleared the container was later identified and the container itself found. Despite being under a UN arms embargo since 1992, Somalia has had steady access to illicit weapons, especially through maritime shipments. Large quantities of illicit firearms have flooded the Puntland state of Somalia, through the Gulf of Aden and the port of Bossaso, arming al-Shabaab, Da'esh, and other armed groups (UNODC Issue Paper 1/2022, 'Firearms and Ammunition Trafficking in Eastern Africa'). In most of these trafficking cases, government officials have accepted bribes or turned a blind eye to the illicit act, allowing firearms to flow onto the black market (ENACT 2021). Government officials at land borders, given the notoriety and permeability of African borders, are more disposed to such acts of opprobrium. Corruption can also involve the activities of shipping and transport company officials, who have been known to facilitate the entry of illegal weapons at ports. Africa's porous borders make effective control of illegal firearms proliferation a herculean task.

From the analysis above, it is clear that the illicit firearms market in Africa is facilitated by a range of political and economic factors. The political economy of illicit weapons proliferation finds expression in profiteering and power. Non-state actors desirous of carving territorial spaces out of existing boundaries in Africa use firearms to legitimize a governance architecture based on the instrumentality of force. For example, in Nigeria's north-east, Boko Haram and Islamic State in West Africa (ISWAP) have used weapons obtained from both grey and black markets to wage a deadly war against the state since 2010.

Actors in the Illicit Firearms Market in Africa

As shown in Figure 6.1, Africa's illicit firearms markets is intricate, with a range of entangled actors, including state and non-state actors, actively involved in the grey and black firearms markets. These actors include terrorist groups, armed groups and militia organizations, transnational organized

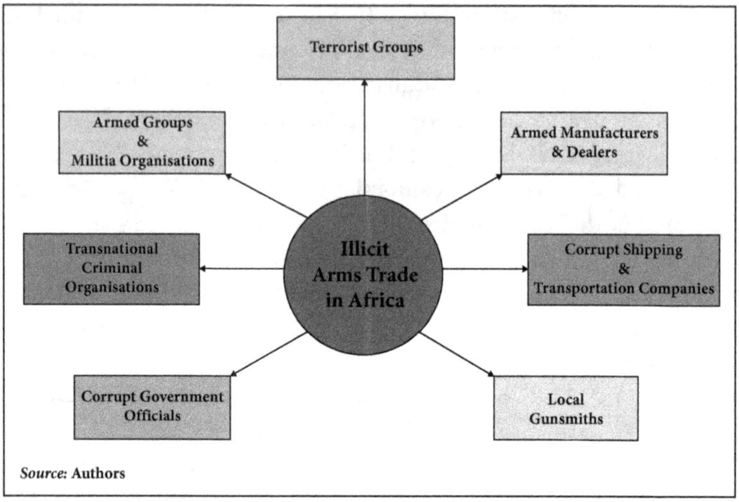

Figure 6.1 Actors in the illicit firearms trade in Africa

criminal groups, arms manufacturers and dealers, corrupt shipping and transportation companies, corrupt government officials, local gunsmiths, and international arms traffickers, among others.

Several armed, rebel, and terror groups in Africa are major drivers of the illicit firearms trade. As of 2021, there were over twenty armed groups in Africa, with five notoriously active corridors: the Sahel, Somalia, Lake Chad Basin, Mozambique, and North Africa (African Centre for Strategic Studies 2020). The operations of these armed groups reinforce the continued flow of illicit firearms and other weapons, compromising states' capacity to guarantee national security and development in the process.

Meanwhile, those notoriously active arms corridors are exploited by illegal arms traffickers and war merchants in the cross-border transnational illicit arms trade. The blossoming African 'arms-preneurship' is partly driven by the active engagement of mercenaries or soldiers of fortune in the continent's theatres of conflict (Taylor 2022). 'Arms-preneurship' refers to the flourishing illicit arms markets in the various corridors on the continent and the myriad of actors that participate in the illicit trade. Actors involved in the illicit arms trade are not limited to criminal groups but also state-embedded actors, terrorist groups, insurgents, local craftsmen, artisans, and other citizens used as mules. Africa has a rich history of mercenaries' involvement in its conflicts. From the Cold War era, when mercenaries were hired to support governments or regimes in several African countries, such as Namibia, Angola, and Congo-Brazzaville, to the armed local militias enlisted by multinational oil companies to offer protection services for critical energy assets, as was the case with Chevron in Southern Sudan in the early 1980s, to the contemporary variants hired to provide strategic planning, intelligence-gathering, troop training, and weapons supply, mercenaries in Africa's conflict zones have become embedded in states' security infrastructure as purveyors of arms (Taylor 2022). Such groups include the Russian Wagner Group, South African Dyck Advisory Group (DAG), United States' CACI and Academi, France's Secopex, Great Britain's Aegis Defence Services, Ukraine's Omega Consulting Group, and Germany's Xeless and Asgaard. The growing influence of these war merchants has exacerbated the proliferation of illicit firearms in Africa.

Given their transnational nature and high profitability, illicit firearms markets provide a rallying hub for transnational criminal syndicates involved in drug trafficking, human smuggling, and other illicit activities. These groups often diversify their operations by participating in the illegal firearms trade, but they require access to an active illicit firearms market to carry out their nefarious acts in an overlapping and mutually reinforcing relationship.

Money laundering is an integral part of the illicit firearms trade. In terms of actors, financial institutions and those who work for these institutions are usually conscripted into illicit financing of the trade in firearms, rendering financial tracking and tracing by law enforcement extremely difficult (Falode and Chukwuemeka 2022). The resilience of violent extremist groups such as al-Qaeda in the Maghreb (AQIM), al-Shabaab, Boko Haram Terrorist (BHT) and the Islamic State of West Africa Province (ISWAP) highlights the inextricable connection between illicit firearms trafficking and illicit financial flows. For example, Boko Haram's proceeds from criminal activities such as kidnapping for ransom, banditry and cattle rustling, drug trafficking, armed robbery, maritime piracy and armed robbery at sea, and illegal fishing, have been ploughed into weapons acquisition.

Interconnections Between Illicit Firearms Markets and Organized Crime in Africa

The connections between the illicit firearms market and organized crime in Africa are complex and opaque. Both firearms proliferation and organized crime exist and operate in a mutually reinforcing relationship anchored on economies of armed conflict (see Figures 6.2 and 6.3). Africa's expanding theatres of conflicts are reinforced by the activities of illicit firearms traffickers whose activities are in themselves organized crimes, but also facilitate

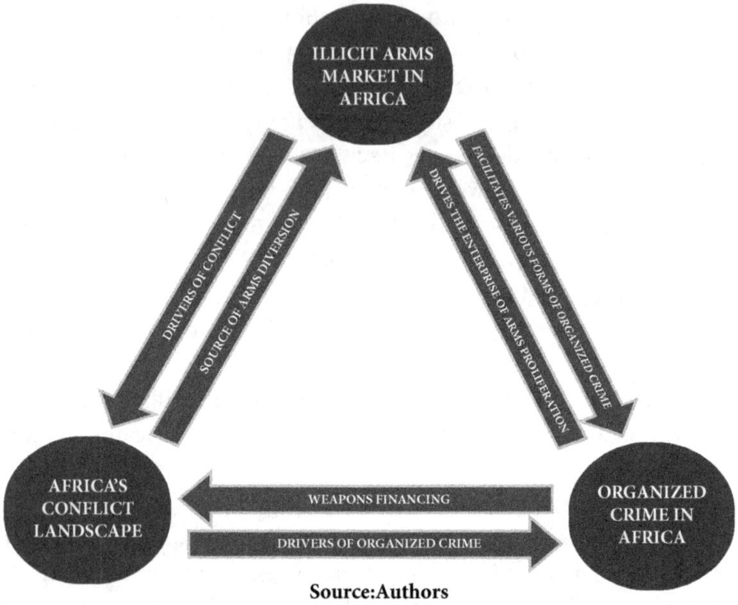

Figure 6.2 Organized crime–illicit firearms–conflicts nexus

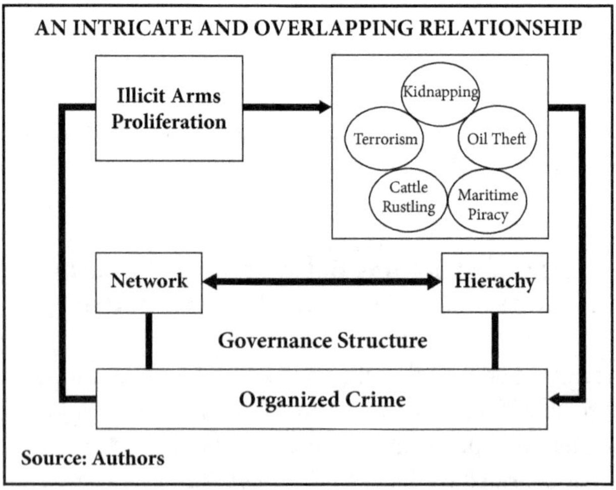

Figure 6.3 The relationship between organized crime and illicit arms trafficking

other illicit activities such as human trafficking, drug trafficking, and piracy. As noted previously in this chapter, this means the illicit firearms markets serve as both a means to an end and an end in itself. As a means to end, the illicit firearms markets provide a steady stream of SALWs that enable the commission and sustenance of other illicit enterprises. As an end, the markets make it possible for purveyors of illicit arms and their clientele to have easy access to weapons they can use to defend and protect their enterprises. Figure 6.2 shows the overlapping and mutually beneficial relationship of firearms proliferation, organized crime, and conflict. As the diagram shows, the availability of illicit firearms plays a critical role not only in influencing the operations and modus operandi of organized criminal groups, but also shapes how the illicit firearms economy operates. The diagram illustrates that illicit firearms underpin much of organized crime, and that firearms and ammunition trafficking strengthen and expand illicit markets, especially in Africa. The illicit activities of organized criminal groups generate resources to buy firearms, which are then used to support and protect organized criminal activities.

Building on Pinson (2022), across Africa, a triangle of connections is discernible from the linkages between firearms proliferation, organized crime, and the conflict environment that nourishes each component individually and collectively. First, Africa's conflicts represent markets for illicit firearms. This is because most, if not all conflicts in Africa are between state and non-state actors. Non-state actors, unlike their state counterpart, do not have access to the legitimate international arms markets. Therefore, the illicit firearms markets provide the bridge to meeting their demand for firearms. The flow of firearms into conflict zones helps to ensure that the demand for firearms by a range of belligerents is met. In other words, Africa's conflict zones are the major sources of illicit firearms primarily through diversion from legitimate markets and stockpiles.

Africa's conflict zones are a source of firearms, ensuring a steady supply of illicit arms that are transferred to other volatile and conflict-ravaged zones across the continent. In this regard, Africa's conflict zones lie at the intersection of both the demand and supply of illicit firearms. And lastly, significant opportunities for the diversion of firearms to the illicit market also exist in Africa's conflict-ravaged zones. With armed groups and other non-state actors seeking to diversify the sources of illicit firearms flows, organized criminal groups become channels for such illicit trafficking, funnelling and conveying illegally acquired weapons across Africa's theatre of conflicts. Organized criminal groups appear to dominate the illicit firearms trade, from production to shipment and retail components. The fallout of such domineering influence is a rich black market for firearms, sustained by conflicts.

The flow of uncontrolled firearms plays a crucial role in the activities of networks of organized crime groups across Africa. There is a convergence of organized crime and armed conflict, including violent extremism, in places like the Sahel, Libya, and Somalia. Indeed, the various armed conflicts that dot the continent provide a ready market for weapons in both grey and black markets. For example, pirates use illicit firearms in the Horn of Africa and the Gulf of Guinea region to attack and seize ships and to kidnap crews for ransom (Willima and Ramachela 2023). Indeed, the ransom economy has been a major driver of maritime piracy and kidnapping in the Niger Delta region of Nigeria since the global crude oil price plunge in 2020 (Balogun and Adesanya 2022).

Illicit firearms shape the activities of organized criminal groups, giving them more social, economic, and political power, as well as transforming criminal landscapes and enabling other illicit markets to thrive. In summary, organized crime and firearms markets tend to benefit and reinforce each other.

The ready availability of firearms in some regions has led to an arms race in which criminal groups invest their profits into 'out-gunning' their rivals and legitimate security forces (Lacher 2012). As members of such groups recognized there were profits to be made in the illicit firearms market, they began to establish themselves as brokers, using profits from a range of illicit markets to buy and sell firearms not only to and from their members but also other criminal groups at huge mark-ups (Lacher 2012). In the Niger Delta region of Nigeria, the proliferation of illegal firearms has enabled smaller gangs to compete with both rival organized criminal groups and the security forces. (Hazen and Horner 2007).

Impacts of Illicit Firearms Markets on Africa's Security

Illicit firearms flows have a multi-dimensional impact across Africa. In the realm of security and development, illicit arms reinforce the continent's conflict landscape, and the impact of terrorist and organized criminal activities and other security threats. According to the United States Agency for International Development (TOCTA 2022), illicit arms have contributed significantly to the continuous cycle of violence and instability in Africa, with about 50 per cent of illicit firearms used in internal conflicts and interpersonal crimes such as armed robbery. In a similar vein, since 2000, Africa has seen an increase in election-related political violence, with fifteen African countries ravaged by post-election violence and conflict, suggestive of a nexus between the availability of uncontrolled firearms and political violence (Adeniyi 2017). Election-related violence adds to the rising conflict profile in Ethiopia, Somalia, Libya, the Sahel region of West Africa, CAR, and the DRC, where a range of drivers of insecurity, such as rebellion, civil war, secessionist agitations, and farmer–herder conflicts have significantly threatened security and sustainable development across these regions.

The proliferation of illicit firearms not only escalates Africa's conflict landscape but also weaponizes hostilities among non-state actors and criminal organizations, thereby expanding the scope and territoriality of illicit activities. The commission of crimes such as kidnapping, extortion, armed robbery, assassinations, and poaching in several parts of Africa has been reinforced by the steady supply and availability of illicit firearms (Falode 2021).

Illicit weapons proliferation and the activities of organized crime groups have also accentuated the challenge of forced migration and internal displacements in several war-torn African countries. In the CAR, DRC, Lake Chad Basin, Mali, Somalia, Sudan, and Nigeria there have been large numbers of internally displaced persons and refugees. For example, about 2.8 million people have been displaced by the activities of Boko Haram in the Lake Chad Basin (Adeniyi 2017).

The proliferation of firearms in Africa has contributed to protracted conflicts and state collapse in Somalia, Libya, and the Sahel region (Oghuvbu 2020). In several of these states, the institutions of state and governance infrastructure have basically collapsed as diverse armed criminal groups and other non-state actors have assumed administrative, social, and economic responsibilities usually met by legitimate states. These failed states have then become conduits and markets for illicit firearms. Importantly, in these milieux, illicit firearms are instrumentalized to foster authority and power especially by non-state actors.

Policy Recommendations

A range of policy recommendations flow from the foregoing discussion about illicit firearms markets and the operation of organized criminal groups across Africa. To effectively check the proliferation of illicit firearms and disrupt organized criminality, African states will need to establish a continent-wide intergovernmental agency that will monitor the flow of firearms across the continent. Such an agency can be created from any of the existing continental or regional organizations. For example, the Economic Community of West African States (ECOWAS) has a range of programmes operating at the regional level akin to this: the ECOWAS Convention on Small Arms and Light Weapons, their Ammunition, and other Related Materials (2006); the West African Action Network against Small Arms (WAANSA); and the ECOWAS Programme for the Control of Small Arms (ECOSAP) (ECOWAS 2016) Further, inter-agency intelligence-sharing hubs must be established. This will ensure that there is real-time actionable information about the flow of firearms across the continent.

Secondly, each country must create a firearms registry. This will facilitate monitoring of the illicit flows of legitimate firearms into the grey market. This may also have the knock-on effect of dissuading state actors from offloading their weapons in the grey market for profit. This is crucial to check diversion of weapons from states' armouries to both the black and grey markets. Crucially, it may make it easier for states to keep track of SALWs produced by craftsmen and artisans in their countries. To make this work, governments will have to provide a modicum of legitimacy for artisanal producers. Making their production legitimate will mean that respective governments will need to grant them operational or production licences. In this way, governments will be better able to monitor the local production of firearms.

Thirdly, a concerted effort must be made to staunch the flow of firearms to non-state actors. This will necessarily involve the deployment of technology and kinetic military operations across borders. Finally, since unimpeded access to finance is the backbone of both illicit markets and organized criminal activities, African states must toughen and enforce their anti-money laundering laws, especially with respect to firearms trafficking. Financial institutions, especially those known as 'fintech', must be equipped and mandated to prevent illegitimate actors and criminal groups from using their channels and resources to move profits generated by illicit activities. This will impede the flow of funds into the firearms markets and rob these illegitimate and non-state actors of the financial incentive to participate in the illicit firearm economy.

Conclusions

From the foregoing, we can conclude that there is an inextricable link between the illicit market for firearms and organized crime in Africa. This interconnectedness has ensured the outbreak and sustenance of conflicts with the attendant negative impacts on socio-economic, political, and human development. The chapter identified the important drivers of the illicit firearms market in Africa and further links this to the activities of organized criminal groups. The effect of the activities of the non-state and embedded state actors in the illicit arms markets is a major factor for the incessant conflicts across the continent. Additionally, the unimpeded flow and exchange of illicit arms in both the black and grey markets have a knock-on effect to other illicit activities like drug trafficking and mineral trafficking across Africa. Furthermore, the easy access by criminal groups to virtually untraceable SALWs have made it possible for malign non-state actors to effectively challenge the authority of African governments. To effectively curb the activities of these criminal groups and check the unhindered flow of arms into the illicit markets, African governments must pool their resources, tackle corruption, and create a central and easily accessible registry for local, national, regional, and continental arms produced across Africa.

References

Adeniyi, Adesoji. 2017. 'The Human Cost of Uncontrolled Arms in Africa: Cross-National Research on Seven African Countries'. Oxfam Research Reports. https://www-cdn.oxfam.org/s3fs-public/file_attachments/rr-human-cost-uncontrolled-arms-africa-080317-en.pdf Accessed 23 Jul. 2024.

Adewuyi, Taiye, and Daful, Gideon. 2021. 'Mapping of Conflicts and Small Arms and Light Weapons Proliferations in Africa'. In *The Palgrave Handbook of Small Arms and Conflicts in Africa* edited by Tar, Usman, and Onwurah Chukwurah. Switzerland: Springer-Nature. https://doi.org/10.1007/978-3-030-62183-4_7 Accessed 23 Jul. 2024.

Africa Check. 2020. 'FACTSHEET: South Africa's Crime Statistics for 2019/2020'. https://africacheck.org/fact-checks/factsheets/factsheet-south-africas-crime-statistics-201920 Accessed 23 Jul. 2024.

African Centre for Strategic Studies. 2020. 'Countering Transnational Organized Crime' (13–17 Jan. 2020). https://africacenter.org/programs/ctoc/#:~:text=The%20Africa%20Center's%20countering%20transnational,state%20responses%20to%20TOC%20 Accessed 23 Jul. 2024.

Agbegbedi, Oghenevwoke. 2022. 'Small Arms and Light Weapons Proliferation and Gun Violence in West African Sub-Region'. *Wukari International Studies Journal* 6 (2): p. 12. https://wissjournals.com.ng/index.php/wiss/article/view/56#:~:text=Findings%20revealed%20that%20the%20porous,destruction%20of%20lives%20and%20properties Accessed 23 Jul. 2024.

Bahadur, Jay. 2021. 'An Iranian Fingerprint? Tracing Type 56-1 Assault Rifles in Somalia'. Global Initiative Against Organized Crime. https://globalinitiative.net/analysis/iran-firearms-somalia/ Accessed 23 Jul. 2024.

Baiywe, Leke. 2021. 'Local Blacksmiths now Manufacture AK-47, says Defence Agency'. https://punchng.com/local-blacksmiths-now-manufacture-ak-47-says-defence-agency/#google_vignette Accessed 28 May2024.

Balogun, Wasiu, and Adesanya, Olusegun. 2022. '"A Sea of Troubles": Oil Theft. Crude Economy and the Business of Organized Energy Crime in the Gulf of Guinea'. *African Journal of Stability and Development* 14(1 & 2). https://journals.abuad.edu.ng/index.php/ajsd/article/view/113 Accessed 28 Oct. 2024

Bhalla, Nita. 2018. 'U.N. Sounds Alarm on South Sudan as Africa's Biggest Refugee Crisis Looms'. *Reuters*. https://www.reuters.com/article/us-southsudan-aid-refugees/u-n-sounds-alarm-on-south-sudan-as-africas-biggest-refugee-crisis-looms-idUSKBN1FL687/ Accessed 23 Jul. 2024.

Christopher, Louise. 2011. 'The Social Impacts of Light Weapons Availability and Proliferation'. International Alert, A Discussion Paper for UNIDIR. In Small Arms and light Weapons Proliferation in the Early 21st Century: The Nigerian Case. *International Journal of development and Sustainability*, by Moses, John and Ngoma, Julius, vol. 6, no. 17: 1640. https://isdsnet.com/ijds-v6n11-10.pdf Accessed 23 Jul. 2024

Economic Community of West African States (ECOWAS). 2016. 'ECOWAS Policy Framework for Security Sector Reform and Governance'. https://ecowas.int/wp-content/uploads/2022/08/ecowas-policy-framework-on-ssrg-english-adopted-1.pdf Accessed 23 Jul. 2024.

Ejiofor, Promise. 2022a. 'Beyond Ungoverned Spaces: Connecting the Dots between Relative Deprivation, Banditry and Violence in Nigeria'. *African Security* 15 (2): pp. 111–141. https://doi.org/10.1080/19392206.2022.2061320 Accessed 23 Jul. 2024.

Ejiofor, Promise. 2022b. 'Assessment of the Impact of Ungoverned Spaces on Insurgency in Borno State, Nigeria'. *Ghana Journal of Geography* 13 (2): pp. 31–65. https://www.ajol.info/index.php/gjg/article/view/213164Accessed 23 Jul. 2024.

Enhancing Africa's Response to Transnational Organized Crime (ENACT). 2021a. 'Organized Crime Index 2021. How has Organized Crime in Africa Changed Since 2019'. https://globalinitiative.net/analysis/organised-crime-index-africa-2021/ Accessed 23 Jul. 2024.

Enhancing Africa's Response to Transnational Organized Crime (ENACT). 2021b. 'Africa Organized Crime Index 2021: Evolution of Crime in a COVID World—A Comparative Analysis of Organized Crime in Africa, 2019-2021'. https://enact-africa.s3.amazonaws.com/site/uploads/2021-11-25-oci-final.pdf Accessed 23 Jul. 2024.

Enhancing Africa's Response to Transnational Organized Crime (ENACT). 2023. 'Africa Organized Crime Index, 2023'. https://africa.ocindex.net/assets/downloads/english/enact_report_2023.pdf Accessed 23 Jul. 2024.

Falode, Adewunmi. 2020. 'Small Arms and Light Weapons (SALW) and Transnational Crime in Africa'. *Vestnik RUDN International Relations* 20 (1): pp. 158–169. https://papers.ssrn.com/sol3/papers.cfm?abstract_id=3564629 Accessed 23 Jul. 2024.

Falode, Adewunmi. 2021. 'Guns, Arms Trade and Transnational Crime in Africa'. In *The Palgrave Handbook of Small Arms and Conflicts in Africa* edited by Tar, Usman, Charles Onwurah, U.A. Tar, and C.P. Onwurah, pp. 411–425. Springer Nature. https://link.springer.com/chapter/10.1007/978-3-030-62183-4_20 Accessed 23 Jul. 2024.

Falode, Adewunmi, and Chukwuemeka, Nnemeka. 2022. 'Countering Terrorism and Criminal Financing in Nigeria: Strategic Options'. *Razon Critica* 13. https://doi.org/10.21789/25007807.1861 Accessed 23 Jul. 2024.

Falode, Adewunmi, and Faseke, Babajimi. 2024. 'Transnational Crime'. In *Handbook of African Defence and Armed Forces* edited by Marco Wyss and Evert Kleynhans. Oxford: Oxford University Press (forthcoming).

Global Initiative Against Transnational Organized Crime, GIATOC. 2022. Annual Report. https://globalinitiative.net/analysis/annnual-report-2022/ Accessed 23 Jul. 2024.

Haysom, Simone. 2018. 'Where Crime Compounds Conflict: Understanding Northern Mozambique's Vulnerabilities'. Global Initiative Against Transnational Organized Crime. Switzerland. https://globalinitiative.net/wp-content/uploads/2018/10/TGIATOC-North-Mozambique-Report-WEB.pdf Accessed 23 Jul. 2024.

Hazen, Jennifer, and Horner, Jonas. 2007. 'Small Arms, Armed Violence and Insecurity in Nigeria: The Niger Delta in Perspective'. *Small Arms Survey*. https://www.smallarmssurvey.org/sites/default/files/resources/SAS-OP20-Nigeria.pdf Accessed 23 Jul. 24.

Hirsh, Michael. 2023. 'How AI will Revolutionize Warfare'. *Foreign Policy*. https://foreignpolicy.com/2023/04/11/ai-arms-race-artificial-intelligence-chatgpt-military-technology/ Accessed 23 Jul. 2024.

Irish-Qhobosheane, J. 2021. 'Counting the Cost of Firearm Violence: How to Silence the Guns? Southern Africa's Illegal Firearms Markets'. Global Initiative Against Transnational Organized Crime. https://globalinitiative.net/wp-content/uploads/2021/09/GITOC-ESA-Obs-How-to-silence-the-guns-Southern-Africas-illegal-firearms-markets.pdf Accessed 23 Jul. 2024.

ISS. 2023. 'An Ocean of Weapons: Arms Smuggling to Somalia'. Institute for Security Studies. https://issafrica.org/iss-today/an-ocean-of-weapons-arms-smuggling-to-somalia Accessed 23 Jul. 2024.

Jesse, Genevieve. 2023. 'Arms Trafficking: Fuelling Conflict in Sahel'. *The International Affairs Review*. https://www.iar-gwu.org/print-archive/ikjtfxf3nmqgd0np1ht10mvkfron6n-bykaf-ey3hc-rfbxp-dpte8-klmp4 Accessed 23 Jul. 2024.

Karp, Aaron. 1994. 'The Rise of Black and Gray Markets'. *American Academy of Political and Social Science* 535: p. 179. https://www.jstor.org/stable/1048134 Accessed 23 Jul. 2024.

Kinsella, David. 2014. 'Illicit Arms Transfer to Africa and the Prominence of the Former Soviet Bloc: A Social Network Analysis'. *Crime, Law and Social Change* 62(2). https://link.springer.com/article/10.1007/s10611-014-9531-9 Accessed 23 Jul. 2024.

Lacher, Wolfram. 2012. 'Organized Crime and Conflict in the Sahel-Sahara Region'. *The Carnegie Papers*. Carnegie Endowment for International Peace. https://carnegieendowment.org/files/sahel_sahara.pdfAccessed 23 Jul. 2024.

Malami, Salisu, Abdullah, Anita, and Yusoff, Mohamed. 2021. 'The Proliferation of Small Arms and Light Weapons in Nigeria: Corruption a Major Challenge'. *Malaysian Journal of Law and Society* 29. https://www.arcjournals.org/pdfs/ijhcs/v3-i3/4.pdf Accessed 23 Jul. 2024.

Mangan, Fiona, and Nowak, Mathias. 2019. 'The West Africa-Sahel Connection: Mapping Cross-border Arms Trafficking.' Small Arms Survey, Briefing Paper. https://www.smallarmssurvey.org/sites/default/files/resources/SAS-BP-West-Africa-Sahel-Connection.pdf Accessed 23 Jul. 2024.

Mercado, Guillermo. 2022. 'Arms Trafficking and Organized Crime: Global Trade, Local Impacts'. The Global Initiative Against Transnational Organized Crime. Switzerland. https://globalinitiative.net/analysis/arms-trafficking-and-organized-crime/ Accessed 23 Jul. 2024.

Nowak, Mathias, and Gsell, Aaron. 2018. 'Handmade and Deadly: Craft Production of Small Arms in Nigeria'. *Small Arms Survey*. https://www.smallarmssurvey.org/sites/default/files/resources/SAS-BP-Nigeria-craft-weapons.pdf Accessed 23 Jul. 2024.

'Observatory of Illicit Economies in Eastern and Southern Africa'. 2022. *Global Initiative*, January-February, https://globalinitiative.net/wp-content/uploads/2022/03/ESA-Obs-Risk-Bulletin-23.pdf Accessed 23 Jul. 2024.

Oghuvbu, Augustine. 2020. 'Arms Trading and Weapons Proliferation in Africa: Implications for Nigeria'. *Public Security and Public Order* 25. https://doi.org/10.13165/PSPO-20-25-18 Accessed 23 Jul. 2024.

Pinson, Lauren. 2022. 'Addressing the Linkages between Illicit Arms, Organized Crime and Armed Conflict'. United Nations Institute for Disarmament Research. United Nations Office on Drugs and Crime (UNODC). https://www.unodc.org/documents/firearms-protocol/2022/UNIDIR-UNODC_Adressing_the_linkages_between_illict_arms_organized_crime_and_armed_conflict.pdf Accessed 23 Jul. 2024.

Schmdt, Elizabeth. 2013. 'Nationalism, Decolonization, and the Cold War, 1945–1991'. In *Foreign Intervention in Africa: From the Cold War to the War on Terror*, pp. 18–33. Cambridge: Cambridge University Press. https://doi.org/10.1017/CBO9781139021371 Accessed 23 Jul. 2024.

Shihundu, Felix. 2022. 'Libya: Arms Proliferation and Armed Groups. The Libyan Conflict Revisited'. *Conflict Studies Quarterly* 38: p. 64. DOI:10.24193/csq.38.4 Accessed 23 Jul. 2024.

'Small Arms and Light Weapons: Africa'. 2020. Religions for Peace. https://www.rfp.org/wp-content/uploads/2020/10/Small-Arms-and-Light-Weapons-Africa-English.pdf Accessed 23 Jul. 2024.

Small Arms Survey. 2017. *Annual Report 2017*. https://smallarmssurvey.org/resource/annual-report-2017 Accessed 23 Jul. 2024.

Small Arms Survey. 2018. *Annual Report 2018*. https://smallarmssurvey.org/resource/annual-report-2018 Accessed 23 Jul. 2024.

Small Arms Survey. 2019. *Annual Report 2019*. https://smallarmssurvey.org/highlight/small-arms-survey-annual-report-2019 Accessed 23 Jul. 2024.

Small Arms Survey. 2020. Global Firearms Holding. *Small Arms Survey*. https://www.smallarmssurvey.org/database/global-firearms-holdings#:~:text=The%20Small%20Arms%20Survey%20estimates%20that%20of%20the,per%20cent%29%20are%20owned%20by%20law%20enforcement%20agencies. Accessed 23 Jul. 2024.

Small Arms Survey. 2022. *Annual Report 2022*. https://www.smallarmssurvey.org/sites/default/files/resources/SAS-ANNUAL-REPORT-2022.pdf Accessed 23 Jul. 2024

Stockholm International Peace Research Institute, SIPRI. 2020. *SIPRI Yearbook 2020*. Armaments, Disarmament and International Security. https://www.sipri.org/yearbook/2020 Accessed 23 Jul. 2024.

Stockholm International Peace Research Institute, SIPRI. 2022. *SIPRI Yearbook 2022*. Armaments, Disarmament and International Security. https://www.sipri.org/sites/default/files/YB22%2010%20World%20Nuclear%20Forces.pdf Accessed 23 Jul. 2024.

Stockholm International Peace Research Institute, SIPRI. 2023. *SIPRI Yearbook 2023*. Armaments, Disarmament and International Security. https://www.sipri.org/media/press-release/2023/states-invest-nuclear-arsenals-geopolitical-relations-deteriorate-new-sipri-yearbook-out-now Accessed 23 Jul. 2024.

Taylor, David. 2022. *Combatants in African Conflicts: Professionals, Praetorians, Militias, Insurgents and Mercenaries*. Abingdon: Routledge.

TOCTA. 2022. 'Firearms Trafficking in the Sahel. Transnational Organized Crime Threat Assessment. United Nations Office on Drug and Crime'. https://www.unodc.org/documents/data-and-analysis/tocta_sahel/TOCTA_Sahel_firearms_2023.pdf Accessed 23 Jul. 2024.

Ugwuibo, Onyemaechi, Idoko, Cordelia, Nwogbo, David, and Ezinne, Paul. 2023. 'Nigeria Ports and Arms Smuggling'. *The Journal of Territorial and Maritime Studies* 10(1): pp.38–59. https://www.jstor.org/stable/48713707 Accessed 23 Jul. 2024.

United Nations Office on Drug and Crime (UNODC). 2005. *Transnational Organized Crime in West Africa*. https://www.unodc.org/pdf/transnational_crime_west-africa-05.pdf Accessed 23 Jul. 2024.

United Nations Office on Drug and Crime (UNODC). 2010. *The Globalization of Crime: A Transnational Organized Crime Threat Assessment (TOCTA)*. https://www.unodc.org/documents/data-and-analysis/tocta/TOCTA_Report_2010_low_res.pdf Accessed 23 Jul. 2024.

United Nations Office on Drug and Crime (UNODC). 2020. 'Global Study on Firearms Trafficking 2020'. 2020_REPORT_Global_Study_on_Firearms_Trafficking_2020_web3.pdf Accessed 23 Jul. 2024.

United Nations Office on Drug and Crime (UNODC). 2023. *An Aid to Strategic Reponses to Organized Crime in East and Southern Africa: Foreign Policy Brief*. Geneva: United Nations Office of Drugs and Crime. https://sherloc.unodc.org/cld/uploads/pdf/2305764E-eBook.pdf Accessed 23 Jul. 2024.

Varisco, Edoardo, Wezeman, Pieter, and Kuimova, Alexander. 2022. *Illicit Small Arms and Light Weapons in Sub-Saharan Africa*. Stockholm International Research Peace Institute. https://www.sipri.org/publications/2022/policy-reports/illicit-small-arms-and-light-weapons-sub-saharan-africa-using-un-reports-arms-embargoes-identify Accessed 23 Jul. 2024.

Willima, David, and Ramachela, Tshegofatso. 2023. 'An Ocean of Weapons: Arms Smuggling to Somalia'. Institute for Security Studies. https://issafrica.org/iss-today/an-ocean-of-weapons-arms-smuggling-to-somalia Accessed 23 Jul. 2024.

Wood, Brian, and Danssaert, Peter. 2020. 'Africa and the 'Grey Market'. *Good Governance Africa*. https://gga.org/africa-and-the-grey-market/ Accessed 23 Jul. 2024.

Zweifel, Mary. 2012. 'Taking up Arms'. *Peace Review: A Journal of Social Justice* 24(1): pp. 108–113. https://doi.org/10.1080/10402659.2012.651041 Accessed 23 Jul. 2024.

7

Not Just a Ballistic Affair

Firearms Trafficking, Crime, and Violence in the Caribbean

*Nicolas Florquin, Simon Anderson, Anne-Séverine Fabre, Callixtus Joseph, and Joy St. John**

The Caribbean region suffers from high levels of violent crime by global standards. Homicide rates for 2020 among the member states of the Caribbean Community (CARICOM) were almost three times the world average (Fabre et al. 2023, 36). More recently, the situation deteriorated markedly in several countries, including Antigua and Barbuda, the Bahamas, Jamaica, Saint Lucia, St Vincent and the Grenadines, and Trinidad and Tobago, which all recorded steep increases in their homicide rates between 2020 and 2022 (Maharaj et al. 2024, Table 11). Moreover, more than half of the region's homicides in 2020 involved the use of a firearm. The proportion of gun homicides reaches even higher levels in several states that are the most affected by violence: 90 per cent in Jamaica, 84 per cent in Haiti, 78 per cent in Trinidad and Tobago, and 75 per cent in the Bahamas (Fabre et al. 2023, 38). Notwithstanding some significant national-level variations, gun violence is overall an important contributor to the Caribbean's high levels of crime and violence.

In addition to causing human casualties, firearms-related violence imposes high costs on the Caribbean society, which means that scarce resources

* The authors are grateful to Maria Garcia-Joseph and to the many individuals and institutions that contributed indirectly to this chapter through their work on the Caribbean Firearms Study, as acknowledged in Fabre et al. (2023, 8–9). They include but are not limited to the German Federal Foreign Office, CARICOM IMPACS, CARPHA, the Small Arms Survey, the George Alleyne Chronic Disease Research Centre at the University of the West Indies, the Research Institute for Social Sciences at Anton de Kom University, Arquebus Solutions, Joeleita Agard, Mark Antrobus, Gianluca Boo, André Desmarais, Rufus Ferdinand, Georgiana Gordon-Strachan, Danielle Jemmott, Michael Jones, Aaron Karp, Reginald King, Matt Schroeder, Randy Seepersad, Natasha Sobers, Jason Toppin, Elizabeth Ward, and Hugh Wong.

Nicolas Florquin, Simon Anderson, Anne-Séverine Fabre, Callixtus Joseph, and Joy St. John, *Not Just a Ballistic Affair* In: *Illicit Firearms Markets and Organized Crime*. Edited by: David Bright, Oxford University Press. © Oxford University Press 2025. DOI: 10.1093/9780198902409.003.0008 are taken away from other important public services such as health, education, and infrastructure. For instance, research has found that treating a single firearms injury can cost between two to eleven times the annual per capita health spending of the Bahamas, Barbados, and Jamaica (Fabre et al. 2023, 144). The pervasive use of firearms in the Caribbean has significant repercussions not only for crime rates but also for public health and economic stability across the region. In Haiti, escalating gang-related violence has heavily disrupted health operations—healthcare workers have been shot, injured, or kidnapped, leading to the closure or suspension of health facilities due to concerns for the safety of patients and personnel. Pharmacies have also been burned down, affecting the supply of medicine (St John 2024)

This chapter aims to shed light on the linkages between illicit firearms markets, organized crime, and firearms-related violence in the Caribbean context. Although the relationship between gangs, drugs, and firearms is often more complex than commonly assumed, gangs and other organized criminal groups are undeniably actors in the Caribbean gun violence equation that deserve further study (Baird, Bishop, and Kerrigan 2023). The policy discourse surrounding this issue has intensified, following CARICOM Heads of Government's April 2023 declaration of crime and violence as a public health emergency, underscoring the critical need to address the dual challenges of gangs and illicit firearms proliferation (CARICOM 2023). This chapter therefore contributes to these discussions by exploring the nexus between firearms, crime, and violence, including the role of gangs and organized crime groups; it analyses the dynamics of illicit firearms trafficking in the Caribbean region, including the types of weapons, sources, and techniques involved; and identifies challenges and efforts in countering illicit firearms trafficking and associated crime and violence in the region.

The chapter draws in part on research undertaken as part of the Caribbean Firearms Study, which is a joint report by the CARICOM Implementation Agency for Crime and Security (IMPACS) and the Small Arms Survey (see Fabre et al. 2023). Sources consulted therefore include official datasets (relating both to seized illicit weapons and gun crime data) shared by Caribbean state agencies and those of other 'source' countries; qualitative interviews with seventy-seven inmates serving firearms-related sentences in Belize, Suriname, and Trinidad and Tobago; US court documents relating to outbound cases of firearms trafficking to the Caribbean; and research on gunshot wounds undertaken in hospitals in the Bahamas, Barbados, and Jamaica (Fabre et al. 2023, 28–31).

The chapter also incorporates more recently published scientific literature, reports by specialized United Nations bodies and agencies, and press reports in order to update the analysis and delve deeper into issues of particular relevance to this volume. While most of the data and analysis focuses on the fifteen member states and six associate members of CARICOM, complementary data from other countries in the region is also included where available.

The chapter is divided into three main substantive sections. It first examines the actors involved in firearms trafficking and related violence, and the associated impacts on public health and societies. The chapter then delves more deeply into the main types of illicit firearms circulating in the Caribbean, before documenting current knowledge about the sources and trafficking methods used for acquiring illicit firearms in the region. The final section concludes with a discussion of the chapter's policy implications.

Actors and Impacts

This section discusses the actors involved in firearms trafficking and misuse in the Caribbean. It then examines the impacts of firearms-related violence on Caribbean societies, with a specific focus on the public health dimensions.

Actors

The Latin America and Caribbean region as a whole is affected by a range of socio-economic drivers of crime, including social inequalities, poverty, urbanization, impunity, and delayed justice provision (Jaitman and Machin 2016, 3; Eller 2024, 1). Situated between South and North America, the Caribbean is also exposed to a number of transnational security issues—including drug trafficking, gang violence, and organized crime—that illicit firearms can exacerbate (Fabre et al. 2023, 35, 41). The Caribbean emerged as a regional drug trafficking route in the 1990s as Colombian cartels fragmented and Mexican drug trafficking organizations rose as key players. These developments coincided with a boom in homicides at the turn of the millennium in countries such as Trinidad and Tobago, where gangs and organized criminal groups engaged in this trade and benefited from drug-related firearms flows (Baird, Bishop, and Kerrigan 2023, 2).

The relationship between drugs, gangs, organized crime groups, and illicit firearms in the Caribbean has been less systematic in more recent years, however. In Trinidad and Tobago, homicide rates continued increasing in the 2010s despite reductions in the regional drug trade—which by then had been partly rerouted from the Caribbean to Central America. Gangs nevertheless continued contributing to lethal violence, suggesting that 'residual' firearms and local cultures of violence in Trinidad and Tobago have also contributed to the increasing homicide rates (Baird, Bishop, and Kerrigan 2023, 2–3). The disconnect between drug trafficking and lethal violence observed in Trinidad and Tobago stands in contrast with the more recent situation in Europe. Indeed, the 2016 peace agreement in Colombia is reported to have contributed to the fragmentation of organized criminal groups controlling the cocaine trade in Colombia. This fragmentation enabled smaller European trafficking networks to gain access to the wholesale cocaine market, thereby creating new competition for established organized criminal groups and contributing to an increase in drug-related violence among these actors in Europe (De Schutter and Duquet 2023; and see Chapter 10 for discussion of firearms trafficking networks).

On the other hand, a longstanding 'guns for drugs' trafficking route between Haiti and Jamaica—two countries particularly affected by both gang- and gun-related violence—has existed since the early 2000s. Recent estimates suggest this barter trade may be worth \$1.3–1.7 million a year (UNSC 2024, 9-10). As a result of diminishing state capacities, Haitian gangs have grown into powerful criminal organizations. As of early 2024, Haitian gangs controlled swathes of territory including domestic trading routes, maritime ports, and other critical infrastructure that allowed them to move illicit firearms, drugs, and other illicit goods with impunity (UNSC 2024).

While gang-related violence in the Caribbean tends to occur in urban settings, rural settings are also affected in some countries such as in Haiti.[1] In Jamaica, gangs account for 70 per cent of all homicides, most of which involve the use of a firearm (Fabre et al. 2023, 38, 41). Haiti, Jamaica, and Trinidad and Tobago reportedly have more than 100 gangs each, largely due to the fragmentation of existing groups (Fabre et al. 2023, 41).

[1] The UN reported in 2023 that gang violence in rural areas north of Port-au-Prince accelerated sharply after July 2022, and that between 'January 2022 and October 2023, more than 1,690 people were killed, injured or kidnapped in these rural localities, some 100 km north of the capital, Port-au-Prince'. See OHCHR (2023, 13–15).

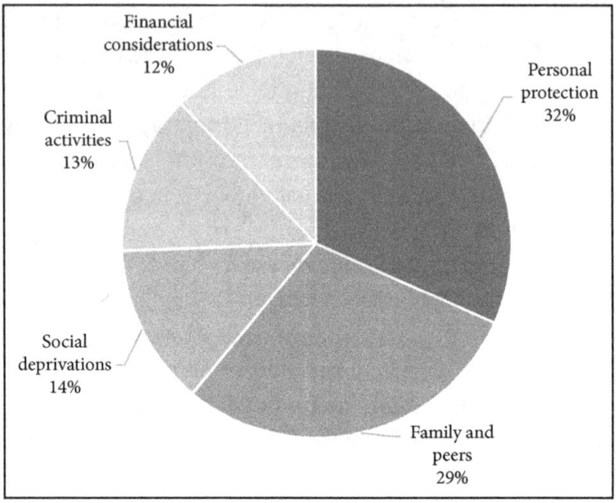

Figure 7.1 Motives for acquiring an illicit firearm, based on interviews with 77 inmates in Belize, Suriname, and Trinidad and Tobago
Source: Fabre et al. (2023, 41), reproduced with permission from CARICOM IMPACS and Small Arms Survey.

While gang-related dynamics of formation and influence are often context-specific, a common feature is the involvement of young men as both the main perpetrators and victims of gang-related violence (Fabre et al. 2023, 38). Although men tend to dominate gangs while women often act as 'peace-makers', women and girls are also affected by, or sometimes even complicit in, certain gang activities—ranging from warning male gang members of the movements of police and rival groups to direct involvement in scamming schemes (Levy, 2012, 34–36; Weekes, 2023, 24–25). Research has also shown that 'engaging with gangs makes women highly vulnerable to sexual and gender-based violence' (Baird, Bishop, and Kerrigan 2022, 635).

In this context, young people's exposure to and perceptions of firearms from an early age are causes for concern. Qualitative interviews with inmates in Belize, Suriname, and Trinidad and Tobago revealed that personal protection, family and peers, and criminal activities were their main motivations for acquiring illicit firearms (Figure 7.1; see also Chapter 11 of this volume). Half of the surveyed inmates reported having accessed a firearm while they were adolescents—the youngest explained how he found a firearm in his neighbourhood and played with it regularly from the age of six (Fabre et al. 2023, 41). According to investigative media reporting, local gangs and their younger members in particular seem most interested in the 'bigger' firearms, namely semi-automatic rifles and pistols converted to automatic fire (*The Trinidad & Tobago Guardian* 2023; see also below on conversion devices).

Impacts and Costs

As reflected in this chapter's introduction, firearms-related homicides contribute significantly to the high rates of lethal violence observed in the Caribbean region. Mortality data compiled by the Caribbean Public Health Agency (CARPHA) for 2019 across fifteen CARPHA member states shows that firearms-related deaths also contribute to high regional levels of mortality overall, and particularly among youth. In this sample, firearms-related deaths accounted on average for 47 per cent of all deaths in the 15–24 age group.[2] Based on an examination of death certificates and International Classification of Diseases (ICD) codes, 39 per cent of 153 recorded lethal firearms-related assaults (i.e. homicides) involved the use of a handgun, while 61 per cent involved the discharge of another type of firearm or an unspecified firearm. These trends raise public policy concerns about so many lives being lost among one of the region's most productive age groups. The data also highlights the need for better coordination and information exchange between the security, forensic, and public health sectors to better classify and document the different types of firearms resulting in these deaths.

In addition to inflicting death and injuries, crime and violence have a range of impacts on the short and long term that also feature complex economic, social, and psychological dimensions. These impacts affect societies at the individual, family, community, and society levels. It is therefore particularly challenging to try to assess such consequences comprehensively.

One approach to document these impacts involves estimating the monetary value of a range of direct costs resulting from violence that require payments from individuals or institutions, and indirect costs that capture lost resources and opportunities (Fabre et al. 2023, 127). Previous crime-costing estimates in the Caribbean have accounted for the victims' loss in

[2] The data is based on a review of 25,513 validated death certificates of persons of all ages from fifteen CARPHA member states (Anguilla, Antigua and Barbuda, Aruba, Belize, British Virgin Islands, Cayman Islands, Dominica, Grenada, Guyana, Montserrat, Saint Kitts and Nevis, Saint Lucia, Saint Vincent and the Grenadines, Trinidad and Tobago, and Turks and Caicos Islands). This data set did not include Jamaica, where the proportion of firearms-related deaths among youth is expected to be even higher. Data shared through correspondence by the Health Information, Communicable Diseases and Emergency Response (HCE) department at CARPHA, 11 April 2024.

quality of life, forgone income due to incarceration, private sector expenses for security and crime prevention, and public spending on police services, the judiciary system, and the administration of prisons. One regional study estimated these costs to amount to up to 4.8 per cent of GDP in the Bahamas, 2.7 per cent in Barbados, 4 per cent in Jamaica, and 3.5 per cent in Trinidad and Tobago in 2014—which were higher estimates than seen in the United States, for instance (Jaitman and Torre 2017, 26–27). Crime and violence therefore consume a significant proportion of Caribbean countries' revenue stream.

A focus on the direct medical costs incurred by the victims makes it possible to more specifically evaluate the costs of firearms-related violence. Based on a review of medical notes concerning 298 victims of violence-related injuries in the Bahamas, Barbados, and Jamaica in 2019,[3] the Caribbean Firearms Study compared the costs generated by firearms-related violence with those of violence involving other weapons or 'mechanisms'. It found that on average, gunshot wounds tend to result in higher medical costs than injuries caused by knives or other objects (Fabre et al. 2023, 126). This finding is consistent with previous costing studies, as well as with other literature that finds that the type of weapon used affects the severity of the violent outcome and, by extension, its costs to society (see Florquin 2021).

Moreover, the Caribbean Firearms Study documented that the average medical expenditure required to treat a single firearm injury was equivalent to between two and eleven times the annual per capita public health spending in the three countries under review (Fabre et al. 2023, 144). Even so, these findings are underestimates, given that patients' medical records were often incomplete or missing (Fabre et al. 2023, 139). They nevertheless illustrate the significant burden that gunshot wounds impose on Caribbean societies, whose scarce resources therefore need to be diverted from other public priorities to care for the consequences of firearms misuse.

A Regional Typology of Illicit Firearms

This section documents the main types of illicit firearms circulating in the Caribbean. The analysis covers the main types of firearms—including revolvers, pistols, rifles and carbines, shotguns, and machine guns—as well as

[3] The George Alleyne Chronic Disease Research Centre at the University of the West Indies coordinated this field work.

their parts, accessories, and ammunition. The term 'illicit' refers to weapons and ammunition that are held, modified, produced, transferred, or used in violation of national or international law (Schroeder 2014, 246). Three main characteristics are highlighted here: the prominence of handguns, the emerging threat posed by a range of privately made firearms, and the circulation of conversion devices that transform handguns and rifles into more lethal fully automatic weapons.

Handguns (Still) Prevail Over Rifles

Handguns (i.e. pistols and revolvers) and their associated ammunition are overall the most prominent category of illicit weapon in the Caribbean, presumably due to their concealable nature and—for the time being—greater availability on illicit markets. Drawing from a range of international and national official sources, the Caribbean Firearms Study concluded that handguns represent—by a margin—the main category of illicit firearms documented in the region. For instance, 88 per cent of firearms tracing requests submitted by Caribbean countries to INTERPOL in 2015–21 concerned handguns (primarily pistols), while only 5 per cent referred to rifles. Similarly, 87 per cent of tracing requests submitted to tracing to the US Bureau of Alcohol, Tobacco, Firearms, and Explosives (ATF) from 2016–20 concerned handguns, compared with just 4 per cent of rifles (Fabre et al. 2023, 70).

Ballistic data on 1,429 cartridges fired at the scenes of violent crime—i.e. homicides, attempted homicides and assaults—in ten Caribbean countries and territories from 2016 to 2021 similarly showed the dominance of calibres typically used with handguns. In fact, the five ammunition calibres most frequently recovered at the crime scenes were all primarily destined for use with pistols and accounted for 91 per cent of the entire dataset (Fabre et al. 2023, 104–105).

Remarkably, the makes and models of the most commonly seized handguns are also quite consistent across the sub-region (Fabre et al. 2023, 67): Glock, Taurus, Beretta, and Smith & Wesson pistols systematically top the list of seizures Table 7.1). These findings suggest that the pool of illicit firearms in the Caribbean is rather consistent across the region and that contextual factors, such as different Caribbean countries' relative proximity to neighbouring firearms-producing states in South, Central or North America, have only a limited impact on the pool of available illicit firearms.

Table 7.1 Top Makes of Seized Pistols Submitted for Tracing by States in Different Subregions of the Caribbean, 2015–21

Northern Caribbean states*		**Caribbean states located in or near South America****	
Brand	**Percentage (n = 568)**	**Brand**	**Percentage (n = 1,296)**
Glock	27%	Glock	29%
Taurus	20%	Smith & Wesson	13%
Smith & Wesson	11%	Beretta	12%
Beretta	5%	Taurus	10%
Ruger	3%	Tanfoglio	4%
SIG Sauer	3%	Weihrauch	3%
Bersa	3%	Rossi	3%
FN	3%	JA Industries***	3%
Colt	2%	Walther	3%
Springfield	2%	Ruger	2%
Other	21%	Other	18%

Notes:

* Data in this column includes seizures in the following states: Bermuda, the Cayman Islands, the Dominican Republic, Haiti, Jamaica, and Turks and Caicos.

** Data in this column includes seizures in the following states: Aruba, Curacao, Guyana, St Lucia, and Trinidad and Tobago.

*** Bryco and Jennings firearms are included in this figure.

Source: Written correspondence with INTERPOL official, 18 April 2022. Table elaborated based on Fabre et al. (2023, 73), with permission from CARICOM IMPACS and Small Arms Survey.

Although rifles still represent a small proportion of seizures overall, Caribbean law enforcement agencies have expressed growing concerns over their proliferation and misuse (Jones 2023). This is the case notably in Trinidad and Tobago, where significant seizures have taken place recently (*The Trinidad & Tobago Guardian* 2023). Another case in point is Haiti, where 15 per cent of firearms submitted for tracing to US ATF during 2016–20 were rifles—a much higher rate compared with the rest of the Caribbean (Fabre et al. 2023, 68). According to the UN Panel of Experts on

Haiti, Haitian gangs have recently intensified their procurement efforts towards semi-automatic rifles. Twenty-three per cent of 191 firearms seized by Haitian authorities between October 2022 and July 2023 were rifles, which is significantly higher than the regional rates observed above (UNSC 2023, para. 93).

What mostly distinguishes Haiti from the rest of the Caribbean is the gangs' demand for and acquisition of military-grade weapons—including 0.50 cal/12.7 mm sniper rifles—usually not seen outside of state control (Roll 2024). For instance, the UN Panel documented instances of gang use of 7.62 x 51 mm belt-fed light machine guns and 12.7 x 99 mm ammunition for use with heavy machine guns or sniper rifles (UNSC 2023, para. 94). In one notorious trafficking case, the leader of the Haitian gang known as '400 Mawozo' and his Florida-based co-defendant pleaded guilty to the trafficking of a 0.50 cal military rifle along with at least twenty-three other firearms—including AK-47s, AR-15s, an M4 carbine rifle, and an M1A rifle—'in containers disguised as food and household goods' that were shipped from the United States to Haiti. 400 Mawozo is notorious for its involvement in gang violence in Haiti, including the alleged kidnapping of fourteen US citizens in 2021 (US DOJ 2024).

Overall, these trends suggest that while illicit handguns still prevail, the Caribbean is becoming increasingly vulnerable to expanding demand for and trafficking in military-style rifles. Still, as a whole the region fares better than other countries in Central and North America, where rates of rifle seizures remain much higher. The percentage of rifles among firearms submitted for tracing to US ATF by Caribbean countries was 4 per cent for 2016–20, compared with 29 per cent for Mexico, 41 per cent for Canada, and 47 per cent for Honduras (Fabre et al., 68–69).

The Growing Threat of Privately Made Firearms

Existing evidence illustrates the growing threat posed by privately made firearms (PMFs) as a source of illicit weapons in the region (see Yarina and Florquin 2024). The US government defines a PMF as 'a firearm, including a frame or receiver, assembled by a person other than a licensed manufacturer, and not containing a serial number or other identifying marking placed by a licensed manufacturer at the time the firearm was produced' (Office of the US Federal Register 2022, 24664).

Although current data limitations make it difficult to assess the exact magnitude of the PMF threat to the Caribbean, authorities have documented these weapons in several countries. The seized PMFs have included crude homemade shotguns, converted flare guns, as well as 'ghost guns' assembled from factory-produced parts and partially finished receivers, which are readily available in the United States (see Fabre et al. 2023; *Loop* 2023b; *The Gleaner* 2023; and TTPS 2023). Computer numerical control (CNC) milled lower receivers used to assemble PMFs have also been seized in several countries, including in Haiti and Trinidad and Tobago (UNSC 2023, para. 102; TTPS 2023). Due to the region's proximity to the United States, the Caribbean appears particularly vulnerable to new types of ghost guns, which are often more difficult to detect and trace than industry-made firearms, as they are often smuggled in parts and do not carry serial numbers.

In August 2023, Trinidad and Tobago became the first Caribbean country to report seizing 3D-printed firearms (*Loop* 2023a; see Chapter 8 for more detailed discussion of 3D-printed firearms). The 3D-printing of firearms poses profound challenges to law enforcement and arms control. Indeed, it provides criminals with the capability to manufacture untraceable and increasingly capable and reliable weapons rather than resorting to illicit markets and trafficking, which are activities the police can more easily detect and investigate (see Schroeder et al. 2023). Although PMFs, overall, still represent a relatively small percentage of illicit firearms in the Caribbean, they are likely to pose a growing threat in the near future that law enforcement and policy-makers need to be well prepared to confront.

Proliferation of Conversion Devices

Illicit accessories known as 'conversion devices' that transform semi-automatic pistols and rifles into fully automatic weapons also circulate in the region. In the United States, seized conversion devices have been imported from China, or have been fabricated at home or in small workshops (Fabre et al. 2023, 99). They have also contributed to a 49 per cent increase in 'suspected automatic gunfire in 2022 in portions of 127 [US] cities', as fully automatic pistols are being seen by teenagers as 'status symbol[s] that provide[ ] a competitive advantage' (*City of Chicago v. Glock Inc.* 2024, 13–14).

Few Caribbean countries have publicly reported seizing conversion devices to date, but this could be due to a lack of awareness, detection, and reporting by the authorities. Indeed, conversion devices are small, simple, and easy-to-install components that do not look anything like firearms or their main components. Law enforcement and border control officials not familiar with these items may therefore not necessarily know how to identify and detect them.

Still, conversion devices have begun circulating in the Caribbean region. This is the case in Trinidad and Tobago, where they were documented in twelve separate seizure incidents between 2020 and 2021 (Fabre et al. 2023, 100). The police in Saint Lucia similarly reported seizing several conversion devices in 2023 (*The Voice* 2023). Investigative media reports and key informants suggest that pistols converted to fully automatic in this way are in high demand among local gangs in Trinidad and Tobago as well as in Jamaica (*The Trinidad & Tobago Guardian* 2023).[4] The proliferation of these devices is a worrying development, as it potentially provides automatic fire capabilities to certain types of rifles and to more concealable handguns, and therefore increases the risk of a single shooting incident resulting in multiple casualties and injuries (including among non-involved bystanders).

Sources and Trafficking Methods for Illicit Firearms

This section reviews the main sources of illicit firearms in the Caribbean region. Trafficking from abroad appears to be the main source, and the methods used by traffickers are becoming better documented. Although it is not a primary source of illicit weapons, the diversion of legal firearms—including ammunition—is also taking place in the region.

Trafficking Sources

The United States stands out as a major source of firearms trafficked to the Caribbean region (Fabre et al. 2023, 18; *The Economist* 2023). US-sourced firearms end up in the region in different ways. In some cases, the firearms are trafficked directly from the US domestic market to the region. Under this scenario, US-based traffickers tend to acquire 'firearms from different sellers through straw purchases, falsely representing the identities of the actual

[4] Participant inputs into the inception meeting of the Advisory Committee of Regional Experts to support the project: 'Pathway to Policy: Integrating Security and Public Health Responses to Firearms Trafficking and Violence in the Caribbean', Barbados, 20–21 November 2023.

purchasers and recipients of the firearms, as well as their ultimate destination' (US DOJ 2023). The Bahamas, for instance, has traced more than 90 per cent of the firearms used in homicides to US manufacturers and retailers. Antigua and Barbuda, the Bahamas, Haiti, and Jamaica have identified the state of Florida as a significant source of trafficked firearms, followed by other coastal states (Fabre et al. 2023, 76). Neighbouring US territories—including the US Virgin Islands, St Martin, and Puerto Rico—are also a source of firearms trafficking to the Caribbean, and notably to the British Virgin Islands (Fabre et al. 2023, 76).

The United States also appears to be a source of illicit ammunition used in the region. US-produced ammunition accounted for almost half (48 per cent) of a sample of 1,429 cartridges recovered at the scenes of violent crime in ten Caribbean countries and territories from 2016 to 2021. In Jamaica, the proportion of US-made ammunition used in similar crimes even reached 83 per cent (Fabre et al. 2023, 108). It is nevertheless possible that at least some of this ammunition was first exported legally either to the Caribbean or a third country, before being diverted in or trafficked into the Caribbean. Indeed, due to the limited markings applied on industrially produced cartridges, it is difficult to trace illicit ammunition and identify its last legal owner.

Trafficking sources are not limited to the United States, however. Firearms smuggled from Venezuela are also of concern, given that country's large weapons stockpile and ongoing political and economic instability. Firearms were reportedly trafficked from Venezuela to several countries, including Trinidad and Tobago as well as to Curaçao, where weapons of Venezuelan origin account for about 20 per cent of the firearms seized in recent years (Fabre et al. 2023, 78–79, 112; *The Trinidad & Tobago Guardian* 2023). Other reported sources of trafficked firearms have included Argentina, Brazil, Colombia, Costa Rica, the Dominican Republic, French Guiana, Guadeloupe, Honduras, Nicaragua, and St Maarten. They also include inter-island trafficking between nearly half the twenty CARICOM member states and associate members as of April 2023 (Fabre et al. 2023, 79; UNSC 2023, para. 103; 2024, 8).

Unlike weapons, the types of ammunition used in violent crime tend to vary according to the sub-region (Figure 7.2). While US-produced ammunition is by far the most prominently used by violent criminals in the northern (70 per cent) and south-eastern Caribbean (60 per cent), the picture is more mixed in the French territories, where more than half of recovered ammunition was manufactured outside the US. In Belize (categorized as the western Caribbean in Figure 7.2), a CARICOM member state, ammunition produced

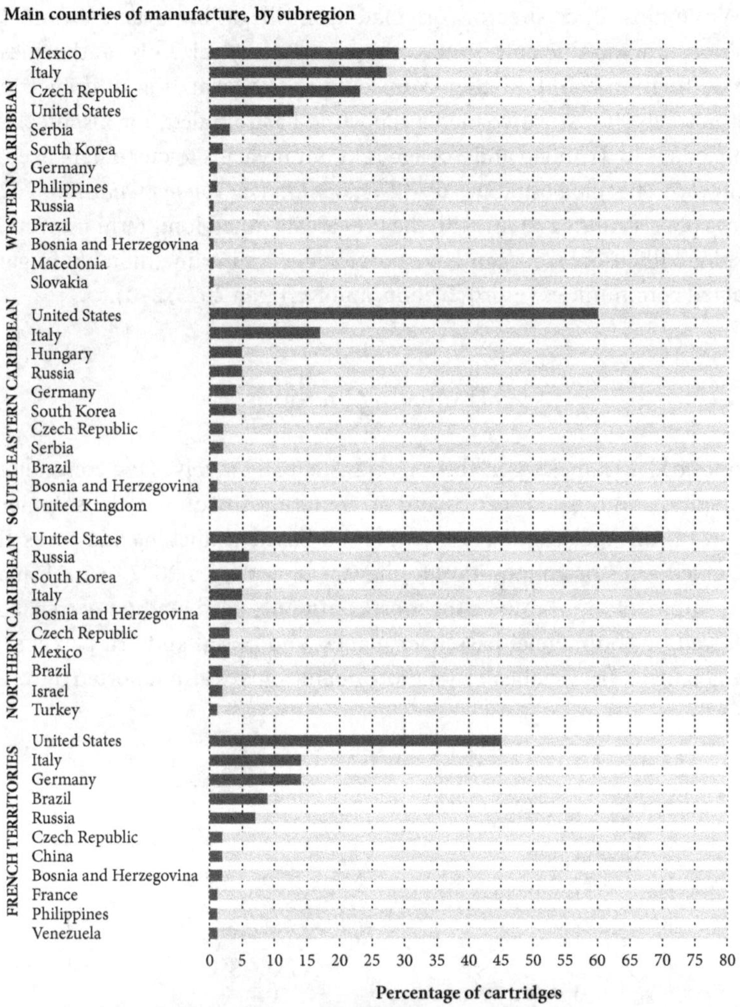

Figure 7.2 Top Ten identified countries of manufacture of 1,429 cartridges used in violent crime incidents in the ten Caribbean countries and territories under review, by subregion, 2016–21

Source: Fabre et al. (2023, 109), reproduced with permission from CARICOM IMPACS and Small Arms Survey.

in neighbouring Mexico represented the largest share (29 per cent) of cartridges recovered from crime scenes, with US-made ammunition ranking fourth (Fabre et al. 2023, 108–115). These patterns suggest that proximity to producing countries influences ammunition trafficking flows.

While most illicit firearms originate from illegal imports, the trafficked weapons are durable and—unless they are rapidly seized by authorities in the destination country—they contribute to the formation of domestic illicit markets. Investigative media reporting has revealed, for instance, that some gangs in Trinidad and Tobago rent out firearms to customers needing them for a specific period or 'job' (*The Trinidad & Tobago Guardian* 2023). These observations concur with the previously noted long-term impact that 'residual' illicit firearms can have on violence and crime, notably in gang-affected communities (Baird, Bishop, and Kerrigan 2023, 2–3).

Trafficking Methods

Cross-border trafficking in the region principally involves the concealment of small quantities of firearms and ammunition in commercial shipments. Based on an analysis of twenty-nine US-based trafficking networks that smuggled arms or ammunition to the Caribbean from 2007 to 2021, maritime shipments appear to be the most commonly used method of transport, followed by commercial passenger planes, and postal and fast parcel services (Figure 7.3). Caribbean law enforcement sources also reported the use of

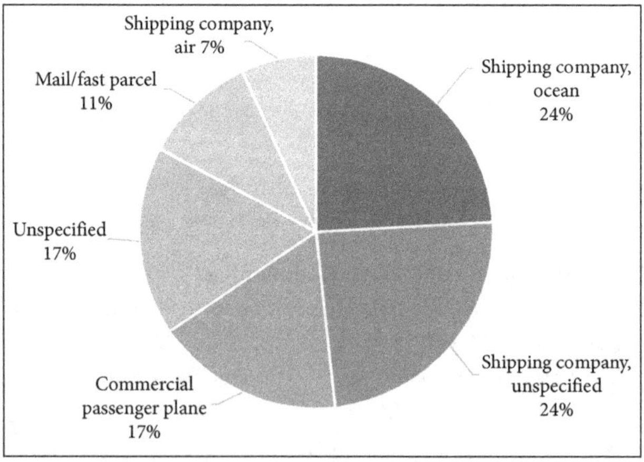

Figure 7.3 Modes of transport used for trafficking firearms and ammunition from the United States to the Caribbean, 2010–21

Source: Fabre et al. (2023, 80), reproduced with permission from CARICOM IMPACS and Small Arms Survey.

private maritime vessels such as yachts and speedboats by traffickers (Fabre et al. 2023, 81).

Smuggled firearms and ammunition can be hidden in a range of household items—including peanut butter jars, cereal boxes, refrigerators, televisions, and toolboxes—that are then packed in containers, in cars and car parts, or hidden within foul-smelling cargo to deter inspections. Smuggling networks use several techniques to conceal the illicit nature of their transactions. When procuring firearms on the US market, they may use false addresses on firearms sales documents, purchase only one or two firearms at a time and from different sellers, and communicate using code names with their clients. Smugglers also obliterate serial numbers, declare the firearms they ship as other types of items, and use aliases in shipping documents (Fabre et al. 2023, 82–87).

Haiti also suffers primarily from small-scale 'ant trafficking' that typically involves only a few firearms at a time. Shipments to Haiti appear to have gained in frequency, however, and some cases have comprised relatively large quantities. A January 2022 seizure, for instance, recovered twenty-three firearms and 120,000 rounds of ammunition in a single shipment (UNSC 2023, para. 88). Haitian trafficking networks appear to use similar techniques as in the rest of the Caribbean and involve a range of actors, including 'straw buyers in the United States, money carriers, freight forwarders, government officials and small illicit market traders in Haiti selling to the highest bidders' (UNSC 2023, para. 89).

Overall, the methods used to traffic firearms in the Caribbean are relatively simple. They have been successful despite their lack of sophistication due to the vast amounts of commercial shipments moving to and within the region, which makes the control of all consignments impossible for the authorities.

Diversion of Legal Weapons

The region's relatively strict controls over and low levels of legal possession of firearms seem to provide limited opportunities for criminals to divert legal weapons to the illicit markets. Indeed, the Caribbean region averages about 1.6 registered firearms per 100 residents, which is a low rate of legal civilian firearm ownership by international standards (Fabre et al. 2023, 43–64). Interviews with inmates in Belize, Suriname, and Trinidad and Tobago seemed to confirm the prevalence of foreign sources as the main way to acquire illicit firearms in the region (twenty-seven respondents), with few respondents (two) reporting the use of domestic sources (Fabre et al. 2023, 74).

Diversion of legal firearms nevertheless occurs in the region, even if on a smaller scale than cross-border trafficking. In Haiti, close to 2,500 police firearms were lost or stolen between 2012 and 2023, contributing to the arming of local criminals and gangs. While Haitian gangs often target the police to steal their firearms, there have been cases of police officers illegally selling their ammunition (UNSC 2023, paras 106–107). Authorities in Haiti also lack the resources to effectively monitor firearms that are registered to civilians and private security companies, which makes this materiel vulnerable to diversion (UNSC 2023, para. 109).

Moreover, ATF data shows that almost a quarter of firearms seized in the Caribbean and that were traced to the US during 2017–20 were legally exported to entities outside the United States, before they were diverted in or trafficked to the Caribbean. The Dominican Republic and Belize stand out as two countries in the region where a high proportion of seized firearms have been traced to authorized foreign importers of US weapons (Fabre et al. 2023, 76). Publicly available ATF data does not reveal whether these importers are located in the Caribbean or other regions, however. More research is therefore needed to better understand this pattern of diversion.

Several sources indicate that the region's legally held ammunition may be more vulnerable to diversion than its firearms. Most of the interviewed inmates in Belize, Suriname, and Trinidad and Tobago who contributed information on this topic reported acquiring their ammunition together with firearms (twenty-four respondents). Almost as many interviewees reported sourcing ammunition in local communities through community members, shops, and 'the street' (twenty respondents) (Fabre et al. 2023, 122). Interviews with law enforcement officials also revealed concerns over ammunition sold at shooting ranges, which can be challenging to fully account for. In Barbados, for instance, at least two persons were arrested and charged for buying ammunition from shooting ranges and selling it on the street (Fabre et al. 2023, 124).

In Trinidad and Tobago, authorities have investigated cases of ammunition marked as belonging to the Trinidad and Tobago Police Service and Trinidad and Tobago Regiment, and that were subsequently used in crime. While investigations were still ongoing at the time of writing, national forensic experts suggested the spent cartridges may have initially been sold to and used in shooting ranges. The spent casings were then possibly recycled by criminals to produce functioning homemade or reloaded ammunition (*The Trinidad Express* 2023). There is evidence of the use of self-loaded ammunition elsewhere in the Caribbean. Indeed, spent ammunition produced by companies that specialize in the production of empty casings have been recovered at crime scenes. Ammunition primers and loading equipment have also been seized en-route to the Caribbean (Fabre et al. 2023, 124).

Policy Implications

This chapter has examined firearms trafficking in the Caribbean in a regional context of rising homicide rates that surpass the world average by a ratio of three to one and the escalating political, humanitarian, and security crisis in Haiti. It documented context-specific and complex relationships between illicit firearms, drug trafficking, organized crime, and gang-related violence. Demographically, young men are both the primary perpetrators and direct victims of firearms misuse. Geographically, firearms violence mainly affects urban settings, and notably so in communities where cultures of violence have long been exacerbated by gangs and the availability of illicit firearms. The situation in Haiti stands out as an outlier, however, as gang-related violence is expanding beyond the capital city and into rural areas.

The chapter showed that while the Caribbean remains less exposed than some of its neighbours to the proliferation of weapons of particular concern such as rifles, the situation could quickly deteriorate. The evolving security crisis and proliferation of military-grade firearms in Haiti, the trafficking in parts used for assembling new generations of privately made firearms, and the illicit conversion of handguns and rifles to automatic fire are creating new regional security and public health challenges for containing gun-related crime and violence. Continued deterioration of the regional security environment would have profoundly negative consequences for the region—not only for the individuals involved in or victimized by the violence, but also for Caribbean societies as a whole who will need to divert increasing amounts of public and private resources to contain and respond to the violence.

On 18 April 2023, the CARICOM heads of government declared crime and violence to be a public health emergency and committed to a multi-sectoral and whole-of-society approach for addressing these challenges. The series of measures they called for included overhauling the criminal justice system, strengthening regional forensic capabilities and intelligence-sharing, promoting the regional harmonization of laws, applying pressure on US gun manufacturers and retailers, empowering and engaging young people, and supporting communities and victims (CARICOM 2023). Recognizing that 'the roots of antisocial behaviour go back to one's childhood', some governments have suggested that preventative measures also be put in place from a very early age, such as early warning systems that enable 'governments and their social partners to act as soon as red flags of antisocial behaviour' appear. Establishing such a prevention system would involve 'redefining the roles and functions of [the] police, . . . schools, and . . . primary and secondary healthcare facilities' (OPM Saint Lucia 2024).

Several measures to curtail the supply of illicit firearms are already being pushed forward. In 2020, CARICOM member states and the Dominican Republic adopted the Caribbean Firearms Roadmap, which contains a series of priority actions to strengthen weapons and ammunition controls and boost capacities to detect and tackle firearms trafficking by 2030 (CARICOM IMPACS and UNLIREC 2020). The United States also strengthened its cooperation and intelligence-sharing with the region, reinforced its counter-trafficking legislation and increased its capacities to prosecute US-based traffickers, as well as provided related funding and training to Caribbean countries (Lee 2023; US DOS 2024).

The region, through CARICOM IMPACS, is actively enhancing its firearms-related crime intelligence capacities, particularly with initiatives such as the establishment of the CARICOM Crime Gun Intelligence Unit. (see CARICOM 2024). This strategic development is essential for effectively monitoring trafficking networks, identifying smuggling routes, and addressing emerging forms of illicit firearms, thereby supporting law enforcement agencies and public prosecutors across the Caribbean in efforts to remove illegal firearms from circulation, reduce gun violence, and strengthen the prosecution of firearm-related offenses.

Despite advancements in the digital age, many processes across the region remain largely analogue, underscoring the urgent need for digital transformation to enhance early warning and monitoring systems. However, this transformation requires more than just technology: it demands well trained human resources; streamlined, robust systems; and cross-sectoral connectivity to fully realize its potential. Strengthening the regional intelligence picture on illicit firearms will be critical for anticipating the impact of emerging threats—including concerns over a possible increase in the availability of high powered and fully automatic weapons—which pose significant risks to both crime control and public health.

Enhanced digitalization will improve data analysis capabilities, enabling the collection, analysis, and dissemination of real-time information on illicit firearms trends across various societal sectors, including—but not limited to—the security sector. This broader, multisectoral approach is crucial to ensure that timely, evidence-based prevention and mitigation strategies are effectively implemented across the region.

In light of the Caribbean region's specific geographical configuration and vulnerabilities, ongoing efforts to limit the supply of illicit firearms will not prove sufficient on their own to reduce violence levels meaningfully. As noted by Patel et al. (2022), comprehensive and multi-sectoral approaches are essential for rolling back in a sustainable manner the 'violence-supportive norms' that contribute to sustaining firearms-related violence. Implementing a whole-of-society approach as articulated by the heads of government will require Caribbean countries to invest in systems to identify and monitor risk and protective factors related to firearms trafficking and gun violence. Governments and their civil society partners will also need to design, test, and evaluate violence prevention initiatives that simultaneously address the root factors of violence and reduce access to illicit firearms. When doing so, programme designers should carefully take into consideration and build upon the lessons learned from previous relevant efforts in the region (Ward and Sutton 2024, 2).

Conclusions

The key to success in the region's efforts to reduce firearms-related crime and violence lies in its ability to translate the ambitious political commitments made to date into concrete, well-coordinated, and measurable actions (see Griffith 2023). Firearms-related violence in the Caribbean is not intractable, and can be prevented or, at minimum, reduced, similar to how public health efforts have prevented many infectious diseases. The factors that contribute to violent responses—whether they are factors of attitude and behaviour or related to larger social, economic, political, and cultural conditions—can be changed. There is an urgent need to de-normalize violence and crime. Illicit firearms—as the primary and highly symbolic mechanism used in violence in the Caribbean—are part of this normalization process and should therefore be tackled simultaneously.

References

Baird, Adam, Bishop, Matthew Louis, and Kerrigan, Dylan. 2022. '"Breaking Bad"? Gangs, Masculinities, and Murder in Trinidad'. *International Feminist Journal of Politics* 24 (4): pp. 632–657. https://doi.org/10.1080/14616742.2021.1931395 Accessed 23 Jul. 2024.

Baird, Adam, Bishop, Matthew Louis, and Kerrigan, Dylan. 2023. 'Differentiating the Local Impact of Global Drugs and Weapons Trafficking: How Do Gangs Mediate "Residual Violence" to Sustain Trinidad's Homicide Boom?' *Political Geography* 106 (102966): pp. 1–16. https://doi.org/10.1016/j.polgeo.2023.102966 Accessed 23 Jul. 2024.

CARICOM. 2023. 'Declaration by Heads of Government on Crime and Violence as a Public Health Issue—Trinidad and Tobago' (18 Apr. 2023), https://safecaribbean.caricom.org/declaration-by-heads-of-government-on-crime-and-violence-as-a-public-health-issue-trinidad-and-tobago-18-april-2023/ Accessed 23 Jul. 2024.

CARICOM. 2024. '"Trafficking of Illegal Weapons into any Nation is a Breach of its Borders" SKN PM'. Press Release (30 Apr.2024), https://caricom.org/trafficking-of-illegal-weapons-into-any-nation-is-a-direct-breach-of-its-borders-skn-pm/ Accessed 23 Jul. 2024.

CARICOM IMPACS (Caribbean Community Implementation Agency for Crime and Security) and UNLIREC (United Nations Regional Centre for Peace, Disarmament and Development in Latin America and the Caribbean). 2020. *Roadmap for Implementing the Caribbean Priority Actions on the Illicit Proliferation of Firearms and Ammunition across the Caribbean in a Sustainable Manner by 2030*. https://www.pgaction.org/pdf/2022/unlirec-caribbean-firearms-roadmap-presentation-to-pga-oct-2022.pdf Accessed 27 Jul. 2024.

City of Chicago v Glock Inc. 2024. 'Civil Action No. 2024CH02216. Complaint and Demand for Jury Trial'. Filed 19 March. https://everytownlaw.org/documents/2024/03/3052.pdf/ Accessed 23 Jul. 2024.

De Schutter, Astrid, and Duquet, Nils. 2023. *The Nexus Between Drug Markets and Gun Violence in the European Union*. Lisbon: European Monitoring Centre for Drugs and Drug Addiction. October. https://vlaamsvredesinstituut.eu/en/report/the-nexus-between-drug-markets-and-gun-violence-in-the-european-union/ Accessed 23 Jul. 2024.

Eller, Jack David. 2024. 'In the Shadow of the Giant: Gun Violence in Latin America and the Caribbean'. In *Gun Violence and Prevention - Connections, Cultures, and Consequences*, edited by Jack David Eller, pp. 1–18. London: IntechOpen. https://www.intechopen.com/online-first/1171308 Accessed 23 Jul. 2024.

Fabre, Anne-Séverine, Florquin, Nicolas, Karp, Aaron, and Schroeder, Matt. 2023. *Weapons Compass: The Caribbean Firearms Study*. Port of Spain and Geneva: CARICOM IMPACS and Small Arms Survey. https://www.smallarmssurvey.org/resource/weapons-compass-caribbean-firearms-study Accessed 23 Jul. 2024.

Florquin, Nicolas. 2021. 'Gun Violence: Insights from International Research'. *Global Crime*. https://doi.org/10.1080/17440572.2021.1997741 Accessed 23 Jul. 2024.

Griffith, Ivelaw Loyd. 2023. *The Crime Conundrum in the Caribbean*. Report. Washington DC: The Global Americans. https://theglobalamericans.org/wp-content/uploads/2023/05/The-Crime-Conundrum-in-the-Caribbean-Ivelaw-Griffith.pdf Accessed 23 Jul. 2024.

Jaitman, Laura, and Machin, Stephen. 2016. 'Crime and Violence in Latin America and the Caribbean: Towards Evidence-Based Policies'. *CentrePiece* Winter 2015/16. London: Centre for Economic Performance at the London School of Economics and Political Science. https://cep.lse.ac.uk/pubs/download/cp461.pdf Accessed 23 Jul. 2024.

Jaitman, Laura, and Torre, Iván. 2017. 'A Systematic Approach to Measuring the Costs of Crime in 17 Latin American and Caribbean Countries'. In *The Costs of Crime and Violence: New Evidence and Insights in Latin America and the Caribbean*, edited by Laura Jaitman, pp. 19–29. Washington. DC: IDB.

Jones, Esther. 2023. 'The Tropical Journey of a Firearm'. *Caribbean Investigative Journalism Network* (2 Aug. 2023), https://www.cijn.org/the-tropical-journey-of-a-firearm/ Accessed 23 Jul. 2024.

Lee, A.L. 2023. 'Harris Announces $100M Initiative to Fight Climate Change, Arms Smuggling in Caribbean' *United Press International* (8 Jun. 2023), https://www.upi.com/Top_News/US/2023/06/08/bahamas-Harris-announces-new-initiatives-on-climate-firearms-smuggling/5201686227899/ Accessed 23 Jul. 2024.

Levy, H. 2012. *Youth Violence and Organized Crime in Jamaica: Causes and Counter-Measures.* Technical report. Kingston: The University of the West Indies (UWI) – Institute of Criminal Justice and Security.

Loop. 2023a. '3D Printed Guns Seized in Raid on Caparo House' (30 Aug 2023), https://tt.loopnews.com/content/3d-printed-guns-seized-raid-caparo-house Accessed 23 Jul. 2024.

Loop. 2023b. 'American Jailed for Trafficking 'Ghost Guns' to Dominican Republic' (31 Dec. 2023), https://caribbean.loopnews.com/content/american-jailed-trafficking-ghost-guns-dominican-republic?utm_campaign=American%20jailed%20for%20trafficking%20%27ghost%20guns%E2%80%99%20to%20Dominican%20Republic&utm_medium=push&utm_source=firebase&utm_content=web Accessed 23 Jul. 2024.

Maharaj, Sandeep, et al. 2024. 'A Public Health Approach to Reducing Violence Within the CARICOM Region'. *Frontiers in Public Health* 12 (15 Feb. 2024), https://doi.org/10.3389/fpubh.2024.1344387 Accessed 23 Jul. 2024.

Office of the High Commissioner for Human Rights (OHCHR). 2023. *Criminal Violence Extends Beyond Port-au-Prince.* Geneva and Port-au-Prince: OHCHR and BINUH. https://www.ohchr.org/sites/default/files/documents/countries/haiti/Haiti-report-criminal-violence-artibonite-2023-EN.pdf Accessed 23 Jul. 2024.

Office of the Prime Minister of Saint Lucia (OPM Saint Lucia). 2024. 'Key Note Address at the 68th Annual Health Research Conference'. https://opmsaintlucia.com/news/speeches/key-note-address-at-the-68th-annual-heath-research-conference?fbclid=IwZXh0bgNhZW0CMTEAAR0wMTKzi7KJ0eHALKX7G-01m7axN65JA1RNmBuRgkD03NniXcE93jmMS10_aem_Af5S_3dsfKvdhh_zfLCG1Yk20fZ8dNwriYn0gmEHLCfHIENUhwLR-8sRGV-cq7u4yO2klH6wY8EVgqE4-KSXcYQ5 Accessed 23 Jul. 2024.

Office of the US Federal Register. 2022. 'Definition of "Frame or Receiver" and Identification of Firearms'. *Federal Register* 87 (80) (26 Apr. 2024).

Patel, Jay, et al. 2022. 'Firearm Injury—A Preventable Public Health Issue'. *The Lancet Public Health.* 7 (11): pp. E976–E982. November. https://doi.org/10.1016/S2468-2667(22)00233-X Accessed 23 Jul. 2024.

Roll, Nicholas. 2024. 'Behind Haiti Violence, Smuggled Guns From The US'. Agence France Presse News (15 Mar. 2024), https://www.barrons.com/news/behind-haiti-violence-smuggled-guns-from-the-us-1a45c61d Accessed 23 Jul. 2024.

Schroeder, Matt. 2014. 'On the Record: Illicit Weapons in the United States'. In *Small Arms Survey 2014: Women and Guns*, pp. 241–273. Cambridge: Cambridge University Press.

Schroeder, Matt, Florquin, Nicolas, Fabre, Anne-Séverine, and Varisco, Andrea. 2023. *Privately Made Firearms in the European Union.* Project INSIGHT research report. Brussels and Geneva: Flemish Peace Institute and Small Arms Survey.

St. John, Joy. 2024. Opening Statement by Executive Director of the Caribbean Public Health Agency (CARPHA), at the 68th CARPHA Research Conference, Saint Lucia, 25 April 2024.

The Economist. 2023. 'The Caribbean is Awash With Illegal American Guns' (5 Oct. 2023), https://www.economist.com/the-americas/2023/10/05/the-caribbean-is-awash-with-illegal-american-guns Accessed 23 Jul. 2024.

The Gleaner. 2023. 'Antigua and Barbuda Police Discover 3D Printed "Ghost Guns"' (5 Sep. 2023), https://jamaica-gleaner.com/article/caribbean/20230905/antigua-and-barbuda-police-discover-3d-printed-ghost-guns Accessed 23 Jul. 2024.

The Trinidad Express. 2023. 'Police, Defence Force Bullets on Crime Scenes' (10 Dec. 2023), https://trinidadexpress.com/news/local/police-defence-force-bullets-on-crime-scenes/article_1836cdfa-970c-11ee-aad2-a7e66b8b03be.html Accessed 23 Jul. 2024.

The Trinidad & Tobago Guardian. 2023. 'Guns Rampage ... more than $129M in Illegal Firearms Recovered in 9 Years' (5 Nov. 2023), https://www.guardian.co.tt/news/guns-rampage--more-than-129m-in-illegal-firearms-recovered-in-9-years-6.2.1844265.d6d337c961 Accessed 23 Jul. 2024.

The Voice. 2023. 'Device Used to Convert Semi-Automatic Weapon into Fully Automatic Weapon Found' (28 Oct. 2023), https://thevoiceslu.com/2023/10/device-used-to-convert-semi-automatic-weapon-into-fully-automatic-weapon-found/ Accessed 23 Jul. 2024.

Trinidad and Tobago Police Service (TTPS). 2023. 'More Firearms, Ammo Seized in Santa Cruz'. Official Facebook account [Facebook post] (18 Oct. 2023), https://www.facebook.com/PoliceServiceTT/posts/pfbid02rkTedMkFtmYofPtA4VLK6JEkJRpAekALnpKp4tP5H6xCXUHFxoqFt2VSeFJNaKabl Accessed 23 Jul. 2024.

United Nations Office on Drugs and Crime (UNODC). 2023. *Haiti's Criminal Markets: Mapping Trends in Firearms and Drug Trafficking.* Vienna: UNODC. https://www.unodc.org/documents/data-and-analysis/toc/Haiti_assessment_UNODC.pdf Accessed 24 Jul. 2024.

United Nations Security Council (UNSC). 2023. *Final Report of the Panel of Experts on Haiti Submitted Pursuant to Resolution 2653 (2022).* S/2023/674 of 15 September. https://documents.un.org/doc/undoc/gen/n23/246/28/pdf/n2324628.pdf?token=Bb5YQBnocv8yKzgHZV&fe=true Accessed 23 Jul. 2024.

United Nations Security Council (UNSC). 2024. Report of the United Nations Office on Drugs and Crime pursuant to paragraph 9 of Security Council resolution 2692 (2023). S/2024/79 of 17 January. https://digitallibrary.un.org/record/4025603?v=pdf&ln=en Accessed 27 Jul. 204.

United States Department of Justice (US DOJ). 2023. 'Two Members of Caribbean Arms Trafficking Ring Sentenced To More Than Four Years In Prison'. Press Release (28 Jul. 2023), https://www.justice.gov/usao-mdfl/pr/two-members-caribbean-arms-trafficking-ring-sentenced-more-four-years-prison Accessed 23 Jul. 2024.

United States Department of Justice (US DOJ). 2024. '"King" of Violent Haitian Gang Pleads Guilty to Gun Smuggling and Money Laundering After Government's Case'. Press Release (1 Feb. 2024), https://www.justice.gov/opa/pr/king-violent-haitian-gang-pleads-guilty-gun-smuggling-and-money-laundering-after-governments Accessed 23 Jul. 2024.

United States Department of State (US DOS). 2024. 'U.S.-Caribbean Engagement to Counter Firearms Trafficking'. Fact Sheet (1 Mar. 2024), https://www.state.gov/u-s-caribbean-engagement-to-counter-firearms-trafficking/ Accessed 23 Jul. 2024.

Ward, Elizabeth, and Sutton, Heather. 2024. 'Violence in the Caribbean: A Public Health Emergency'. *West Indies Medical Journal* 71 (Suppl. 1): pp. 1–4. https://www.mona.uwi.edu/fms/wimj/article/4046 Accessed 23 Jul. 2024.

Weekes, T. 2023. 'Duration and Variation of Active Gangs in Jamaican Communities'. *Journal of Gang Research* 30: pp. 11–36.

Yarina, Y., and Florquin, N. 2024. *Dangerous Devices: Privately Made Firearms in the Caribbean.* https://www.smallarmssurvey.org/sites/default/files/resources/SAS-Situation-Update-2024-Caribbean-PMFs-EN.pdf Accessed 23 Jul. 2024.

PART II

INTERSECTIONS BETWEEN ILLICIT FIREARMS MARKETS AND ORGANIZED CRIME

8

Firearms Technology and Organized Crime

Assessing the Threat

Monique Mann, David Bright, and Ashley Allen

3D-Printing and Firearms

3D-printing (3DP) is used to create a three-dimensional (3D) object by layering materials (usually thermoplastics, but they can also include metals) according to the directions contained within a digital design file or blueprint called a computer aided design (CAD) file (Meyer 2013). These files can be readily downloaded from the surface web (Schaufelbühl et al. 2023), on (dark) market forums, and shared via online networks. A key innovation in 3D-printing is its low cost and simplicity, given 3D-printers are all-in-one devices that do not require modification and can print anything, provided a design file exists (Daly et al. 2021). Like many new technologies there are socially positive applications of 3D-printing, as well as potential nefarious uses such as the manufacture of firearms (Daly et al. 2021). The accessibility of these files and the relative ease of printing firearms raises concerns about the potential for the covert use of such technology by organized criminal groups.

Our examination in this chapter unfolds across four steps. First, we present a brief overview and history of 3DP firearms. Second, we consider laws that criminalize the possession and dissemination of design files, present cases where individuals have been charged and/or prosecuted for this offence in one Australian jurisdiction, and situate this analysis in the context of organized criminal activity. Third, we present our findings in relation to the online availability and dissemination of digital design files and the policies of the platforms that host them. Finally, we consider the merits of a range of legal, policy, and regulatory responses that could be implemented to restrict access to digital design files for the manufacture of 3DP firearms.

Monique Mann, David Bright, and Ashley Allen, *Firearms Technology and Organized Crime* In: *Illicit Firearms Markets and Organized Crime*. Edited by: David Bright, Oxford University Press.
 DOI: 10.1093/9780198902409.003.0009

The costs of 3DP firearms have been rapidly decreasing. For example, in Australia in 2024, a 3D-printer can be purchased for A$200 and a filament is cheap at A$20 per 1 kilogram. Some 3D-printers are capable of printing lower receivers for rifles and frames for Glock handguns at a rate of one every thirty-five minutes (Wintemute 2021). 3DP firearms can include handguns, rifles, and machine guns, representing the range of firearms known to be in demand from members of organized criminal groups (Bright et al. 2023). Although 3DP firearms are constructed mostly from plastic, until recently they required two metal parts (the firing pin and the bullet) to be operational (Daly and Mann 2018). However, recent advances in 3D-printing and materials mean that guns can now be made entirely of plastic, leading to further difficulty in terms of detection. There are also 'modular-type guns' that are interchangeable, allowing for customization, including hybrid guns consisting of both conventional and 3DP components.

The digital design files for firearms that can be downloaded from the Internet and online chat rooms provide instructions and guidance (Wintemute 2021). Schaufelbühl et al. (2023) conducted a systematic study of the availability of 3DP design files on the surface web between 2021 and 2023. They identified 2,133 design files (of which many were duplicates) for 3DP firearms through online searches and via social media accounts of prominent members of the 3DP firearms online community. They note that while the number of design files they were able to access, download, and catalogue was substantial, 'it is not exhaustive' (Schaufelbühl et al. 2023, 3). It also does not include design files accessible through the dark web or files exchanged via peer-to-peer file sharing software. The categorization of design files consisted of fully 3DP firearms (F3DP), parts kits completions (PKC), and hybrid firearms. According to their classification system, firearms are F3DP if 'all essential parts of the 3D-printed firearm, such as the barrel, frame and breech, are printed, and only a few non-printed parts that are needed for their basic functioning (e.g. a nail as a firing pin or rubber bands to operate the moving parts)'. They classified hybrid firearms as '3D-printed firearms containing non-printed parts that are intended to increase reliability (e.g., metal tubes as barrels or other reinforcements)' (Schaufelbühl et al. 2023, 2). According to this classification scheme, there were over 1,500 PKC design files, such as receivers and frames for firearms (Schaufelbühl et al. 2023, 5). A key finding was the increasing publication of design files for hybrid and PKC design files. The number of design files collected and catalogued by Schaufelbühl et al. (2023, 5) shows:

> an acceleration of the activity and an increase in the number of publications in the last few years. This trend is largely due to the PKC designs

> which increased strongly in 2019 before declining somewhat in 2020. This trend was followed by another massive increase, due to the releases of many remixes of already existing PKC firearms. Releases of hybrid firearms have also increased steadily in recent years, but to a lesser extent than PKC.

Schaufelbühl et al. (2024) continued their research on 3DP guns through analysis of global press reports. They identified an exponential increase in 3DP guns reported in the media between 2014 and 2023. The majority of the occurrences of 3DP guns were PKC designs (47 per cent, n = 87), followed by hybrid firearms (34 per cent, n = 64), and 3DP parts (23 per cent, n = 43). Only 8 per cent (n = 14) of the 3DP guns were F3PD. These findings are significant and illustrate some of the challenges in regulating 3DP, as components or parts of firearms can be printed, which may be more difficult to legislate against, detect, and ultimately control, compared with F3DP firearms. Firearms hybridity is a key issue to consider, and the threat that these types of designs pose has been documented by law enforcement agencies. For example, the UK Home Office (2023) held consultation on strengthening law enforcement responses to organized crime which considers new offences, to criminalize the making, modifying, supplying, offering to supply, and possession of articles for use in organized crime such as 3DP guns. In the consultation documents, the UK NCA reported that hybrid firearms designs represent the most significant threat:

> The NCA has reported that it is highly likely that hybrid firearm designs, where 3D-printed components are combined with easily accessible metal non-firearms parts, represent the most significant threat from 3D-printing technologies in criminal firearms manufacture. Self-loading hybrid weapons, assembled from approximately 80% printed parts, have been seized in the UK. As the quality of 3D-printed weapons improve, it is highly likely that viable hybrid firearms will increasingly feature in UK criminality. UK Home Office (2023)

In addition to hybridity, several other factors combine to render 3DP firearms (and components) a significant threat to public safety. As outlined above, 3DP firearms have evolved to become relatively cheap and easily accessible. These firearms are essentially untraceable as they do not have serial numbers like factory manufactured guns, nor do they leave ballistic evidence in the same way as conventional firearms, which may have consequences for investigations and the operation of police information systems.[1] Members of organized criminal groups tend to prefer untraceable firearms such as those without serial numbers or with serial numbers removed (Bright et al. 2023), suggesting that there may be demand for 3DP firearms among members of such groups if other options are no longer viable or where forensic analyses render attempts to remove serial numbers unviable. Given the covert nature of 3DP firearms, they could represent a viable option for individuals who are not licensed to own a firearm, and those under Firearms Prohibition Orders (or control orders more broadly, i.e. protection orders, domestic violence, or personal safety intervention orders etc.), including members of organized criminal groups such as outlaw motorcycle clubs (OMCGs). As 3DP firearms and their components are made mostly from plastics, they are not detectable using standard security protocols such as metal detectors, which may also render them attractive to members of organized criminal groups. The modularized nature of 3DP guns and gun parts is concerning, in that firearms can be retrofitted with 3DP parts. 3DP firearms are also easier to dismantle and destroy compared with more durable metal-based firearms. Again, this characteristic of 3DP firearms may enhance their attractiveness to members of criminal groups, who often dispose of firearms following their use in crime (Bright et al. 2023). The main risks to society regarding 3DP guns and associated digital design files relate primarily to the ease of manufacturing guns within an otherwise heavily regulated firearms context such as in Australia.

Digital Design Files

The rise in 3DP firearms has occurred partly due to the ready accessibility of digital design files. The first design file for a 3DP firearm, known as 'the Liberator', was published online by the US company Defense Distributed. The design file for the Liberator was downloaded more than 100,000 times within the first two days of publication (Daly et al. 2021), triggering action by the US State Department Directorate of Defense Trade Controls (Daly

[1] When a projectile or bullet is fired from a firearm, the barrel leaves (microscopic) marks on the projectile or bullet. Forensic ballistic analysis enables the cataloguing and consequently tracing of firearms that have been used across multiple incidents. This enables law enforcement to connect the use of firearms across crimes for intelligence and investigative purposes. Internationally, police information systems have been established to facilitate this, such as, for example, the Australian Ballistic Information Network (ABIN).

et al. 2021). Cody Wilson—the creator of the Liberator and founder of Defense Distributed—launched appeals based on the First (free speech) and Second (the right of the people to keep and bear arms) Amendments to the US Constitution. This was followed by a series of events including an initial settlement with the US Department of Justice (under the Trump administration) which was met with an injunction to prevent publication (Daly et al. 2021).

A protracted legal process continued and resulted in the introduction and passage of the Bipartisan Safer Communities Act 2022 (US). This amended the definition of a firearm (to include hybrid parts) and introduced requirements for commercial manufacturers to 'become licensed and include serial numbers on the kits' frame or receiver, and [that] commercial sellers of these kits must become federally licensed and run background checks prior to a sale', irrespective of how the firearms were manufactured, including by 3D-printing (White House 2022). At the time of writing, legal challenges and appeals by commercial manufacturers are ongoing. Most recently, in October 2023, the US Supreme Court ruled in *Garland v Blackhawk Manufacturing Group* that they must comply with the new regulations, while further appeals are underway, possibly to the US Supreme Court (see: Associated Press 2023; Chung 2023; Reichmann 2023; The Guardian 2023). Significantly, the legal challenges centre on the requirements for commercial manufacturers (or platforms disseminating the design files) to be registered and to conduct background checks, and for the inclusion of serial numbers, rather than the legality or permissibility of publishing 3DP design files. There are a range of interesting arguments in relation to the regulation and censorship of (harmful) online content and tensions with individual rights which are constitutionally and jurisdictionally bound (e.g. the right of the people to keep and bear arms does not exist in Australia or most jurisdictions outside of the US) (Daly et al. 2021). It is with this in mind that we turn to an overview of laws that have been introduced to criminalize the possession of design files for 3DP firearms and their components.

Law

Legislative responses to 3DP firearms have varied internationally and continue to evolve. Daly et al. (2021) categorize international legislative and government responses to 3DP guns into three main approaches: (1) explicit criminalization of the manufacture of 3DP firearms; (2) licensing or registration schemes for 3DP firearms; and (3) introduction of new offences for possession of design files for 3DP firearms. There is variation in Australian regimes across states. New South Wales was the first jurisdiction internationally to criminalize the possession of 3DP firearms and digital design files (Daly et al. 2021).

Internationally, Spain and Germany have laws to criminalize dissemination of information concerning 3DP guns, such as the design files, rather than possession of them (Daly et al. 2021). More recently, in 2021, Singapore created new offences relating to possession of design files (Guns, Explosives and Weapons Control Bill 2020 (Singapore); Listek 2021). What is interesting in the Singaporean law is the definition of a firearm and related exclusions. For example, 3DP accessories such as silencers or suppressors are not included. Proposals are being considered in New York state to criminalize the possession of digital blueprints (Max 2023), akin to the New South Wales model, however noting the complexities with other US legal developments, as discussed above.

In 2022, the Australian jurisdiction of Western Australia introduced the Firearms Amendment Act 2022 (WA) that criminalizes both the possession and dissemination of firearms technology, defined as (div. 4 s. 23AG):

(a) a thing that is programmed, configured or otherwise enabled—
  (i) to carry out a step in the manufacture or repair of a firearm, major firearm part, prohibited firearm accessory or ammunition; or
  (ii) without limiting subparagraph (i), to change an object into a component of a firearm, major firearm part, prohibited firearm accessory or ammunition;
(b) any type of digital or electronic reproduction of a technical drawing of the design of a firearm, major firearm part, prohibited firearm accessory or ammunition;
(c) a plan, drawing, instruction, template or computer program, in digital or electronic form, for the manufacture or repair of a firearm, major firearm part, prohibited firearm accessory or ammunition;
(d) a hard copy of a digital or electronic thing referred to in paragraph (b) or (c).

As per the above definition, the law also applies to *an instruction* for manufacture, which could extend to instructional manuals, videos, and discussion forums that provide instructions on how to manufacture firearms technology. The law also criminalizes the unauthorized dissemination (Firearms Amendment Act 2022 (WA), div. 4 s. 23AJ) of firearms technology. Dissemination is defined as sending, supplying, exhibiting, transmitting or communicating firearms technology, making available for access by electronic or other means, or entering into an agreement to conduct such activities (Firearms Amendment Act 2022 (WA), div. 4 s. 23AJ (2)). This *may* have implications for persons or platforms disseminating design files for 3DP firearms, however, for individuals located outside WA, this would require extra-territorial enforcement.

Other Australian jurisdictions, including Tasmania and South Australia, are currently considering or in the process of criminalizing the possession of digital blueprints that can be used to manufacture 3DP firearms (Firearms Amendment (Community Safety) Bill 2023 (TAS) which inserts a new offence in s. 119A of the Firearms Act 1996 (TAS), concerning the possession of digital blueprints (see also Tasmania Police 2023). South Australia Police is proceeding with a request to the government to introduce an offence for possession of digital blueprint which 'would enable police to take action in the first instance; that is, during the possession of the blueprints, before any firearms are constructed' (South Australia Police 2023). However, it is important to recognize that criminalizing possession of a blueprint does not address issues of the availability of the design files, as it does not prevent access to them.

We focus on the Firearms and Weapons Prohibition Legislation Amendment Act 2015 (NSW) as the first (internationally) to criminalize the possession of a digital blueprint for 3DP guns and as it has been in force for nine years, with a series of individuals charged and/or prosecuted. We focus on cases where individuals have been charged and/or prosecuted for the possession of digital blueprints rather than possession of 3DP firearms more broadly as our aim is to examine how law enforcement are using this specific offence and drawing lessons. Further, individuals who have been charged and/or prosecuted with possession of the design files are arguably more likely to be involved with downloading the design files for the manufacture of 3DP weapons. This law defines a blueprint as 'any type of digital or electronic reproduction of a technical drawing of the design of an object' (s. 51F(3)). This is a broad definition (i.e. an object) and can be contrasted with Western Australia's approach.

According to the Firearms Act 1996 (NSW), amended by the Firearms and Weapons Prohibition Legislation Amendment Act 2015 (NSW), a firearm 'means a gun, or other weapon, that is (or at any time was) capable of propelling a projectile by means of an explosive, and includes a blank fire firearm, or an air gun, but does not include a paintball marker within the meaning of the Paintball Act 2018 (NSW) or anything declared by the regulations not to be a firearm' (div. 4 Definitions, Firearms Act 1996 (NSW)). Firearm part 'means a barrel, breech, pistol slide, frame, receiver, cylinder, trigger mechanism, operating mechanism or magazine designed as, or reasonably capable of forming, part of a firearm' (div. 4 Definitions), and the manufacture of a firearm includes assembling a firearm from firearm parts (pt. 6 s. 50A(5). There are specific provisions that relate to imitation firearms, and the Firearms Act 1996 (NSW) applies in the same way to imitation firearms, with exceptions, such as an imitation firearm is *not* required to be registered (pt. 1 s. 4D). An imitation firearm is 'an imitation of a pistol that is taken to be a pistol' (pt. 1 s. 4D(2)(a)), and an imitation firearm is a firearm that is taken to be a prohibited firearm (pt. 1 s. 4D(2)(b)). An imitation firearm means 'an object that, regardless of its color, weight or composition or the presence or absence of any moveable parts, substantially duplicates in appearance a firearm but that is not a firearm' (pt. 1 s. 4D(3)). An imitation firearm '*does not include any such object that is produced and identified as a children's toy*' (pt. 1 s. 4D(4)) (emphasis added).

Under the New South Wales laws, possession is also taken to include 'control of the blueprint held in a computer that is in the possession of another person, whether the computer is inside or outside of this jurisdiction [New South Wales]' (s. 51F(3)(b)), for instance, where the blueprint may be held in the cloud or on a server outside of New South Wales. This adds interesting extraterritorial complexity, and the scope of the law may potentially apply outside of the physical jurisdiction of New South Wales (provided the blueprint can be controlled or accessed from New South Wales). As explored below, we have only identified cases involving the possession of digital blueprints for 3DP firearms where the individual has been physically present in New South Wales. This is not to say, however, that there are other instances where the New South Wales law may apply to those located outside of the jurisdiction of New South Wales, if the blueprint can be accessed from the jurisdiction of New South Wales. Extraterritorial application of laws criminalizing the possession and dissemination of design files or firearms technology requires further study. The New South Wales law can also be compared with the more recent Western Australia law that relates to firearms technology and criminalizes both *possession* and *dissemination* of such technology.

Review of 3DP Firearms Cases

To explore cases in which New South Wales Police have used the offence that a person must not possess or control a digital blueprint, we searched media reports, police media statements, and legal cases between 2017 and 2023 (the offence was introduced in 2015 and the first case was two years later in 2017). These cases do not include those where 3DP firearms themselves were located, and there was no separate charge for possession of digital blueprint reported (see Table 8.1).

These cases suggest that detection is happening mostly offline, for example by the Australian Border Force during attempted importation of other firearms parts, or threats made to Members of Parliament, as evident in cases 2–5. There are connections to sovereign citizen and right-wing extremism (cases 2 and 3), and 'organized crime' such as drug trafficking (case 5). The outlier here appears to be case 1 where imitation firearms were manufactured for the purpose of cosplay and detection occurred online as the individual advertised the imitation firearms for sale on Facebook. This raises questions about the legal and definitional scope of what constitutes a firearm, imitation firearm, and the digital blueprints for them. It is significant that police have charged individuals with links to extremism, terrorism, and drug trafficking. These types of offences present significant risks to public safety, and we examine these below in terms of connections to organized crime, drawing from research and media reports that have identified links between 3DP firearms and organized crime.

3DP Firearms and Organized Crime

As per the cases above, police have identified both organized criminal groups involved in drug trafficking and extremists with 3D-printers and 3DP firearms in their possession. In this chapter, our focus is specifically on organized criminal groups, however we recognize that members of extremist groups present a significant threat. This is because they are less likely to be able to access the Australian illicit market for firearms (compared to organized criminal groups), it is difficult and risky to import firearms and their parts (as evident by offline detection in the cases described above), and therefore extremists may see the potential to print firearms as an attractive and low risk option. Isolated extremists may lack the necessary social networks to facilitate access to an illicit firearm. There has been growing concern in the US

Table 8.1 Case Summaries for Possession of Digital Blueprints

Case and reference	Date	Case Summary	Outcome	Lessons
Case 1 (Mitchell 2018)	April 2017	An individual made replica guns for cosplay, advertised one on Facebook 'buy swap sell' for AUD $1 million. This triggered law enforcement attention and a search of property. Police found several replica guns and more than 400 digital blueprints, the guns were not capable of being loaded or fired.	12-month suspended sentence. Risk to the community was deemed to be low.	Online detection Cosplay Guns not functional
Case 2 (Syal 2023)	November 2018	A 'sovereign citizen' subject to extended supervision order (ESO) under the Terrorism (High Risk Offenders) Act 2017 (NSW) came to law enforcement attention after threats were made to a NSW politician in 2017. This led to a police search and it was found that across 2017 digital blueprints were downloaded including for a plastic sub-machine gun, plastic semi-automatic pistol, among other weapons. Firearms were tested and in working condition, police found USB with 411 digital blueprints for 3DP firearms or parts.	Pleaded guilty to possession of 411 digital blueprints for the manufacture of twelve different firearms.	Detection offline via threats made to Member of Parliament. Connection to sovereign citizen movement and terrorism.
Case 3 (Hotham 2021; Hunter 2021)	September 2021	Individual charged for possession of digital blueprint located on phone. Police state person had been importing items for manufacturing firearms and came to law enforcement attention as the Australian Border Force intercepted a package containing a firearm component. NSW joint counter-terrorism team identified the individual as a right-wing extremist.	Pleaded guilty October 2021.	Connections to right-wing extremism Detection offline via importation

Case 4 (AFP 2022)	March 2022	As part of Australian Federal Police and Border Force Operation, ABF examined imported parcel and arrested an individual. Police seized a 3D-printer, spools of 3D filament and electronic devices. AFP allegedly found files on a SD card for a semi-automatic firearm and a 3DP assault rifle, and the individual was charged with possession of digital blueprint.	Case outcome unknown.	Detection offline via importation
Case 5 (Rajen 2023)	May 2023	Two individuals were arrested, one was charged with manufacturing a prohibited firearm without a licence/permit and possessing a digital blueprint. The other individual was charged with numerous other firearms offences, and drug offences.	Case outcome unknown.	Connections with drug possession and supply Organized offending.
Case 6 (The National Tribune 2023)	August 2023	An individual came to the attention of law enforcement following a joint AFP and ABF operation and investigation into the importation of firearm parts. Charged with eighteen offences, including one count of possessing digital blueprint for the manufacture of firearms.	Case outcome unknown.	Detection offline via importation

Note: Cases have been de-identified to protect individual identity, especially in cases that have not been finalized by a finding of guilt and noting the possibility of subsequent appeal against criminal conviction. All information is drawn from publicly accessible sources such as media reporting and court records and to the best of our knowledge is correct at the time of writing. This research did not require human research ethical approval as all information presented is drawn from 'open-source' public records.

about the risks posed by extremist groups such as white supremist groups accessing and producing 3DP firearms (Stephens 2021).

Previous research has established that to mitigate risks of being connected with a crime, members of organized criminal groups seek weapons that have not been used in crime previously, and often discard a firearm after it has been used in a crime (Bright et al. 2023). Furthermore, research has shown criminals are aware that police can trace firearms and, therefore, will in some cases seek a firearm that has had the serial number obliterated. Of course, it should be noted that this may impact the traceability of the firearm itself as the serial number has been removed, however forensic analysis may still be able to identify and trace a firearm from ballistic evidence discharged from it. 3DP firearms may offer risk mitigation with respect to firearms possession and use that may render them more attractive to organized criminal group members, in that there is an absence of serial numbers, together with control of the manufacture process and therefore a guarantee the firearm has no criminal history, and the capability to destroy the firearm (i.e. melting it) following use in a crime. Further, the costs associated with manufacturing 3DP firearms (or hybrid parts and components) may be cheaper than accessing a firearm via the black market. Such costs would mainly involve the initial 'set-up' costs of purchasing the 3D-printer(s), which may even include industrial-scale metal 3DP capabilities.

Nonetheless, 3DP firearms are not currently the firearms of choice for organized criminal groups. There appear to be two main reasons for this, at least in Australia. First, access to factory manufactured firearms remains relatively easy for criminally connected individuals (Bright et al. 2023). Second, factory manufactured firearms are considered functionally reliable, while 3DP technology currently involves inherent risks in the use of 3DP firearms (i.e. single shot, risks of injury to the shooter). Of course, if these factors change, for example, improvements in 3DP reliability and/or withering supply of factory manufactured firearms, we may see more demand for 3DP firearms among members of organized criminal groups.

Notwithstanding the overall low demand for 3DP firearms among members of organized criminal groups, there are some anecdotal reports of such groups using 3DP firearms. For example, in New South Wales in 2021, a man was alleged to be selling 3DP firearms to members of the Comanchero OMCG (AFP 2021). However, seizures of 3DP guns comprise a small proportion of overall illicit firearms seized by law enforcement in Australia and connected to organized criminal groups, although there is currently limited empirical evidence concerning firearms seizures.

The potential for hybrid 3DP firearm components such as flash suppressors and/or silencers to be fitted to traditional firearms may also be appealing to organized criminal groups who have access to firearms but not necessarily accessories or other desired functions. As outlined above, this has been identified by international police agencies as a major emerging threat. It appears that some groups may be dabbling in 3DP firearms, perhaps as a diversification tactic to ensure continued access to firearms. For example, there is evidence that some organized criminal groups such as OMCGs have used 3D-printers to manufacture firearms (Simpson 2016). In New Zealand, it has been reported that 3DP firearms, including semi-automatic weapons, have been found in the possession of gang members (Kapitan 2021). It is in this context that we explore the availability of design files for various types of 3DP firearms (and parts) on the surface web as this provides organized criminal groups the ability to manufacture such weapons (see also Chapter 9 for a discussion of access to illicit firearms via the dark web). Understanding the availability and platforms that host or disseminate design files and their associated policies may enable the design of improved policy and preventative responses to thwart organized criminal groups' ability to manufacture 3DP firearms.

Dissemination of Digital Design Files

As mentioned previously, there is one existing study on the availability of 3DP firearm designs on the surface web (Schaufelbühl et al. 2023). Using a similar methodology, we collected an evidence based of the availability of design files on the surface web, including updated results. We conducted a systematic search of publicly available (i.e. surface web) platforms that host 3DP design files. Unlike Schaufelbühl et al. (2023), we did not draw from social media or platforms such as Reddit, nor identify any persons of interest. We did not pay for or download any design files. Rather, the focus of our study was identifying the main or most prominent hosting platforms and exploring their policies about the dissemination of 3DP weapons (if available), and a cursory examination of the types of design files available on them as relevant to legal definitional complexity (i.e. hybrid designs, imitation firearms, and toy firearms). We collected qualitative information about the platforms (such as geographical location), as this has consequences for regulating online content given jurisdictionally bound laws and policies.

Data collection began in mid-September 2023 across a two-week duration and captured more recent data than the Schaufelbühl et al. (2023) study. Search terms included: design files for 3DP guns, real gun stl files, 3DP gun files, firearms printing free download, 3DP gun CAD download, 3DP gun components, firearms, gun, weapon, pistol, magazine, rifle, modification, accessory, hybrid, and CAD and 3DP. Searches continued until saturation. A summary of the findings is presented in Table 8.2 below; as this is exploratory research and due to practical constraints, we have limited our presentation of findings to the most prominent platforms (i.e. those that recurrently appeared on page 1 Google results using the search terms above).

Geographical location was identified by examining the 'About' or 'Contact us' pages. Frequently, geographical location was not readily identifiable using public source information. We also explored whether the platform listed blueprints for entire 3DP firearm models or parts. The type of design file available was recorded as displayed on the platforms. Almost all platforms showed images of the firearm and/or components. Imagery complemented our research as it helped determine what material the 3DP firearm blueprints were for (e.g. plastic, metal, or both). We considered this information to attempt to differentiate between 3DP firearm files, and those for imitation/fantasy gaming, which at times proved challenging as functionality is not always evident from the appearance of a firearm. We recorded any additional information such as whether platforms appeared to display 3DP design files for imitation/fantasy purposes and the availability of DIY kits.

We located thirty-one unique platforms, mostly hosted in the US and Europe, that provide ready access to design files for a range of 3DP weapons. These provided access to both functional firearms and imitation fantasy/gaming 3DP firearm files, and with a considerable range of design files.

Consistent with the findings of Schaufelbühl et al. (2023), we were able to easily locate (i.e. on page 1 of Google search results using obvious search terms) numerous platforms that disseminate a range of design files for 3DP firearms and parts. These included design files for both plastic and metal 3DP firearms; a concerning development, given advances in 3DP metal printing and the functionality and durability of metal weapons over plastic (e.g. that may provide greater reliability and allow multiple rounds to be fired etc.). We located a range of platforms that have design files for imitation firearms. This raises the question of legal definitions of firearms and their component parts, and has implications for the parameters of what is (il)legal (as discussed above, with variation in the legal definitions across Australian states, and international jurisdictions, such as Singapore). Further, we were

Table 8.2 Top Platforms Disseminating Design Files

Platform number	Location	Design Files Available	Plastic or metal	Platform Policies, Terms of Use or Conditions
Platform 1	Europe; US; Asia & Oceania	Rifle; Sniper rifle; Colt; Machine gun; Pistol; Revolver; Grenade launcher; Shotgun	Both	'In particular, but not limited to, the creation of firearms. . . . *will be refused* by DEIDENTIFIED' (emphasis added) (Cults 3D 2023).
Platform 2	US	Pistol; Rifle; Pistol-Caliber; Carbine; Revolver; SMG; Derringer; Shotgun; Launcher; Signal Launcher; Machine Gun; Anti Materiel Rifle; Landmine; Airsoft/BB Gun; Pepperbox; Airgun; Blowgun; Flare gun; Grenade; Arrow Launcher; Grenade; Launcher; Cannon; Flamethrower; Pengun; Crossbow; Tranquilizer gun; Wristgun; Zipgun.	Both	'DEIDENTIFIED is an online information library and CAD model marketplace. We *are dedicated to the advancement of, and education concerning, American gunsmithing, and the protection of the Second Amendment*' (emphasis added) (DEFCAD 2020).
Platform 3	US	Rifle; Pistol; Magazine; Firearm Accessories.	Both	'You agree to use it only for the purposes intended and as permitted by these Terms, any additional contracts with us, and *applicable laws, regulations, and generally accepted online practices and industry guidelines*' (emphasis added) (3D Gun Builder 2022).

(continued)

Table 8.2 Continued

Platform number	Location	Design Files Available	Plastic or metal	Platform Policies, Terms of Use or Conditions
Platform 4	Unknown	Pistol; Glock; Handgun; Machine gun; Sub-machine gun.	Both	Not available
Platform 5	Unknown	Pistol; Revolver; Shotgun.	Both	'You are entirely responsible for all content that you upload, post or otherwise transmit via the Site. You agree *not to upload, post or otherwise transmit via the site any content that is printable 3D models, which are replicas or realistic depictions of weapons*' (emphasis added). 'Sellers may not upload product or add content that v*iolates any international or domestic law, statute, ordinance, or regulation*' (emphasis added) (cgtrader 2011–2024).
Platform 6	Unknown	Pistol; Blowgun; Rifle; Semi-auto revolver; Machine gun.	Both	'DEIDENTIFIED is *not responsible for the content* provided by other websites and furthermore *not responsible for the accuracy of the content or function*' (emphasis added) (Yeggi 2013).

Platform 7	US	Rifle; Pistol; Shotgun; Sniper.	Both	'The Site may be *subject to the U.S. export laws* and *the export or import laws of other countries*. You agree to comply strictly with all such laws and, in particular: (a) obtain any export, re-export, or import authorizations required by U.S.; (b) *not design, develop or produce missile,* chemical/biological, or nuclear *weaponry*; and (c) not provide, re-route, or otherwise package the Site to prohibited countries and entities identified in the U.S. export regulations' (emphasis added) (TurboSquid 2021).
Platform 8	US	Pistol; Magazine.	Both	'You agree not to use the website: in any way that *violates any applicable federal, state, local or international law or regulation*' (emphasis added) (Ghost Guns 2021).
Platform 9	Unknown	Sling gun; Rubber band gun; Pistol holder; Magazine holder; Nerf gun.	Both	Not available
Platform 10	US	Bombshell gun; Machine gun; Swivel gun.	Plastic	'You also certify that any 3D file ('3D Model') uploaded to DEIDENTIFIED *does not violate any federal law or regulation including those pertaining to firearms*' (emphasis added).

(*continued*)

Table 8.2 Continued

Platform number	Location	Design Files Available	Plastic or metal	Platform Policies, Terms of Use or Conditions
				'Weapons Do's DEIDENTIFIED *does produce external accessories for guns and gun games (airsoft, paintball) that do not reproduce core functions.* DEIDENTIFIED *does produce cosplay-type guns* that cannot be reasonably confused with real life firearms' (emphasis added). 'Weapons Don'ts DEIDENTIFIED *does not produce guns, realistic gun replicas, or gun games (airsoft, paintball).* This *includes parts that make up guns or could be assembled into guns or realistic gun replicas (including grips with integrated magazine wells).* It also includes parts whose manufacture *is specifically regulated such as silencers/suppressors. Parts are anything that are required for the gun to load and fire a projectile safely.* Gun replicas *longer than 10cm are likely to be flagged for additional review.* DEIDENTIFIED does *not produce conversion kit parts for guns, gun replicas, or gun games.* DEIDENTIFIED *does not produce magazines for guns, gun replicas, or gun games*' (emphasis added) (Shapeways 2023).

Platform 11	Unknown	Machine gun; Sub-machine gun; Twin pellet gun.	Plastic	'You agree that you will not under any circumstances: *use the service for any unlawful purpose or for the promotion of illegal activities*' (emphasis added) (Repables 2014).
Platform 12	US	Handgun prop; Scatter gun; Rubber band gun; Paintball gun.	Plastic	'You agree not to use the Site to upload, collect or display Content that is *unlawful*, threatening or abusive, *harmful*, vulgar, misleading, pornographic, sexually explicit, obscene, or which promotes racism or hatred' (emphasis added) (Redpah 2024).

Note: While the platforms we have identified are all publicly accessible on the surface web using Google, we have de-identified them in the reporting of this research. This is to ensure that we do not promote or publish identifiable websites, platforms and domains that are disseminating potentially illegal content (depending on jurisdiction, as the design files for 3DP firearms are not universally criminalized), incite or facilitate illegal or harmful activity, or potentially cause harm to businesses.

able to identify and access a range of additional information and resources such as instructional manuals, video tutorials, and chat forums that can be used to facilitate the manufacture of firearms. As discussed above, this type of instructional material would fall within the Western Australia firearms technology law.

When able to identify the geographical location where the platform was hosted, we found that most of the 'top' platforms are emanating from the US. This is perhaps unsurprising, given that 3DP firearms have their origins in the US and given the more liberal approach there to gun control. Some platforms were specific to and specialized in the publication of design files for 3DP firearms, and we also identified platforms that offered a wider variety of CAD files.

We identified some variation in the policies of the platforms. Of the twelve most prominent platforms disseminating design files of 3DP firearms as in Table 8.2, there were key distinctions in their policies. For example, platforms explicitly prohibited design files for the manufacture of firearms (Platform 1, to some extent Platform 5), others had policies prohibiting violation of *relevant* laws and regulations (Platform 3, 5, 7, 8, and 10–12; again, these may not be meaningful as the dissemination of design files for 3DP weapons is not universally criminalized). Interestingly, the policies of Platform 7 referred to export and import laws and regulations, and the policy of Platform 10 limited design files to firearms that were solely for cosplay. One platform was explicitly concerned with realizing Second Amendment rights (Platform 2), and one denied liability for content shared on the platform (Platform 6). One platform indicated that there are review mechanisms in place, specifically for replicas longer than 10 cm (Platform 10). Finally, two platforms did not have any identifiable policies concerning 3DP firearms or design files (Platforms 4 and 9). There is evidence that platforms that explicitly prohibited the dissemination of design files for 3DP firearms in their policies had design files available for download. This may indicate that in the respective jurisdictions this does not contravene local or relevant laws (even though online dissemination of information extends across national borders and jurisdictions) and/or the platforms are not actively enforcing their own policies. This raises the question as to whether platforms should be responsible for self-regulation in terms of *designing* and *enforcing* their own policies, or whether external enforcement is more appropriate. Based on these findings, we turn to consider potentials for policy, prevention, and policing.

Policy, Prevention, and Policing

Like Schaufelbühl et al. (2023), our findings show that there is widespread online availability of a range of plastic and metal digital design files for 3DP firearms. This is concerning, given the potential risks of organized crime groups use of 3DP firearms, and especially given the low cost and ease of covert manufacture. In this concluding section, we consider avenues that may mitigate such risks, and consider options for policy, preventative, and policing responses.

Police responding to individuals downloading and possessing digital design files through criminalization is a reactive and resource-intensive approach that is likely to be ineffective in preventing the manufacture of firearms. This is compounded by jurisdictional idiosyncrasies in the legal definition of firearms. There are complexities involved in regulating the Internet as a cross/trans/multi-jurisdictional sphere, and limits to extraterritorial enforcement where legal and constitutional frameworks vary (Daly et al. 2021). This would potentially require extraterritorial enforcement, legal harmonization (e.g. via the firearms protocol to the United Nations Convention on Transnational Organised Crime), or local attempts to block platforms. It is worth reiterating that unlike some forms of content (such as child exploitation material, CEM) the design files for 3DP firearms are not universally criminalized and, indeed, in jurisdictions such as the US are legally permissible (notwithstanding current challenges to requiring background checks, serial numbers, and registration, as discussed above). This is not to argue that criminalization is not important (e.g. for deterrence or the prosecution of such offences). Rather, measures that aim to prevent the dissemination and regulate access to harmful online content are likely to be more effective.

One avenue to consider is giving attention to the policies of web hosting platforms, as this may offer possibilities for preventing access to design files in jurisdictions where they are criminalized. Our review of platform policies showed variation and inconsistencies in policies. Therefore, one potential approach could be requiring platforms to have standardized policies, including external enforcement. This could also involve, for example, geo-blocking or local censorship of platforms where the possession or dissemination of 3DP design files are criminalized, however noting that such attempts can be readily circumvented through virtual private networks (VPNs) and Tor (i.e. the dark web). The use of VPNs and Tor requires greater technological sophistication than Google searches, and therefore may limit access to those who lack the skill and determination to obfuscate their (geo) location. Another avenue could include requiring provision of identification and residency documents, registration, and conducting background checks. However, it could be argued that the proverbial horse has already bolted, with widespread availability of design files which can be shared and hosted in a multitude of other file-sharing sites, peer-to-peer networks, and the dark web. We can reasonably anticipate that if organized criminal groups are highly motivated then they can delve deeper than the surface web. Other forms of subterfuge could be adopted, such as flooding the Internet with design files that are not functional or potentially even malfunction, but this may raise ethical issues (e.g. potential to cause injury). Further, hash values might be used to eradicate digital design files from the Internet (Daly et al. 2021). Hash values are binary codes associated with images and files and are already used by law enforcement agencies and technology companies to detect and remove CEM from the Internet.

Other avenues to prevent access to design files for 3DP firearms could, for example, involve online safety laws such as the Online Safety Act 2021 (Cth). In the Australian context, the Australian Online Safety Codes seek to regulate and limit access to harmful online content via industry codes and are championed by the Office of the eSafety Commissioner (eSafety Commissioner 2024). This model could be an opportunity to require platforms to have and enforce policies concerning the dissemination of design files for 3DP firearms. Given the focus on crime and safety in the Online Safety Codes, it is surprising that design files for 3DP firearms are absent.

In addition to these potential preventative measures, our review of cases points towards possible policing strategies. From the small sample of cases that we were able to identify in media or court reporting, detection of the possession of design files was occurring offline, for example when individuals attempted to import other firearms components and 3DP technology (such as printers). This could indicate that greater scrutiny of the import of 3DP printers or associated materials could provide insight into those manufacturing firearms. There have been some attempts internationally to require registration of 3D-printers, and suggestions that 3D-printers could be programmed to not print design files for 3DP firearms (Daly et al. 2021). Another approach could be enhanced surveillance and intelligence-led policing, including monitoring of the IP addresses and the metadata of those that are visiting platforms that host design files for 3DP firearms (acknowledging there are serious critiques about mandatory metadata retention laws, Mann et al. 2018). However, again, there are methods of concealing IP addresses and circumventing metadata retention. Other intelligence-led approaches could involve additional monitoring of or restrictions being imposed on individuals subject to control orders, restricting access to platforms that disseminate design files.

Limitations and Future Directions

There are, of course, limitations with cases reported in the media or public domain as this is unlikely to be comprehensive, especially in areas of terrorism and organized crime where police may not release security related information publicly. The cases that we have presented in this chapter are illustrative examples of what is on the public record and not a complete assessment of all cases where police have used the offence, or indeed, where digital design files have been downloaded and not detected by police. There is likely to be information that is not reported, and this may influence the inferences drawn. The main limitation of the search of hosting platforms is that it only concerns the surface web and not the dark web or other peer-to-peer file-sharing sites. A further challenge was identifying the geographic location where the platforms were physically located. Further, the availability of design files for 3DP weapons on the dark web requires further study, especially given attempts to regulate and control their dissemination on the surface web.

There is a need for future research on organized crime (and extremist) groups' use of 3DP firearms and the conditions that may increase or disrupt this. Technologies, as well as legal frameworks, are constantly evolving, and there is a need to study the impacts of such developments on firearms crime. For example, the impact of the recent US requirements for commercial manufacturers (or platforms) being registered, requiring serial numbers, and conducting background checks is yet to be seen on the global accessibility of design files for 3DP firearms on the surface web, and is an important area for longitudinal study. Further, the extraterritorial enforcement of the criminalization of the possession (or control) and dissemination of design files is another area worthy of criminological and legal investigation.

Conclusions

As part of our approach to this chapter we located thirty-one platforms that disseminate a range of design files for 3DP firearms and their component parts. The risk of organized crime groups using 3DP weapons is an emerging threat, and we have identified cases where individuals potentially connected to organized criminal groups have been charged with the possession of design files for 3DP firearms (in the Australian state of New South Wales). There are several factors that could influence organized criminal groups seeking to use 3DP firearms at a greater rate. First, where the technology of 3DP firearms advances to a point where they are more reliable (e.g. advances in metal 3DP), organized criminal groups may take more interest. Second, where the costs of reliable 3DP firearms are significantly lower than factory-made firearms, demand for 3DP firearms by organized criminal groups may increase. And third, where the supply of firearms (or specific types of firearms sought by these groups) becomes more limited, criminal groups may shift to 3DP firearms. Given the serious risks, there is an immediate need to regulate the ready availability of digital design files or blueprints for 3DP firearms. However, there are complexities of developing and enforcing public policy and law given the multi-jurisdictional nature of the Internet, disharmonious nature of law and legal definitions, the challenges of regulating online platforms and content, and the potential for circumvention. Further research is required to more fully understand the interplay between organized offending and emerging technologies to inform law, policy, prevention, and policing practice.

References

Associated Press. 2023. 'The Supreme Court Orders Makers of Gun Parts to Comply with Rules on Ghost Guns' (17 Oct. 2023). https://apnews.com/article/supreme-court-ghost-guns-biden-administration-c61 9b0212be94de9ff043e3a0040b1da Accessed 24 Jul. 2024.

Australian Federal Police (AFP). 2021. 'National Anti-Gangs Squad Seizes More Firearms, Cash and Drugs from OMCGs'. *AFP Media Release* (2 Dec. 2021). https://www.afp.gov.au/news-centre/media-release/national-anti-gangs-squad-seizes-more-firearms-cash-and-drugs-omcgs#:~:text=Police%20will%20allege%20a%2038,%27%20%E2%80%93%20F*%20Gun%20Control Accessed 23 Jul. 2024.

Australian Federal Police (AFP). 2022. 'Port Macquarie Man Charged Over Firearms Blueprints'. *AFP Media Release* (30 Mar. 2022). https://www.afp.gov.au/news-centre/media-release/port-macquarie-man-charged-over-firearm-blueprints Accessed 23 Jul. 2024.

Bright, David, et al. 2023. '"I Know a Guy and He's Got Guns Galore": Accessing Crime Guns in the Australian Illicit Firearms Market'. *Deviant Behavior* 44 (5): pp. 671–689.

cgtrader. 2011–2024. 'General Terms and Conditions'. https://www.cgtrader.com/pages/terms-and-conditions Accessed 23 Jul. 2024.

Chung, Andrew. 2023. 'Supreme Court Blocks Judge's Order Allowing 'Ghost Gun' Sales'. *Reuters* (17 Oct. 2023). https://www.reuters.com/legal/us-supreme-court-blocks-judges-order-allowing-ghost-gun-sales-2023-10-16/#:~:text=The%20justices%20lif ted%20Fort%20Worth,Blackhawk%20Manufacturing%20and%20Defense%20Distributed Accessed 23 Jul. 2024.

Cults 3D. 2023. 'Terms and Conditions' (9 Jun. 2023). https://cults3d.com/en/legal Accessed 23 Jul. 2024.

Daly, Angela, and Mann, Monique. 2018. '3D Printing, Policing and Crime'. QUT Crime Justice and Social Democracy Research Centre Briefing Paper Series, 1.

Daly, Angela, et al. 2021. '3D Printing, Policing and Crime'. *Policing and Society* 31 (1): pp. 37–51.

DEFCAD. 2020. 'Terms of Service' (24 Nov. 2020), https://defcad.com/terms-of-service/ Accessed 24 Jul. 2024.

eSafety Commissioner. 2024. 'Industry Codes and Standards'. https://www.esafety.gov.au/industry/codes Accessed 24 Jul. 2024.

Ghost Guns. 2021. 'Website Terms of Use' (5 Jan. 2021). https://ghostguns.com/website-terms-of-use/ Accessed 24. Jul. 2024.

Hotham, F. 2021. 'Orange Man Enters Guilty Plea on Serious Firearms Charge'. *The Orange App* (6 Oct. 2021). https://theorangeapp.com.au/news-sport/news/orange-man-enters-guilty-plea-on-serious-fire-arms-charges?id=615cac3a00a99c002b7d1920.

Hunter, Fergus. 2021. 'Alleged Right-Wing Extremist Charged Over Blueprint to 3D-Print a Gun'. *The Sydney Morning Herald* (12 Sep. 2021). https://www.smh.com.au/national/nsw/alleged-right-wing-extremist-arrested-over-blueprint-to-3d-print-a-gun-20210913-p58r80.html Accessed 24 Jul. 2024.

Kapitan, Craig. 2021. 'Gang Member Accused of Having 3D-Printed Semi-Automatic Weapon'. *New Zealand Herald* (8 Nov. 2021). https://www.nzherald.co.nz/nz/gang-member-accused-of-having-3d-printed-semi-automatic-weapon/D7NOQGYCD2LSVFDYPVFLNELYIA/ Accessed 24 Jul. 2024.

Listek, Vanesa. 2021. 'New Singapore law Criminalizes Possession of Blueprints for 3D-Printing Guns', *3DPrint.com* (6 Jan. 2021). https://3dprint.com/277588/new-singapore-law-criminalizes-possession-of-blueprints-for-3d-printing-guns/#:~:text=Singapore%20moved%20to%20control%20digital,gun%20parts%20without%20a%20license Accessed 24 Jul. 2024.

Mann, Monique, et al. 2018. 'The Limits of (Digital) Constitutionalism? Exploring the Privacy-Security (Im)balance in Australia'. *International Communication Gazette* 80 (4): pp. 369–384.

Max, Samantha. 2023. 'Proposed NY Law Would Crack Down on People Who Use 3D Printers to Make Guns at Home', *Gothamist* (5 Jun. 2023). https://gothamist.com/news/proposed-ny-law-would-crack-down-on-people-who-use-3d-printers-to-make-guns-at-home Accessed 24 Jul. 2024.

Meyer, Jean-Yves. 2013. 'The Basin of the Danaides: How 3-D Printing Will Push the Limits of International Gun Control and Digital Freedom of Speech in the Twenty-First Century'. *Denver Journal of International Law & Police* 41: p. 555.

Mitchell, Georgina. 2018. 'Sicen Sun Given 12-Month Suspended Sentence for 3D-Printed Prop Guns'. *The Sydney Morning Herald* (21 Aug. 2018). https://www.smh.com.au/national/nsw/sicen-sun-given-12-month-suspended-sentence-for-3d-printing-prop-guns-20180821-p4zyro.html Accessed 24 Jul. 2024.

Rajen, Shri Gayathirie. 2023. 'Riverina Men Denied Bail Over Alleged Involvement in Illegal Manufacture of Firearms'. *Regional Riverina* (17 May 2023). https://regionriverina.com.au/riverina-men-denied-bail-over-alleged-involement-in-illegal-manufacture-of-firearms/29148/ Accessed 24 Jul. 2024.

Redpah. 2024. 'End User License Agreement'. https://www.redpah.com/terms Accessed 24 Jul. 2024.

Reichmann, Kelsey. 2023. 'Supreme Court says Biden Administration Can Keep Ghost Gun Rules, For Now'. *Courthouse News Service* (16 Oct. 2023). https://www.courthousenews.com/supreme-court-says-biden-administration-can-keep-ghost-gun-rules-for-now/ Accessed 24 Jul. 2024.

Repables. 2014. 'Repables LLC. Terms of Use' (18 Mar. 2014). https://repables.com/licenseagreement/ Accessed 24 Jul. 2024.

Schaufelbühl, Stefan, et al. 2023. 'Investigating the Availability of 3D-Printed Designs on the Clear Web'. *Forensic Science International: Synergy* 7: pp. 1–9.

Schaufelbühl, Stefan, et al. 2024. 'The Emergence of 3D-Printed: An Analysis of Media and Law Enforcement Reports'. *Forensic Science International: Synergy* 8: pp. 1–10.

Shapeways. 2023. 'Terms and Conditions' (12 Dec. 2023). https://www.shapeways.com/terms_and_conditions Accessed 24 Jul. 2024.

Simpson, Campbell. 2016. 'Australian Police Seized 3D-Printers For Building Guns'. https://www.gizmodo.com.au/2016/05/australian-police-seized-3d-printers-for-building-guns-in-a-melbourne-raid/ Accessed 24 Jul. 2024.

South Australia Police. 2023. 'Legislation—3D Blueprints'. https://www.police.sa.gov.au/services-and-events/firearms-and-weapons/consultation-3d-blueprints Accessed 24 Jul. 2024.

Stephens, Alain. 2021. 'Ghost Gun Government Report'. https://www.thetrace.org/2021/08/ghost-gun-government-report-3d-print-extremism-terrorism/ Accessed 24 Jul. 2024.

Syal, Rajeev. 2023. 'NCA Calls for Possession of 3D-Printed Gun Blueprints to be Made Illegal'. *The Guardian* (31 Oct. 2023). https://www.theguardian.com/world/2023/oct/31/nca-calls-for-possession-of-3d-printed-gun-blueprints-to-be-made Accessed 24 Jul. 2024.

Tasmania Police. 2023. 'Firearms Amendment (Community Safety) Bill 2023'. https://fas.police.tas.gov.au/firearms-2023/ Accessed 24 Jul. 2024.

The Guardian. 2023. 'US Supreme Court Blocks "Ghost Gun" Makers Again from Selling At-Home Kits' (16 Oct. 2023). https://www.theguardian.com/us-news/2023/oct/16/us-supreme-court-ghost-gun-ban-firearms-texas-manufacturers Accessed 24 Jul. 2024.

The National Tribune. 2023. 'AFP and ABF Target Firearms Parts Importation' (2 Sep. 2023). https://www.nationaltribune.com.au/afp-and-abf-target-firearm-parts-importation/ Accessed 23 Jul. 2024.

3D Gun Builder. 2022. 'Terms and Conditions'. https://3dgunbuilder.com/terms-conditions/ Accessed 24 Jul. 2024.

TurboSquid. 2021. 'Terms of Use' (10 May 2021). https://support.turbosquid.com/hc/en-us/articles/230094927-Terms-of-Use Accessed 24 Jul. 2024.

UK Home Office. 2023. 'Strengthening the Law Enforcement Response to Serious and Organised Crime'. *Gov.uk* (24 Jan. 2023), https://www.gov.uk/government/consultations/strengthening-the-law-enforcement-response-to-serious-and-organised-crime Accessed 24 Jul. 2024.

White House. 2022. 'Fact Sheet: The Biden Administration Cracks Down on Ghost Guns, Ensures that ATF Has the Leadership it Needs to Enforce Our Gun Laws'. *White House Briefing Room* (11 Apr. 2022). https://www.whitehouse.gov/briefing-room/statements-releases/2022/04/11/fact-sheet-the-biden-administration-cracks-down-on-ghost-guns-ensures-that-atf-has-the-leadership-it-needs-to-enforce-our-gun-laws/ Accessed 24 Jul. 2024.

Wintemute, Garen J. 2021. 'Ghost Guns: Spookier Than You Think They Are'. *Injury Epidemiology* 8 (1): pp. 1–3.

Yeggi. 2013. Terms of Use (Mar. 2013). https://www.yeggi.com/int/terms-of-use Accessed 24 Jul. 2024.

Laws Cited

Bipartisan Safer Communities Act 2022 (US)
Firearms Act 1996 (NSW)
Firearms Act 1996 (TAS)
Firearms Amendment (Community Safety) Bill 2023 (TAS)
Firearms Amendment Act 2022 (WA)
Firearms and Weapons Prohibition Legislation Amendment Act 2015 (NSW)
Guns, Explosives and Weapons Control Bill 2020 (Singapore)
NY State Senate Bill 2023-S7364
Online Safety Act 2021 (Cth)
Paintball Act 2018 (NSW)

Cases Cited

Garland v Blackhawk Manufacturing Group (2023)
NSW v Hardy [2021] NSWSC 900

9

Illicit Firearms Markets Accessible Through the Dark Web

David Décary-Hétu, Arielle Chainé, and Étienne Blais[*]

The US Bureau of Alcohol, Tobacco, Firearms, and Explosives (ATF) defines a firearm as 'any weapon, including a starter gun, which will or is designed to or may readily be converted to expel a projectile by the action of an explosive' (Bureau of Alcohol, Tobacco, Firearms, and Explosives 2018). This includes several categories such as shotguns, rifles, handguns, machine guns, as well as explosive devices. Each of these firearms is classified for legal and judicial purposes depending on various characteristics, such as its level of lethality, its configuration, and its portability (United Nations Office on Drugs and Crime 2020).

In addition to the categorization of the different types of firearms, components are just as important to understand the external and internal mechanisms of a weapon. While there can be hundreds of parts in a firearm, the main ones are the barrel, magazine, handguard, pistol grip, trigger, and the trigger guard. Different components can be replaced, thereby affecting the proper identification of a firearm. For example, individuals who do not want their weapon to be traced back to them can change their firearm's barrel, making it impossible to link it to a bullet that was fired, as the markings of the new barrel deviate from those of the original one. This trend is fuelled by criminally minded individuals that adopt a 'build-your-own' approach towards the production and trade of firearms parts and components (UNODC 2020). Build-your-own firearms extends to firearms assembled at home with legal parts, and even using a 3D-printer (Wintemute 2021; see also Chapter 8). This recent development enables the printing of components of firearms and even the production in large quantities of illicit weapons with no serial

* This chapter was funded by the Research Chair on gun violence prevention in the Montreal region (FRQSC).

David Décary-Hétu, Arielle Chainé, and Étienne Blais, *Illicit Firearms Markets Accessible Through the Dark Web* In: *Illicit Firearms Markets and Organized Crime*. Edited by: David Bright, Oxford University Press. © Oxford University Press 2025. DOI: 10.1093/9780198902409.003.0010 numbers (Bright et al. 2023). Another obfuscation technique is the removal of the serial number stamped on a firearm. A serial number serves as a unique identifier and facilitates the tracking of a firearm, identifying its manufacturer and assisting law enforcement in investigations. In 2019 alone, the ATF reported more than 10,000 ghost guns recovered by various law enforcement agencies. Gang members and people who sell drugs tend to pay higher sums for firearms with obliterated serial numbers, specifically high-calibre semi-automatic pistols (Hureau and Braga 2018).

A small but still significant contributor to the illicit firearms markets is the illegal purchases facilitated by platforms only accessible through the dark web. These platforms are designed like e-commerce websites where products are offered for sale and paid for in cryptocurrencies. The transactions can be local, regional, or international. In the former case, local dead drops, where vendors hide their products at a specific location and then send the GPS coordinates to their buyers, is a known method for the illicit trade of firearms facilitated by the dark web. However, for regional and international sales of firearms, parcel mail use is identified as the key modus operandi used by dark web marketplace vendors. While there is little empirical research exploring the nature of those sites, firearms illegally purchased online have been linked to acts of terrorism and organized crime violence (Broadhurst et al. 2020). An American-based crime gang appears to have succeeded in shipping more than fifty parcels of hidden firearms inside electronic devices, destined for customers who bought those weapons on dark web illicit markets. A teenager who was supposedly planning a shooting spree targeting his former classmates in the UK acquired a Glock semi-automatic pistol with ammunition using the dark web. Following a tip-off, he described to authorities that acquiring the handgun was as easy as 'buying a bar of chocolate' (Paoli et al. 2017). Some firearms illegally purchased on dark web marketplaces have been used to successfully kill individuals, such as in the November 2015 Paris terrorist attacks and the 2016 Munich shooting (Paoli et al. 2017). See Chapter 12 of this book for a discussion of illicit firearms access by terrorist groups.

This chapter brings to light that the dark web remains a small and somewhat stagnant marketplace for illicit firearms. When comparing data collected in late 2023 to that collected in recent years (Paoli et al. 2017; Copeland et al. 2019; Holt and Lee 2022; Holt et al. 2022), it appears that availability and price have not changed much. The platforms may differ from year to year, but the constraints of the illicit firearms market remain the same. In this chapter, we begin by reviewing the current state of knowledge on the dark web and illicit firearms. We then present our dataset, carefully collected over many shops. From each shop, all the listings were extracted and coded. Finally, we analyse our dataset and present implications for policy makers.

Illicit Firearms on the Dark Web

Most illicit firearms are believed to originate from legitimate markets before being diverted to the illicit markets (Hureau and Braga 2018). Bright et al. (2023) conducted interviews with individuals incarcerated for convictions for serious gun-related crimes in Australia, identifying six means of illegally acquiring a firearm. These means include using family members and friends, obtaining a firearms licence for a trusted third-party who acts as an intermediary for the purchase, and using contacts from within one's organized crime group. Theft, straw purchasing, and manufacturing—although less often exploited—are also mentioned in the interviews. Personal relationships and connections are the most valuable resources when seeking to acquire a gun (Bright et al. 2023; Hureau and Braga 2018; Morselli 2013). Hureau and Braga (2018) find similar means and report transactions, both cash and trade, with friends, family members, and street circles as being the most common when illicitly acquiring a firearm. Theft is also considered a significant source of acquisition, as not all purchases are premeditated; many illicit transactions are made up of opportunistic acquisitions, mainly when individuals connect with organized crime groups as well as street gangs (Morselli 2013). Markets are fluid, as firearms are repeatedly bought and sold, thereby complicating efforts of law enforcement to trace them back to their source (Cook et al. 2019).

While (licit and illicit) acquisitions of firearms via the internet were uncommon just a few years ago, the Covid-19 pandemic raised interest in this distribution channel, as travelling and in-person meetings became uncommon (Bright et al. 2023). The internet offers many layers of communication which provide more or less anonymity. The regular internet, or clear web, is the most open and accessible, as all of its contents are searchable with search engines (Holt and Lee 2022). Anyone illicitly advertising a firearm is therefore only a Google search away. The deep web refers to all the content that is not indexed by search engines, namely the information behind a pay or login wall (Perrat 2018). Individuals must have accounts and credentials to access the websites that illicitly advertise firearms on the deep web. Finally, the dark web is a communication channel that anonymizes the parties in a conversation so that it is difficult to trace the location of anyone involved. The dark web is used to access certain platforms that require visitors to hide their identity and location. There are many dark webs, and the most popular by far is the Tor network (Perrat 2018). The Tor network uses an onion structure of proxies to make it difficult to know who is hosting a website, chat room or social media, where its content is hosted, and who is visiting it (Dingledine et al. 2004). It has been open to the public since 2003 and, while it can be and is used for legitimate purposes, it is estimated that 48 per cent of its 30,000 sites offer illegal goods and services for sale (Perrat 2018). As an anonymous communication channel, the dark web has facilitated international firearms trafficking by enabling seamless anonymous communication across borders (Paoli et al. 2017). Sites only accessible through the dark web cannot be found on traditional search engines (Holt and Lee 2022).

Since they are unregulated, markets accessible through the dark web offer the opportunity to illegally purchase firearms and prohibited weapons for ineligible individuals (i.e. those with criminal records or mental health issues). The anonymity provided by the Tor network means that firearms restrictions and regulations are difficult to enforce, and that few if any checks are made before an illicit firearms sale (O'Malley et al. 2019). The use of anonymous online markets remains niche, and a relatively new component of the illicit firearm trade (Broadhurst 2020). Cryptomarkets and single-vendor shops, also known as single-vendor markets, are the two main sources of firearms through the dark web (Rhumorbarbe et al. 2018). Cryptomarkets are large merchant platforms where an administrator enforces the social regulation it sets forth. The administrator selects multiple independent vendors who, in return, give up a commission on their sales to the platform's administrator. Cryptomarkets offer protection for buyers as they provide escrow services, holding on to their payment until they receive their purchase; buyers receive a refund if they do not receive their order. All payments are made in cryptocurrencies and communications are end-to-end encrypted. To root out opportunistic vendors, each vendor receives a score based on reviews from past customers (Holt and Lee 2022).

Single-vendor shops are operated by a single seller who deals directly with customers. There are no commission cuts or third-party services, and the reliability of these shops is much more difficult to assess (Laferrière and Décary-Hétu 2023). Indeed, anyone can put up a single-vendor shop online and advertise it on forums. There is no telling, however, if the products are really for sale, nor if they are of the advertised quality. While the anonymity of individuals might provide a sense of protection against conventional law enforcement efforts, there is evidence of scamming on single-vendor shops. Some are sting operations created by multiple international law enforcement agencies in response to the threat of untraceable and unregistered firearms, and meant to collect information about potential buyers. Authorities are known to disrupt the flow of illicit firearms trades with fake seller profiles to undermine the trust of buyers in dark web vendors (Holt and Lee 2022). While there are some cases where firearms sales were facilitated by the dark web, Paoli et al. (2017) found that scams were more common than real sales. Since single-vendor shops operate without any third-party oversight, customers may be more at risk of being scammed (Paoli et al. 2017). Cryptomarkets usually have a large user base and there are many discussions on forums about the reliability of cryptomarkets, and of their vendors. Unreliable vendors are supposed to be rooted out very quickly. Certain cryptomarkets have employed the tactic of recycling reviews and comments across multiple listings, creating the illusion of extensive feedback and customer engagement across their platform (Holt and Lee 2022). Cryptomarket administrators have also been known to steal from their participants, and to let law enforcement slip through their net, and become vendors on their platform. Therefore, some administrators prohibit the sale of weapons (and child exploitation material) on their cryptomarkets, to prevent attracting too much attention from authorities and thereby avoiding a market shutdown (Bright et al. 2023). There are therefore challenges to trust both on cryptomarkets and single-vendor shops. Still, some single-vendor shops have managed to build a more significant reputation than some cryptomarkets (Holt and Lee 2022).

Holt and Lee (2022) analysed thirteen single-vendor shops and six cryptomarkets to identify a comprehensive understanding of the crime script analysis for obtaining a firearm from a platform only accessible through the dark web. Their findings suggest that firearms trafficking using the dark web is organized around five main steps: (1) the vendor advertising firearms and providing reasons for purchasing firearms; (2) customer accessing merchant platforms through the dark web and connecting with vendors; (3) customer and vendor interacting via emails, messages, or other electronic means; (4) customer placing the order and vendor shipping the firearms; and (5) customer receiving products (Holt and Lee 2022, 518). The purchase of firearms on sites only accessible through the dark web is similar to acquiring other illicit goods, such as drugs and stolen identity documents, although it is less common due to the greater risk of parcels being detected by mail service inspectors in transit (Holt and Lee 2022). The anonymity, relatively easy access, and challenges when regulating the cryptomarkets and single-vendor shops enable customers to purchase anything, from semi-automatic pistols to rocket launchers. This gap allows buyers and sellers to trade on an international scale, increasing the prevalence of illicit and untraceable firearms (O'Malley et al. 2019).

A huge challenge for all vendors is the packaging and delivery of the firearm to the buyer's address. Holt et al. (2022) report shipping methods in a sample of 287 firearms from twenty different vendor shops. Of those listings, half of the handguns and 69 per cent of long guns had detailed shipping instructions, indicating the lengths to which some buyers go to remain undetected by law enforcement during transit. Given that most firearms trafficking on cryptomarkets is international, with shipping to worldwide destinations, a significant challenge for both academia and law enforcement is to pinpoint the locations of both vendors and buyers (Paoli et al. 2017).

While firearms sales represent only 1 per cent of all illicit goods advertised on cryptomarkets, the average estimated revenue of their vendors is around $80,000 per month. Due to the illicit activities and the advantage of buying weapons while remaining anonymous, firearms purchased from cryptomarkets and single-vendor shops are more expensive than those from conventional firearms trades. Paoli et al. (2017) estimated that 136 transactions related to firearms were made on sixty different sites only accessible through the dark web, with prices significantly greater than the manufacturer's suggested retail price (MSRP). The standard accepted payment for transactions is cryptocurrencies, such as Bitcoin, which maintain the anonymity of both the buyer and the seller (Copeland et al. 2019). Holt et al. (2022) established the average advertised price of a handgun at $742 and $1,085 for a long gun. In 2020, twenty vendors, both single-vendor shops and cryptomarkets, accounted for 66 per cent of the total firearms trade value of all markets, which was estimated at roughly $2.5 million (Broadhurst et al. 2020).

In 2017, 811 weapons, including 339 firearms, were reported by Paoli et al. (2017) to be on sale on twelve cryptomarkets. Of those firearms, 84 per cent were handguns, while knives and batons (22 per cent), digital products (27 per cent), ammunition (7 per cent), and explosives (1 per cent) made up the other weapons. These findings corroborate those of Copeland et al. (2019) who identified seventy-seven handguns out of 105 (73 per cent) firearms advertisements across six single-vendor shops. The remaining 27 per cent consisted of long guns (rifles and shotguns), handguns, mostly semi-automatic pistols like Glocks. The latter are the most commonly available by sellers due to their light weight, stealth packaging, and straightforward assembly, although a 'build-your-own' approach seems rare within the buyers' community, who tend to prefer fully assembled and functioning firearms (Broadhurst et al. 2020). In their sample, Copeland et al. (2019) found well-known firearms from manufacturers such as Colt, Smith & Wesson, Glock, and Beretta being sold under common street names similar to those in the licit markets, suggesting that they may have been purchased legally and then introduced onto the cryptomarkets and single-vendor shops. They primarily featured North Atlantic Treaty Organization (NATO) or Western ammunition calibre specifications in their listings. Ammunition is rarely listed on its own and is often purchased directly with the firearm, hinting that the sellers might have access to a broader range of suppliers, including for parts, components, and accessories (Paoli et al. 2017).

Current Study

The illicit firearms markets have understandably attracted much attention from researchers over the past decades (Hureau and Braga 2018; Pierce et al. 2004; Braga et al. 2002). Firearms violence comes with extremely high societal costs (Lee et al. 2014; Werbick et al. 2021) and was responsible for 79 per cent of all homicides in the US in 2019–20 (Kegler et al. 2022). The US national homicide rate is increasing quickly and is being fuelled by a surge in firearms-related violence. In comparison to countries such as Canada, Australia, the United Kingdom, and New Zealand, the US has a relatively lenient gun control policy. The variation in the different states' regulations facilitates national firearms trafficking as guns are acquired in states with less restrictive regulations and smuggled into states with more restrictive regulations (Braga et al. 2021). In addition, many states' regulations also offer the opportunity to legally acquire guns and resell them in unregulated transactions (Braga et al. 2021), perhaps through the dark web. In turn, the dark web could represent an interesting source of acquisitions for individuals located in jurisdictions with restrictive gun regulations such as Canada, Australia, and the United Kingdom. While studies suggest that it is relatively easy to illegally acquire a gun through one's social network, some would-be purchasers struggle to find firearms as vendors are suspicious of undercover cops and do not sell firearms to strangers (Morselli 2002; 2013).

The dark web may not be a panacea to circumvent gun control regulations found in different jurisdictions, as there are several challenges associated with firearms transactions facilitated by the dark web. Firearms are difficult to hide in packages because of their size and weight (Paoli et al. 2017), which could lead to interception and seizure by law enforcement. Size and weight also contribute to the high cost of firearms, through the costs of shipping heavy packages internationally. The dark web markets are also unstable (van Buskirk et al. 2017; Afilipoaie and Shortis 2018) due to numerous routine disruptions to their illicit activities. These disruptions include the seizure of dark web markets by law enforcement, the theft of deposits by market administrators, and the technical issues that are inherent with hosting content only accessible through the dark web. The dark web has, however, proven to be a source of firearms (Broadhurst et al. 2020; Holt and Lee 2022) that needs to be studied if we are to understand the role it plays in the illicit markets of firearms.

This chapter fits within the replication paradigm in that it seeks to assess the availability of firearms through platforms accessible only through the dark web. It builds on past research on the dark web and firearms and seeks to update the supply side of this illicit firearm market. Dark web merchants are known to evolve quickly over time (Soska and Christin 2015), and constant attention need to be invested in updating our understanding of this distribution channel. Martin et al. (2018) demonstrated, for example, how a change in opioid regulations affected what was distributed through the dark web, possibly increasing its share of the illicit opioid markets.

The data for this chapter comes from an in-depth indexing of the firearms markets accessible through the dark web. We used traditional search engines (Google, DuckDuckGo, Bing), directories (e.g. dark.fail) and dark web search engines (e.g. Ahmia) using multiple combinations of keywords to identify cryptomarkets and single-vendor shops advertising the sale of firearms. We used keywords such as *firearms, weapons,* and *guns* as well as popular firearm brands such as *Glock, Colt* and *Kalashnikov.* We identified thirty-four platforms that advertised firearms illicitly through the dark web. For each platform, we manually collected the following details for the weapons: 1) product name; 2) category; 3) manufacturer; 4) price (in USD); 5) description; 6) firearm is new or used; 7) name of seller, if on cryptomarkets. A total of 1,016 firearms were collected in December 2023, when the data collection occurred.

We present in the results section below the descriptive statistics on data that was collected on the firearms. Our aim is to describe the type of firearms being advertised, the characteristics and prices of these firearms. This will provide empirical evidence for future comparison with other distribution channels for illicit firearms for two main reasons. First, information on the demand side could not be collected from these advertisements. Single-vendor shops do not advertise the number of sales for each product, and even if they were to do so, it would be difficult to trust these numbers as the shop owners have a vested interest in artificially increasing these numbers. Second, cryptomarkets have unofficially banned firearms so as not to draw too much attention from law enforcement (Bright et al. 2023). Due in large part to the disruption efforts by law enforcement, Chainalysis (2023) has shown that the dark web sales for illicit goods and services are not increasing at the same pace as before, Cryptomarkets were valuable open-information sources as they provided sales figures for each product, managed by their 'neutral' administrators. These sales figures could be trusted more than those from single-vendor shops. Researchers lost access to this precious data for the most part with the unofficial ban on firearms. Recent research by Blais et al. (2022) demonstrates that firearms have all but disappeared from cryptomarkets over the past few years, although a few items are still for sale. Given the small number of advertisements collected on cryptomarkets, we provide no information in this chapter on the demand side of the firearms illicit markets facilitated by the dark web.

Results

We found a total of 1,016 advertisements related to firearms accessible on thirty-four platforms only accessible through the dark web. While this information was not systematically reported, one advertisement could contain more than one weapon or gun-related products. For instance, some handguns were sold along with magazines and ammunition. Advertisements sometimes revealed information about stocks of weapons. Platforms advertised between one and 307 products (mean = 30; S.D. = 59). The average platform therefore offered a somewhat large variety of products. Table 9.1 presents the types of products advertised for sale.

Most listings were for handguns (58.9 per cent) and long guns (21.9 per cent). Most firearms (87.0 per cent) were automatic or semi-automatic. Ammunition alone was also a popular product, with 7.6 per cent of all listings. Based on information found in the description of the product, ammunition was sold alongside firearms in 55.2 per cent of advertisements. Only three advertisements specifically indicated that firearms were not for

Table 9.1 Types of Products Advertised for Sale Through the Dark Web

Type	N	%
Handgun	598	58.9%
Long gun	222	21.9%
Ammunition	77	7.6%
PDF (instructions for building)	31	3.1%
Suppressor	21	2.1%
Holster	16	1.6%
Scope	17	1.7%
Vest	11	1.1%
Explosives	9	0.9%
Handgun part	3	0.3%
Taser	3	0.3%
Anti-tank weapon	2	0.2%
Rocket launcher	2	0.2%
Grenade	1	0.1%
Light	1	0.1%
3D gun	1	0.1%
Magazine	1	0.1%
TOTAL	**1,016**	**100.0%**

shipping but for dead drop only (not presented in Table 9.1). Platforms also advertised firearms components (e.g. handgun part, scope, suppressor) that might be easier to export due to their smaller size, and therefore likely lower detection rate. This has, however, yet to be confirmed by empirical research. Other lethal weapons included explosives and even rocket launchers and grenades. The PDF type refers to plans for individuals to build their own guns and prepare their own ammunition. These PDF files are not sufficient in and of themselves to build your own firearm. 3D-printers and manufactured metal pieces may be necessary to build a firearm, depending on the design (see Chapter 8).

Table 9.2 presents the manufacturer of the firearms for sale. These results indicate whether firearms for sale through the dark web were initially manufactured by legitimate producers or privately manufactured.

The name of the manufacturer was available for 779 of the 820 firearms (handguns and long guns), suggesting that at best 5 per cent of guns were not industrially manufactured. Table 9.2 indicates that 72.9 per cent of all advertisements involved the products of only fourteen manufacturers. These are the only manufacturers for which more that ten advertisements were found. Glock, Sig Sauer, Beretta, and Ruger represented 16.9 per cent, 7.2 per cent, 6.7 per cent, and 6.7 per cent or all advertisements, respectively. These findings indicate that most firearms found on the dark web originate from well-established manufacturers. Only one firearm was precisely advertised as a 3D gun made of polymer.

Table 9.2 Manufacturer of Firearms for Sale on Platforms Accessible Through the Dark Web

Manufacturer	N	%
Glock	132	16.9%
SIG Sauer	56	7.2%
Ruger	52	6.7%
Beretta	52	6.7%
CZ	39	5.0%
Colt	38	4.9%
Smith & Wesson	35	4.5%
Walther	33	4.3%
Heckler & Koch	29	3.7%
Springfield Armory	25	3.2%
Taurus	24	3.1%
FN	23	3.0%
Kimber	17	2.2%
Mossberg	13	1.7%
Other brands/Unknown	211	26.9%
Total	779	100.0%

Table 9.3 presents the prices for firearms in general, by category, and depending on whether the firearms are new or used.

Table 9.3 shows that, on average, a firearm was sold for $953.90. Prices varied between $199.00 and $11,180.00. The standard deviation ($996.00) and median ($763.00) indicate large variations in prices. In fact, about 80 per cent of all advertised firearms were offered for less than $1,000; the mean was influenced by some firearms that were sold at a very high price. For instance, one CheyTac M200, which is a military-type weapon renowned for its excellent precision and long-range capability, was advertised for $11,188.00. An MK48, a belt-fed machine gun for military operations, was advertised for $10,000.00.

Table 9.3 indicates that long guns were generally more expensive than handguns, with respective median prices of $708.50 and $1,037.80. Few variations were observed between new and used guns. New and used handguns were both advertised at a median price of $708.50. The median price for new long guns was $1,484.60 and $1,144.50 for used ones. Additional analyses suggest that the price for long guns was not necessarily influenced by the 'new or used' status, but rather by the characteristics of the firearm. Non-automatic weapons such as bolt-action rifles or lever-action rifles were on average more expensive than automatic or semi-automatic long guns ($1,937.10 vs. $1,344.80). Bolt-action rifles were quite expensive; they are precision weapons used in military or special forces operations. Automatic or semi-automatic handguns were advertised on average at $755.50 against $760.00 for non-automatic handguns (i.e. revolvers) (not shown in Table 9.3).

Table 9.3 Prices of Firearms[a]

	All firearms	**All handguns**	**All long guns**	**Handguns**		**Long guns**	
				New	**Used**	**New**	**Used**
N	819	597	222	532	65	213	9
Mean	953.9	756.0	1,486.2	762.2	705.2	1,484.6	1523.6
Median	763.0	708.5	1,037.8	708.5	708.5	1,000.0	1144.5
St. Dev.	996.0	410.9	1,681.1	432.2	139.1	1,706.2	962.6
Min	199.0	199.0	249.0	199.0	249.0	249.0	799.0
Max	11,188.0	5,800.0	11,188.0	5,800.0	1,253.0	11,188.0	3,180.0

[a] Analysis based on 819 observations. Data was missing for one case.

Figure 9.1 Wordcloud of product descriptions

Taking a more qualitative approach, it appears as though the markets provide very little information about the products they advertise. Listings included a median of sixteen words (min = 1; max = 505). These descriptions comprised the name of the product, and the bundled products (e.g. scope, ammunition). They also provided limited information on who can purchase the weapons, how it should be used, and if there were important things to know about the firearm.

Figure 9.1 presents the main words used to describe the firearms for sale. Figure 9.1 also provides the most important keywords that could be used in future research to identify firearms for sale. The most important words were not necessarily firearms themselves, but rather *rounds*, *trigger*, *magazine*, and *box*. These results suggest that the sellers list the parts that are included with firearms, but do not put all the emphasis on the firearms themselves. Important keywords also included popular manufacturers such as Glock, Ruger, and Beretta, and types of firearms such as 9 mm, pistol, and rifle.

Discussion

The dark web was believed at first to be a paradigm-shifting innovation that would transform illicit markets for drugs, but also for guns, malware, and many other illicit products (Aldridge and Décary-Hétu 2014). This chapter built on past research to understand the recent evolution of dark web-facilitated firearms transactions. Recent publications had found that cryptomarkets were not popular sources of illicit firearms, as this trade attracted too much attention from law enforcement (Blais et al. 2022).

Cryptomarket administrators have long banned the sale of poison, and more recently fentanyl-related products and firearms. These measures aim to mitigate the risk of law enforcement intervention and reduce the length of potential sentences for those convicted. We similarly find that cryptomarkets are not commonly used to advertise firearms, and that single-vendor shops are much more popular from a supply side.

When comparing prices with Holt and Lee (2022), we find very similar prices in our datasets. Combined, these results suggest first that inflation has not been reflected on sales facilitated by the dark web. This would be surprising, as the dark web prices for illicit products have traditionally reflected the street price for the same items, though often with a 'security premium' for the use of anonymity technologies that should in theory reduce the risks of arrests (Broséus et al. 2017). An alternative explanation is that the same websites that were advertising years ago are still in operation with minimal to no alterations. These platforms could actually be sting operations designed to lure potential buyers into sharing their data. Such a strategy is evidenced in Warren et al. (2020), where law enforcement operated a platform to infect its users and identify them. Paoli et al. (2017) suggested that sting operations were being deployed on the dark web, and this would explain why prices are static. The operators of the platforms are either gone, or glad to keep the low prices to lure in more unsuspecting customers. Another possibility is that the website operators are long gone, and that these merchant websites are no longer supported even though they remain online. Future research should consider engaging with the platform administrators to investigate if these prices are accurate, and how they could remain stable for so long. Another factor that warrants further examination along those lines is the fact that used guns are not much cheaper than new guns. Bright et al. (2023) found that there are many risks to reusing a firearm, and that new firearms could therefore in theory fetch higher prices.

The dark web unfortunately remains somewhat of a mystery as to the size and scope of the illicit firearms market it facilitates. This challenge has plagued past research (Broadhurst et al. 2020; Holt et al. 2022) that can at best only estimate the number of sales occurring through the dark web. Paoli et al. (2017) managed to complete an extensive review of the illicit sales of firearms online and found little evidence that the market was significant in size and scope. Given the quality of the websites that we indexed, and the small number of listings and information available, it would be surprising if this had changed over the past few years. The same challenge regarding the shipping of firearms (Holt et al. 2022) remains. In fact, Blais et al. (2022) found that several shipped firearms were intercepted by postal services or border agencies, and planned deliveries permitted to arrest the buyer. Although the Hydra marketplace in Russia offered drops where vendors would hide their products in a park, or a dark alley, and then send the coordinates to their buyers who could fetch the package, our results suggest that this strategy was quite uncommon. This means however that the sales must be local, and that the vendor can trap the buyer by giving them wrong directions. It remains to be seen if there would ever be a market for dead drops for firearms, and if so, in what country. The ease with which firearms can often be found in the streets of some jurisdictions (Braga et al. 2021) makes the dark web a less interesting distribution channel for many offenders. A recent publication by Oosthoek et al. (2023) suggests that tracking cryptocurrency wallets of single-vendor shops could potentially leak information about the demand side, though that methodology has yet to be applied to single-vendor shops that specialize in firearms.

Through this study, little could be gleaned about the role of organized crime groups in the illicit trafficking of firearms through the dark web. An interesting question to investigate in future research will be the role of organized crime in dark web illicit transactions. Single-vendor shops usually only advertise one type of product: firearms. This is not typical of large, organized crime groups, which often advertise online a large range of products (e.g. drugs, stolen financial information, firearms). We found no evidence or clear indication that organized crime groups were involved in this trade. These groups probably already have distribution channels for their firearms, and may rely more on personal relationships, rather than distant and anonymous online communications. Past research has suggested that organized crime groups have obtained illegal firearms using darknet marketplaces (Europol 2016) and that one of the main sources of illegal weapons for organized crime groups may be the dark web (Europol n.d.). These sources however are not relying on a clear methodology that could be replicated. Still, handguns appear as popular weapons both for organized crime groups (Hureau and Braga 2018) and for sale on the dark web, which suggests some sort of alignment between the potential demand and the supply. There has been evidence of criminal groups being active on other online channels, such as Telegram (Schaufelbühl et al. 2024; Ubbink 2019) and further research will need to investigate their implication in dark web vendor shops. With its significant resources, the adoption of the dark web by organized crime groups could seriously increase the number of firearms illicitly bought and sold through the dark web. For this to happen however, traditional distribution channels would likely have to be seriously disrupted, leading to a repositioning of actors.

Policy Implications

One could argue that the dark web should not be a priority for law enforcement agencies, as relatively few guns are advertised. Cryptomarket administrators have already banned sales of firearms to reduce arrest risks. Some cues also indicate that some platforms could indeed be sting operations. A careful monitoring of firearms offers and sales on the dark web could however be useful. Firearms are different from other services or products found on the dark web such as illicit drugs. Firearms are durable and often shared by offenders, suggesting that the relatively thin firearms market (the supply side) on the dark web could correspond to the demand side. Firearms recovered on crime scenes are sometimes close to fifty years old and still operational (Blais and Morselli 2014). Gang members are also known to have stocks of firearms; they have direct connections to well-established gun traffickers and can order large quantities of guns (Braga et al. 2021). Firearms found on the dark web share characteristics of guns prized by offenders and gang members, which are concealable handguns but also hard-to-conceal shoulder weapons with strong firepower (e.g. assault or military-style) with included ammunition (Wachtel 1998; Webster et al. 2002; Wintemute et al. 2004).

Guns found on the dark web are also industrially manufactured, indicating that prevention efforts should target the 'source' where the firearm was originally diverted from the primary market. Hence, the literature suggests that several guns originate from jurisdictions with lenient gun control policies (Hureau and Braga 2018). Tightening gun control laws could contribute to the prevention of firearms trafficking. In an era of globalisation and because of the transnational nature of firearms transactions facilitated by the dark web, international guidelines or resolutions should be adopted to prevent firearms trafficking and its collateral harm. Coordinated efforts should also be facilitated by some memorandum of understanding or international agreements as the sharing of information by police forces and border agencies allow to seize parcels with guns and arrest traffickers as well as buyers (Blais et al. 2022). Accordingly, additional efforts or actual efforts should at least be maintained to detect parcels with concealed guns or other related products. At last, several PDF files containing instructions to build firearms were put up for sale through the dark web. Tools and parts necessary to build firearms are often sold in several shops without any restrictions. Canada recently modified its legislation on firearms (see Bill C-21) to include in the definition of a firearm parts previously unregulated that could only be used to build firearms. This change was motivated by the growing number of privately manufactured firearms seized at crime scenes.

Legislators and law enforcement agencies would also do well to dispel the myth that the dark web is a secure and efficient platform from which to purchase illicit firearms. The dark web is depicted publicly as a state-free environment where anything can be purchased. While this is true, by highlighting the challenges, and the small number of actors involved, it may be possible to deter some people from using these platforms to purchase a firearm. Following the demise of Silk Road, the first large dark web cryptomarket, an enduring news report wave had told people that cheap drugs could be bought anonymously through the dark web. This news had brought a new generation of customers to cryptomarkets, and the same mistake should not be repeated. When speaking in public, government officials and law enforcement officers should be wary of praising indirectly the efficiency that the dark web affords.

Conclusion

The examination of the dark web as a conduit for illicit firearms transactions reveals a complex, albeit limited, landscape that is both influenced by and reflects broader trends in both legal and illegal firearm markets. Despite the inherent anonymity and the potential for global reach offered by the dark web, it remains a marginal player in the broader context of firearms trafficking. This is evidenced by the relatively stable prices and availability of firearms on these platforms, suggesting a market that is neither expanding nor becoming more accessible, despite technological advances and the potential for anonymity. The findings underscore the persistent challenge of tracking and curbing the flow of illegal firearms, particularly those facilitated through the dark web. While the platforms provide a method to circumvent traditional surveillance and tracking by law enforcement, their actual impact on the availability of illicit firearms appears limited. The predominance of scams, sting operations, and the logistical challenges of shipping firearms discretely further complicate transactions, thereby dampening the scale of operations and the effectiveness of the dark web as a reliable source of illicit firearms. Moreover, the enduring presence of industrially manufactured firearms suggests that significant sources of illicit firearms are likely diverted from legitimate markets. This highlights the importance of stringent controls and robust monitoring within the legal manufacturing and distribution channels. Strengthening regulations, improving international cooperation, and enhancing enforcement mechanisms to track and intercept illegal transactions are critical steps toward mitigating the risks associated with firearm trafficking. As policy makers and law enforcement agencies consider the implications of these findings, it is imperative that efforts are focused not only on curbing the immediate challenges posed by the dark web but also on addressing the underlying issues that facilitate the diversion of firearms from legal to illegal markets. By prioritizing comprehensive strategies that encompass both technological and regulatory measures, there is potential to significantly reduce the impact of the dark web on the global illicit firearms trade, thus enhancing public safety and security.

References

Afilipoaie, A., and Shortis, P. 2018. 'Crypto-market Enforcement-new Strategy and Tactics'. https://cointhinktank.com/upload/Crypto-Market-Enforcemnet-New-Strategy-and-Tactics.pdf Accessed 24 Jul. 2024.

Aldridge, Judith, and Décary-Hétu, David. 2014. 'Not an 'Ebay for Drugs': the Cryptomarket 'Silk Road' as a Paradigm Shifting Criminal Innovation'. https://ssrn.com/abstract=2436643 or http://dx.doi.org/10.2139/ssrn.2436643 Accessed 24 Jul. 2024.

Blais, Etienne, et al. 2022. 'Le marché des armes à feu illicites au Québec: stratégies et sources d'approvisionnement'. Report prepared for the Public Safety Quebec. Montreal: Université de Montréal. https://www.researchgate.net/publication/365714976_Le_marche_des_armes_a_feu_au_Quebec_strategies_et_sources_d'approvisionnement Accessed 27 Jul. 2024.

Braga, Anthony A., et al. 2002. "The Illegal Supply of Firearms'. *Crime and Justice* 29: pp.319–352. https://doi.org/10.1086/652223 Accessed 24 Jul. 2024.

Braga, A. A., Brunson, R. K., Cook, P. J., Turchan, B., and Wade, B. 2021. 'Underground Gun Markets and the Flow of Illegal Guns into the Bronx and Brooklyn: A Mixed Methods Analysis'. *Journal of Urban Health* 98: pp. 596–608. https://doi.org/10.1007/s11524-020-00477-z Accessed 24 Jul. 2024.

Bright, David, et al. 2023. '"I Know a Guy and He's Got Guns Galore": Accessing Crime Guns in the Australian Illicit Firearms Market'. *Deviant Behavior* 44 (5): pp. 671–689. https://doi.org/10.1080/01639625.2022.2086838. Accessed 24 Jul. 2024.

Broadhurst, Roderic, et al. 2020. 'Illicit Firearms and Other Weapons on Darknet Markets' (SSRN Scholarly Paper ID 3653619). *Social Science Research Network*. https://www.aic.gov.au/sites/default/files/2021-03/ti622_illicit_firearms_and_other_weapons_on_darknet_markets.pdf Accessed 27 Jul. 2024.

Broséus, Julian, et al. 2017. 'A Geographical Analysis of Trafficking on a Popular Darknet Market'. *Forensic Science International* 277: pp. 88–102. DOI: 10.1016/j.forsciint.2017.05.021 Accessed 24 Jul. 2024.

Bureau of Alcohol, Tobacco, Firearms, and Explosives. 2018. *Firearms Guides: Importation & Verification of Firearms, Ammunition, and Firearms (Gun Control Act Definitions).* https://www.atf.gov/firearms/firearms-guides-importation-verification-firearms-ammunition-gun-control-act-definitions Accessed 24 Jul. 2024.

Chainalaysis. 2023. *Crypto Crime Report.* https://go.chainalysis.com/crypto-crime-2024.html Accessed 24 Jul. 2024.

Cook, Philip J., Pollack, Harold A., and White, Kailey. 2019. 'The Last Link: From Gun Acquisition to Criminal Use'. *Journal of Urban Health* 96 (5): pp. 784–791.

Copeland, Christopher, Mikaela Wallin, and Thomas J Holt. 2019. 'Assessing the Practices and Products of Darkweb Firearm Vendors'. *Deviant Behavior* 41: pp. 1–20. DOI:10.1080/01639625.2019.1596465. Accessed 24 Jul. 2024.

Dingledine, Roger, Mathewson, Nick, and Syverson, Paul F. 2004. 'Tor: The Second-Generation Onion Router'. *USENIX security symposium* 4: pp. 303–320.

Europol. n.d. *Illicit Firearms Trafficking.* https://www.europol.europa.eu/crime-areas/illicit-firearms-trafficking Accessed 24 Jul. 2024

Europol. 2016. *Trafficking of Firearms.* https://www.europol.europa.eu/socta/2017/trafficking-of-firearms.html Accessed 24 Jul. 2024.

Europol. 2020. *Global Action Against Mail-Order Gun Traffickers.* https://www.europol.europa.eu/media-press/newsroom/news/global-action-against-mail-order-gun-traffickers Accessed 24 Jul. 2024.

Holt, Thomas, and Lee, Jin Ree. 2022. A Crime Script Model Of Dark Web Firearms Purchasing. *American Journal of Criminal Justice* 48; pp. 509–529.

Holt, Thomas, Lee, Jin Ree, and Smirnova, Olga. 2022. 'An Assessment of the State of Firearm Sales on the Dark Web'. *Journal of Crime and Justice.* https://www.tandfonline.com/doi/full/10.1080/0735648X.2022.2058062 Accessed 24 Jul. 2024.

Hureau, David M., and Braga, Anthony A. 2018. 'The Trade in Tools: The Market for Illicit Guns in High-Risk Networks'. *Criminology* 56 (3): pp. 510–545.

Kegler, Scott R., et al. 2022. 'Vital Signs: Changes in Firearm Homicide and Suicide Rates—United States, 2019–2020'. *Morbidity and Mortality Weekly Report* 71 (19): p. 656.

Laferrière, Dominique, and Décary-Hétu, David. 2023. 'Examining the Uncharted Dark Web: Trust Signalling On Single Vendor Shops'. *Deviant Behavior* 44 (1): pp. 37–56.

Lee, Jarone, et al. 2014. 'The Economic Cost of Firearm-Related Injuries in the United States from 2006 to 2010'. *Surgery* 155 (5): pp. 894–898.

Martin, James, et al. 2018. 'Effect of Restricting The Legal Supply of Prescription Opioids on Buying through Online Illicit Marketplaces: Interrupted Time Series Analysis'. *British Medical Journal.* https://pubmed.ncbi.nlm.nih.gov/29899119/ Accessed 24 Jul. 2024.

Morselli, Carlo. 2002. 'The Relational Dynamics in Illegal Firearm Transactions'. *Canadian Journal of Criminology* 44 (3): pp. 255–276.

Morselli, Carlo. 2013. 'Assessing Network Patterns in Illegal Firearm Markets'. In *Transnational Organized Crime*, edited by M.E. Beare, pp. 375–396. London: Routledge.

Morselli, Carlo, and Blais, Dominik. 2014. 'The Mobility of Stolen Guns in Quebec'. *European Journal of Criminology* 20: pp. 379–397.

O'Malley, Roberta, et al. 2019. 'The Dark Web as a Platform for Crime: An Exploration of Illicit Drug, Firearm, CSAM, and Cybercrime Markets' (pp. 1–27). DOI:10.1007/978-3-319-90307-1_17-1 Accessed 24 Jul. 2024.

Oosthoek, Kris, Van Staalduinen, Mark, and Smaragdakis, Georgios. 2023. 'Quantifying Dark Web Shops' Illicit Revenue'. *IEEE Access* 11: pp. 4794–4808.

Paoli, Giacomo, et al. 2017. 'Behind the Curtain: The Illicit Trade of Firearms, Explosives and Ammunition on the Dark Web'. *RAND Corporation*. https://www.rand.org/pubs/research_reports/RR2091.html Accessed 24 Jul. 2024.

Perrat, Jean-François. 2018. Un « deep/dark web »? 'Les métaphores de la profondeur et de l'ombre sur le réseau Tor'. *Networks and Communication Studies* 32(1): pp. 61–86. https://doi.org/10.4000/netcom.3134 Accessed 24 Jul. 2024.

Pierce, Glenn L., et al. 2004. 'Characteristics and Dynamics of Illegal Firearms Markets: Implications for a Supply-Side Enforcement Strategy'. *Justice Quarterly* 21 (2): pp. 391–422.

Rhumorbarbe, Damien, et al. 2018. 'Characterising the Online Weapons Trafficking on Cryptomarkets'. *Forensic Science International* 283: pp. 16–20.

Schaufelbühl, Stefan, et al. 2024. 'The Emergence of 3D-Printed Firearms: An Analysis of Media and Law Enforcement Reports'. *Forensic Science International* 8. https://doi.org/10.1016/j.fsisyn.2024.100464 Accessed 24 Jul. 2024

Soska, Kyle, and Christin, Nicolas. 2015. 'Measuring the Longitudinal Evolution of the Online Anonymous Marketplace Ecosystem'. *24th USENIX security symposium (USENIX security 15)* pp. 33–48. https://www.usenix.org/system/files/sec15-paper-soska-updated_v2.pdf Accessed 24 Jul. 2024.

Ubbink, Jeroen. 2019. 'Characterization of Illegal Dark Web Arms Markets. Guns and the Dark Web'. Masters Thesis. Eindhoven University of Technology.

United Nations Office on Drugs and Crime (UNODC). 2020. *Global Study on Firearms 2020.* https://www.unodc.org/documents/data-and-analysis/Firearms/2020_REPORT_Global_Study_on_Firearms_Trafficking_2020_web.pdf Accessed 24 Jul. 2024.

Van Buskirk, Joe, et al. 2017. 'The Recovery of Online Drug Markets Following Law Enforcement and Other Disruptions'. *Drug and Alcohol Dependence* 173: pp. 159–162.

Wachtel, Julius. 1998. 'Sources of Crime Guns in Los Angeles, California'. *Policing: An International Journal of Police Strategies and Management* 21 (2): pp. 220–239.

Warren, Ian, Mann, Monique, and Molnar, Adam. 2020. 'Lawful Illegality: Authorizing Extraterritorial Police Surveillance'. *Surveillance & Society* 18 (3): pp. 357–369.

Webster, Daniel W., et al. 2002. 'How Delinquent Youth Acquire Guns: Initial Versus Most Recent Gun Acquisitions'. *Journal of Urban Health* 79 (1): pp. 60–69.

Werbick, Meghan, et al. 2021. 'Firearm Violence: A Neglected "Global Health" Issue'. *Globalization and Health* 17: pp. 1–5.

Wintemute, Garen J., et al. 2004. 'The Life Cycle of Crime Guns: A Description Based on Guns Recovered From People in California'. *Annals of Emergency Medicine* 43 (6): pp. 733–742.

Wintemute, Garen J. 2021. 'Ghost Guns: Spookier Than You Think They Are'. *Injury Epidemiology* 8(13): pp. 1–3. https://doi.org/10.1186/s40621-021-00306-0 Accessed 24 Jul. 2024.

10

A Multiplex Network Perspective on Illicit Firearms Trafficking

Fenna van der Wijk, David Bright, and Freddie Kootstra

Illicit Firearms Trafficking

Illicit firearms trafficking is a transnational problem affecting communities worldwide. A variety of factors, such as armed conflict, crime, and violence, contribute to demand for different quantities of illicit firearms (United Nations Office on Drugs and Crime (UNODC 2019). Therefore, within the illicit firearms market, a distinction exists between large- and small-scale trafficking. Large-scale firearms trafficking is often linked to the shipment of container loads of firearms to conflict zones and embargoed or banned destinations around the world (UNODC 2015; 2019; Squires 2021). In contrast, small-scale firearms trafficking facilitates the procurement of smaller numbers of firearms for criminal activities, personal protection, and collection (Savona and Mancuso 2017; UNODC 2020a). The focus of this chapter is on trafficking of firearms on the small scale, for criminal use, in the European context. Issues related to trafficking of firearms for warfare will not be discussed.

Small-scale firearms trafficking for criminal use is mostly based on demand for firearms for instrumental and symbolic purposes by organized criminal groups (Spapens 2007; Savona and Mancuso 2017). Although various actors are involved (e.g. corrupt officials and professionals, hobbyists and amateurs, outlawmotorcycle gangs (OMGs), and criminal youth groups), the supply of firearms is primarily conducted by organized criminal groups (OCGs) and those affiliated with such groups (EUCPN Secretariat 2016; Buscemi et al. 2018; Sneddon 2021; Liem and Krüsselmann 2022). Due to a lack of law enforcement attention and reliable data, obtaining a clear picture of the criminal groups involved in illicit firearms trafficking has proven to be difficult (Savona and Mancuso 2017; Duquet and Goris 2018).

Fenna van der Wijk, David Bright, and Freddie Kootstra, *A Multiplex Network Perspective on Illicit Firearms Trafficking* In: *Illicit Firearms Markets and Organized Crime*. Edited by: David Bright, Oxford University Press. © Oxford University Press 2025. DOI: 10.1093/9780198902409.003.0011

Most criminal groups engage in firearms trafficking in addition to other illicit activities (UNODC 2015; Squires 2021). Those other trafficking activities, particularly drug trafficking, provide OCGs with well-established networks, routes, personnel, and skills that are directly transferable to trafficking illicit firearms (Savona and Mancuso 2017; UNODC 2020b; 2024; De Schutter and Duquet 2023). In comparison to illicit drug trafficking, which is characterized by high profit margins, the trafficking of firearms is not so lucrative. Therefore, it tends to be a supplementary rather than a primary source of income for the OCGs involved (EUCPN 2016; Duquet and van Alstein 2016; De Schutter and Duquet 2023). Moreover, firearms are generally trafficked for reasons other than monetary profit, such as to facilitate access to firearms for other criminal activities (e.g. armed robbery), crimes involving threats of violence, and for the protection of illicit marketplaces, illicit commodities, and money (Savona and Mancuso 2017).

Although little is known about the structure of firearms trafficking groups, European reports state that criminal groups involved in firearms trafficking are often (very) small and work together for a limited amount of time (Spapens and Bruinsma 2002; Duquet and van Alstein 2016). Generally, these groups are loosely structured and constitute highly flexible and horizontal, or non-hierarchical, networks (Buscemi et al. 2018). The flexibility of firearms trafficking networks allows them to maximize profit and quickly adapt to changing circumstances, such as law enforcement interventions (Bright et al. 2018). Connections between actors are often established based on pre-existing connections, for example with family and friends (Buscemi et al. 2018; UNODC 2020b; De Schutter and Duquet 2023). The core of those groups consists of an importer (in the destination country), a supplier (in the source country) and couriers that do the cross-border transport (Spapens 2007). The firearms are eventually sold through a network of intermediaries in the country of destination (Spapens and Bruinsma 2002; Duquet and van Alstein 2016).

Given the paucity of previous research on the structure of criminal groups that engage in illicit firearms trafficking, we draw from research in analogous trafficking contexts. Across a range of illicit markets including illicit drugs (e.g. Bright et al. 2012), trafficking in people (Campana 2020), vehicle rebirthing (Morselli and Roy 2008), and firearms (e.g. Duquet and van Alstein 2016), small loosely connected groups of criminals appear to be involved. Research tends to show that these groups show characteristics that include three primary structures: hierarchies, markets, and networks (von Lampe 2015). These three forms of social structure differ in key ways. They are best conceptualized as ideal forms of social organization, but in the real world these different structures often overlap with each other such that groups can show elements of one or more of these social structures.

First, hierarchies involve some type of authority structure within a group with a chain of command from leaders down to those who undertake activities under instruction of those above in the hierarchy. Hierarchies are characterized by dominance and power asymmetry, where lower-ranked members tend to do the risky work. Second, market-based structures are driven by market forces, such as supply and demand, and are characterized by one-off transactions with no expectation of future transactions (Savona and Mancuso 2017). This results in impersonal and short-term transactional relationships. And third, networks are loose non-hierarchical structures that can facilitate trust and resource/skill pooling. Network structure can help the group to balance efficiency and security of their operations (Morselli 2007).

In reality, scholars converge on the finding that criminal groups are often comprised of social structures that incorporate two or three of these types of social organization (e.g. network configurations with some hierarchical elements; see Bright et al. 2012). In this chapter, social network analysis (SNA) will be used to explore the relative presence of these three forms of social organization within a group that engaged in firearms trafficking.

The Network Perspective and Social Network Analysis (SNA)

The network perspective draws on theory and analysis to explore patterns of connection. The structure of these connections or *ties* emerges as a complete network from the individual dyadic relationships between pairs of entities which are usually referred to as *nodes* (e.g. between individuals in a group). In the case of social configurations such as groups of people, researchers use social network analysis to identify patterns in social structures in the context of the overall functioning or operation of the group (e.g. an organized criminal group). In social networks, the nodes are usually people who are referred to as *actors*. A network can be conceptualized as the actors (i.e. nodes) that comprise the social group, the ties between the actors (e.g. criminal) and the emerging patterns and structures of the connections between actors. SNA can be described as a set of analytical techniques that can be used to visualize or map the network and to explore patterns of ties between actors (e.g. see Borgatti et al. 2018). For example, SNA can be used to identify actors who are particularly active or influential in the network. SNA can also be used to identify actors who are strategically positioned between other actors (often called 'brokers') who have the capacity to mobilize resources, transfer information, or share knowledge more efficiently.

Network ties can be directed or undirected. For undirected ties, there is no direction represented by the tie and the connection between the two actors applies equally to both actors. Directed ties, on the other hand, represent the direction of the relationship or exchange. For example, in an organized criminal group, Person A (a firearms dealer) may provide illicit firearms to Person B (a buyer), but the exchange of firearms does not move in the other direction. Actors within social networks can possess a range of attributes (e.g. skills, knowledge) and/or resources (e.g. money, goods). These characteristics can be referred to as actor-level attributes and can be considered as the human capital that is possessed by network actors. Previous research on criminal networks has examined particular roles that individuals play in the network (e.g. courier, dealer; see Bright et al. 2015). Where there are multiple types of ties or many different actor attributes, SNA can examine these different ties and attributes separately or as an aggregate, sometimes referred to as multiplex network analysis. We discuss this approach in the next section.

Social network analysis has been used to study a range of organized crime groups including mafia groups (e.g. Calderoni 2013) and outlaw motorcycle gangs (e.g. Bright et al. 2023; Coutinho et al. 2020) and a range of illicit trafficking contexts, including people (e.g. Campana 2018), illicit drugs (e.g. Bright et al. 2012), and stolen motor vehicles (see Morselli and Roy 2008), in addition to a range of other illicit commodities. SNA has also been employed in related fields such as the study of terrorism and extremism (e.g. Bright et al. 2020a; 2020b). A few studies (e.g. Bichler and Malm 2013; Leuprecht and Aulthouse 2014) have used SNA to study the trafficking of illicit firearms and we turn to these studies later in this chapter.

Multiplex Networks

Human interactions are inherently complex and often comprise multiple affiliations (e.g. friendship, kinship, criminal). Therefore, most social networks are *multiplex networks*, meaning that actors are connected via a range of different types of ties. To use a relatively simple example, ties might be of two types, indicating that two actors are both friends and co-offenders involved in illicit firearms trafficking.

Uniplex SNA, using only single tie types, can miss important information about the network such as whether ties between actors are characterized by single or multiple relations (see Robins 2009). In the case of criminal groups, researchers and law enforcement practitioners alike could be 'missing critical insights into the behaviour, strengths, and weaknesses of social networks by ignoring the multidimensionality of human relationships' (Hamill et al. 2008 28). Similarly, SNA metrics such as centrality ties between actors are valued equally (Schwartz and Rouselle 2009). That is, actors with identical centrality scores would be considered equally important, without consideration of other key data such as the range of tie types that exist between any two actors in the network. Indeed, SNA conducted on multiplex networks may reveal important actors and network structures that emerge from the multidimensionality present in relationships between actors.

Data that describes multiple relations among the same set of actors is called 'multiplex data' (e.g. see Hanneman and Riddle 2013). One approach to using multiplex data is the construction of a 'super-sociomatrix' formed by merging several matrices, in which each matrix or layer corresponds to one type of relation or tie (see Magnani et al. 2013; Magnani and Rossi 2013). A matrix contains all the actors in the network layer and information about the presence (indicated by a 1) or absence of ties (indicated by a 0) between pairs of actors. Similarly, Hamill et al. (2008) recommend the use of several network layers in which different types of connections between actors are analysed separately.

Multiplex network approaches have been employed previously to study the social structure of an organized crime group (Smith and Papachristos 2016), drug trafficking (Bright et al. 2015), and political corruption (Diviák et al. 2019). To date, no study has used a multiplex network approach to study firearms trafficking, most likely due to a lack of rich data to support such analyses. To our knowledge, this study is the first to do so.

Social Network Research on Firearms Trafficking

Given the general scarcity of scientific knowledge on firearms trafficking, it is not surprising that there are only a few studies in which SNA has been applied to groups involved in firearms trafficking. The majority of these focus on large-scale firearms trafficking, trafficking to embargoed destinations and/or firearms trafficking networks in which the actors are countries or states (Curwen 2007; Kinsella 2004; 2006; 2013; 2014; Bichler and Malm 2013). Others focus on small-scale firearms trafficking and/or criminal groups, where the actors in the network are individuals (Morselli 2012; Leuprecht and Aulthouse 2014; van Wanrooij and Sapulete 2019). Because this is the focus of our chapter, these studies will be briefly discussed.

Morselli (2012) studied the personal networks of twenty incarcerated and non-incarcerated illicit firearms acquirers. In line with earlier findings, the networks of most respondents were either open or brokered, meaning that they were able to acquire firearms through direct contact with a multitude of suppliers, or indirectly through close and trusted intermediaries. Leuprecht and Aulthouse (2014) mapped the structure of six cross-border firearms trafficking networks. Two took the form of simple chains in which two or three actors were involved, another three were hubs consisting of multiple peripheral actors connected to one or two central actor(s), and one was a more complex multiplayer network featuring multiple central actors. Van Wanrooij and Sapulete (2019) explored the network of forty firearms dealers, firearms possessors, and terrorism suspects. The network consisted of twenty-two separate components (a component is a group of connected actors), where one component with fifty-five actors contained all identified firearms dealers. The dealers were located in the periphery of the overall network.

While these studies reveal important characteristics of network structure and identify key actors in the networks, each suffers weaknesses in terms of reliability and robustness due to evidence from public sources (e.g. new articles and police reports) and primary data from police databases (Morselli 2012; Leuprecht and Aulthouse 2014; van Wanrooij and Sapulete 2019). In this chapter, we contribute to the growing literature on illicit firearms trafficking networks by using a multiplex network approach to examine the structure and social dynamics of a group involved in trafficking firearms. The aims of the study were to examine the network structure of a criminal group involved in firearms trafficking with a focus on the flows of commodities (firearms, money, equipment) and the interactions (orders, planning, negotiation) between actors. To accomplish this, we employed a multiplex approach to examine the structure of different network layers.

Method

Data Collection

In this study, we extracted data from case files constructed in the course of a Dutch police investigation.[i] The group of suspects (N = 14) who were detected as part of this investigation was primarily involved in the trafficking of firearms, explosives, and ammunition. The case files consisted of a range of documents containing information obtained from telephone intercepts, listening devices, GPS tracking devices, text and chat messages, camera observations, forensic investigations, suspect interrogations, and witness statements.

Data Processing

Two sets of information were collected from the case files: (1) data about the involvement, skills, and resources of the individual actors regarding firearms trafficking, and (2) details about the relationships between actors. Coding of ties between actors was conducted in two steps. First, a relational tie was considered extant between any pair of actors where there was any evidence of a criminally relevant connection between them, for example, where a pair of actors co-offended, texted, or called each other on the phone, or were seen together. This resulted in a network of forty-two actors, who were directly or indirectly related to the criminal group, and 112 undirected ties between them. Undirected ties are by nature bidirectional (mutual), while directed ties have a specific direction (one-way).

Next, criteria were formulated for determining what types of ties were present between actors. After reading the case files in detail, six tie types (three commodities and three dynamics) emerged from the data. These types and their criteria are shown in Table 10.1. We coded two types of ties between actors. First, based on the types of commodities exchanged and second based on the social dynamics between actors. Commodity ties represent ties across which actors exchanged firearms, money, and equipment. These were all directed ties to show directionality of commodity

[i] Permission to access the case files of the investigation was provided by the Dutch Ministry of Justice and Security. This study is registered in the research portal of the Faculty of Behavioural and Social Sciences of the University of Groningen (SOC-2324-S-0005).

Table 10.1 Description of the Different Tie Types Identified in the Network

Tie type		Description	Criteria
Commodities	Firearms	Actor A gives a quantity of firearms to actor B*	Firearms, detonators, explosives, and/or ammunition
	Money	Actor A gives a sum of money to actor B	Cash or transfer, not always in exchange for firearms
	Equipment	Actor A provides a piece of equipment to actor B	E.g. wires, phones
Dynamics	Orders	Actor A gives orders to actor B	Actor A tells (or asks) actor B (in a pressing manner) to do something or gives actor B an assignment which could be any task (i.e. not always related to firearms trafficking) as long as there is a consistent pattern
	Negotiation	Actor A negotiates about firearms with actor B	Actor A and actor B are involved in discussing supply and demand of firearms (and prices, if available)**
	Planning	Actor A and actor B plan a specific activity related to firearms trafficking (e.g. a firearms transaction or transport) together	Actor A and actor B are planning a specific activity related to the firearms trafficking process in the future (e.g. meeting to prepare a firearms transport and scheduling a meeting or preparing for a firearms transaction)
Unknown		Actor A and actor B are connected but the nature of the tie is unknown	No information concerning the six link types between actor A and actor B

* A tie would be typed as 'firearms' when person A physically delivers a firearm to person B. Sometimes firearms were delivered by multiple actors, e.g. three actors, so that from all these three actors a separate 'firearms' tie would go from them (actors A, B, and C) to the buyer (person D): (person A to person D, person B to person D, and person C to person D).

** In case there was only information about demand (actor A gets in contact with actor B (seller) and asks for a firearm) this was not counted as a negotiation tie.

exchanges. The second category of ties represent social dynamics between actors including giving orders, negotiating, and planning. Of these three tie types, negotiation and planning were undirected, while giving orders was directed to show which actor was giving orders and which actor was receiving orders.

For analytical purposes, the 112 undirected ties in the network were treated as 224 directed ties. The undirected ties (negotiation and planning) were counted twice. This was done in order to analyse these ties together with the other directed ties (firearms, money, equipment, and orders). There was sufficient information to classify the tie types of 105 of all (224) known ties (47 per cent) while for 119 ties (53 per cent) the tie type remained unknown due to insufficient information. We then created seven matrices: six for the six different tie types and one for the merged network. The merged network consists of all actors and all ties including those ties of which the tie type remained unknown. Each matrix contains all actors and indicates whether a tie exists between each pair of actors in the dataset.

Social Network Analysis

The software package UCINET was used to analyse the six individual network layers or tie types and the merged network (Borgatti et al. 2002). The visualizations in this study were created by using the visdcc package (https://pypi.org/project/visdcc/) within the programming language Python (Van Rossum and Drake 2009). To calculate measures on the network level for the individual network layers and only for the actors present in those layers, actors that had no tie (either sending or receiving) in a layer were removed from the corresponding matrix. Because of this, the matrices for the different tie types were of varying sizes in terms of number of actors (and ties). Specifically, *density, degree centralization, indegree centralization, outdegree centralization* and *average degree* were calculated. *Density* is the ratio of the number of existing ties to the number of possible ties between actors in a network. *Degree centralization* indicates the extent to which a network is centralized around one or a few specific actors. *In-/outdegree centralization* measures the extent to which the incoming/outgoing ties of actors in a network are concentrated around one or a few specific actors. *Average degree* is simply the average number of ties of the actors in a network.

At the actor level, *degree centrality* and *betweenness centrality* were calculated for all actors to identify the most prominent actors in the firearms trafficking network (Morselli 2009; 2013). *Degree centrality* refers to the number of ties each actor has with other actors, and can be interpreted to indicate those actors who are most active and influential in the network. *Betweenness centrality* measures the number of times an actor is on the shortest path between pairs of actors, and can reveal actors who are brokers (i.e. connecting otherwise disconnected actors).

Results and Discussion

The merged network and the six individual network layers were analysed separately. The six network layers comprised of three layers based on ties representing the commodities exchanged and three layers based on ties representing the social dynamics between actors. Figure 10.1 displays a network

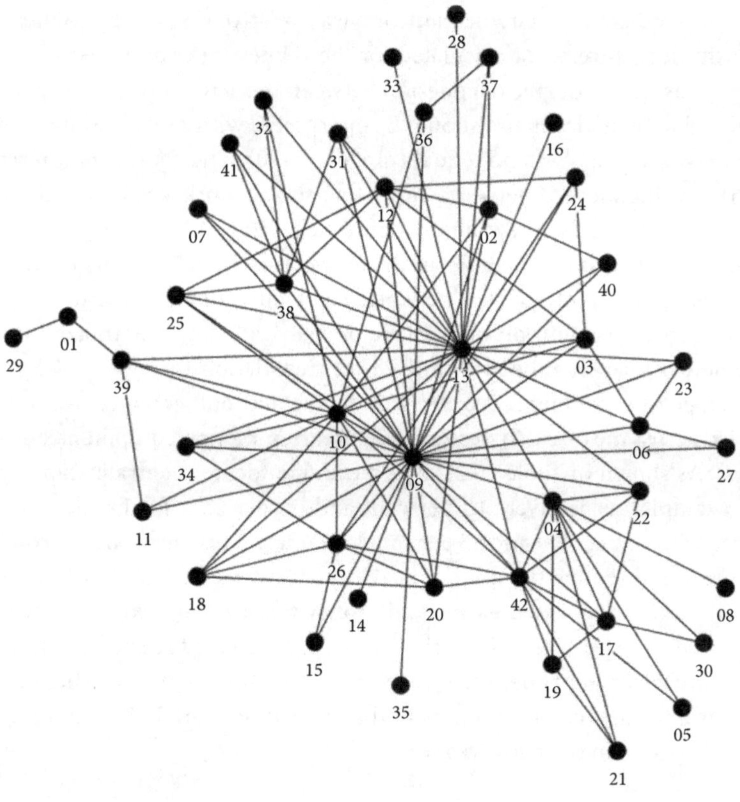

Figure 10.1 The merged network

map or visualization of the merged firearms trafficking network. This network includes all tie types, including those of unknown type. The merged network consisted of forty-two actors and 224 ties. The actors in the network were all connected to each other, forming a 'connected component'. Figures 10.2a–10.2f show network maps of each of the six network layers, highlighting the actors present in each layer, set against the merged network in the background. Also here, the actors involved in the separate layers formed connected components, except for the layer of negotiation which consisted of four discrete components.

Table 10.2 shows the descriptive measures at the network level for the merged network and the network layers. In terms of relative number of actors and ties, the largest network layers were the layers of planning (twenty actors) and the exchange of firearms (nineteen actors) while the smallest network layer was the exchange of equipment (five actors). The density of the merged network was 0.13, which means that 13 per cent of all possible ties between actors in the firearms trafficking network were present, indicating that the network was relatively sparsely connected. Density scores were not calculated for the six network layers because they only measure the degree of cohesion between the actors present in each individual network layer and should be interpreted with caution as the size of the network layers was not equal (range = 5–20). The centralization score (0.61) for the merged network shows that the network was highly centralized around one or a few highly connected actor(s), often referred to as 'hubs'. At first glance, the hubs in the network seem to be actors 09 and 13 (located in the centre of the network, see Figure 10.1). We return to this finding in the section on network actor metrics below. Centralization for the network layers ranged from 0.21 for negotiation through to 1 for the exchange of equipment. Scores for indegree and outdegree centralization varied across the directed tie types (i.e. firearms, money, equipment, and orders). As shown in Table 10.2, indegree and outdegree centralization were, for example, respectively 15 per cent and 38 per cent for firearms, compared with 11 per cent and 53 per cent for money. This means that incoming firearms and money ties are not heavily concentrated around one or a few actor(s), but outgoing firearms and money ties are more concentrated. In other words, while there is a variety of actors receiving firearms and money, there are fewer actors delivering firearms or sending money to other actors. The average degree of the actors in the merged network is 5.33 and ranges from 0.8 to 1.9 in the network layers.

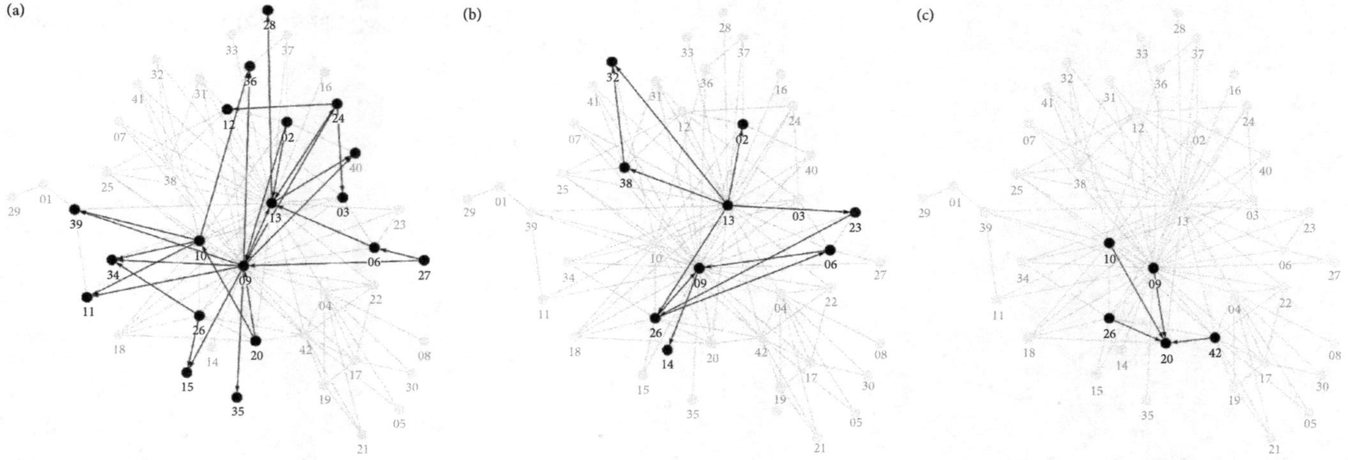

Figure 10.2 (a) Firearms, (b) Money, (c) Equipment

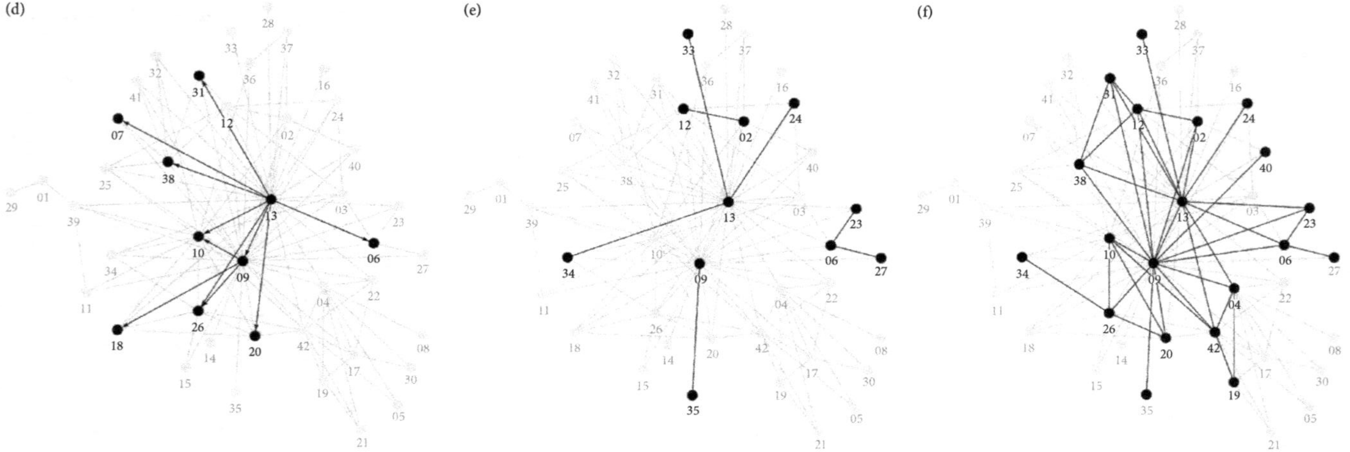

Figure 10.2 (d) Orders, (e) Negotiation, (f) Planning.

Table 10.2 Descriptive Metrics for the Merged Network and the Network Layers

		Network layers					
Metrics	**Merged network**	**Firearms**	**Money**	**Equipment**	**Orders**	**Negotiation**	**Planning**
Actors	42	19	9	5	10	11	20
Ties	224	28	11	4	11	14	76
Components	1	1	1	1	1	4	1
Avg. degree	5.33	1.47	1.22	0.80	1.10	1.27	1.90
C*	.61	.57	.41	1	.81	.21	.60
C (in)	-	.15	.11	1	.11	-	-
C (out)	-	.38	.53	.06	.85	-	-

*C indicates degree centralization

Table 10.3, together with the Figures 10.2a–10.2f, displays the number of network layers as well as which specific layers each actor is present in. There were twelve actors (29 per cent) that did not appear in any of the six network layers (i.e. none of their ties are typed). Similarly, there were twelve actors (29 per cent) that belonged to only one network layer (half of which to firearms). Only one actor, actor 09 (one of the two network hubs), was involved in all layers. The three actors 06, 13 (the other hub), and 26 were each involved in five network layers.

Additionally, Table 10.3 shows the degree centrality and betweenness centrality scores for all the actors in the merged network and the different network layers. The analysis of the merged network identifies actors 09 and 13 as being highest on degree centrality (respectively twenty-nine and twenty-seven undirected ties) and betweenness centrality (respectively 348 and 297). When analysing the network layers separately, these actors were present in all layers, except for actor 09 in the layer of equipment. Consistent with their position in the merged network, both actors were also highest on degree and betweenness centrality in half of the network layers (firearms, orders and planning). Actor 13 gives orders to eight other actors in the network and actor 09 gives orders to three others, while receiving orders only from actor 13. This suggests that there were some hierarchical structures within the network, where actor 13 seems to be the boss and actor 09 his right-hand man. Additionally, actor 13 is most prominent in the money layer, in terms of sending money (outdegree = 5), as well as in the negotiation layer

Table 10.3 Degree and Betweenness Centrality Scores of all Actors in the Merged Network and Different Network Layers

	Merged network		Firearms			Money			Equipment			Orders			Negotiation		Planning		Total
Actors	Degree	Betweenness	Indegree	Outdegree	Betweenness	Indegree	Outdegree	Betweenness	Indegree	Outdegree	Betweenness	Indegree	Outdegree	Betweenness	Degree	Betweenness	Degree	Betweenness	Network layers
01	2	40.00																	0
02	6	4.15	0	2	0.00	1	0	0.00							1	0.00	3	0.00	4
03	6	1.53	1	0	0.00														1
04	10	108.37															4	7.50	1
05	2	0.00																	0
06	5	3.83	1	1	2.50	1	1	0.00				1	0	0.00	2	1.00	4	18.00	5
07	3	0.00										1	0	0.00					1
08	1	0.00																	0
09	29	348.47	4	8	44.50	2	1	4.00	0	1	0.00	1	3	1.00	1	0.00	14	97.67	6

10	14	44.02	1	4	2.00				0	1	0.00	2	0	0.00			4	2.50	4
11	3	0.00	2	0	0.00														1
12	8	3.67	1	0	0.00										1	0.00	5	0.67	3
13	27	297.41	4	3	30.00	0	5	0.00				0	8	0.00	3	3.00	11	52.17	5
14	1	0.00				1	0	0.00											1
15	2	0.00	2	0	0.00														1
16	1	0.00																	0
17	6	17.35																	0
18	5	0.00										1	0	0.00					1
19	4	0.33															2	0.00	1
20	6	0.61	0	2	0.00				4	0	0.00	1	0	0.00			3	0.00	4
21	3	0.00																	0
22	5	1.31																	0
23	3	0.00				1	1	0.00							1	0.00	3	0.00	3

(continued)

Table 10.3 Continued

	Merged network		Firearms			Money			Equipment			Orders			Negotiation		Planning		Total
24	4	0.00	1	4	26.00										1	0.00	1	0.00	3
25	5	0.45																	0
26	8	7.90	0	2	0.00	2	2	6.00	0	1	0.00	2	0	0.00			4	18.00	5
27	2	0.00	0	2	0.00										1	0.00	1	0.00	3
28	1	0.00	1	0	0.00														1
29	1	0.00																	0
30	2	0.00																	0
31	4	0.00										1	0	0.00			4	0.00	2
32	3	0.25				2	0	0.00											1
33	1	0.00													1	0.00	1	0.00	2
34	4	0.00	3	0	0.00										1	0.00	1	0.00	3
35	1	0.00	1	0	0.00										1	0.00	1	0.00	3

36	3	2.29	2	0	0.00														1
37	3	1.67																	0
38	8	6.51				1	1	0.00				1	0	0.00			4	0.00	3
39	5	79.48	2	0	0.00														1
40	3	0.00	2	0	0.00												1	0.00	2
41	3	0.00																	0
42	11	66.41							0	1	0.00						5	11.50	2
Total	42		19			9			5			10			11		20		

(degree = 3). This suggests that this actor played a key role in the flow of money in the trafficking network.

Interestingly, one actor was not central in the merged network, but emerged as central in a specific network layer. Actor 24 only has four (undirected) ties in the merged network, but this actor delivered firearms to four others (degree = 4), received (a) firearm(s) from one other actor. Additionally, the betweenness centrality scores suggest he was a broker (betweenness = 26.00), making him an important actor in the firearms layer.

Table 10.4 shows all combinations of two or three tie types that were present between pairs of actors. No pairs of actors were involved in four or more tie types. The majority of dyads (71 or 68 per cent), share only one type. However, some pairs of actors (thirty-four ties; 32 per cent) were involved in more than one type of tie. There were no ties in which more than one type of commodity (i.e. firearms, money, and equipment) flowed from one actor

Table 10.4 Combinations of Tie Types Present Between Pairs of Actors

Combinations	**Number of ties**	**Pairs of actors**
Two tie types: dynamics		
Orders, planning	5	09 – 10, 09 – 26, 13 – 06, 13 – 09, 13 – 31
Negotiation, planning	8	02 – 12, 06 – 23, 06 – 27, 12 – 02, 13 – 33, 23 – 06, 33 – 13, 35 – 09
Two tie types: commodities & dynamics		
Orders, money	1	13 – 26
Planning, money	4	06 – 09, 13 – 02, 13 – 23, 26 – 09
Planning, equipment	3	09 – 20, 10 – 20, 26 – 20
Planning, firearms	8	02 – 09, 02 – 13, 06 – 13, 09 – 13, 09 – 40, 20 – 09, 20 – 10, 26 – 34
Three tie types		
Planning, orders, money	1	13 – 38
Planning, negotiation, firearms	4	09 – 35, 13 – 24, 24 – 13, 27 – 06
Total	34	

to another. Moreover, there were no pairs of actors between which one type of commodity (e.g. firearms) was sent from A to B and another type (e.g. money) from B to A (in return).

Conclusion

This chapter shows that a multiplex network approach can provide a deeper and more nuanced understanding of the structure and operation of a firearms trafficking network. It helps to capture the complexity and range of resource exchanges and social interactions in the trafficking group, even though the group was relatively small. Six individual network layers or types of ties were identified, three of which related to resource exchanges (firearms, money, and equipment) and three of which related to social interactions (orders, planning, and negotiation). Despite only being able to determine the type of 47 per cent of the ties in the firearms trafficking network, we found that 43 per cent of the actors were present in two or more network layers. Only 12 per cent of the actors did not appear in any of the six network layers. Moreover, 32 per cent of dyads in the network were characterized by more than one type of tie. The combination of the tie types of negotiation and planning, and planning and exchange of firearms occurred the most (both eight times). These results are in line with previous research that found that criminal networks are characterized by multiple types of ties (Bright et al. 2015; Smith and Papachristos 2016).

The overall network was sparsely connected but highly centralized around two actors or hubs (actor 09 and 13). These hubs were also central in the majority of the network layers. However, through analysing the network layers separately, another central actor (actor 24) was identified. Although this actor did not score high on degree nor betweenness in the merged network, he had a prominent position in the firearms exchange layer, indicating that the multiplex approach may reveal important information not detected in more traditional network approaches. The analysis of the aggregated (i.e. merged) network alone may lead to over- or underestimation of the importance of some actors. This study confirms that 'an actor may be central in one dimension but peripheral in others, incorrectly making him seem unimportant in the overall aggregated simplex network' (Diviák et al. 2019).

In light of the social organization of criminal groups (i.e. hierarchies, markets, and networks), this firearms trafficking group had a clear network structure with elements of hierarchy embedded within that structure. These elements become apparent in the analysis of the merged network as well as the analysis of the orders network layer: the two hubs (actor 09 and 13) were connected to the majority of the other actors in the network and were the actors giving orders. This is consistent with the finding that criminal groups can be composed of hybrid types of social organization (e.g. a hybrid of networks and hierarchies; see Bright et al. 2012). In terms of the efficiency/security trade-off, the network was able to operate efficiently due to its centralized structure but consequently was less secure and therefore vulnerable to detection and disruption. Pure market-based social structures were not a dominant form of interaction in the network. Although one-off transactions occurred, the high levels of interpersonal trust required in the illicit commodity exchange appeared to result in relationships that endured beyond a single transaction.

Limitations

This study was the first to apply a multiplex network approach to a firearms trafficking network that was subject to police investigation. Information from the investigation allowed us to map the trafficking network in great detail. However, there are a few limitations. First, in some cases it was impossible to type ties between actors as 'firearm(s) exchanged' because the exact route of the firearm (e.g. from person A to B, to C) was unknown, even though there was information about the exchange of firearms. Second, the finding that actors 09 and 13 were the hubs and that these actors were involved in six and five network layers, respectively, could perhaps be attributed to the fact that these actors were the main focus of the investigation. However, the twelve other initial suspects are scattered around the network in terms of their position. That is, not all actors are central and some are peripheral. Moreover, there are actors that emerged as central while the investigation was not initially focused on them. Third, equipment is an odd layer in the sense that this represents only one incident where four actors brought equipment to one other actor.

Policy Implications

The outcomes of this chapter can be translated into a number of implications for policy and policing practice. First, if police seek to target a specific network layer (e.g. the flow of firearms), a multiplex approach is needed to identify the actors that are important in that network layer. In other words, using multiplex approaches can help the police to target key actors in more nuanced ways compared with strategies that emerge from more traditional network approaches. Second, policies more broadly need to target different network layers in order to be most effective. Our results show the benefit of deconstructing firearms trafficking into key elements or parts (e.g. the system of exchange of resources, the social structures that facilitate such trafficking). Policies will be most effective when they involve a suite of strategies that target various points across the structure and dynamics of the illicit trafficking of firearms, including the resource exchanges (i.e. the organized criminal activities) and the social connections between actors (i.e. the organized criminal groups). For example, policies should target and disrupt not only the flows of illicit firearms but also the flows of money. Such targeting should focus not only on the resources themselves but on the key actors who facilitate such resource exchanges, including planning and operation. We note that 'following the money' has proven an effective approach for law enforcement in analogous areas like illicit drug trafficking (see Levi 2015). Third, police should target not only those actors who appear to be at the top of any assumed hierarchy, but also those actors who are key for other reasons; for example, those central within the flows of money or involved in the exchange of multiple (or important) resources. Finally, analysts and policing should include social network analysis in their repertoire of intelligence analysis when studying or investigating criminal groups. SNA provides a set of analytical techniques that can be used to measure the degree of cohesion, map the structure of the group and exchange of resources, and identify the actors who are particularly important in a firearms trafficking network. This suggests that training in SNA should be embedded within professional development opportunities offered to intelligence analysts within policing agencies across the world, including analysts responsible for offering support to investigations related to firearms trafficking.

References

Bichler, Gisela, and Malm, Aili. 2013. 'Small Arms, Big Guns: A Dynamic Model of Illicit Market Opportunity'. *Global Crime* 14 (2–3): pp. 261–286. doi: 10.1080/17440572.2013.787928 Accessed 26 Jul 2024.

Borgatti, Steve, Everett, Martin G., and Freeman, Lin. 2002. *UCINET 6 for Windows: Software for Social Network Analysis*. Harvard: Analytic Technologies.

Borgatti, Stephen P., Everett, Martin G., and Johnson Jeffrey C. 2018. *Analyzing Social Networks*, 2nd edn. London: Sage.

Bright, David A., Hughes, Caitlin E., and Chalmers, Jenny. 2012. 'Illuminating Dark Networks: A Social Network Analysis of an Australian Drug Trafficking Syndicate'. *Crime, Law and Social Change* 57: pp. 151–176.

Bright, David A., et al. 2015. 'The Use of Actor-Level Attributes and Centrality Measures to Identify Key Actors: A Case Study of an Australian Drug Trafficking Network'. *Journal of Contemporary Criminal Justice* 31 (3): pp. 262–278.

Bright, David, Koskinen, Johan, and Malm, Aaili. 2018. 'Illicit Network Dynamics: The Formation and Evolution of a Drug Trafficking Network'. *Journal of Quantitative Criminology* 35: pp. 237–258.

Bright, David, Whelan, Chad, and Harris-Hogan, Shandon. 2020a. 'Exploring the Hidden Social Networks of "Lone Actor" Terrorists'. *Crime, Law and Social Change* 74: pp. 491–508.

Bright, David, Whelan, Chad, and Harris-Hogan, Shandon. 2020b. 'On the Durability of Terrorist Networks: Revealing the Hidden Connections Between Jihadist Cells'. *Studies in Conflict & Terrorism* 43 (7): pp. 638–656.

Bright, David, et al. 2023. 'Investigating the Dynamics of Outlaw Motorcycle Gang Co-Offending Networks: The Utility of Relational Hyper Event Models'. *Journal of Quantitative Criminology* pp. 1–43. https://link.springer.com/article/10.1007/s10940-023-09576-x Accessed 26 Jul. 2024.

Buscemi, Francesco, et al. 2018. 'Illicit Firearms Proliferation in the EU Periphery: The Case of Ukraine'. In *Triggering Terror: Illicit Gun Markets and Firearms Acquisition of Terrorist Networks in Europe*, edited by Nils Duquet, pp. 461–480. Flemish Peace Institute. https://vlaamsvredesinstituut.eu/safte/files/boek_safte_bw_lowres.pdf Accessed 26 Jul. 2024.

Calderoni, Francesco. 2013. 'Strategic Positioning in Mafia Networks'. In *Crime and Networks*, edited by Carlo Morselli, pp. 163–181. New York: Routledge.

Campana, Paolo. 2018. 'Out of Africa: The Organization of Migrant Smuggling across the Mediterranean'. *European Journal of Criminology* 15 (4): pp.481–502.

Campana, Paolo. 2020. 'Human Smuggling: Structure and Mechanisms'. *Crime and Justice* 49: pp. 471–519.

Coutinho, James A, et al. 2020. 'Multilevel Determinants of Collaboration Between Organised Criminal Groups'. *Social Networks* 63: pp. 56–69.

Curwen, Philip. 2007. 'The Social Networks of Small Arms Proliferation: Mapping an Aviation Enabled Chain'. Master's thesis, Naval Postgraduate School.

De Schutter, Astrid, and Duquet, Nils. 2023. 'The Nexus Between Drug Markets and Gun Violence in the European Union'. *European Monitoring Centre for Drugs and Drug Addiction*. https://www.emcdda.europa.eu/system/files/documents/2023-11/edmr_firearms-background-paper_final_0.pdf Accessed 26 Jul. 2024.

Diviák, Tomáš, Dijkstra, Jan Kornelis, and Snijders, Tom A.B. 2019. 'Structure, Multiplexity, and Centrality in a Corruption Network: The Czech Rath Affair'. *Trends in Organized Crime* 22: pp. 274–297.

Duquet, Nils, and Goris, Kevin. 2018. 'The Illicit Gun Market in Belgium: A Lethal Cocktail of Criminal Supply and Terrorist Demand'. In *Triggering Terror: Illicit Gun Markets and Firearms Acquisition of Terrorist Networks in Europe*, edited by Nils Duquet, pp. 21–79. Flemish Peace Institute. https://vlaamsvredesinstituut.eu/wp-content/uploads/2019/07/boek_safte_bw_lowres.pdf Accessed 26 Jul. 2024.

Duquet, Nils, and van Alstein, Maarten. 2016. *Guns For Sale: The Belgian Illicit Gun market in a European Perspective*. Flemish Peace Institute. https://vlaamsvredesinstituut.eu/wp-content/uploads/2019/03/guns-for-sale-report.pdf Accessed 26 Jul. 2024.

EUCPN Secretariat (eds). 2016. 'Trafficking in Illicit Firearms: A Global and European Overview'. EUCPN Theoretical Paper Series. Brussels: European Crime Prevention Network.

Hamill, Jonathan, et al. 2008. 'Analysis of Layered Social Networks'. *IOSphere* (January): pp. 27–33. https://scholar.afit.edu/cgi/viewcontent.cgi?article=4343&context=etd Accessed 26 Jul. 2024.

Hanneman, Robert A., and Riddle, Mark. 2013. *Introduction to Social Network Methods.* Chapter 16: 'Multiplex Relations'. https://faculty.ucr.edu/~hanneman/nettext/C16_Multi_Plex.html. Accessed 26 Jul. 2024.

Kinsella, David Todd 2004. 'Mapping the Small Arms Trade: Insights From Social Network Analysis'. *Political Science Faculty Publications and Presentations.* 21. https://pdxscholar.library.pdx.edu/polisci_fac/21 Accessed 26 Jul. 2024.

Kinsella, David. 2006. 'The Black Market in Small Arms: Examining a Social Network'. *Contemporary Security Policy* 27: pp. 100–117.

Kinsella, David. 2013. 'The Illicit Arms Trade in Asia: A Social Network Analysis'. *Political Science Faculty Publications and Presentations.* 22. https://pdxscholar.library.pdx.edu/polisci_fac/22 Accessed 26 Jul. 2024.

Kinsella, David. 2014. 'Illicit Arms Transfers to Africa and the Prominence of the Former Soviet Bloc: A Social Network Analysis'. *Crime, Law and Social Change* 62 (2): pp. 523–547.

Leuprecht, Christian, and Aulthouse, Andrew. 2014. 'Guns for Hire: North America's Intra-Continental Gun Trafficking Networks'. *Criminology, Criminal Justice, Law & Society* 15 (3): pp. 57–74. https://ccjls.scholasticahq.com/article/421-guns-for-hire-north-america-s-intra-continental-gun-trafficking-networks Accessed 26 Jul. 2024.

Levi, Michael. 2015. 'Money for Crime and Money from Crime: Financing Crime and Laundering Crime Proceeds'. *European Journal on Criminal Policy and Research* 21 (2): pp. 275–297.

Liem, Marieke, and Krüsselmann, Katharina. 2022. *The Way of the Gun: Firearm trafficking and its Impact on Violence in the Netherlands.* Flemish Peace Institute. https://vlaamsvredesinstituut.eu/wp-content/uploads/2022/11/TARGET_Netherlands5.pdf Accessed 26 Jul 2024.

Magnani, Matteo, and Rossi, Luca. 2013. 'Formation of Multiple Networks'. In *Social Computing, Behavior-Cultural Modeling and Prediction*, edited by Ariel Greenberg, William Kennedy, and Nathan Bos, pp. 257–264. Berlin: Springer.

Magnani, Matteo, Micenková, Barbora, and Rossi, Luca. 2013. 'Combinatorial Analysis of Multiple Networks'. https://arxiv.org/abs/1303.4986 Accessed 26 Jul. 2024.

Morselli, Carlo. 2007. 'The Efficiency/Security Trade-Off in Criminal Networks'. *Social Networks* 29: pp. 143–153.

Morselli, Carlo. 2009. *Inside Criminal Networks.* New York: Springer.

Morselli, Carlo. 2012. 'Assessing Network Patterns in Illegal Firearms Markets'. *Crime, Law and Social Change* 57: pp. 129–149.

Morselli, Carlo. 2013. *Crime and Networks.* New York: Routledge.

Morselli, Carlo, and Roy, Julie. 2008. 'Brokerage Qualifications in Ringing Operations'. *Criminology* 46: pp. 71–98.

Robins, Garry. 2009. 'Understanding Individual Behaviors within Covert Networks: The Interplay of Individual Qualities, Psychological Predispositions, and Network Effects'. *Trends in Organized Crime* 12 (2): pp. 166–187.

Savona, Ernesto U., and Mancuso, Marina. 2017. *Fighting Illicit Firearms Trafficking Routes and Actors at European level.* Final Report of Project FIRE (www.fireproject.eu). Milano: Transcrime—Università Cattolica del Sacro Cuore.

Schwartz, Daniel M., and Rouselle, Tony. 2009. 'Using Social Network Analysis to Target Criminal Networks'. *Trends in Organized Crime* 12: pp. 188–207.

Smith, Chris M., and Papachristos, Andrew V. 2016. 'Trust Thy Crooked Neighbor: Multiplexity in Chicago Organized Crime Networks'. *American Sociological Review* 81 (4): pp. 644–667..

Sneddon, Simon. 2021. 'Firearms, Terrorism and Organized crime'. In *Firearms: Global Perspectives on Consequences, Crime and Control*, edited by Helen Poole, and Simon Sneddon, pp. 98–110. New York: Routledge.

Spapens, Toine. 2007. 'Trafficking in Illicit Firearms for Criminal Purposes within the European Union'. *European Journal of Crime, Criminal Law and Criminal Justice* 15 (3): pp. 359–381.

Spapens, Toine, and Bruinsma, Monique Y. 2002. *Smokkel van Handvuurwapens vanuit Voormalige Oostbloklanden naar Nederland.* IVA Tilburg. https://repository.wodc.nl/bitstream/handle/20.500.12832/1337/01.022-volledige-tekst_tcm28-66803.pdf?sequence=2&isAllowed=y Accessed 26 Jul. 2024.

Squires, Peter. 2021. 'Illegal Firearms, Illicit Markets and Weapon Trafficking'. In *Firearms: Global Perspectives on Consequences, Crime and Control*, edited by Helen Poole, and Simon Sneddon, pp. 51–71. New York: Routledge. https://doi.org/10.4324/9780429316951-4 Accessed 26 Jul. 2024

United Nations Office on Drugs and Crime (UNODC). 2015. *Study on Firearms 2015: A Study on the Transnational Nature of and Routes and Modus Operandi Used in Trafficking Firearms.* https://www.unodc.org/documents/firearms-protocol/UNODC_Study_on_Firearms_WEB.pdf Accessed 26 Jul. 2024.

United Nations Office on Drugs and Crime (UNODC). 2019. *University Module Series: Firearms. Module 4: The Illicit Market in Firearms.* https://www.unodc.org/documents/e4j/Module_04_-_The_Illicit_Market_in_Firearms_FINAL.pdf. Accessed 26 Jul. 2024.

United Nations Office on Drugs and Crime (UNODC). 2020a. *Global Study on Firearms Trafficking 2020.* United Nations publication, Sales No. E.20.IV.1. https://www.unodc.org/unodc/en/firearms-protocol/firearms-study.html Accessed 26 Jul. 2024.

United Nations Office on Drugs and Crime (UNODC). 2020b. *Illicit Trafficking in Firearms, their Parts, Components and Ammunition to, from and across the European Union: Regional Analysis Report.* https://www.unodc.org/documents/firearms-protocol/2020/UNODC-EU-Report-A8_FINAL.pdf Accessed 26 Jul. 2024.

United Nations Office on Drugs and Crime (UNODC). 2024. *Firearms and Drugs: Partners in Transnational Crime.* https://vlaamsvredesinstituut.eu/wp-content/uploads/2024/03/Issue-paper-on-firearms-drugs-links_final.pdf Accessed 26 Jul. 2024.

Van Rossum, Guido, and Drake, Fred L. 2009. *Python 3 Reference Manual.* Scotts Valley: CreateSpace.

Van Wanrooij, Niels, and Sapulete, Saraï. 2019. 'Do Firearms Link Organised Crime and Terrorism in the Netherlands? A Social Network Analysis Exploration'. In *Constructing and Organising Crime in Europe*, edited by Petrus van Duyne, Alexey Serdyuk, Georgios Antonopoulos, Jackie Harvey, and Klaus von Lampe, pp. 289–312. Den Haag: Eleven International Publishing.

Von Lampe, Klaus. 2015. *Organized Crime: Analyzing Illegal Activities, Criminal Structures, and Extra-legal Governance.* Thousand Oaks: Sage.

11

'If You Get into the Business, You Have to Arm Up'

The Possession, Display and Discharge of Firearms by Members of Organized Criminal Groups

*David Bright and Mark Halsey**

While there is an extensive literature examining organized crime, illicit markets, and the organizational structures of criminal groups (e.g. Pearson and Hobbs 2001; Morselli and Roy 2008; Hornsby and Hobbs 2007), there is limited research focused on the use of firearms in illicit markets and by members of criminal groups (example sources). Even ethnographic research on organized crime and illicit markets seldomly references illicit firearms (e.g. Anderson 1999; Bourgois 1996). Responding to this paucity of research at the intersection of illicit markets, organized crime, and illicit firearms use, this chapter explores the range of factors that drive associates and members of organized criminal groups to carry, display, and discharge firearms in the commission of crimes broadly categorised under the umbrella of 'organized criminal activities'. First, we review the existing literature on the use of firearms by associates and members of organized criminal groups. We then provide an overview of our methods and approach before presenting our results using a thematic analysis of interviews with incarcerated offenders. Finally, we discuss the results in the context of previous research and proffer some implications for policy and practice.

* This work was supported by the Australian Research Council under DP150100619 'Understanding and preventing gun violence: A qualitative study'.

David Bright and Mark Halsey, *'If You Get into the Business, You Have to Arm Up'* In: *Illicit Firearms Markets and Organized Crime*. Edited by: David Bright, Oxford University Press.
 DOI: 10.1093/9780198902409.003.0012

The Use of Illicit Firearms by Members of Organized Criminal Groups

Unlike other illicit commodities (e.g. illicit drugs), firearms are durable. Most firearms, if looked after, can circulate in illicit markets for decades, being sold and re-sold many times over during their lifespan (Savona and Mancuso 2017; Goldsmith et al. 2022). Firearms may be used only once or a few times by an offender, before being sold or otherwise passed on to a new user (see Bright et al. 2023). The acquisition of illicit firearms within the context of membership of gangs and organized criminal groups is often based on social networks and contacts (e.g. Cook et al. 2007; Bright et al. 2023). For example, interviews with gang members in Chicago revealed that many affiliates joined and/or maintained membership of a gang primarily to facilitate access to firearms (Cook et al. 2007). In some instances, illicit firearms are provided to members by senior members with instructions to undertake specific tasks such as transporting illicit drugs (e.g. Cook et al. 2007; Bright et al. 2023).

Some research has identified trends in preferences for firearms among those involved in organized criminal activities. Different guns are selected for different purposes based on specific characteristics. For example, handguns are generally chosen for concealability, power, and capacity for rapid reloading (Blumstein 2002; Hales et al. 2006; Lizotte et al. 2000; Wright and Rossi 1994). In contrast, long-arms (e.g. rifles and shotguns) are generally selected due to ease of availability and their capacity for intimidation (Hales et al. 2006; Newbold 1999). Firearm selection may also be driven by attempts to seek higher status in criminal milieux (e.g. larger, more powerful guns are associated with higher status; Cook et al. 2007). In addition, there is some evidence that firearms with automatic or semi-automatic modes possess a 'symbolic value' that 'conform(s) to gangster stereotype(s)' (Hales et al. 2006, 55).

Carrying, Displaying, and Discharging Firearms

Research has converged on a finding that the primary reasons for carrying, displaying, and discharging a firearm are bifurcated into: (1) symbolic purposes such as kudos and status, and (2) instrumental purposes such as personal protection, robbery, and violence (see Marshall et al. 2005; Hales et al. 2006). We now briefly explore instrumental and symbolic motivations to use illicit firearms in the context of organized crime and illicit markets.

Instrumental Motives

Some firearms are purchased as 'criminal tools', for instance, to commit armed robberies (Spapens 2007; Hales et al. 2006). Possessing and displaying a gun can facilitate other criminal objectives, such as ensuring compliance during armed robberies (e.g. Luckenbill 1981). Firearms can enhance the perceived strength of older or weaker members, allowing them to carry out acts that would otherwise be impossible (Kleck and McElrath 1991). Carrying and displaying firearms has instrumental value that facilitates the commission of a range of criminal activities, especially those involving violence and coercion (Savona and Mancuso 2017). Being armed with a firearm, even a cheap or malfunctioning gun, can achieve the desired effect of inducing a sense of fear and intimidation (Overton 2016). Displaying and threatening others with a firearm (even without discharging the gun) is often enough to achieve an intimidatory effect (Cook et al. 2007). Indeed, for many members and affiliates of organized criminal groups, the use of firearms may be limited to display (e.g. Cook et al. 2007).

In illicit drug markets, drug dealers are vulnerable to robberies (of drugs and money) and will consequently carry firearms for protection (Marshall et al. 2005). Firearms are used by gangs and those affiliated with organized crime groups to protect people and assets (e.g. illicit drugs; Savona and Mancuso 2017). Those involved in the illicit drug trade will also use firearms to enforce collection of unpaid debts and to protect territory (Marshall et al. 2005). Firearms are also used instrumentally by members of organized criminal groups to establish and maintain control of illicit markets (e.g. Markoswki et al. 2009; Davis et al. 2001). The nature of the use of firearms by members of criminal groups may depend on the market level in which they operate. For street gangs involved in retail level drug distribution, the use of firearms is focused on controlling local drug markets as well as carrying out armed robberies (Hales et al. 2006). Organized criminal groups engaged in middle-market level activities use firearms for more serious armed robberies and quasi-legitimate criminal enterprises like event security (Hales et al. 2006).

Symbolic motives

In addition to the instrumental value of guns, some gun users denote symbolic significance to firearms (e.g. Savona and Mancuso 2017), including the physical aesthetic value of the gun itself (e.g. Goldsmith et al. 2022). For example, gun ownership and use can enhance masculine status, particularly among young men (Blumstein 2002). In criminal milieux, possessing and displaying firearms can build respect and generate perceptions of power, status, and threat (Savona and Mancuso 2017). Indeed, without possession of a firearm, individuals in these organized criminal milieux may be concerned that they will not be feared or taken seriously.

The symbolic value of firearms to members of organized criminal groups is related to three main themes: 1) the ascendancy of criminal role models (including portrayals in the media—e.g. movies, news, books); 2) emergence of illicit drug markets; and 3) cultures of gang/crew membership (Hales et al. 2006). Carrying firearms can symbolise the wealth and criminal authority of particular persons or groups, amassed through drug trafficking and armed robberies (Hales et al. 2006; Cook et al. 2007).

Of course, some uses of firearms can involve both instrumental and symbolic motivations. One example of this is the use of firearms to achieve ascendancy in inter-group conflicts (e.g. Hales et al. 2006). These conflicts can be focused on disputes about territory or markets, including perceived threats to status and/or being 'disrespected' in inter-group interactions or business dealings (Hales et al. 2006). Even relatively trivial disputes may culminate in shootings as the availability of firearms increases threat levels and a 'shoot or be shot' culture that can trigger pre-emptive violence between members (Hales et al. 2006). Regarding conflict between criminal groups, Green et al. (2017) found that social contagion of shootings—a type of 'tit-for-tat' effect—was responsible for 63.1 per cent of gun violence episodes in gang-related contexts. This chapter aims to examine the various drivers and manifestations of carrying, displaying, and discharging firearms in organized crime contexts by analysing interviews with convicted crime gun users in Australia.

Method

The conceptual framework of this study is based on the tradition of qualitative studies of offending contexts, including approaches that rely on in-depth interviews with so-called 'difficult to reach' populations (Bourgois 1996; Contreras 2013; Halsey and Deegan 2015; Morselli 2009). In-depth interviews can be fruitful when the central objective is to understand the motivations and meanings of particular behaviours or events and to examine the influence of a range of contextual factors (Hales, Lewis, and Silverstone 2006).

All interviews (n = 75) were conducted with prisoners incarcerated across sixteen correctional centres in two Australian states (South Australia and New South Wales).[1] Both states have well-documented problems with firearms-related and organized crime (Bricknell 2012).

A purposive sampling technique guided the recruitment of participants. Three broad groups formed the primary targets of interviews: drug traffickers, members of gangs including organized criminal groups, and armed robbers. These 'ideal' interview categories were selected in order to examine the variety of uses of firearms in organized criminal activities and by members and associates of organized criminal groups. To be eligible for interview, participants had to be eighteen years or older and incarcerated in South Australia or New South Wales with an earliest possible release date of 1 January 2019 (to ensure accessibility during the period of fieldwork), be serving or have previously served time for major firearms-related offences, and be willing to be interviewed about the significance of guns in different stages of their own life course and/or that of the criminal networks/gangs to which they belong/once belonged. Once an inmate agreed to be interviewed, interviews were scheduled, and inmates were then visited by the researchers at the prison at which they were incarcerated. At this meeting, consent forms were presented to inmates, and those who consented to participate in the study were interviewed.

Of the seventy-five interviewees, seventy-four were male and one was female, and they ranged from twenty-three to seventy-eight years of age, with a mean age of forty-one years old. Twenty-eight (37 per cent) of the people interviewed had left school before commencing Year 10. Forty-three (57 per cent) identified as Caucasian; six (8 per cent) as Aboriginal or Torres Strait Islander Australians and sixteen (21 per cent) as from a Culturally and Linguistically Diverse Background (ten participants or 13 per cent did not declare their cultural background). Individual prison sentences ranged from one and a half years to life. The average full-length sentence was eleven years. With respect to time served in prison prior to interview, the range was six months to twenty-two years, with a median of 4.8 years. While some interviewees were serving their first custodial sentence, others had spent much of their adult lives (and a considerable portion of their teenage years) in custody.

[1] Ethics approval for the study was provided by the Social and Behavioural Research Ethics Committee at Flinders University (#6849), the Ethics Committee of the South Australian Department for Correctional Services (CEN/15/0323) and the Ethics Committee of Corrective Services New South Wales (D16/320488).

Interviews were conducted between October 2015 and December 2018 and ranged in duration from thirty minutes to three hours. Interviews were audio recorded and transcribed verbatim. A grounded approach (Glaser 1992) to data analysis was adopted. Full transcripts of interviews were read in detail by the authors and additionally analysed in NVivo producing several key themes and subthemes.

Results

We now expand on the themes that emerged from interviews related to the use of firearms in organized criminal activities (e.g. drug dealing) and by members of organized criminal groups (e.g. outlaw motorcycle gangs, or OMCGs). The following themes are discussed sequentially below: (1) firearms preferences; (2) firearms and power, status, and reputation; (2) organized criminal groups and firearms; (3) conflict between groups and the use of firearms; (4) illicit drug trafficking and the use of firearms; (5) personal protection using firearms; and (6) thefts ('rip-offs') from illicit drug dealers using firearms.

Firearm Preferences

Some participants reported that organized crime groups have access to a range of automatic weapons which are illegal to purchase and possess in Australia. For example, Participant 41 (hereafter P41) who was an OMCG associate and used his employment with a shipping organisation to facilitate drug deals with multiple OMCG clubs, noted that: 'Between the late 90s till now... it went from shotties [shotguns] and revolvers and just shitty old guns from the farm to fucking automatic weapons' (P41). He told of powerful automatic weapons being available to members of his group: 'I've seen some nice ones with laser fucking scopes and shit on them ... you know, at certain friends of mine houses that have bought them and then on-sold them' (P41). This same participant also made reference to higher-quality weapons being increasingly available and used more regularly: 'Years ago a lot of bikies might have had a handgun but they could always get shotguns and fucking old SKSs and SLRs. If there was a bikie turf war or something they'd get them. But from 2000 onwards, it's not just your shitty old revolvers and shotties. You're talking AKs and machine guns that are brand new' (P41).

P12 spent time 'hanging around' his older brother's gang, who would often get into fights with rival gangs. He spoke about the wide range of firearms that were available: 'They had handguns, a pump action, AK-47' (P12). P68 also witnessed an improvement in the type of firearms he could access, and this was linked to making more money from dealing: 'Well, at first they were cut-down rifles or cut-down shotguns. But once I knew people who sold a lot of drugs and made a lot of money, I started seeing pistols. Smaller, easier weapons, that are worth a bit more. Pistols are worth more than rifles and shotguns. They are harder to get. Just 'cause they're easier to conceal. And they got more bullets in the clip. Boom, boom, boom, you know. A shotgun or rifles only have a couple of bullets. And you can't walk around with a rifle' (P68). P62 had close connections with high-level members of an Italian Mafia group. He referred to a range of weapons to which the group had access: 'We had machine guns . . .we had anything you can think of. Glocks, brand new' (P62).

Power, Status, and Reputation

Some participants described the feeling of power that carrying and displaying a firearm can induce, especially in situations involving conflict and violence. For example, P26 discussed guns as promoting one's status in the criminal milieu: 'There's people who are scared for hand-to-hand combat and a gun makes them feel they're in more power and they could beat a six-foot bloke by just shooting him' (P26). Similarly, according to participant 38: 'I was only little. I couldn't handle a six-foot bloke that's 120 kilos. He's going to put it all over me. But if I pull a gun he's going to back up' (P38).

Others who were members of organized criminal groups described the use of firearms to develop and enhance their reputation for strength and potential for violence. A component of this was fashioning a reputation for being willing to display and if necessary, to discharge a firearm. According to P37, 'You weren't a someone unless you had a gun or access to a gun. So, you had to have it. All the guys I hung with had a gun or access to one' (P37). P28 explained how he used a firearm to cement the reputation of his associates (high-level drug traffickers) on whose behalf he was collecting debts. He threatened and fired a Beretta pistol at someone who owed money to associates of his who ran a drug dealing enterprise: 'I was happy that I'd done it because now everyone knows not to fuck with them, you know what I mean? Rumours were getting around, "Don't fuck with them. They got a bloke with them who's got a gun"' (P28).

P32 described garnering a reputation for being armed and being willing to shoot to defend himself. He told us that this meant his enemies would 'think twice' before coming to his house to threaten or attack him: 'None of them would think about coming to my house. They will ask around. . . . [it's] that reputation thing. They will know "If we go there we have to bally up [be armed with guns]. 'Cause he's going to come out and start shooting". People have to know that or they will try and take a piece of you' (P32). Similarly, P69 was a drug dealer who discussed his use of a gun to protect his money and drugs: 'It was important for others to know that I have a gun and for others to know that I'm the man who'll use it' (P69).

Organized Criminal Groups and Firearms

For some interviewees, it was important to have possession of a gun or easy access to one, but not necessary to carry one regularly. P21, who was involved in middle market drug trafficking, talked about those who carry and display firearms for no reason and those who can get access to a gun when it is actually needed: 'I've met some people that liked to show their gun off, liked people to know he had it, and there are the ones that will take it to show off, use it everywhere, and I think that's just stupid. But . . . generally, I'd say that guns are there and they're put away and then when they're needed either for a dispute or for this or for that they're got and whatever happens, happens. They're sorted and then they're put away. It's not a day-to-day carrying' (P21). Similarly, according to P36: 'It's all about showing off. They're just show-offs. "I've got something better" and that's all it's about' (P36). Being a gang member often meant you could not risk having guns at your home or on your person due to law enforcement targeting. P41 told us OMCG members would not carry the guns themselves but store them somewhere close and accessible: 'One of your good mates lives two doors down or an old lady (and) you've told her you want to store some paint tins in her shed out the back. Anything, you know. Because if something kicks off war-wise with them [rivals], you got to be able to have them ready' (P41). For other interviewees, carrying a gun was a necessary part of the criminal lifestyle. For example, P61 also spoke of the need to carry guns in the lifestyle of crime gangs and drug dealing: 'They've armed themselves up . . . because they have to because, at end of the day, it's a business. It's like, "I can't walk out of the house without it". Guys like us, we live on the edge. Especially in this game you always look over your shoulder' (P61).

Many participants discussed OMCGs either because they were members/ex-members or had dealings with them. For example, P35 talked about OMCGs controlling drug trafficking operations in some areas: 'OMCG members used guns to protect the drug trade, enforce power onto the streets, to have people scared of them. It's about power and about intimidation. It's about scaring people and letting people know that we are running the town around here' (P35). P14 was affiliated with an OMCG, and he would always carry a gun: 'I always had guns. When I was out there, I always had pistols' (P14). P61 was involved with OMCG leadership, enforcement, and drug dealing. He described the need to carry a gun because of his membership of a crime group and dealing drugs: 'When I was sixteen, seventeen I had to carry a gun. It's part of the game. I mean, it's like any trade you do. . . It's like any business in life. You're going to have a gun. A firearm comes with the lifestyle' (P61).

In joining OMCGs, individuals were required to defer to leadership and complete any tasks assigned to them. For example, according to P60: 'You just don't go straight to the top. . . .Got to start somewhere . . . Start as a nominee. Like, you just start off as a shit kicker, basically. They say, "Go and shoot this person". If you want to be somebody in their outlaw motorcycle gang you got to do it' (P60). P35 described how some OMCGs would provide associates with a gun and instructions on tasks to be completed: 'These cunts [OMCG members] will give you the gun and say, "I know where there's a job. There's $50,000 in the safe"' (P35). Similarly, P59 recounted how on joining an OMCG one of his friends was provided with an AK-47: 'I hung around with a couple of bad kids and their fathers were drug dealers and bikies and we managed to get our hands on a few guns. At first it was just single shots and, muck around with a couple of little rifles. Then my mate rings me up. He's got an AK-47 and he goes, "I'm going to war. I'm a bikie now"' (P59).

P61, who was involved with an Italian Mafia group, explained how later in life he elected not to carry a gun, instead employing a bodyguard who would have possession of a gun: 'As I got older I thought that maybe I don't want to do gaol for fucking guns. Maybe it's better to hire a bodyguard to carry that. And, you know, if you come to harm me he can kill you' (P61).

Conflict Between Organized Criminal Groups

Some interview participants discussed inter-group rivalry and conflict as a major driver of possession and use of firearms. Again, OMCG clubs featured in these discussions. For example, P60 said that once you were member of an

OMCG club you were expected to participate in their fights and that firearms featured in these disputes: 'If there's a war going on between two rival clubs, you're going to get shot' (P60). P17 described conflicts between rival OMCG clubs involving drive-by shootings: 'It started off when the New Boyz and the Hells Angels had a drama and houses were getting shot up [i.e. drive-by shootings]' (P17). P59, who would do jobs for OMCG clubs to pay off drug debts, found himself in the middle of an OMCG dispute involving firearms: 'Apparently my mate got shot and killed and I thought, "Fuck". Because I owe these guys money. I think it was about nine grand. I didn't know what to do. Next thing you know I'm walking around with a phone and I've got all their guns in my roof and they're going to war with the Comancheros and I'm mates with a lot of the Comancheros' (P59).

Participants discussed the use of firearms to settle conflicts between rival OMCG clubs but also between members of the same OMCG club. For example, P31 referred to personality conflicts that resulted in guns being used: 'It was over something trivial, and I'd obviously hurt the bloke's ego and it boiled out of control from there. So, next thing they're telling me they're going to spray me [with bullets]. So now where do we go from here? Do I get you first or you, do you get me?' (P31). P69 spoke of competition between different groups for territory: 'They did [push back], of course. But they couldn't compete. I had a couple of shootouts with them. I let them know that I'm not going to tolerate this shit. I heard that they're going to try to rob the dealers who deal in those apartment blocks' (P69).

Interviewees described a type of arms race related to intergroup conflict and a need to maintain superiority over rival groups with respect to firearms. According to P25: 'If they've got guns, you've got to have a gun. If you're going to stay in that world, you've got to [have guns], even just as a deterrent' (P25). P73 described different groups accumulating firearms in preparation for conflict: 'All of a sudden you'll hear: "This group are arming up so if you know anyone that's got any guns then let us know". Because they going to buy them all' (P73). P36 told us that some groups would accumulate caches of firearms for use in inter-group disputes: 'Each group will have their armoury which will be kept in a certain safe place. And if the shit really is going to hit the fan that's what they'll use. So it's group against group' (P36).

Firearms as Protection

P26 described the need for protection when plying one's wares in illicit drug markets: 'It [a gun] made you feel protected. And once the money was involved, then how to protect yourself in that scene was having a gun' (P26). Similarly, P36 described the nexus between involvement in the drug trade and the need for protection: 'It's definitely the criminal activity that promotes carrying the firearm. And pretty much these days it's all around the drug trade and you're either buying or selling. And you carry the gun if you're buying drugs 'cause you don't want to get ripped off and if you're selling the drugs you're carrying a firearm so you don't get robbed' (P36). P13 also believed that drugs and the money associated with it was the biggest reason to need a gun: 'Drugs is [the main reason] to need protection. Someone can just walk in, and I've got all these drugs here. I've got all this money here' (P13).

Often, guns were carried for protection because of an expectation that other participants in illicit markets would also be carrying a gun. P10 told us: 'In the back of my mind he was [carrying a gun]. People don't want to go and do their own dirty work and they [might] want to try and fucking stand over me or something like that' (P10). P18, who was an associate of a crime gang, argued that guns were purely for protection: 'I [carry a gun] to protect myself ... I'm not holding it to go around and hurt people. I've got to defend myself' (P18). P61 also explained that this was the only way he thought he could continue his lifestyle: 'You carry it round just like Armaguard will protect the money but we're protecting our lives. So that's why you carry the gun' (P61).

P32 told us that the risk of being robbed increased as the quantity of drugs and money in one's possession increased: 'Sooner or later, if you're making enough money and people know about it, someone's going to come. If you're not man enough to hold onto it you don't deserve it. There's another saying: "If you're not blasting you're not lasting"'(P32). P51 shared similar sentiments, expressing the suspicion and paranoia that drives gun-carrying in illicit markets: 'When you meet up with someone to sell something, you want [the gun] there. Half the time they're not meeting up with you just to buy the drugs. They're going to try and rob you. So that's where a lot of guns are coming out. Protection' (P51).

Some participants described situations in which they escalated from carrying a gun to displaying their firearm in order to protect themselves or to deter an imminent threat. For example, P64 was asked what would cause him to display or fire their gun: 'Someone kicking. . . your door in, trying to rob you. Half of them aren't after the drugs but after your cash. So, they try and stand over you' (P64). P10 also told us that he would display his gun if he felt threatened: 'I've been in a situation where I've had to pull it out and show that I will use it. [If] somebody wanted to rob you with your drugs or your cash' (P10).

P56 carried a gun due to conflicts with a local OMCG club. On one occasion he displayed it during a meeting with representatives of the club at which he was ambushed: 'Six cunts come out of the bush, and I pulled [my gun] on them and then I thought, "Who's going to come first?" and, they didn't want to really step forward' (P56).

Interviewees told us that when guns were displayed, the goal was usually to scare people. Nonetheless, many interviewees reported that they would discharge their gun if necessary. For example, according to P27: 'I never used it on no one. I used to carry it 'cause I was selling drugs. I used to just carry it around, scared a few people. I pulled it out on a few people. I wasn't going to, I wasn't going to shoot necessarily, unless I had to. If they had come at me I would have shot them' (P27). Similarly, P21 said: 'When you pull a gun on people, they're not going to keep coming at you . . . and if they do, you stop them pretty quick' (P21).

Illicit Drug Trafficking and Firearms

Many participants described the nexus between involvement in illicit drug dealing and firearms. For P61 a firearm was a tool that was a necessary part of the illicit drug trade: 'If you get into the business you have to arm up, you had to protect yourself. It's like a trade. Whatever job you have, there's going to be tools involved. For this business it's a gun' (P61). This was also backed up by P23: 'A lot of drug dealers purchase [guns] because of their safety' (P23).

P64 felt he needed to carry a gun because he was a member of an OMCG and a drug dealer: 'The more I got involved with drugs, the more I got involved with guns. Then I started affiliating with bikers, some individual bikie clubs. The more bad I seemed to get, the more I carried a fucking piece. The more drugs you were involved with, the more you needed a gun and that's just how it went' (P64).

P33 also explained the need for a gun when working as a drug dealer: 'When you're drug dealing, everyone doesn't always get along. When you sell drugs there's always someone that's jealous or there's always someone that's sick, hanging out [for drugs] that's going to do something to get the drugs. So that's the sort of risk you take in this sort of game' (P33). Similarly, P38 told us that: 'Anyone who has got anything to do with any sort of drug,

I don't care if it's just, like, a couple of pills, I'm telling you these days they got a gun on them' (P38). Similarly, P28 stated: 'When you're dealing, like kilos [of drugs], it's always better to have a gun in case someone gets that bright idea, "Oh, I might rob him". A lot of them that deal big [amounts], I'd say nearly all of them have guns' (P28).

Interviewees also highlighted the way illicit drug consumption amplified unpredictable behaviour around the use of guns and that this ultimately increased the risks of people being shot. For example, P14 said: 'You're high on coke or you're high on ice. You're moving a major ice, major coke deal and you're off your tree. And you start becoming paranoid, and it becomes dangerous. You've got a gun 'cause you don't want to get robbed. You know, you might have $20,000 worth, so you carry a gun 'cause you're paranoid. You think, the bloke you're selling to, you don't really know him that well. You might have been set up. There's a bloke in here [prison], who has gone to do a drug deal, on ice. He met somebody at [suburb], but he's dropped his mate off before he's pulled up to meet the dealer. And the dealer's rocked up by himself, hopped in the car and his mate was fried, watching, making sure everything goes down nice and smooth. And then his mate's spun out and run back, jumped in the back seat and went fucking bang [shot and killed the dealer]' (P14).

Robberies of Drug Dealers

P36 described the risks of being robbed when trafficking large quantities of illicit drugs: '[It's a] very dangerous place to play in these days. If you're getting involved with the drug trade, you need to come armed. There's been a spate of home invasions [and] just about every home invasion's revolved around a drug dealer and these blokes that get together in their gangs and they don't want to do the hard yards. They'd just rather pull a gun on you, run in, kick your door in, bash you and take what you got. And that's why just about every major drug dealer now is armed to the teeth' (P36).

Many participants acknowledged that they had engaged in robbing drug dealers to generate income. Drug dealers were generally viewed as easy targets who would not report such robberies to the police. For example, P35 described stealing from drug dealers as an easy way to acquire both drugs and money quickly: 'I used to rob the little time drug dealer, and then I met some big boys, and I thought, "Fuck robbing these little cunts for half a gram. I'm going to go and get fucking kilos". There's houses with millions [of dollars] in them and they will just go, "Here's 50 grand. Leave me alone for a week"' (P35).

P44 would target high-level drug dealers: 'I did rip-offs. They're not just shitty street dealers. They're making 150 grand a week profit. They're doing very well for themselves. Most of them were just "run houses", you know, where they sort out the drugs, distribute the drugs. And then we'd just come in, kick the door and all of us are armed' (P44). P46 also did rip-offs of drug dealers: 'So we've gone there, and we're armed with guns. We've got guns 'cause I know the bloke's got guns on the premises. It was home invasion. A shot was fired, and all the heroes backed off. We got pseudo[ephedrine] and money' (P46).

P46 argued that part of the reason dealers were an easy target was because they wouldn't report the robbery to police: 'That's what most crims do these days. They'd rather go and get a dealer because when they're robbing dealers they're not going to tell on us because they're dealing drugs. What, are they going to go to the police and say, "He robbed me for my drugs"?' (P46).

Some participants began carrying guns after a personal experience of being robbed or threatened. P19 learnt the importance of carrying a gun when he was in his late teens and was robbed while he was with a friend who was a drug dealer: 'He was a drug dealer and we were going to go drop drugs off to someone and he's gone to give the drugs over and the dude's pulled a gun out on both of us to take the drugs' (P19). Similarly, P26 was robbed while drug dealing at age seventeen and then decided to start carrying a handgun: 'I never pulled it on innocent people though, it was always amongst other drug dealers . . . if they're trying to rob me or something' (P26).

Debt Collection and Retribution

Guns were often used for debt collection in illicit markets. For example, P27 told us: 'A bloke owed [money], about four grand. We knocked on the door and no one would answer. We heard the back door open. So, this bloke's taken off out the back. We run around the back and at the back of the house is a paddock and we seen the bloke. My mate shot him. A couple of times' (P27). P28 also described how he used firearms to collect debts: 'One person refused to pay his debt and the problem escalated. This bloke was massive, and I remember feeling intimidated and we had an argument and it got to the point where I pulled [my gun] out and just started shooting at him' (P28). P33 also used guns for collecting drug debts and described the infliction of gunshot injuries as one way to punish lack of payment: 'My friends have asked for help where I would go sort some dramas out, not kill them but just shoot them, not in the kneecap but just below, so the wound's not too bad' (P33). In a more extreme example, P14 reported that when someone did not pay for a drug delivery, the response was swift and fatal: 'I give six ounces of heroin to him. I got ripped off. He got killed [because he] didn't pay. The people that were involved with me are serious fucking people' (P14).

Discussion

There are many implications stemming from the narrative excerpts and themes relayed above. Here, though, we home in on three key issues. The first, and perhaps most obvious matter, concerns the inextricable overlap between illicit firearm possession and illicit drugs. It is, in the world of organized crime as well as less 'serious' criminal worlds, fundamentally expected that key actors (dealers, suppliers, stand-over people, debt collectors) will be carrying a firearm. And if not carrying on their person, such weapons will be in very close or ready proximity should the occasion call for it. This is a situation, we would contend, driven as much by the continuing prohibition surrounding particular substances ('ice', heroin, cocaine, MDMA, etc.) as it is by the dynamics and subcultural rules of criminal life. The criminalization of illicit drug markets—as a mountain of hard research evidence attests (example sources)—literally creates the conditions and possibilities for the 'rip-off', debt collection, and battles more generally around who or which group commands the higher status or power. Consequently, it also creates the conditions for personal injury or death for criminal actors and innocent by-standers. Any serious effort to come to grips with gun crime (in Australia and elsewhere) needs to grapple head on with the undeniable connection of firearms to organized crime and the local and global markets for illicit drugs. There are, in short, serious unintended consequences to the criminalization of particular substances and the attraction to, and inappropriate display and discharge of firearms is demonstrably one of them.

The second issue to emerge concerns the curious (and possibly inverse) relationship between criminal actors' illicit possession, display, and discharge of firearms, and their 'natural' stock of personal fortitude or strength. Far from being accomplished players in the organized crime world, it is clear many participants rely on firearm possession and threat of use as a means to compensate for their poor underworld standing (and, in certain cases, their own small or weak physical stature). Firearms, particularly shotguns and pistols, therefore become objects for generating instant (as opposed to hard-won) social gravitas and respect. This is a fast-tracked type of masculinity with correlative benefits accrued within the organized crime world (e.g. enhanced strength or status). Illicit possession and display of firearms does something, therefore, to its subject (i.e. to the firearm user) as well as to those staring, so to speak, down the barrel of a gun (i.e. to the victims). It is a performative act that is as much 'inward'-facing as outward-facing in terms of its impact. Participants' declarations of new-found confidence when in possession of a firearm is concrete evidence of this effect. The antidote to such situations would necessarily involve a complex array of strategies—but it would undoubtedly involve the more democratic distribution of legitimate opportunity structures in, especially, many of the poorer socio-economic areas across Australia and elsewhere. These areas, after all, are the known ground for recruitment of vulnerable people (predominantly young men) who cannot get a foothold in legitimate social and economic networks (see Rose 2000). This is not to say that some people—even in the face of multiple legitimate pathways to employment—do not consciously choose a life within organized criminal groups. We acknowledge such choices are indeed made. But even here they are heavily structured by a multitude of micro, meso and macro factors that push up hard against the idea of a truly sovereign subject (or individual). The push and pull factors at work in such contexts are obviously in need of further exploration.

The third and final issue relates to the relative impunity with which most members of organized criminal groups operate. Australia has some of the strictest firearm regulations in the world. And yet we also have incontrovertible evidence regarding the relative ease of firearm procurement for criminal actors—and in relation to a wide variety and calibres of firearm. This is a worrying situation. Theft from farms, theft from gun clubs and gun shops, theft of firearms from private urban dwellings, through to organized importation rackets, are all part and parcel of the Australian criminal landscape. How might we best tackle the problem? At a basic level, the problem can be approached as one involving supply or demand. The former necessarily involves better intelligence (especially around key players and of the grey market), more frequent interdiction of firearm shipments from overseas and across the country, greater restrictions on manufacturers (in terms of the quantity, type and calibre of weapons permitted to be made and subsequently sold), as well as more stringently enforced regulations relating to the storage of firearms in private residences, gun clubs, and licensed dealers. We recognise, though, that situational solutions (target hardening, removal and surveillance) will not solve the problem. Coming to grips with the demand or motivation to own or (illegally) possess a firearm (or many thereof) has to be firmly in the mix as well. Why do people need or want firearms? That seemingly simple question requires a multitude of responses in accordance with the category of user (e.g. hunter, farmer, law enforcer, collector, vet, controller of vermin, professional shooter, standover man/debt collector, drug dealer/supplier) and their geographical location (urban, rural, remote).

The question regarding demand for firearms is really one about limiting *nefarious* demand for such. What might it take, for example, for an OMCG member to resist arming themselves or to desist from illicitly carrying, displaying, or using a firearm? Again, this is complex question. Boland et al. (2021, 7) note that OMCGs provide a strong sense of 'brotherhood, loyalty and camaraderie'. Those values, it would seem, need to take root in new contexts beyond gang membership in order for desistance from gang life to achieve real momentum. Meaningful or sustained desistance (whether from gun crime specifically or repeat offending more generally) requires, more particularly, that three interrelated dimensions (i.e. primary, secondary, and tertiary) be addressed (see Patton and Farrall 2021). Primary desistance involves the cessation of the behaviour in question; a binary scenario where either offending stops or it persists. Sometimes a prison sentence is the only thing capable of ensuring the primary element occurs—on other occasions it happens through a series of micro-decisions or change in circumstances. Secondary desistance involves the complex cognitive shift from viewing oneself as an offender (as an outsider, as deviant, as fundamentally Other) to viewing oneself as a non-offender or conventional citizen. That might involve help from professionals as suppliers of cognitive behavioural therapy or help from peers and family as sources of encouragement or as role models. Tertiary desistance—perhaps the most neglected but most important of the three dimensions—involves the collective stance of the community toward the reformed or desisting person. People do not desist from crime so much as they desist *into* pro-social non-criminal milieux (McNeill 2012, 13). Accordingly, it is the community which can provide the key critical places and social contexts where the stigma of a criminal past is non-existent and where opportunities to cement the process of personal change abound. Tertiary desistance is therefore being fully accepted and validated by legitimate actors. What all this means is that getting people to desist involves a multi-dimensional approach. People—especially OMCG members looking to get out of the life—have to know there is something beyond their current circumstance that they can risk leaping (or desisting) into. There is also evidence to suggest that desistance might be best facilitated when it is achieved in concert with like others. Here, co-offenders might draw courage from one another as co-desisters—something which is only just starting to get some traction (Halsey and Mizzi 2023).

Policy Implications

In summary, a number of key policy implications flow from our results. First, there is a need to further limit the availability of firearms, even in countries like Australia which have tight restrictions on firearms purchasing via legitimate routes. This should include interventions that track and reduce the availability of black and grey market firearms (e.g. via thefts), as well as enhanced tracking and tracing of all firearms (e.g. via state and national registers). Second, there is a pressing need to reduce the attraction of organized crime and firearms crime by addressing motivations for entry, especially for youth. These interventions should cater to the range of motivations from financial motivations through to those that relate to social status and identity. These interventions should be supplemented by policy levers that increase the risks and reduce the rewards of firearm crime, at least with respect to how such risk and rewards are perceived by actors within organized criminal milieux. Third, given the covert nature of much firearms crime, especially that conducted within organized criminal contexts, intelligence collection is key to prevention and disruption. Access to illicit firearms occurs via tight, trusted networks that are extremely difficult for law enforcement to penetrate. Intelligence collection and analysis is not only key to disruption but is also important in the collection and collation of aggregate data (e.g. to facilitate estimates of the size of the black and grey markets for firearms). Finally, there should be a multi-agency strategy to facilitate desistance from organized crime and firearms crime. This should include policies and practices that encourage desistance from crime and provide pathways out of illicit gun crime, policies that address the economic, affective, and social drivers of organized crime and firearm crime, and interventions within social networks that facilitate 'replacement self' and leverage social capital to encourage desistance from crime.

Conclusions

To close the chapter, and by way of summary, we offer a few primary conclusions about the possession, display, and discharge of firearms by members of organized criminal groups. First, from a 'rational' perspective, members of organized criminal groups will weigh the risks and rewards of possessing, displaying, and discharging firearms. As we heard from our participants, the perceived need to carry and use a gun (often for personal protection) often outweighs the perceived risks of detection and punishment. Second, firearms possess strong symbolic value in the lives of members of organized criminal groups. They facilitate personal identity of being strong and tough and represent a powerful deterrent for other actors in organized criminal milieux. Second, arms races within and between organized criminal groups, and a related desire to 'outgun' one's rivals, stoke demand for firearms including demand for higher calibre and automatic firearms. Third, the perceived need for personal protection in illicit contexts drives demand for handguns because they are more concealable compared with other firearms. Ironically, it is the concealable nature of handguns that helps to drive the demand for handguns. In circular logic, some of our participants indicated they needed to carry a handgun in the event that those they were interacting with were also carrying one. Finally, there is a very clear nexus between participation in illicit markets (especially the market for illicit drugs) and the possession, display, and discharge of firearms by members of organized criminal groups. Operating within this nexus of illicit drugs and illicit firearms, one is presented with situations which feature high risks (e.g. of personal injury and death) and inflated levels of unpredictability. Participants of illicit markets use firearms in attempts to regain some sense of personal control in the context of inherently chaotic experiences.

References

Anderson, E. 1999. *The Code of the Streets: Decency, Violence, and the Moral Life of the Inner City*. New York: W.W. Norton & Company, Inc.

Blumstein, Alfred. 2002. 'Youth, Guns, and Violent Crime'. *The Future of Children* 12 (2): pp. 39–53.

Bourgois, P. 1996. *In Search of Respect: Selling Crack in El Barrio*. Cambridge: Cambridge University Press.

Bricknell, Samantha. 2012. *Firearm Trafficking and Serious and Organized Crime Gangs'.* Canberra: Australian Institute of Criminology Report, Research and Public Police Series, Australian Institute of Criminology.

Bright, David, et al. 2023. '"I Know a Guy and He's Got Guns Galore": Accessing Crime Guns in the Australian Illicit Firearms Market'. *Deviant Behavior* 44 (5): pp. 671–689.

Contreras, R. 2013. *The Stickup Kids: Race, Drugs, Violence, and the American Dream.* University of California Press.

Cook, Philip, et al. 2007. 'Underground Gun Markets'. *The Economic Journal* 117 (524): pp. 588–618.

Davis, Ian, Hirst, Chrissie, and Bernado, Mariani. 2001. *Organized Crime, Corruption and Illicit Arms Trafficking in an Enlarged EU.* London: Saferworld.

Goldsmith, Andrew, Halsey, Mark, and Bright, David. 2022. 'Taking Crime Guns Seriously: A Socio-Material Perspective'. *Criminology & Criminal Justice* 22: pp. 462–479.

Green, Ben, Horel, Thibaut, and Papachristos Andrew V. 2017. 'Modeling Contagion Through Social Networks to Explain and Predict Gunshot Violence in Chicago, 2006 to 2014'. *JAMA Internal Medicine* 177 (3): pp. 326–333.

Hales, Gavin, Lewis, Chris, and Silverstone, Daniel. 2006. *Gun Crime: The Market in and Use of Illegal Firearms* (Home Office Research Study 298). London: Home Office Research and Statistics Directorate.

Halsey, M., Deegan, S., Halsey, M., and Deegan, S. 2015. Catastrophic Turn. *Young Offenders: Crime, Prison and Struggles for Desistance*, 127–176.

Halsey, Mark, and Jenna, Mizzi. 2023. 'Co-desistance From Crime: Engaging The Pro-Social Dimensions of Co-offending'. *The British Journal of Criminology* 63 (1): pp. 134–150.

Hornsby, Rob, and Hobbs, Dick. 2007. 'A Zone of Ambiguity: The Political Economy of Cigarette Bootlegging'. *The British Journal of Criminology* 47 (4): pp. 551–571.

Kleck, Gary, and McElrath, Karen. 1991. 'The Effects of Weaponry on Human Violence'. *Social Forces* 69 (3): pp. 669–692.

Lizotte, Alan J. et al. 2000. 'Factors Influencing Gun Carrying Among Young Urban Males Over The Adolescent-Young Adult Life Course'. *Criminology* 38 (3): pp. 811–834.

Luckenbill, David F. 1982. 'Compliance under Threat of Severe Punishment'. *Social Forces* 60 (3): pp. 811–825.

Markowski, Stefan, et al. 2009. 'Multi-Channel Supply Chain For Illicit Small Arms'. *Defence and Peace Economics* 20 (3): pp. 171–191.

Marshall, Ben, Webb, Barry, and Tilley, Nick. 2005. *Rationalisation of Current Research on Guns, Gangs and Other Weapons: Phase 1.* London: Jill Dando Institute of Crime Science, University College London.

McNeill, Fergus. 2012. 'Four Forms of "Offender" Rehabilitation: Towards an Interdisciplinary Perspective'. *Legal and Criminological Psychology* 17 (1): pp. 18–36.

Morselli, Carlo, and Roy, Julie. 2008. 'Brokerage Qualifications in Ringing Operations'. *Criminology* 461: pp. 71–97.

Newbold, Greg. 1999. 'The Criminal Use of Firearms in New Zealand'. *Australian & New Zealand Journal of Criminology* 32 (1): pp. 61–78.

Overton, Iain. 2016. *The Way of the Gun: A Bloody Journey into the World of Firearms.* McClelland and Stewart.

Patton, David, and Farrall, Stephen. 2021. 'Desistance: A Utopian Perspective'. *The Howard Journal of Crime and Justice* 60 (4): pp. 209–231.

Pearson, Geoffrey. and Hobbs, Dick. 2001. *Middle Market Drug Distribution.* Home Office research study 227. Home Office research and statistics directorate. London. https://eprints.lse.ac.uk/13878/1/Middle_market_drug_distribution.pdf Accessed 7 Jul. 2024.

Rose, Nikolas 2000. 'Government and Control'. *The British Journal of Criminology* 40 (2): pp. 321–339. http://www.jstor.org/stable/23638480 Accessed 26 Jul. 2024.

Savona, Ernesto U, and Mancuso, Marina. 2017. *Fighting Illicit Firearms Trafficking Routes and Actors at European Level.* Final Report of Project FIRE.

Spapens, Toine. 2007. 'Trafficking in Illicit Firearms For Criminal Purposes Within the European Union'. *European Journal of Crime, Criminal Law and Criminal Justice* 15 (3): pp. 359–381.

Wright, James D., and Rossi, Peter H. 1994. *Armed and Considered Dangerous: A Survey of Felons and their Firearms.* New York: Aldine de Gruytner.

12

Firearms, Conflict, and Terrorism

A Violent Nexus

Annelies Pauwels and Nils Duquet

Concerns about the possession and use of firearms by terrorists have led to a number of international and regional policy initiatives aimed at preventing and countering terrorist access to such weapons, such as the United Nations Security Council Resolutions 2370 and 2482. A better understanding of how terrorist organizations[1] acquire firearms is needed to increase the effectiveness of such initiatives. This chapter aims to contribute to this understanding by answering two research questions: (i) How do terrorist groups gain access to firearms? (ii) What role do firearms play in furthering the tactical and strategic objectives of these groups?

The chapter presents three case studies of terrorist acquisition of firearms in different regions of the world: the Taliban in Afghanistan, Jama'a Nusrat al-Islam wa al-Muslimin' (JNIM) and the Islamic State Sahel Province (ISSP) in the Central Sahel, and terrorist networks and lone actors in the European Union (see Chapter 10 for a discussion of trafficking networks and access to illicit firearms).

In this chapter, and through the three case studies, we make and test two central claims, each of which is directly related to one of the research questions. The first claim is that conflicts play an important role in facilitating terrorist access to firearms. Conflicts attract large numbers of firearms; this is

[1] There is no universal agreement on the definition of terrorism. In this chapter, by the term 'terrorist organization' we refer to a group that engages in acts of terror. The UN General Assembly in Resolution 49/60 states that 'Criminal acts intended or calculated to provoke a state of terror in the general public, a group of persons or particular persons for political purposes are in any circumstance unjustifiable, whatever the considerations of a political, philosophical, ideological, racial, ethnic, religious or any other nature that may be invoked to justify them' (United Nations General Assembly 1995). This chapter covers a lot of different types of organizations, groups, and individuals—some of which are included in the UN sanctions list, while others are not. This diversity aligns with the research purpose of the chapter to examine the acquisition and use of firearms by terrorist organizations in various contexts and settings.

Annelies Pauwels and Nils Duquet, *Firearms, Conflict, and Terrorism* In: *Illicit Firearms Markets and Organized Crime*. Edited by: David Bright, Oxford University Press. © Oxford University Press 2025.
DOI: 10.1093/9780198902409.003.0013

a logical dynamic inherent in violent conflicts. However, the easy availability of firearms in a given region also provides terrorists with many opportunities to acquire those firearms. We argue that the conflict-firearms-terrorism nexus materializes in different ways. It may be more direct and immediate, for example, in the case of a recent or ongoing conflict, or where a terrorist group is one of the parties in the conflict. It can also occur over a longer period, for example, in the case of an old conflict, or when a terrorist group is not involved in the conflict.

In this respect, the selection of our case studies provides a good starting point for analysis. The case studies cover regions that have been at war for years or even decades. Afghanistan, for example, has been at the centre of communist, Western, local warlord, and global jihadist wars for more than forty years. At the same time, our analysis includes a case study of the European Union, which has remained largely free of large-scale violent conflict on its territory for more than seventy years, with some notable exceptions such as the Troubles in Northern Ireland and the Basque conflict.

The second assertion is that firearms play a critical role in advancing the long-term and strategic goals of a terrorist group. In doing so, we go beyond the usual assessments of the immediate and direct benefits that the possession and use of weapons can bring to a terrorist organization. In particular, we look at the role of firearms in terrorist state-building and governance efforts. Over the past twenty-five years, and in particular in post-2011 Middle East, state-building and governance have become an increasingly important part of the strategic objectives of a number of (mainly jihadi) terrorist organizations (Lia 2015; Ladbury et al. 2016; Rupesinghe et al. 2021).

State-building is a complex process involving a number of different domains. It involves, for example, the need to acquire and control a specific territory and to monopolize the use of legitimate force. It also involves a political process of building institutions and maintaining relations with the population in a particular territory. Jihadist groups generally use two types of methods to further this process: their tactics aim to both terrorize and win the hearts and minds of those living in the territories they seek to control. In this chapter, we argue that firearms play a crucial role in all of these areas of terrorist state-building.

The case studies in this chapter present terrorist organizations that have made varying degrees of progress in their territorial and state-building objectives. The Taliban, for example, after waging a twenty-year insurgency against the Afghan government and NATO-led coalition forces, recently became the de facto ruling government of Afghanistan. The Taliban themselves are now facing insurgencies from the Islamic State Khorasan Province, on the one hand, and actors associated with the former government, of which the National Resistance Front is the largest faction, on the other (International Crisis Group 2022).

In the Sahel, both the JNIM and the ISSP have advanced territorial and governance claims. However, they have had limited success in establishing jihadi governance. Both groups remain primarily engaged in terrorist operations and have not managed to effectively control much territory. Other non-state armed groups remain present in the region, such as rebel groups fighting for independence or greater autonomy, and militias and self-defence groups formed in opposition to the rebels and jihadists (Anders 2015, 157). These groups also operate with a high degree of fluidity and pragmatism, which may hinder their long-term strategic goals. Finally, the case study of terrorist groups in the European Union is an outlier in this regard. Given the strong institutional, societal, and security framework in which they operate, terrorist groups have little room for manoeuvre to effectively engage in state-building efforts.

The Taliban in Afghanistan

How Did the Taliban Obtain Firearms?

Firearms are widespread in Afghanistan; they are mainly conflict-legacy products and have been introduced from abroad, for example, by the Soviet Army during the Soviet-Afghan war (1979–89) or by the US and its NATO allies during their twenty-year presence (2002–21) (Pirseyedi 2000, 13–37; Schroeder 2024). In this case study, we examine how the Taliban gained access to firearms, both during their insurgency against the Islamic Republic of Afghanistan and after they regained control of Afghanistan in 2021.

Given the widespread circulation of weapons in the country, the Taliban had several viable options for gaining access to weapons. A first source of weapons for the Taliban was the takeover of active stocks held by the Afghan security forces. This occurred not only through individual battlefield captures or thefts but also through the overrunning of vulnerable Afghan security checkpoints and facilities. Analysts at Conflict Armament Research found that many of the weapons seized from the Taliban had previously been supplied by the US to the Afghan security forces (Conflict Armament Research 2021). There is considerable confusion about the number of weapons transferred to the Afghan security forces over the past two decades, but a recent analysis by Small Arms Survey, based on a US Department of Defense (DoD) report, suggests that the US transferred 427,015 small arms and light weapons (SALW) between 2005 and 2021. The analysis also indicates that more than thirty other countries have transferred more than 300,000 SALW over the past two decades (Schroeder 2024). As highlighted in the same analysis, shortcomings in both US and Afghan arms control mechanisms—including inadequate record-keeping of equipment transfers and monitoring of weapons losses—facilitated the Taliban's access to this arsenal of Afghan security forces.

While this was the case in the years just before they took control of Kabul, the withdrawal of the US forces in August 2021 left the Taliban again with access to large military equipment caches (Mehra et al. 2022). The above-mentioned US DoD report estimated that nearly three-quarters of the 427,015 SALW procured by the DoD remained in Afghanistan (Schroeder 2024). A large amount of the Afghan National Defense and Security Forces (ANDSF) equipment is believed to have fallen into the hands of the Taliban. According to a Taliban official, the group has taken possession of more than 300,000 light weapons, 26,000 heavy weapons, and some 61,000 military vehicles (Special Inspector General for Afghanistan Reconstruction 2023, 65).

Not only have the Taliban managed to capture military equipment intended for other actors in Afghanistan, but they have also on occasion been the direct recipients of arms supplies from foreign donors. The Taliban is one of the Islamist factions that emerged from the collective of mujahideen and Afghan warlords that received weapons from foreign governments during the Soviet-Afghan war, as part of the proxy war between the US and the Soviet Union. Even after the war with the Soviet Union—both during the ensuing civil war and under the Taliban's rule—the Taliban continued to receive weapons and other military equipment, particularly from Pakistan, Iran, and Russia (Schroden 2021).

The Taliban have also supplemented their arsenal with weapons from illicit cross-border trafficking. Trafficking is particularly prevalent across the country's porous borders with Pakistan, Iran, and Tajikistan. Local manufacturing centres, such as the town of Darra Adam Khel in Khyber Pakhtunkhwa, a region just across the border in Pakistan, play an important role in the illicit trade. Firearms manufacturing has been an established practice in this region for more than 200 years, and it is estimated that nearly 10,000 families depend on local arms production for their livelihoods. While some of these locally produced firearms—modelled after popular Chinese, Russian, Turkish, and US weapons—are extremely well made and difficult to distinguish from the originals, others are poorly made and notorious for their low quality and unreliability. These weapons are popular with civilians because of their low cost and widespread availability. The smuggling of firearms is facilitated by the availability of numerous routes for this type of transaction, close tribal and kinship ties and support for the trade, and rampant corruption within the police force (Malik 2016).

Use of Firearms to Gain Territorial Control

Firearms play a crucial part in the Taliban's state-building project, which has entered a new, more advanced phase since the group took over Kabul in the summer of 2021. Firearms play an important role in many of the critical elements underpinning their state-building attempt, both in terms of the direct and indirect benefits they bring.

Firearms acquired by the Taliban have played a significant role in their battlefield offensives and terrorist and guerrilla operations. Both the quantity and quality of the weapons were important. The possession of a large number of weapons may have been necessary to arm and supply the organization's growing fighting force, which appears to have expanded significantly in the years prior to the takeover of Kabul (Schroden 2021). On the other hand, the more advanced military equipment captured through the overrunning of Afghan security checkpoints gave Taliban fighters an immediate advantage on the battlefield; ANDSF fighters now had to fight against an opponent with equally advanced weaponry. These spoils also had a cumulative effect, as the weapons were then used to launch attacks on more hardened installations and sensitive targets (Schroden 2021; Snow 2017a).

However, SALW also served a more indirect purpose for the Taliban prior to their takeover of Kabul. For example, they served as a powerful recruiting pitch to attract new members, and were a useful tool in their psychological warfare during the final offensives before taking Kabul in 2021; propaganda with images of captured military equipment on the battlefield was aimed at undermining morale and cohesion of the resisting Afghan security forces (Snow 2017b; Special Inspector General for Afghanistan Reconstruction 2023, 3).

Even after the Taliban took control of Kabul and became the de facto ruling government in Afghanistan, obtaining and maintaining access to weapons continues to play a crucial role in their state-building efforts. For example, they attempt to limit the weapons circulating in Afghanistan in order to remain the sole and legitimate user of force. For this reason, the Taliban have adopted policies and measures aimed at curbing the proliferation of weapons and limiting the access of other actors inside (and outside) the country to firearms. Some of these policies have been highlighted in a recent report by International Crisis Group on Afghanistan's security challenges under the Taliban. For example, in the summer of 2021, as their forces began to capture large swathes of territory, the Taliban announced a general amnesty—applicable to everyone who refrained from fighting them—aimed at encouraging former enemies to help rebuild state institutions, including the Taliban's security forces.

The Taliban have also made attempts at widespread disarmament, including house-to-house searches to confiscate privately held weapons, and have enhanced rules to register or request weapons. While the authorities justified the searches as a crime-fighting measure, the weapons may also have been seized with the aim of pre-empting opposition plans to launch offensives, by reducing their firepower (International Crisis Group 2022).

The Taliban's efforts to gain greater control over the proliferation of small arms in the country have in part been thwarted by local power dynamics. For example, powerful commanders tend not to agree to register their weapons (Schroden 2021, 22). This tension shows how weapons are also an important diplomatic tool for the Taliban in their efforts to establish the political processes that link state and society, such as the rules that determine the distribution of power and wealth. The Taliban are struggling to find the right balance of power between the centre and the periphery (Thier 2020; Madadi 2022). Before they came to power, they led a highly decentralized insurgency: they allowed a lot of leeway to regional commanders to run the war in their areas as they saw fit (Watkins 2020, 16). Now they are struggling to transform into a centralized government; asking trusted and influential commanders to give up their autonomy and follow orders could risk serious resistance, fragmentation, and commanders defecting to other insurgent groups (Madadi 2022; Jackson et al. 2023).

Weapons are an important factor in the accumulation of wealth for the Taliban, in terms of both the direct and indirect financial income they can provide. For example, research into the arms smuggling markets in southern, eastern, and northern Afghanistan and in neighbouring Pakistan suggests that Taliban operatives partially control and tax these black markets. This contrasts with the above-mentioned official policy of curbing the arms trade, which analysts say is only partially implemented. Traders in these ad hoc bazaars in border areas operate with Taliban arms permits and licences, and low-level Taliban fighters have been observed selling and trading weapons (Fleischner 2023, 4; Fleischner and Khan 2024).

Possession of weapons also provides the Taliban with indirect sources of financial income. They are also an excellent means of coercion, enabling many other income-generating activities. While for many years the Taliban relied on the opium trade as a source of financial income, more recently the organization has diversified its sources of cash flow, for example, into other streams of illicit trade (such as methamphetamines, illegal mining, and timber trade), kidnapping for ransom and extortions, and the imposition of taxes on checkpoints, infrastructure, and utilities under its control (United Nations Security Council 2020, 14–16). Firearms are essential to carry out these activities, especially in a region where many other militant and criminal groups are active (Demuynck et al. 2020, 8).

Last but not least, state-building also involves aligning with or managing societal expectations about state-society relations, i.e. what the state should do and what the terms of the state–society relationship should be. The Taliban has also used their weapons to subjugate the population under their command. In their first months in power, the Taliban—predominantly a Pashtun ethnic group with an ethno-nationalist outlook—cracked down on other ethnic, tribal, and religious groups they suspected of supporting the insurgency or otherwise fomenting anti-Taliban sentiment. More recently, the group has adopted more varied and nuanced ways of trying to assert control over the population, recognizing that heavy-handed tactics (on their own) can create a backlash that drives Afghans to support their opponents (International Crisis Group 2022, 20).

JNIM and ISSP in the Central Sahel

How do JNIM and ISSP Acquire Firearms?

The Central Sahel is a region that has been at the centre of a surge in jihadi activity in recent years. Researchers have highlighted the fluidity and pragmatism with which jihadist and other non-state armed groups operate in the region. For instance, it is difficult to establish a clear line of demarcation that separates *strictu sensu* jihadist militia from ethnic-based armed gangs and traffickers of weapons, drugs, and human beings. This mixture of roles is directly proportional to the mixture of interests between the different groups which, for mutual benefit, need mutual support (see Di Liddo 2019). Nevertheless, two main jihadi groups can be identified. The first is the Jama'a Nusrat al-Islam wa al-Muslimin' (JNIM)—a jihadist 'cartel' that brings together and coordinates the activities of various organizations and militias directly or indirectly linked to al-Qaeda. JNIM is the most active armed actor in the Sahel regional conflict. Its influence and reach extend across much of the Central Sahel and into the West African coastal states, having expanded from the group's traditional strongholds in northern and central Mali to the western and southern parts of Mali, most of Burkina Faso, parts of Niger, and the northernmost areas of Benin, Ghana, Côte d'Ivoire, and Togo. The second is the Islamic State Sahel Province (ISSP), the Sahelian affiliate of Islamic State. The ISSP is mainly active in the border areas between Burkina Faso, Mali, and Niger, but it has also been sporadically active in Algeria, Benin, and Niger (Nsaibia 2023a; Nsaibia 2023b).

How do these organizations obtain firearms? Three main sources of arms can be identified. A first source is the active stockpiles of security forces fighting terrorist groups. These include weapons that have been captured, stolen, or looted, either in ambushes on the battlefield or in attacks on military barracks. Some of these weapons were diverted quickly (i.e. in the last decade) after being handed over to national governments in the region (Anders 2015, 166–171).

For example, a Small Arms Survey analysis of weapons recovered from armed groups in northern Mali in 2012–14 shows that the Malian armed forces were the main source of weapons and ammunition for opposition fighters (Anders 2015). This was the case, inter alia, in early campaigns against military bases, such as the attacks in early 2012 on the military bases of Aguelhok, Menaka, and Timbuktu in Mali, carried out by fighters from both rebel and jihadist groups (Jeune Afrique 2013; Dubruelh 2012). More recently, non-state actors have also sought to secure military supplies by attacking military bases. For example, in the face of intensified clashes following the recent withdrawal of UN forces at the request of the ruling junta in Mali, JNIM has launched a new offensive involving a series of large-scale attacks on military positions (Nsaibia 2023c). In November 2023, the group claimed on its media platform to have carried out an attack on a military base near Timbuktu in northern Mali, publishing photos of weapons and ammunition as well as armoured vehicles it claimed to have captured (Agence France-Presse 2023).

A second source of firearms for non-state armed groups are legacy weapons, i.e. firearms that have not been used by government forces in their current conflict with rebel groups and jihadists. Even before the outbreak of the rebellion in northern Mali in 2011–12, rebel groups possessed many weapons that had been diverted from government stockpiles during Mali's forty years of revolutions (Florquin and Pézard 2005). Weapons from Libya also fall into this category. After the fall of the Gaddafi regime in 2011, Tuaregs returning from Libya brought a significant number of weapons with them. During the Libyan revolution, weapons from Gaddafi's vast arsenals had fallen into various hands, including rebel and jihadist groups. Hundreds of Malian Tuaregs who had come to Libya in the previous decades in search of work and better living conditions had brought many of these weapons with them when they returned to Mali to join the local Tuareg separatist movement, the Mouvement National pour la Libération de l'Azawad, or MNLA (Marsh 2017).

After 2013, illicit arms flows from Libya declined due to a combination of national and international initiatives to prevent trafficking, as well as increased domestic demand for arms and ammunition due to the upsurge in fighting in Libya itself (de Tessières 2017, 6; Pellerin 2017, 9). By 2015, most of the flow from Libya had dried up, but as of 2020–21, some new arms flows seem to have resumed, albeit at much lower levels (Anders 2024, 10; Small Arms Survey and UNDP 2022, 90). In addition to weapons from Libya, research has also shown that armed groups in northern Mali possess small arms and related ammunition diverted from stockpiles in other countries in the region, including Algeria, Burkina Faso, Côte d'Ivoire, Guinea, Liberia, Mauritania, Niger, and Sierra Leone, albeit typically in limited quantities (Anders 2015, 177–178).

The trafficking of firearms and other contraband along the trans-Saharan smuggling routes is embedded in local socio-economic dynamics. It is rooted in cross-border tribal relations and is a long-established (and one of the only) sources of income for some local tribes (Anders 2015, 175). There may also be close links between armed insurgent groups and transnational criminal groups in the region. Traffickers form temporary alliances with armed groups to protect and promote their economic interests, and jihadist and other insurgent groups have used trafficking extensively as a means of generating financial income (Anders 2015, 165). Arms trafficking mostly takes place in environments that are difficult for governments to monitor and control, and where regional border control capacities are limited and easily circumvented by traffickers (Marsh 2017, 80).

A third source of firearms for non-state armed groups is the black market. Armed groups opportunistically accumulate material that has been in illicit circulation in Mali for decades. This material may have been diverted to the black market in various ways. For example, non-state actors acquired materiel from new recruits who deserted the army with their weapons, and through misappropriation by state officials, such as when individual soldiers sold their weapons to rebels (Florquin and Pézard 2005, 51). Government policies aimed at providing arms to self-defence units and pro-government militias may also have increased the amount of weapons held by non-state actors in northern Mali. These weapons may then find their way onto the black market and into the hands of rebel and jihadi groups (Anders 2024, 6).

In this context, it is also important to note how components for improvised explosive devices (IEDs)—such as commercial explosives, detonators, detonating cord, and ammonium nitrate—end up on the black market. The use of IEDs in the region increased dramatically between 2014 and 2022, for example, in attacks against national and international security forces, UN peacekeepers, and civilians. Recent analysis by the Small Arms Survey highlights various trafficking and diversion dynamics. For example, IED components are trafficked along the same routes used for decades to smuggle arms, drugs, and people, and are sourced mainly from Ghana and Nigeria. They also enter the black market through the resale of mining or quarrying companies' surpluses on the illicit market, fraud, theft at the companies, or during transport (Small Arms Survey 2023).

How Did Weapons Enhance Jihadist Strategy in Sahel?

Access to more and better weapons significantly improved the operational capabilities of jihadist actors in the Sahel, particularly in the early stages of the insurgency. For example, the weapons brought by Tuareg fighters from Libya who joined the local insurgency in Mali in early 2012 qualitatively improved the military capabilities of insurgent (and terrorist) groups in the region. These weapons were previously unavailable to them or were in short supply. Insurgents now had at their disposal material traditionally associated only with military forces, which played an important role in increasing their mobility and firepower. The destructive power of these weapons enabled rapid territorial advances: within three months, the government had lost control of large areas of northern Mali (Anders 2015; Marsh 2017).

Moreover, access to weapons and subsequent territorial advances in the early years of the Malian insurgency had a cumulative effect. The initial defeat of the Malian army allowed the opposition forces to seize weapons caches abandoned by fleeing soldiers, setting off a cascade in which each capture of weapons and ammunition strengthened the fighters and allowed them to seize yet more caches (Marsh 2017).

Access to more and better weapons has not only advanced the purely military objectives of the jihadists in the region; it has also played a role in a secondary phase, namely the consolidation of power over their areas of operation. Both the JNIM and the ISSP have sought to establish and consolidate territorial control by providing governance—a means of justifying their legitimacy as authorities—to local populations in Mali, Burkina Faso, and Niger. In doing so, the two groups compete with each other and adopt different styles of 'jihadi governance'. Each group seems to express or impose its political will in rather opposite ways. The JNIM adopts a 'soft' approach to governance. The group has offered protection to local communities, refrained from imposing harsh rule on them, and has focused on embedding itself in local dynamics in order to win hearts and minds. The JNIM also seeks to negotiate with various Muslim sects and ethnic groups in order to expand its influence. The ISSP, on the other hand, has sought to consolidate its power by intimidating the local population. The group has ruled according to strict interpretations of Sharia law, often with little regard for local dynamics (Clarke and Zenn 2023; The Soufan Center 2021; Nasr 2021).

The crucial importance of weapons is reflected in various aspects of their governance projects. For example, weapons are an important means of providing local communities with a sense of protection. Both groups are in competition with each other—as well as with government security forces—and the fighting between them has a spillover effect on local communities: local residents are forced to seek protection from either the JNIM or the ISSP against attacks by the other group or affiliated militias. In this sense, weapons are used as a tool to gain sympathy or support from local communities; jihadi groups may use weapons to show individuals or communities that they can protect them. For an individual, the possession of a weapon may be attractive because it can lead to a higher social status or respect, or to a position of dominance. At the community level, however, weapons can be a useful tool to resist threats from other communities, armed groups, or government forces. In Mali, jihadist groups have also often stoked tensions between communities, so that they are ultimately seen as the only real providers of security (Small Arms Survey and UNDP 2022).

Weapons are also needed to compensate for the shortcomings of central governments on security and humanitarian issues. Jihadist movements have presented themselves to local populations and ethnic minorities as the only interlocutors capable of listening to their concerns, solving their problems, and supporting their political agendas. In fact, they have set up alternative and (in some cases) more efficient welfare systems than those of the legitimate states, distributing basic necessities, guaranteeing employment opportunities (through recruitment to the militias), offering free and accessible education to all (through the networks of radical imams and ulemas), and defending the economic rights of the most vulnerable communities, starting with the semi-nomadic Fulani herdsmen (Di Liddo 2019, 47).

Terrorist Networks and Lone Actors in the European Union

How Do they Acquire Weapons?

Terrorists in the European Union tend to obtain their weapons from illegal firearms markets. There have been a number of exceptions where terrorist attacks have been carried out using legally obtained firearms. A high-profile case is the 2011 terrorist attack in Norway. Criminal connections are important for gaining access to weapons on the illicit market. Given the generally closed nature of illicit markets in the EU, only terrorists with the right criminal connections can acquire firearms in this way, especially military-style firearms. Many contemporary jihadi terrorists have such criminal connections (Basra et al. 2016); they have criminal backgrounds (e.g. involvement in armed robbery or drug dealing), often prior to their radicalization, and have used their criminal connections to facilitate the acquisition of firearms (Duquet and Goris 2018, 20–21). While a criminal background may facilitate access to firearms on the illicit market for jihadi terrorists, different patterns of acquisition can be identified in relation to right-wing terrorists. These patterns are discussed below.

Terrorist networks use various supply mechanisms to acquires weapons on the illicit firearms markets in the EU. A first major supply mechanism is the trafficking of weapons from the Western Balkans following the various conflicts in the former Yugoslavia (1991–2001). One example is the frequent possession and use of Kalashnikov-type firearms, such as the Zastava M70 assault rifle, by jihadi terrorists in the EU. Weapons supplied through this mechanism were diverted during the Yugoslav wars: they were often surplus weapons, firearms from looted weapons caches, or weapons that in one way or another ended up in the hands of a wide range of non-state actors during the conflict. However, it is often unclear at what specific point the smuggled firearms now available on European illicit firearms markets first entered the EU, as these weapons usually disappeared from the radar during the wars in the region (Duquet and Goris 2018, 107).

The smuggling of legacy weapons from the former Yugoslavia into EU member states is closely linked to drug trafficking. The two phenomena are interlinked in terms of routes, actors, and modus operandi. Firearms trafficking is mainly a supplementary source of income for the organized crime groups involved, alongside their more lucrative core criminal activities such as drug trafficking. According to Europol, weapons and drugs are often smuggled as part of multi-commodity transfers or hidden in vehicles (De Schutter and Duquet 2023). Some firearms are also smuggled by sea. A significant number of firearms trafficked to Italy, for example, are transported by sea from the Western Balkans to the eastern coast of Italy (Duquet and Goris 2018, 107).

A second supply mechanism for terrorist networks is the exploitation of legal loopholes. This is reflected in the recent trade in converted firearms, some of which originate in EU member states. Converted firearms refer to the modification of objects that are incapable of firing a projectile into ones that can. This includes both the conversion of originally non-lethal imitation firearms (such as alarm weapons and airsoft guns) and the reactivation of firearms previously downgraded to smaller 'Flobert' calibres or modified not to fire live ammunition (such as surplus government weapons modified for the civilian market) (Florquin and King 2018, 14). Converted weapons are often cheap, readily available, and difficult to trace—characteristics that make them attractive to criminals and terrorists alike.

There have been a number of high-profile terrorist attacks in Europe involving converted weapons in recent years, such as the January 2015 terrorist attack in Paris. The perpetrator of the Montrouge and Hypercacher attacks used firearms sold in Slovakia as acoustic expansion weapons—live-firing weapons modified to prevent their use with regular ammunition—before they were reactivated and eventually smuggled to France. A reactivated pistol was also among the weapons seized from the perpetrator of the March 2012 attacks in Toulouse and Montauban, France (Florquin and King 2018, 38).

A third supply mechanism is theft. Several of the recent public mass shootings in the European Union (including terrorist attacks) have been committed with firearms that were previously legally owned, but which entered the illicit domain after a burglary or robbery. For example, the deadly shootings at a cultural centre and a synagogue in Copenhagen in 2015 were committed with an automatic firearm stolen from a volunteer military organization (de Labbey et al. 2021). Also, the above-mentioned attacker in Toulouse and Montauban had used a firearm stolen from a professional sport shooter's home (Duquet and Goris 2018, 200).

A fourth group of supply mechanisms includes a variety of sources for which the use of the Internet is crucial. One example is the online purchase of components via the Internet (sometimes the darknet). These are then delivered by parcel services. It is possible to order specific components (e.g. to replace parts of deactivated weapons that would prevent them from firing) or to order entire firearms that are then delivered in parts (Duquet 2022, 192).

In this context, the use of 'straw purchasers' has also been highlighted: these are mainly legal gun owners who, with the necessary permits, purchase firearms from legal arms dealers on behalf of criminal groups. Once they have acquired these firearms, they may erase the serial numbers and then report the firearms as stolen or lost (UNODC 2020, 24 and 66).

Another source for which the Internet plays a crucial role is the 3D-printing of firearms (see Chapter 8 for a detailed discussion of 3DP firearms). Today, 3D-printed (3DP) firearms fall into one of three categories: fully 3D-printed firearms (F3DP), hybrid 3DP firearms, and parts kit completions (PKCs). F3DPs contain no pressure-bearing non-printed components and few metal components. Most of these firearms can only be used for a limited number of shots before they malfunction. Hybrid 3DP firearms—which is the most frequently observed type in the European context, based on known law enforcement seizures—rely on some readily available and unregulated components such as steel tubing, metal bar stocks, and springs. Hybrid 3D printed firearms offer a comparable performance to some mass-produced firearms. PKCs, the final category, include firearms that have been assembled using a combination of 3DP receivers and factory-made pressure-bearing components, such as the barrel and slide. PKCs tend to be the most reliable type of firearm using 3DP parts (Schaufelbühl et al. 2024; Veilleux-Lepage 2021).

The potential threat of terrorist use of 3DP guns did not manifest itself in a concrete way until the Halle synagogue shooting in 2019. The attacker's arsenal included five improvised firearms, mostly made of steel, aluminium, and wood, but with some 3DP components (Veilleux-Lepage 2021). The exponential increase in cases of 3D-printing—particularly in the context of right-wing extremism—may make 3D-printing of firearms an emerging and important source of firearms. Recent cases in the UK, Finland, Ireland, and the Netherlands are evidence of this (Schroeder et al. 2023, 10).

With regards to right-wing extremism, it may be worthwhile highlighting other specific patterns through which terrorist networks can acquire firearms. A first source is the weaponry used by the armed forces of EU member states. This pattern is linked to the presence of members with military backgrounds in the right-wing extremist movements in some European member states. The risk of military equipment being stolen by radicalized military personnel was highlighted in a recent high-profile but unsuccessful attack in Belgium, where an army sergeant misappropriated four rocket launchers and two firearms from a military weapons cache. The target of his attack was a well-known virologist who had been advising the government on policies to deal with the Covid-19 pandemic. The sergeant also had links to a right-wing extremist group, the Flemish Legion (van Dongen et al. 2022). A second source of acquisition specific to the right-wing extremist milieu appears to be the legal acquisition of firearms. In Germany, for example, the domestic intelligence agency revealed in 2021 that more than 1,200 right-wing extremists had firearms licences. The German authorities have also reported that extremists have taken part in target practice, mostly outside Germany (Deutsche Welle 2021). The general fascination with guns in these circles may lead to a significant number of extremists with legal firearms (Koehler 2016). One case of a right-wing terrorist using legally obtained firearms occurred in 2018, when an Italian right-wing extremist targeted six African migrants in Macerata with a legally owned weapon (Duquet and Goris 2018, 139).

How Do Weapons Enhance Terrorist Strategies in Europe?

Terrorist networks in Europe have mainly used weapons for strictly operational purposes. The use of firearms is a preferred—and extremely lethal—tool for carrying out terrorist attacks, whether by right-wing or jihadist networks, or lone actors. Left-wing terrorist groups, on the other hand, also have access to firearms in some countries, but seem to prefer not to acquire them, opting instead for a modus operandi involving arson, letter bombs, sabotage, and intimidation (Duquet and Goris 2018, 141–142). For example, Europol's Trend Report 2022 highlights that most left-wing terrorist attacks have been carried out using improvised incendiary devices, fire accelerators, and IEDs (Europol 2023).

Terrorist networks use firearms both as the primary instrument of violence in attacks and as a facilitating tool to carry out attacks by other means. Good examples of the indirect use of a firearm in carrying out a terrorist attack are the vehicle rammings in Nice and in Berlin in 2016. Both attackers made use of a firearm to obtain their vehicles, which ended up being the main weapon and led to large numbers of casualties.

European terrorist networks do not use firearms as explicitly and extensively as the terrorist organizations in the other two case studies as a means of controlling territory or advancing political, institutional, or societal processes that are embedded in a state-building project. In the other case studies, this is done in a more structural and organized way and on a larger scale. In Europe, however, the use of firearms in building a new state and society remains more anecdotal and less structured. There are instances that hint at such intentions—for example the important role of weapons as outlined in Anders Breivik's manifesto, or the accumulation of firearms beyond a mere operational purpose by some right-wing groups or anti-migrant vigilante groups. However, more research is needed to move beyond this anecdotal level of analysis. Most likely, terrorist groups in Europe have very little room for manoeuvre to effectively engage in state-building efforts, given the strong institutional, societal, and security framework in which they operate. The conditions for effectively occupying and maintaining space may therefore be limited in European member states. However, the situation may be quite different in the online sphere, where many spaces can be found that have been completely taken over by sympathizers or members of extremist or terrorist networks.

In these unregulated online spaces—such as online platforms and imageboards, Telegram channels, and forums on both the surface and dark web (see Chapter 9)—weapons play a central role in advancing the long-term goals of extremist and terrorist movements. Jihadist groups and militant accelerationist movements (such as the Atomwaffen Division and The Base) disseminate and communicate violent content in their propaganda that is not merely instrumental, i.e. aimed at spreading hatred, inciting violence, or glorifying past terrorist attacks—standard elements of terrorist propaganda. The displays of violence and weapons are also symbolic acts. They should be seen as part of their larger apocalyptic worldview, which is embedded in both jihadist and right-wing accelerationist thinking: the idea that there is no salvation for the world as it is and the desire to destroy the existing corrupt world in order to usher in a promised golden age (Argentino et al. 2022, 15–16). In this line of thinking, the violent aesthetics in both types of online propaganda are part of a strategic goal of state-building: posing with weapons is much more than a mere display of military strength or an expression of threat; it contributes to a hypermasculine warrior culture that is considered crucial for building a new world. For a member, posing with weapons is a means of identity formation: a means of becoming a new man—the 'hypermasculine warrior archetype'—who must work to hasten the collapse of society and rebuild a new state and society from its ashes (Argentino et al. 2022, 16).

Policy Implications and Conclusions

This chapter has sought to contribute to our understanding of the acquisition and use of firearms by terrorist organizations by addressing two research questions: (i) How do terrorist networks gain access to firearms? (ii) What role do firearms play in furthering the tactical and strategic objectives of these groups? A meta-analysis of three case studies has helped us to provide answers to these questions and confirms the two claims we made at the beginning of the chapter.

The first claim we made is that conflict plays an important role in facilitating terrorist access to firearms. Our case studies have shown that the conflict—firearms—terrorism nexus operates in different ways. A more direct acquisition of conflict weapons by terrorist groups was highlighted in the Central Sahel case study; many weapons in the possession of jihadist groups in Mali had only recently been delivered to the Malian armed forces fighting the same jihadists.

On the other hand, several case studies have highlighted examples of conflicts that indirectly fuel the acquisition of firearms by terrorists. We have seen that weapons from legacy conflicts make up a significant proportion of the arsenal of various terrorist groups. For example, weapons from the Afghan-Soviet war are still available to the general population or sold on the black market today, decades after the conflict ended, and can be found in the hands of the Taliban and jihadist groups alike.

Even in more peaceful regions, as the case study on the European Union shows, weapons from conflicts in the immediate neighbourhood, in particular the Yugoslav wars of the 1990s, have found their way into the hands of terrorist groups.

When analysing the role of conflict in facilitating terrorist access to firearms, it may also be worthwhile to consider the different dynamics that govern the supply of weapons in the context of these conflicts. For example, arms transfers have often been linked to wider international rivalries and thus seen as a useful diplomatic tool (or, in some cases, part of hybrid warfare) to win over local state and non-state armed actors. Often the accumulation of weapons has been a means for ruling governments to maintain control over internal conflicts that might arise (Krause 1994).

From our analysis, therefore, we can draw five key policy implications aimed at limiting the opportunities for terrorist groups to acquire firearms. States should (i) exercise caution in international arms transfers; (ii) limit the risk of diversion, in particular by improving stockpile management; (iii) deal with conflict-legacy weapons, for example through post-conflict disarmament programmes; (iv) combat trafficking in firearms, ammunition, and related materials; and (v) strongly monitor new technologies that could be used by criminal and terrorist groups to manufacture weapons of an improvised and non-industrial nature.

The second claim we made is that firearms are crucial to terrorist networks not only in terms of the immediate and direct benefits they can bring but also in terms of their role in advancing a group's long-term and strategic goals, particularly state-building and governance efforts. The analysis in the case studies has shown that firearms play a central and cumulative role in furthering the state-building efforts of terrorist movements. Access to weapons is a necessary means of conquering territory, which in turn increases a group's ability to acquire weapons in greater quantities, of higher quality, and sometimes even independently of other actors. All this is crucial not only for territorial control and expansion but also for the political, social, and institutional processes involved in state-building. In doing so, terrorist groups will use weapons both to intimidate and terrorize the local population and to try to win their hearts and minds.

It is clear from our case studies that terrorist groups often operate in areas where there is widespread circulation of weapons, and that they have several ways of gaining access to weapons. One of the main methods of acquisition, as we have seen, is to take over supplies from armed state groups and non-state groups with which they are fighting. Therefore, terrorist networks often do not need to resort to trafficking rings to acquire weapons. Nevertheless, illicit trafficking should be seen as the glue that holds together the various methods of firearms acquisition for terrorist organizations. In conflict regions, weapons are often widely available, but illicit trafficking is necessary for terrorist groups to effectively acquire sufficient firepower to defeat their opponents. Terrorist groups may initially acquire weapons by taking over the stockpiles of other parties to the conflict. However, these weapons need to be supplemented with externally trafficked weapons to give them the strength to overwhelm their opponents. Trafficking also is the glue that binds conflict and non-conflict areas and eras together. Weapons from conflict areas can be trafficked and end up in the hands of terrorist groups in a neighbouring region,or resurface decades after the conflict has ended.

Finally, we can conclude that the availability of firearms—both quantity and quality—enables non-state actors to engage in violent conflict (and thus acquire more weapons), to control territory, and to engage in state-building and governance. Effective and well-functioning state structures are essential for an effective response. As the case study on the European Union shows, terrorist groups there have relatively little room for manoeuvre to acquire and use firearms to further their territorial and governance goals within a strong institutional, political, and social framework, and will therefore seek to adapt. Fragile statehood and the proliferation of firearms are interrelated problems. Dysfunctional states with weak institutions are unable to control the proliferation of firearms, which in turn remain in the region and contribute to state fragility. In order to avoid a vicious circle, any approach should therefore be two-pronged, aimed at both countering the proliferation of weapons and strengthening state structures and institutions, while at the same time addressing the grievances and mistrust of local communities towards the state.

References

Agence France-Presse. 2023. 'Mali Militants Claim to Seize Military Base, Army Denies'. *Voice of America, 25 November 2023.* https://www.voanews.com/a/mali-militants-claim-to-seize-military-base-army-denies-/7370477.html Accessed 29 Apr. 2024.

Anders, Holger. 2015. 'Expanding Arsenals: Insurgent Arms in Northern Mali'. In *Small Arms Survey 2015: Weapons and the World*, edited by Small Arms Survey, pp. 156–169. Cambridge: Cambridge University Press.

Anders, Holger. 2024. *Continuity and Change. Extremist-used Arms in Mali.* Geneva: Small Arms Survey/ Security Assessment in North Africa project. https://www.smallarmssurvey.org/sites/default/files/resources/SAS-SANA-BP-2024-Mali-Extremist-EN.pdf Accessed 29 Apr. 2024.

Argentino, Marc-André, Amarasingam, Amarnath, and Conley, Emmi. 2022. *'One Struggle': Examining Narrative Syncretism between Accelerationists and Salafi-Jihadists.* London: International Centre for the Study of Radicalisation & National Counterterrorism Innovation, Technology, and Education Center.

Basra, Rajan, Neumann, Peter R., and Brunner, Claudia. 2016. *Criminal Pasts, Terrorist Futures: European Jihadist and the New Crime-Terror Nexus.* London: The International Centre for the Study of Radicalisation and Political Violence. https://icsr.info/wp-content/uploads/2016/10/ICSR-Report-Criminal-Pasts-Terrorist-Futures-European-Jihadists-and-the-New-Crime-Terror-Nexus.pdf Accessed 27 Jul. 2024.

Clarke, Colin P., and Zenn, Jacob. 2023. 'Jihadist Terrorism Encroaching on Coastal West Africa, Spilling Over From the Sahel'. *Lawfare*. 5 May 2023. https://www.lawfaremedia.org/article/jihadist-terrorism-encroaching-on-coastal-west-africa-spilling-over-from-the-sahel Accessed 30 Apr. 2024.

Conflict Armament Research. 2021. *Illicit Weapons in Afghanistan. Issue 01: Taliban Seizures of US-Equipment Are Only a Fraction of the Story*. London: Conflict Armament Research Ltd. https://www.conflictarm.com/perspectives/illicit-weapons-in-afghanistan-issue-01/ Accessed 27 Jul. 2024.

de Labbey, Quitterie, Duquet, Nils, and Smets, Lore. 2021. *Project DIVERT: Report. Stealing Precious Steel: Firearms Theft in the European Union*. Brussels: Flemish Peace Institute. https://vlaamsvredesinstituut.eu/wp-content/uploads/2021/05/20210526-DIVERT2-FirearmsTheft.pdf Accessed 29 Apr. 2024.

Demuynck, Méryl, Mehra, Tanya, and Bergema, Reinier. 2020. *The Use of Small Arms & Light Weapons by Terrorist Organisations as a Source of Finance in South and Southeast Asia*. The Hague: International Centre for Counter-Terrorism. https://www.icct.nl/publication/use-small-arms-and-light-weapons-terrorist-organisations-source-finance Accessed 24 Jul. 2024.

De Schutter, Astrid, and Duquet, Nils. 2023. *The Nexus Between Drug Markets and Gun Violence in the European Union*. Brussels: Flemish Peace Institute and European Monitoring Centre for Drugs and Drug Addiction. https://www.euda.europa.eu/drugs-library/nexus-between-drug-markets-and-gun-violence-european-union_en Accessed 27 Jul. 2024.

De Tessières, Savannah. 2017. 'Measuring Illicit Arms Flows, Niger'. *Small Arms Survey*. March 2017. https://www.smallarmssurvey.org/resource/measuring-illicit-arms-flows-niger Accessed 27 Jul. 2024.

Deutsche Welle. 2021. 'Germany: 1,200 Right-Wing Extremists Licensed to Own Weapons'. 2 February 2021. https://www.dw.com/en/germany-1200-right-wing-extremists-licensed-to-own-weapons/a-56416420 Accessed 29 Apr. 2024.

Di Liddo, Marco. 2019. 'The Instability in the Sahel'. In *The Evolution of Radicalisation in the Maghreb in the Aftermath of the Defeat of Daesh*, edited by Lorenzo Marinone, pp. 42–49. Centro Studi Internazionali and ITSTIME. https://www.cesi-italia.org/en/articles/the-evolution-of-radicalisation-in-the-maghreb-in-the-aftermath-of-the-defeat-of-daesh Accessed 29 Apr. 2024.

Dubruelh, Camille. 2012. 'Nord-Mali: des Rebelles Touaregs Attaquent Ménaka'. *Jeune Afrique*. 17 January 2012. https://www.jeuneafrique.com/177703/politique/nord-mali-des-rebelles-touaregs-attaquent-m-naka/ Accessed 30 Apr. 2024.

Duquet, Nils (ed.). 2022. *Project TARGET Country Reports. Pulling the Trigger: Gun Violence in Europe* . Brussels: Flemish Peace Institute. https://vlaamsvredesinstituut.eu/wp-content/uploads/2022/10/TARGET-7CountryReports-FPI-def.pdf Accessed 29 Apr. 2024.

Duquet, Nils, and Goris, Kevin. 2018. *Firearms Acquisition by Terrorists in Europe. Research Findings and Policy Recommendations of Project SAFTE*. Brussels: Flemish Peace Institute. https://flemishpeaceinstitute.eu/safte/files/vrede_syntheserapport_safte_lr.pdf Accessed 29 Apr. 2024.

Europol. 2023. *European Union Terrorism Situation and Trend Report*. Luxembourg: Publications Office of the European Union.

Fleischner, Justine. 2023. 'Arms Smuggling Dynamics under Taliban Rule. Situation update Afghanistan'. *Small Arms Survey*. https://smallarmssurvey.org/sites/default/files/resources/Situation%20Update-Smuggling-Dynamics-under-Taliban-Rule-Final.pdf Accessed 29 Apr. 2024.

Fleischner, Justine, and Khan, Habib. 2024. 'Selective Approval: Taliban Weapons Controls in Afghanistan's Balkh Province. Situation update Afghanistan'. *Small Arms Survey*. May 2024. https://www.smallarmssurvey.org/resource/selective-approval-taliban-weapons-controls-afghanistans-balkh-province. Accessed 23 Oct. 2024.

Florquin, Nicolas, and King, Benjamin. 2018. 'From Legal to Lethal. Converted Firearms in Europe'. *Small Arms Survey*. April 2018. Geneva: Graduate Institute of International and Development Studies. https://www.smallarmssurvey.org/resource/legal-lethal-converted-firearms-europe. Accessed 23 Oct. 2024.

Florquin, Nicolas, and Pézard, Stéphanie. 2005. 'Insurgency, Disarmament, and Insecurity in Northern Mali, 1990–2004'. In *Armed and Aimless: Armed Groups, Guns, and Human Security in the ECOWAS Region*, edited by Nicolas Florquin and Eric G. Berman, pp. 46–77. Geneva: Small Arms Survey.

International Crisis Group. 2022. *Afghanistan's Security Challenges under the Taliban*. Asia Report No. 326. Brussels: International Crisis Group.

Jackson, Ashley, Maiwand, and Weigand, Florian. 2023. 'Taliban Arms Management Practices. Situation Update Afghanistan'. *Small Arms Survey*. June 2023. https://www.smallarmssurvey.org/resource/taliban-arms-management-practices Accessed 29 Apr. 2024.

Jeune Afrique. 2013. *Guerre au Mali: retour sur le drame d'Aguelhok*. 21 October 2013. https://www.jeuneafrique.com/167687/politique/guerre-au-mali-retour-sur-le-drame-d-aguelhok/ Accessed 30 Apr. 2024.

Koehler, Daniel. 2016. *Right-wing Terrorism in the 21st Century: The 'National Socialist Underground' and the History of Terror from the Far-Right in Germany*. Oxon/New York: Routledge.

Krause, Keith. 1994. 'The Arms Trade: Problems and Prospects in the Post-Cold War World'. *The Annals of the American Academy of Political and Social Science* 535: pp. 73–90.

Ladbury, Sarah et al. 2016. 'Jihadi Groups and State-Building: The Case of Boko Haram in Nigeria'. *Stability: International Journal of Security & Development* 5 (1): pp. 1–19.

Lia, Brynjar. 2015. 'Understanding Jihadi Proto-States'. *Perspectives on Terrorism* 9 (4): pp. 31–41. https://www.jstor.org/stable/26297412. Accessed on 31 Apr. 2024.

Madadi, Sayed. 2022. 'Dysfunctional Centralization and Growing Fragility under Taliban Rule'. *Middle East Institute*. 6 September 2022. https://www.mei.edu/publications/dysfunctional-centralization-and-growing-fragility-under-taliban-rule Accessed 29 Apr. 2024.

Malik, Aqab. 2016. 'Darra Adam Khel: "Home Grown" Weapons'. *Air & Space Power Journal-Africa and Francophonie* 7 (1): pp. 73–97. https://www.airuniversity.af.edu/Portals/10/ASPJ_French/journals_E/Volume-07_Issue-1/malik_e.pdf Accessed 29 Apr. 2024.

Marsh, Nicholas. 2017. 'Brothers Came Back with Weapons. The Effects of Arms Proliferation from Libya'. *PRISM* 6 (4): pp. 79–96.

Mehra, Tanya, Demuynck, Méryl, and Wentworth, Matthew. 2022. *Spoils Weapons in Afghanistan: The Taliban's Spoils of War*. The Hague: International Centre for Counter-Terrorism.

Nasr, Wassim. 2021. 'IntelBrief: Negotiating Out of Counterterrorism in the Sahel'. *The Soufan Centre* 6 August 2021. https://thesoufancenter.org/intelbrief-2021-august-6/ Accessed 29 Apr. 2024.

Nsaibia, Héni. 2023a. 'Actor Profile: Jama'at Nusrat al-Islam wal-Muslimin (JNIM)'. *Armed Conflict Location & Event Data Project (ACLED)*. 13 November 2023. https://acleddata.com/2023/11/13/actor-profile-jamaat-nusrat-al-islam-wal-muslimin-jnim/ Accessed 29 Apr. 2024.

Nsaibia, Héni. 2023b. 'Actor Profile: The Islamic State Sahel Province'. *Armed Conflict Location & Event Data Project (ACLED)*. 13 January 2023. https://acleddata.com/2023/01/13/actor-profile-the-islamic-state-sahel-province/ Accessed 29 Apr. 2024.

Nsaibia, Héni. 2023c. 'Fact Sheet: Attacks on Civilians Spike in Mali as Security Deteriorates Across the Sahel'. *Armed Conflict Location & Event Data Project (ACLED)*. 21 September 2023. https://acleddata.com/2023/09/21/fact-sheet-attacks-on-civilians-spike-in-mali-as-security-deteriorates-across-the-sahel/ Accessed 29 Apr. 2024.

Pellerin, Mathieu. 2017. 'Beyond the "Wild West". The Gold Rush in Northern Niger'. *Small Arms Survey*. June 2017. https://www.smallarmssurvey.org/resource/beyond-wild-west-gold-rush-northern-niger Accessed 27 Jul. 2024.

Pirseyedi, Bobi. 2000. *The Small Arms Problem in Central Asia: Features and Implications*. Geneva: United Nations Institute for Disarmament Research. https://unidir.org/files/publication/pdfs/the-small-arms-problem-in-central-asia-features-and-implications-117.pdf Accessed 30 Apr. 2024.

Rupesinghe, Natasja, Naghizadeh, Mikael Hiberg, and Cohen, Corentin. 2021. *Reviewing Jihadist Governance in the Sahel*. Oslo: Norwegian Institute of International Affairs.

Schaufelbühl, Stefan, et al. 2024. 'The Emergence of 3D-Printed Firearms: An Analysis of Media and Law Enforcement Reports'. *Forensic Science International: Synergy* 8: p. 100464. https://www.ncbi.nlm.nih.gov/pmc/articles/PMC10998078/ Accessed 29 Apr. 2024.

Schroden, Jonathan. 2021. 'Afghanistan's Security Forces Versus the Taliban: A Net Assessment'. *CTC Sentinel* 14 (1): pp. 20–29. https://ctc.westpoint.edu/afghanistans-security-forces-versus-the-taliban-a-net-assessment/ Accessed 29 Apr. 2024.

Schroeder, Matt. 2024. 'Calculable Losses? Arms Transfers to Afghanistan 2002–21'. *Small Arms Survey*. 19 January 2024. https://reliefweb.int/report/afghanistan/calculable-losses-arms-transfers-afghanistan-2002-21-january-2024 Accessed 29 Apr. 2024.

Schroeder, Matt, et al. 2023. 'Project Insight Research Report. Privately Made Firearms in the European Union'. *Flemish Peace Institute and Small Arms Survey* 11 December 2023. https://gunviolence.eu/wp-content/uploads/2023/11/Project_INSIGHT_Emerging-Threats_DEF.pdfAccessed 29 Apr. 2024.

Small Arms Survey. 2023. *Out of Control. The Trafficking of Improvised Explosive Device Components and Commercial Explosives in West Africa*. Geneva: Small Arms Survey.

Small Arms Survey and UNDP. 2022. *Perceptions, Vulnerabilities, and Prevention. Violent Extremism Threat Assessment in Selected Regions of the Southern Libyan Borderlands and North-Western Nigeria*. Geneva: Small Arms Survey.

Snow, Shawn. 2017a. 'US Weapons Complicate Afghan war'. *Military Times*. 25 July 2017. https://www.militarytimes.com/flashpoints/2017/07/25/us-weapons-complicate-afghan-war/ Accessed 29 Apr. 2024.

Snow, Shawn. 2017b. 'Taliban Propaganda Showcases US Weapons and Radios as Captured War Spoils'. *Military Times*. 14 August 2017. https://www.militarytimes.com/flashpoints/2017/08/14/taliban-propaganda-showcases-us-weapons-and-radios-as-captured-war-spoils/ Accessed 30 Apr. 2024.

The Soufan Center. 2021. 'IntelBrief: Jihadist Groups Continue to Consolidate Territory Throughout West Africa'. 4 October 2021. https://thesoufancenter.org/intelbrief-2021-october-4/ Accessed 29 Apr. 2024.

Special Inspector General for Afghanistan Reconstruction. 2023. 'Why the Afghan Security Forces Collapsed'. February 2023. https://www.sigar.mil/pdf/evaluations/SIGAR-23-16-IP.pdf Accessed 29 Apr. 2024.

Thier, Alex. 2020. 'The Nature of the Afghan State: Centralization vs. Decentralization'. *Afghan Peace Process Issues Paper*. Washington, DC: United States Institute of Peace. https://www.usip.org/sites/default/files/Afghanistan-Peace-Process_Nature-of-the-Afghan-State_Centralization-vs-Decentralization.pdf Accessed 29 Apr. 2024.

United Nations General Assembly. 1995. Resolution 49/60. Measures to Eliminate International Terrorism. A/RES/49/60 of 17 February.

United Nations Office on Drugs and Crime (UNODC). 2020. *Illicit Trafficking in Firearms, Their Parts, Components and Ammunition to, from and across the European Union*. Vienna: United Nations. https://www.unodc.org/documents/firearms-protocol/2020/UNODC-EU-Report-A8_FINAL.pdf Accessed 29 Apr. 2024.

United Nations Security Council. 2020. *Eleventh Report of the Analytical Support and Sanctions Monitoring Team Submitted Pursuant to Resolution 2501 (2019) Concerning the Taliban and Other Associated Individuals and Entities Constituting a Threat to the Peace, Stability and Security of Afghanistan*. https://www.securitycouncilreport.org/atf/cf/%7B65BFCF9B-6D27-4E9C-8CD3-CF6E4FF96FF9%7D/s_2020_415_e.pdf Accessed 29 Apr. 2024.

Van Dongen, Teun, et al. 2022. *Right-Wing Extremism in the Military: A Typology of the Threat*. The Hague: International Centre for Counter-Terrorism.

Veilleux-Lepage, Yannick. 2021. *CTRL, HATE, PRINT: Terrorists and the Appeal of 3D-Printed Weapons*. The Hague: International Centre for Counter-Terrorism. https://www.icct.nl/publication/ctrl-hate-print-terrorists-and-appeal-3d-printed-weapons Accessed 29 Apr. 2024.

Watkins, Andrew. 2020. 'Taliban Fragmentation. Fact, Fiction, and Future'. *Peaceworks* 160. Washington, DC: United States Institute of Peace. https://www.usip.org/sites/default/files/2020-03/pw_160-taliban_fragmentation_fact_fiction_and_future-pw.pdf Accessed 29 Apr. 2024.

Conclusion

David Bright

In this concluding chapter, I provide an integrated overview of the themes and issues covered across the chapters of the book, including themes related to the regions and countries discussed across Part I and those emerging from the substantive content covered in Part II. In the first section of the chapter, I provide a review of the themes and issues that characterize the interrelationships between organized crime and firearms trafficking across the globe. Emerging from this section of the book are a clear set of potential risks and future trends. There is a need to monitor such trends, foresee potential areas of challenge and risk, and respond effectively to address these emerging and potential risks and threats. In the second section of this concluding chapter, I draw together the policy recommendations across all chapters to construct an integrated policy roadmap for the future for the prevention and intervention of harms that occur at the intersections between firearms trafficking, organized criminal activities, and organized criminal groups.

Chapters contained in this volume have revealed important insights into the social and economic harms that occur at the crossroads of illicit firearms markets, organized crime, and organized criminal groups. The chapters have collated cutting-edge, contemporary scholarship on illicit firearms markets and organized crime contributed by scholars across the globe. Chapters have drawn on multidisciplinary approaches and perspectives to some of the key local, regional, and international issues related to illicit firearms: for example the methods and routes by which firearms enter illicit markets; illicit firearms as facilitators and enablers of other illicit markets and other crime including organized crime; the role of illicit firearms in exacerbating organized crime, and related crime and violence; and national, regional, and international policy responses to illicit firearms markets.

The book has employed a regional lens on illicit firearms markets, while engaging with key emerging themes and challenges at the intersection of illicit firearms markets and organized crime, including the trafficking of

David Bright, *Conclusion* In: *Illicit Firearms Markets and Organized Crime*. Edited by: David Bright, Oxford University Press. © Oxford University Press 2025. DOI: 10.1093/9780198902409.003.0014 firearms by organized criminal groups and the facilitation of other organized criminal activities (e.g. illicit drug trafficking) using illicit firearms. Across the book, chapters have taken a broad, global scope on these issues, while also analysing regional and local harms and impacts. Chapters have also pointed to emerging challenges and threats, including an exploration of potential alternative policy options that are required to address the wicked problem of illicit firearms trafficking. Each chapter incorporated an analysis of relevant policies, and critically examined alternative options that could be employed to prevent and reduce illicit firearms trafficking and associated crime and enhance community safety. In this way, the chapters have each contributed to advances in scholarly and public policy debates within and across regions and countries.

In the first part of the book, the chapters (i.e. Chapters 1 to 7) focused on regional perspectives on illicit firearms markets and intersections with organized crime. Chapter 1, by Anthony Braga, focused on North America. In Chapter 2, Lina Grip contributed a regional analysis of illicit firearms markets in Europe. Chapter 3, written by Michael Picard, focused on firearms trafficking in Asia and South-east Asia. Chapter 4, contributed by Carlos Perez Ricart, provided an analysis of firearms markets and organized crime in Latin and South America. In Chapter 5, written by Piotr Chlebowicz, we turned to Eastern Europe, with an emphasis on the conflict in Ukraine. Chapter 6, contributed by Adewunmi Falode and Wasiu Balogun, directed a regional spotlight on illicit firearms markets and organized crime in Africa. Chapter 7 concluded Part I with a regional analysis of the Caribbean region, written by Nicolas Florquin, Simon Anderson, Anne-Séverine Fabre, Callixtus Joseph, and Joy St. John.

The second part of the book (Chapters 8 to 12) focused on key themes at the intersection between illicit firearms markets and organized crime. In Chapter 8, Monique Mann, David Bright, and Ashley Allen documented some of the emerging risks and vulnerabilities associated with 3D-printed firearms. Chapter 9, written by David Decary-Hetu, Arielle Chainé, and Étienne Blais addressed the emergence of online marketplaces for illicit firearms, including markets on the dark web. In Chapter 10, Fenna van der Wijk, David Bright, and Freddie Koostra used social network analysis to interrogate the structures and dynamics of illicit firearms trafficking. In Chapter 11, David Bright and Mark Halsey examined the use of illicit firearms by members of organized criminal groups who participate in illicit markets. Finally, Chapter 12, written by Nils Duquet and Annelies Pauwels, examined illicit firearms markets and the involvement of terrorist groups.

I now turn to consider the themes that have emerged across the book, by offering an integrative analysis of the dominant themes that have surfaced across the chapters that comprise the two parts of the book.

Emerging Themes

Regional Issues

While there was a great deal of consistency in the findings across chapters, there was also evidence of contextual differences between countries and regions. Some chapters demonstrated the presence of unique conditions within specific countries and regions with respect to illicit firearms markets and the involvement of organized criminal groups. I give four examples below to illustrate the regional and local contexts around the operation of illicit firearms markets.

First, in Eastern Europe, since the 1990s and following the fall of the Soviet Union, organized criminal groups have expanded and sought control over a range of illicit markets. Organized criminal groups have competed for control of markets and trafficking routes, including markets for tobacco, drugs, and firearms. Evidence suggests that involvement in the illicit firearms market is not a primary endeavour or significant income stream for organized criminal groups in Eastern Europe (e.g. Duquet 2022). See Chapter 5 for more discussion of these regional issues related to Eastern Europe, including discussion of the impact of the war in Ukraine.

Second, in South-east Asia the confluence of several factors 'enable and sustain' organized criminal activities, firearms trafficking and other illicit markets (see Chapter 3). These factors include porous borders, institutional corruption, local and regional conflicts, and inconsistent laws and regulations governing goods that are restricted or illicit. In particular, corruption by state officials facilitates access to illicit firearms by organized criminal groups.

Third, the African continent is marked by porous borders between countries and politically fragile states, conditions that facilitate organized criminal activities including firearms trafficking. Conflict, violence, and war across the continent fuels demand for illicit firearms and drives the activities of organized criminal groups. Factors characterising the illicit firearms market in Africa include the following: ongoing conflicts that drive demand for firearms, cross-border trafficking of illicit firearms, diversion of firearms, ungoverned and unregulated spaces, poor regulation and security of firearms, and corruption. Given the political instability and fragility of African states, the actors in Africa's illicit firearms trade include state and non-state actors including armed groups, militia groups, organized criminal groups, corrupt shipping and transportation companies, and corrupt government officials. See Chapter 6 for detailed discussion of illicit firearms markets and illicit firearms trafficking on the African continent.

And fourth, the Caribbean developed into a regional drug trafficking route in the 1990s following the disruption of Colombian cartels and the rise of Mexican organized criminal groups. A reciprocal 'guns for drugs' trafficking route emerged between Haiti and Jamaica, with both countries experiencing significant gang-related firearms violence. Some Caribbean gangs have morphed into powerful organized criminal groups which control territories and illicit markets. See Chapter 7 for details on the illicit firearms markets in the Caribbean.

Motivation for Acquisition of Illicit Firearms

Chapters revealed a range of motivations underlying the acquisition of illicit firearms, including both instrumental motives and motives related to political and social power and influence. For example, the demand for illicit firearms across Africa is driven partly by a need to protect and sustain other illicit activities and enterprises (see Chapter 6). Similarly, when asked about the motivation for acquiring illegal firearms, participants in illicit firearms markets in the United States report the need for protection defined as 'a calculated choice to gain a strategic advantage' (see Chapter 1) in interactions with victims, competitors, or law enforcement agencies. Organized criminal groups represent a key area of demand for illicit firearms in the United States (see Chapter 1). Firearms are demanded as 'tools of the trade' by organized criminal groups in Eastern Europe, with the primary utility of illicit firearms related to enhanced capacity for coercion (e.g. extortion), inflated status within and between organized criminal groups, and protection from perceived threats (see Chapter 5). Firearms can also play an important role as a tool that can assist terrorist groups to achieve their strategic goals. Access to firearms can help terrorist groups achieve their political goals of conquering territory, expanding control and governance, and coercing and intimidating the citizenry into providing support for the terrorist causes (see Chapter 12). In South-east Asia, illicit firearms are sought by traffickers of illicit commodities for protection of group members and illicit goods, and to facilitate the coercion of others (see Chapter 3). Similarly, in Latin America, organized criminal groups use illicit firearms to control illicit markets and associated territories and to engage in extortion (see Chapter 4).

Motivations for carrying and displaying firearms by member of organized criminal groups in Australia include: status and reputation; to control and govern territories and markets; and to gain ascendancy in conflict between competing organized criminal groups. In an Australian context, firearms are sought by members of organized criminal groups to provide protection in a range of contexts, including: interactions in which it is assumed others will be carrying a firearm; protection against thefts (rip-offs) of money and drugs; and protection in the illicit drug trade, especially in the context of competition and rivalry. Some participants of illicit markets in Australia used the coercive power of firearms to rob illicit drug dealers in order to steal drugs and/or money (i.e. to make a profit via theft). Firearms are used by organized criminal group members in Australia as a tool of the trade, for example to collect debts and to engage in retributive 'street justice' for actual or perceived wrongs committed against individual members or groups. Members of organized criminal groups in Australia use firearms to compensate for real or perceived subordinate status in the context of crime and organized crime. Firearms are used as a means to gain status and respect in (organized) criminal milieux. For more details on the use of illicit firearms as 'tools of the trade' by organized criminal groups, see Chapter 11.

Methods of Acquisition of Illicit Firearms

Across the chapters, a range of methods for acquiring illicit firearms were canvassed by authors. Methods of acquisition showed some variety across the different regions and countries that were the focus of chapters. For example, illicit firearms in the United States tend to be acquired through family members, friends, acquaintances, and through networks embedded in illicit markets (e.g. drug dealers; Braga et al. 2002; see Chapter 1). In Europe, the primary sources of illicit firearms for organized criminal groups are: diversion from military and police stockpiles; reactivated firearms; converted firearms (e.g. converted gas pistols); 3DP firearms; and recirculation of illicit firearms through networks (see Chapter 2). The primary sources of illicit firearms across Eastern Europe include the following: firearms sales from legal owners to those who are not authorized to possess the firearms; diversion of firearms from poorly secured warehouses and storage facilities; diversion from military stocks; reactivation of previously deactivated firearms; and conversion of other items (e.g. gas pistols) into firearms (see Chapter 5). In South-east Asia the dominant form of acquisition is diversion from legal markets, followed by craft production of firearms and conversion of other items into firearms (see Chapter 3). For Latin American countries, proximity to the United States and the more liberal access to firearms in the United States is a significant enabler of flows of illicit firearms (see Chapter 4). For example, high-calibre firearms can be purchased in Arizona, Texas or New Mexico and transported to Mexico where there are significant restrictions on the purchase of such firearms (see Chapter 4).

Across the chapters, one consistent finding was that conflict and war consistently result in the leakage of firearms into illicit firearms markets, facilitating access to illicit firearms by members of organized criminal groups. For example, several countries in South-east Asia have accumulated stockpiles of firearms from numerous regional military conflicts and local insurgencies (see Chapter 3). Similarly, in Eastern Europe, during and following the Soviet withdrawal of troops, soldiers and officers sold large numbers of firearms and ammunition which then flowed into the illicit firearms market and into the possession of members of organized criminal groups (see Chapter 5 and also see below on Ukraine). Conflict and war across the African continent also facilitate access to illicit firearms by organized criminal groups and drives other organized criminal activities such as human trafficking, drug trafficking, and piracy (see Chapter 6). Conflicts can facilitate the direct acquisition of firearms by terrorist groups when terrorist groups obtain firearms directly from participants in conflicts, as has occurred in the Central Sahel in Africa. One primary method of acquisition of firearms by members of terrorist groups is to acquire, often by force, the supplies of firearms held by armed groups with whom they are in conflict (see Chapter 12). Conflict can also facilitate the indirect acquisition of firearms. In this case of indirect firearms flows, firearms from legacy conflicts transition into illicit stocks and are ultimately acquired by terrorist groups (as has been seen in, e.g., the Iraq conflicts and the European Union). The ongoing war in Ukraine is a contemporary example of conflict that has significant potential to facilitate flows of firearms into the illicit economy. The conflagration in Ukraine has seen large numbers of firearms imported into the country and the circulation of such firearms to civilians, reservists, and military personnel. These firearms have made their way into the hands of members of organized criminal groups via a number of means, including theft from warehouses and storage facilities. Stocks of firearms in Ukraine have been inflated by importations from countries seeking to support Ukraine, but the extent of security and protection of such firearms from losses, such as theft and diversion, are not well established. For more details on illicit firearms markets and Ukraine, see Chapter 5.

Prices of Illicit Firearms

Some chapters presented information about the prices paid for illicit firearms, often compared with equivalent prices in legitimate markets. For example, evidence from the United States suggests that gang members and members of organized criminal groups pay inflated prices for illicit firearms, compared with prices paid in legitimate markets (Hureau and Braga 2018; and see Chapter 1).

In South-east Asia, inconsistent legislation and restrictions between neighbouring countries can facilitate and provide financial incentives for firearms trafficking. For example, a Glock pistol purchased in Thailand for $450 can be transported to Malaysia and sold for three times the purchase price (see Chapter 3).

Firearms purchased in some contexts were more expensive than others. For example, firearms purchased from online cryptomarkets and single-vendor shops are more expensive than those purchased via more conventional offline markets (even illicit markets). A 'security premium' is paid for anonymous technologies that theoretically reduce the risk of detection and arrest for market participants (Broseus et al. 2017; and see Chapter 9). 3DP firearms are relatively cheap to produce, especially at scale, potentially making them an attractive option for organized criminal groups with the finances to leverage production at increased scale, thus further reducing overall costs (see Chapter 8).

Availability of Illicit Firearms

The availability of illicit firearms showed some variation across countries, regions and contexts. Nonetheless, the dominant finding was that members of organized criminal groups could access illicit firearms with relative ease. In the United States, access to illicit firearms appears to be significantly enhanced for members of gangs or organized criminal groups (Braga et al. 2002; and see Chapter 1). Similarly, in Australia, a country with more restrictive firearms legislation and regulation compared with the United States, participants of illicit markets, members of gangs, and organized criminal groups were able to obtain illicit firearms with relative ease (Bright et al. 2022; and see Chapter 11).

Evidence was provided about the ready availability of illicit firearms in online contexts. For example, design files for 3DP firearms can be downloaded from the clear web (Schaufelbehl et al. 2023) as well as on dark market forums and via online direct transfer. 3D-printing of firearms can be low-cost and relatively easy, requiring little technical knowledge (e.g. Daly et al. 2021). There was evidence of widespread online availability of a range of design files for plastic and metal components for 3DP firearms. For more details on 3DP firearms, see Chapter 8. With respect to availability on the dark web, cryptomarkets and single-vendor shops are the main sources of illicit firearms (Rhumorbarbe et al. 2018). However, firearms represent only 1 per cent of illicit commodities appearing on cryptomarkets, even though the average profits of vendors of illicit firearms is estimated to be around $80k per month (see Chapter 9). Online marketplaces were reported to be particularly common in South-east Asia where online platform appear to be facilitating firearms trafficking, especially via social media platforms and e-commerce websites, including the sale of modified and converted firearms (see Chapter 3).

The Structure of Illicit Markets and Trafficking

Some chapters presented details of the structure of illicit firearms markets, converging on the finding that trafficking within such markets occurred through relatively small, well-connected networks in which interpersonal trust facilitated transactions. Illicit firearms markets in Europe are characterized as being small and primarily involving flows of illicit firearms within Europe. Evidence from Europe also suggests that trafficking has a network structure, with transactions based on trust between individuals and groups, and often involving small numbers of firearms in any single transaction that are smuggled by small numbers of traffickers (known as the 'ant trade'). See

Chapter 2 for more details on the nature of firearms trafficking in Europe. In South-east Asia, the illicit firearms market is comprised of a range of networked actors including organized criminal groups, corrupt government officials, and armed groups (see Chapter 3). Trafficking networks in South-east Asia are described as 'small and highly decentralized', exploiting multiple sources of illicit firearms. In Latin America, the trafficking of illicit firearms is primarily conducted by organized criminal groups, but the supply chains of illicit firearms also include citizens who act as intermediaries supplying firearms to organized criminal groups (see Chapter 4).

A network approach to trafficking showed a range of resource exchanges and social interactions within a Dutch firearm trafficking group (see Chapter 10). The analysis revealed network 'layers' that were related to a range of resource exchange (firearms, money, drugs) and different social dynamics (order, planning, negotiation). Social network analysis showed that a Dutch trafficking network was sparsely connected, centralized around two well-connected actors (also known as 'hubs'). This Dutch illicit firearms trafficking network was found to operate efficiently, but because of its centralized structure, was somewhat low in security, and vulnerable to law enforcement detection and disruption. For more details on the use of a network lens to study illicit trafficking groups, see Chapter 10.

Links between Illicit Firearms Markets and other Illicit Markets

A consistent finding across the book is that illicit firearms markets are interlinked with other illicit markets, and especially with illicit drug markets. This finding holds across countries and regions. For example, in Africa, illicit firearms markets are linked with other illicit markets (e.g. drug trafficking, oil theft, piracy, and wildlife crimes; see Chapter 6). In South-east Asia, illicit firearms facilitate other illicit markets such as drug production and trafficking, illegal casinos, and scam centres (see Chapter 3). In Latin America, illicit firearms markets are predominantly linked with illicit drug markets, especially given the region's centrality in cocaine production (see Chapter 4). However, a range of other illicit markets in Latin American countries are facilitated and controlled through the use of illicit firearms, including kidnapping, people smuggling, and extortion (see Chapter 4). Illicit firearms are used to smuggle a range of illicit commodities across borders, including alcohol, tobacco, and fake currency (see Chapter 3). In Australia, interviews with illicit market participants revealed a strong relationship between the possession of illicit firearms and participation in illicit drug markets (see Chapter 11).

Types of Illicit Firearms

Some chapters presented evidence of demand for specific types of firearms by organized criminal groups, where such demand reflects either enhanced availability of some types of firearms, or that the characteristics of some firearms render them more attractive to members of such groups (e.g. due to their size, look, calibre, or ease of reloading). For example, there is evidence that some gangs and organized criminal groups in South-east Asia, Latin America, and the Caribbean (especially Haiti) are increasingly demanding high-calibre firearms, semi-automatic rifles, and machine guns (UNSC 2023; and see Chapters 3, 4, and 7). Furthermore, again in South-east Asia and the Caribbean, there is evidence of the increasing threat posed by privately made firearms (PMFs) as viable sources of illicit firearms (see Chapters 3 and 7). Turning to types of firearms sought on the dark web, of thirty-four platforms identified that advertised illicit firearms, the majority of listings were for handguns and long guns (accounting for approximately 80 per cent of all firearms listings; see Chapter 9 for more details).

3DP firearms are relatively cheap and easily accessible and are largely untraceable, given the absence of serial numbers. The low cost and ease of manufacture of 3DP firearms may be attractive features to members of organized criminal groups. Some anecdotal evidence suggests that groups such as outlaw motorcycle gangs (OMCGs) have used 3D-printers to print firearms. 3DP firearms are not currently the firearm of choice for organized criminal groups, mainly because factory manufactured firearms are easy to obtain for such groups and are considered more reliable than 3DP firearms (see Chapter 8). Organized criminal groups are known to prefer untraceable firearms, so demand for 3DP firearms by organized criminal groups may increase as there are improvements in the technology and reliability underpinning these firearms. There is, for example, some anecdotal evidence of availability of 3DP firearms across the Caribbean, including some recent documented seizures (Loop 2023; and see Chapter 7).

Some chapters also examined the issue of accessibility of firearm parts and devices. For example, 3DP firearms are often constructed using hybrid kits, or by combining different firearm parts together, some of which are factory produced while others are printed components (see Chapter 8). A further example are conversion devices, accessories that can convert semi-automatic firearms into fully automatic firearms, and which are available in the Caribbean (Fabre et al. 2023; and see Chapter 7). In South-east Asia there is a lucrative online market for firearm parts, and for modified and converted firearms (see Chapter 3).

The range of themes summarized above attest to the complexity of the challenges facing policy makers, law enforcement agencies, intelligence agencies, and security agencies who seek to disrupt illicit firearms markets. I now turn to a discussion of the primary policy recommendations that have emerged across the chapters.

Policy Recommendations

In this section, I draw together a set of policy recommendations based on those rendered by authors across all chapters dealing with policies across localities, regions, countries, and the thematic areas covered throughout the book.

Policies Designed to Limit or Restrict Access to (Illicit) Firearms

Many chapters recommended policies and interventions that are designed to limit or restrict access to firearms more broadly, and illicit firearms more specifically. This includes regionally based options aimed to strengthen controls and restrictions on the availability of firearms and ammunition (see Chapter 7). It also includes interventions that limit access to illicit firearms, for example those designed to limit the proportion of a criminal career across which individuals have ready access to illicit firearms (see Chapter 1). This set of policy recommendations includes those that restrict availability of firearms, including via legitimate routes, even in countries with tight regulations and restrictions, in order to further prevent leakage from legitimate markets into the black market (see Chapter 11). In some countries and regions, there is a pressing need to limit risks of diversion especially via enhancing the security of stockpiles, warehouses, and supply chains (see Chapter 12).

In the context of the emerging threat of 3DP firearms, there were recommendations for governments to compel or incentivize web hosting platforms to include strategies to address availability of 3DP design files in their company policies. This could include, for example, geo-blocking or local censorship targeting design files for firearms, or incorporating requirements for proof of identity or relevant background checks in order to access design files for 3DP firearms (see Chapter 8).

In some regions, such as South-east Asia and Africa, efforts are required to address corruption that can facilitate access to illicit firearms (see Chapters 3 and 6). Strategies could include independent oversight units to counter corruption in law enforcement agencies, and strengthening whistle-blower provisions (see Chapter 3).

Policies that Aim to Increase the Price of Illicit Firearms

One chapter specifically referred to policies that inflate the prices of illicit firearms as a tactic to reduce demand. This includes disruption strategies that aim to increase the price of illicit firearms, inflating the 'effective price' for illicit firearms that includes search time and effort required to locate a specific type of firearm (Braga and Pierce 2005; Moore 1973) (see Chapter 1).

Improved Data Collection and Analysis

Many chapters also referred to the need for improved and coordinated data collection and analysis with respect to firearms and especially illicit firearms. It is critical to collect relevant data in order to paint a valid and reliable picture of the illicit firearm market in cities, regions and countries (see Chapter 11). Indeed, comprehensive and deeper understandings of illicit firearms markets requires the collection and analysis of intelligence about illicit firearms, transactions, and crime committed with illicit firearms. For example, our understandings of illicit firearms markets become compromised when data on recovered illicit firearms and related evidence (e.g. ballistics evidence) are not collected and properly analysed (see Chapter 1). In many regions, there is a need to improve the collection, storage, and analysis of data on firearms, both those held legally and cases of detected/seized illicit firearms (e.g. see Chapters 4 and 5). This type of data, when collected and analysed systematically, can reveal the makes and models of firearms that are in demand by members of organized criminal groups, including any trends in such demand (e.g. see Chapter 5).

It is important to note that these issues regarding data collection and analysis were canvassed with respect to some regions and countries, but also have clear applicability across the globe. An example of this would be the collection of data and intelligence on illicit firearms transactions, especially from Ukraine to other European countries, in order to monitor and respond to emerging trends and threats (see Chapter 5). In Eastern Europe, there is a need for increased funding or forensic laboratory facilities that can analyse seized illicit firearms, tracing the histories of firearms (e.g. via ballistics evidence) including use in organized criminal activities (see Chapter 5). Similarly, in the Caribbean there is an identified need to strengthen forensic capabilities (see Chapter 7). Further enhancement of intelligence capabilities might include improved training of crime analysts within relevant agencies, improving their content area expertise in relevant issues such as illicit firearms trafficking, and intersections with other illicit markets, other organized criminal activity, and organized criminal groups (see Chapter 5). There is a need for firearms registries in each country in order to keep track of legally owned firearms and monitor for diversion, theft, and other flows into the illicit market, including monitoring and intelligence collection on the production of homemade firearms (see Chapter 6).

One chapter specifically canvassed improving intelligence collection and analysis methodologies around network analysis. Social network analysis (SNA) and multiplex network analysis has significant potential to assist law enforcement and security agencies to identify and target key actors in trafficking groups who may be responsible for transactions of specific key resources (e.g. money; see Chapter 10). Crime analysts working for police and security agencies should employ SNA as a tool in their arsenal when collecting and analysing information about firearms trafficking groups (see Chapter 10). Training in SNA and use of relevant software packages such as Analysts Notebook should be part of the standard training for analysts in order to utilize the power of SNA to its full potential (see Chapter 10).

Partnerships and Cooperation

Many chapters referred to the benefits of interagency cooperation and partnerships, including information-sharing between relevant agencies and especially law enforcement, security, and intelligence agencies. Disrupting the trafficking of illicit firearms can be facilitated by improved cooperation between national and international law enforcement agencies and intelligence agencies (see Chapter 5). This includes improving the flow of information on intercepted transactions of illicit firearms between relevant agencies both within and between countries and regions (see Chapter 5), and multilateral sharing of experiences, capacities, and intelligence to enhance efforts to disrupt illicit firearms trafficking (see Chapter 3).

The need for inter-agency cooperation was specifically referenced in relation to some countries and regions. In the United States, for example, there is a pressing need for strategic partnerships between law enforcement agencies and other agencies such as the ATF and other federal and state agencies (see Chapter 1). In Europe, there is a similar need for regional cooperation, for example SEESAC in Europe aims to reduce stockpiles of firearms, limiting access to illicit firearms (see Chapter 2). Other European strategies for cooperation include the European Multidisciplinary Platform Against Criminal Threats (EMPACT) that targets trafficking of illicit firearms via, for example, joint days of action during which a specific broad issue will be identified, and collaborative actions taken (e.g. multiple arrests and seizures; see Chapter 2). In some regions, given regional fragility and political instability, there is a need for an intergovernmental agency to monitor and regulate the flow of firearms across the continent, including methods for tracking and tracing of illicit firearms (see Chapter 6). In Africa, for example, there is an established need for improved intelligence sharing between countries and agencies (e.g. interagency hubs; see Chapter 6). Similarly, in the Caribbean, a key current need is to improve intelligence-sharing between agencies, especially law enforcement and security agencies across the Caribbean region (Chapter 7). In Latin America, countries lack national coordinating agencies for firearms. Instituting such agencies that could then coordinate and collaborate to target illicit firearms trafficking could offer potential beneficial impacts in the region. In South-east Asia, there is a need for expansions in multilateral cooperation, including joint border operations and joint investigations that aim to dismantle transnational criminal networks (see Chapter 3).

Focus on Key Actors and Resources in Firearm Trafficking Networks

To be most effective, policies and interventions should focus on key actors and key resources that are critical to the trafficking of illicit firearms (see Chapter 10). For example, policing interventions may be more effective when they target multiple 'network layers', including the networks of resource exchanges and social dynamics between actors (see Chapter 10). For example, interventions should target not only exchanges of firearms, but also the flows of money and profits (see Chapter 10).

Law enforcement interventions directed at illicit firearms markets should target not only those actors who appear to be at the apex of any hierarchical structures but should also target actors who are important in firearms trafficking networks for reasons other than their hierarchical position. For example, as mentioned previously, interventions should target those in central positions in the flows of money across the network (see Chapter 10). Interventions should also focus on intermediaries or brokers in the illicit supplies of firearms and money (see Chapter 1).

In Latin America, the 'key actor' of relevance from a policy perspective is the United States. Latin American countries could form 'diplomatic coalitions' which seek to advocate for policies that could prevent (or at least restrict) the flows of illicit firearms from the United States.

Policies that Target Specific Types, Makes, and Models of Illicit Firearms

There is a need to focus enforcement, prevention, and disruption strategies on the flows of those firearm types that are most in demand by members of gangs and organized criminal groups, especially those who are involved in serious crime, including violent crime (see Chapter 1). While handguns appear to be the firearm type most preferred by organized criminal groups, demand extends to semi-automatic and fully automatic rifles and machine guns. Policy makers and law enforcement agencies also need to monitor for new trends and any shifts in demand (e.g. potential demand for 3DP firearms in future).

Tracking and Tracing of Illicit Firearms

Tracking and tracing of illicit firearms can contribute to the profiling of the illicit firearms market as well as providing intelligence to law enforcement and security agencies regarding potentially fruitful areas for investigation and disruption strategies. Such strategies can involve tracking and tracing of firearms in the grey and black markets, including tracking of thefts and tracing of firearms used in crime (e.g. the use of national registers for firearms) (see Chapter 11). This includes the tracking and tracing of illicit firearms that have been seized, especially those that have been used in organized criminal activities and related violence (see Chapter 1).

Targeting Financial Flows Connected with Illicit Firearm Trafficking

Policies that seek to address firearms trafficking and interventions that disrupt illicit firearms markets should target not just the flows of illicit firearms, but also financial flows that facilitate the market and often motivate participation (see Chapters 6 and 10). For example, African countries should toughen anti-money laundering laws and provisions especially around firearms trafficking in order to disrupt the flow of profits generated by illicit markets, including profits derived from illicit firearms markets, into legitimate channels (see Chapter 6).

Legislative Change

In some contexts, legislative changes are required in order to effectively address issues of access to illicit firearms. For example, online safety laws could be used to regulate and restrict access to digital design files (see Chapter 8). Legislation could also be employed to mitigate potential future threats. For example, legislative changes that require registration of 3D-printers or mandate that 3D-printers not be capable of printing design files for firearms could prevent future harms related to 3DP firearms (see Chapter 8).

In some countries and regions, there is an urgent need to enhance the consistency of legislation, for example, to close loopholes across countries or regions that can be used to facilitate acquisition of illicit firearms (e.g. see Chapters 2, 3, and 7). For example, there has been cooperation in the European Union across member countries commencing in the 1990s which has been consolidated and strengthened following terrorist attacks in which firearms were employed. Enhancements are required to ensure consistency of legislative approaches in some regions. For example, the harmonizing of legislation across the European Union should focus specifically on trafficking of illicit firearms and the involvement of organized criminal groups (see Chapter 2). There is also a recognized need to harmonize legislation in countries across the Caribbean (see Chapter 7) and South-east Asia (see Chapter 3).

Prevention and Desistance Programmes

Prevention and desistance programmes should target individual-level motivators for participation in illicit firearms markets, organized criminal activities and organized criminal groups. There is a critical need for violence-prevention interventions that can address the genesis of firearms violence and the demand for illicit firearms (see Chapters 4 and 7). These interventions include those that seek to address the motivations, especially for youth, for entry into crime, organized crime, and firearms crime (see Chapter 11). Policy levers should seek to reduce the perceived rewards and enhance the perceived risks of engaging in organized crime and illicit firearms crime. Desistance-style programmes, policies, and interventions should address the range of economic, affective, and social drivers of participation in the illicit firearm market (see Chapter 11). To have the most chance of success, such policy responses must be multipronged and include a range of agencies (criminal justice, health, social services, housing, employment), to facilitate desistance from crime and encourage pathways out of organized crime, illicit firearms crime, and participation in illicit firearms markets (see Chapter 11).

Public Awareness and Marketing Campaigns

Public marketing campaigns can raise awareness of potential threats as well as providing strategic information to the public that can operate as general deterrence. For example, publicising successful investigations and prosecutions of those involved in illicit firearms trafficking can be strategically employed as a method of general deterrence (see Chapter 1). Public awareness campaigns can also be employed to educate citizens on risks posed by illicit firearms, encourage participation in gun buy-back schemes and amnesties, and facilitate collection of intelligence on criminal activities related to trafficking and use of illicit firearms (see Chapter 3).

These campaigns can raise awareness of firearms safety responsibilities and initiatives (e.g. the need to store firearms safely, information on firearms amnesties). Public awareness campaigns can also address specific contexts or supply mechanisms. For example, public awareness campaigns could be used to counter the notion that the dark web offers highly secure and anonymous platform for buyers and sellers of illicit firearms. Such strategies may not only deter potential firearms purchasers from using the dark web, but may also render it more likely that those motivated to acquire an illicit firearm will utilize more conventional, visible methods of acquiring firearms, with enhanced probabilities of detection by law enforcement agencies (see Chapter 9).

International Alliances and Conflict

Given the clear relationship between armed conflict and flows of firearms into illicit markets, there is a critical need to more carefully manage legitimate international firearms transfers and the post-conflict management of firearm stocks. International arms transfers, including between allies, need to be conducted with caution and be closely monitored to prevent diversion of firearms into illicit markets and potentially into the hands of organized criminal groups and terrorist groups (see Chapter 12). There is also a need to address the issue of post-conflict management of firearms, for example via systematic disarmament programmes after a conflict has been concluded (see Chapter 12).

Improvements in State-Building and Development of Democratic Institutions

Fragile states and weak institutions and the trafficking of illicit firearms are intimately connected. Interventions are therefore needed that strengthen the legitimacy and democratic structures of states and state institutions, including addressing citizen mistrust and lack of social cohesion. These interventions are likely to have direct effects on mitigating the threats posed by illicit firearms markets, but can also strengthen other strategies and interventions that seek to disrupt illicit firearms trafficking (see Chapter 12).

Policing Interventions and Strategies

Across the book, a range of specific policing strategies were canvassed that can be used to disrupt illicit firearms markets, particularly in emerging threat areas. These strategies include: techniques which can recover details of obliterated serial numbers of seized illicit firearms and subsequent investigation and tracing of these firearms (see Chapter 1); monitoring of IP addresses for platforms that host design files for 3DP firearms (see Chapter 8); monitoring and intelligence collection of those who have been subject to control orders related to firearms (see Chapter 8); greater scrutiny of importation of 3D-printers that might lead to those who are illegally printing 3DP firearms (see Chapter 8).

Given that the volumes of illicit firearms traded on the dark web are small at present, the dark web should not be a primary focus for prevention and intervention (see Chapter 9). However, given that firearms purchased on the dark web are usually delivered by regular mail, strategies are required that can detect suspicious packages efficiently and effectively. From a deterrence perspective, increasing the risks of detection following the purchase of illicit firearms on the dark web is likely to have a deterrent effect on both buyers and sellers on the dark web (see Chapter 9).

The Need for Policies that Respond to Emerging Trends

Finally, law makers and law enforcement agencies must be constantly vigilant. Illicit firearms trafficking must be recognized as involving dynamic contexts and processes, with a consequent need to identify potential new sources of illicit firearms in order to ensure policy and policing practice can respond with alacrity to new areas of risk (see Chapter 1). This includes monitoring new technologies and trends especially those opportunities that may be used by organized criminal groups and terrorist groups (see Chapter 12) such as 3DP firearms (see Chapter 8) and PMFs (see Chapters 1 and 10), and converted firearms (e.g. see Chapter 3). For example, PMFs are an emerging and potentially dangerous source of illicit firearms for individuals who would not pass relevant background checks and other barriers to legal firearms ownership including members of organized criminal groups (see Chapter 1).

Concluding Comments and the Way Forward

When examining illicit firearms markets and the intersections of these markets with organized criminal activities and organized criminal groups, it is critical to consider international, regional, and local perspectives. It is also important to consider the interplay between illicit firearms markets, other illicit markets, and a wide range of organized criminal activities. Across regions, countries, and contexts, the involvement of organized criminal groups is apparent across all facets of illicit firearms markets, including trafficking, demand, deployment of illicit firearms, and associated acts of crime and violence. Illicit firearms are used by organized criminal groups to assert power, control territories, and govern illicit markets. These activities result in significant social, cultural, environmental, and economic harms across cities, countries, and regions.

Responding effectively to the challenges of illicit firearms markets requires multifaceted policy approaches and broad, cooperative policing approaches. Given the gaps in our knowledge of the operation and dynamics of illicit firearms markets, more research is clearly required at local, regional, and international levels. This research should focus on illicit firearms markets, illicit firearms trafficking, intersections with other organized crime and the involvement of organized criminal groups.

Illicit firearms markets, illicit firearms trafficking and intersections with organized crime are a dynamic set of interactions that demand constant vigilance and the capacity to pivot quickly to deal with emerging threats. Prevention is key, so we need cooperative, multi-agency responses to combat the challenges of illicit firearms markets. It will be critical to carefully monitor emerging trends, identify potential threats, and respond with alacrity in order to enhance the safety and security of communities, regions, and countries across the globe.

References

Braga, Anthony A., and Pierce, Glenn L. 2005. 'Disrupting Illegal Firearms Markets in Boston: The Effects of Operation Ceasefire on the Supply of New Handguns to Criminals'. *Criminology & Public Policy* 4 (4): pp. 717–748.

Braga, Anthony A., et al. 2002. 'The Illegal Supply of Firearms'. In *Crime and Justice: A Review of Research*, vol. 29, edited by Michael Tonry, pp. 319–352. Chicago: University of Chicago Press.

Bright, David, et al. 2022. '"I Know a Guy and He's Got Guns Galore": Accessing Crime Guns in the Australian Illicit Firearms Market'. *Deviant Behavior* 44 (5), pp. 671–689.

Broséus, Julian, et al. 2017. 'A Geographical Analysis of Trafficking on a Popular Darknet Market'. *Forensic Science International* 277: pp. 88–102.

Daly, Angela, et al. 2021. '3D Printing, Policing and Crime'. *Policing and Society* 31 (1): pp. 37–51.

Duquet, Nils (ed.). 2022. *Pulling the Trigger: Gun Violence in Europe. Country Reports.* Project Target. Brussels: Flemish Peace Institute, p. 12.

Fabre, Anne-Séverine, et al. 2023. *Weapons Compass: The Caribbean Firearms Study.* Port of Spain and Geneva: CARICOM IMPACS and Small Arms Survey. https://www.smallarmssurvey.org/resource/weapons-compass-caribbean-firearms-study Accessed 26 Jul. 2024.

Hureau, David M., and Braga, Anthony A. 2018. 'The Trade in Tools: The Market for Illicit Guns in High-Risk Networks'. *Criminology* 56 (3): pp. 510–545.

Loop. 2023. '3D printed guns seized in raid on Caparo house' (30 August 2023). https://tt.loopnews.com/content/3d-printed-guns-seized-raid-caparo-house Accessed 26 Jul. 2024.

Moore, Mark H. 1973. 'Achieving Discrimination in the Effective Price of Heroin'. *American Economic Review* 63 (2): pp. 193–206.

Rhumorbarbe, Damien, et al. 2018. 'Characterising the Online Weapons Trafficking on Cryptomarkets'. *Forensic Science International* 283: pp. 16–20.

Schaufelbühl, Stefan, et al. 2023. 'Investigating the Availability of 3D-Printed Designs on The Clear Web'. *Forensic Science International: Synergy* 7: pp. 1–9.

United Nations Security Council (UNSC). 2023. Final report of the Panel of Experts on Haiti submitted pursuant to resolution 2653 (2022). S/2023/674 of 15 September. https://www.securitycouncilreport.org/atf/cf/%7B65BFCF9B-6D27-4E9C-8CD3-CF6E4FF96FF9%7D/s-2023-647.pdf Accessed 27 Jul. 2024.

Index

For the benefit of digital users, indexed terms that span two pages (e.g., 52–53) may, on occasion, appear on only one of those pages.